European fashion

Manchester University Press

STUDIES IN DESIGN & MATERIAL CULTURE

general editors
Christopher Breward
and
Bill Sherman

founding editor
Paul Greenhalgh

European fashion

The creation of a global industry

Edited by Regina Lee Blaszczyk and Véronique Pouillard

Manchester University Press

Published by Manchester University Press
Altrincham Street, Manchester M1 7JA

www.manchesteruniversitypress.co.uk

British Library Cataloguing-in-Publication Data
A catalogue record for this book is available from the British Library

ISBN   9781526122094 hardback
ISBN   9781526122100 paperback

First published 2018

Sub-editing and picture research by
Mary Schoeser and Diane Mackay
Typeset by
Servis Filmsetting Ltd, Stockport, Cheshire
Printed in Great Britain by
Bell and Bain Ltd, Glasgow

Front cover image: Pierre Cardin coat dress, 1961. Courtesy Hagley Museum and Library.

Contents

Figures

Every effort has been made to obtain permission to reproduce copyright material, and the publisher will be pleased to be informed of any errors and omissions for correction in future editions.

Tables

Notes on contributors

Regina Lee Blaszczyk is Professor of Business History and Leadership Chair in the History of Business and Society at the University of Leeds. Her research focuses on the history of innovation in the creative industries, with reference to consumer society, design, fashion, and retailing. She is the author or editor of twelve books including *Imagining Consumers: Design and Innovation from Wedgwood to Corning* (Hagley Prize for the Best Book in Business History, 2001); *Producing Fashion: Commerce, Culture, and Consumers* (Best of the Best from the University Presses, 2008); *American Consumer Society, 1865–2005: From Hearth to HDTV* (2009); *The Color Revolution* (Sally Hacker Prize for Exceptional Scholarship that Reaches Beyond the Academy, Society for the History of Technology, 2013); *Fashionability: Abraham Moon and the Creation of British Cloth for the Global Market* (2017); with Uwe Spiekermann, *Bright Modernity: Color, Commerce, and Consumer Culture* (2017); and with Ben Wubs, *The Fashion Forecasters: A Hidden History of Color and Trend Prediction* (2018). She was project leader for the Enterprise of Culture, which operated out of the School of History at the University of Leeds from 2013 to 2016.

Florence Brachet Champsaur is a graduate from EM Lyon business school; she holds an MA in Fashion and Creation from Lyon University and an MSc from the Ecole des hautes études en sciences sociales (EHESS). In 2008, she founded and has since managed the heritage department of the Galeries Lafayette Group, where she is also head of patronage activities. She has curated several exhibitions on fashion history and retail, teaches fashion marketing and the history of fashion in postgraduate programmes, and has also worked as retail manager for Givenchy and as a freelance consultant in fashion marketing. Currently completing her PhD at EHESS on department stores and the history of retailing in the area of fashion and luxury goods, she has published on fashion and business history in *Business History*, *Business and Economic History*, and *Entreprises et Histoire*. Her latest book published in French is *From Grand Bazar de l'Hôtel de Ville to Le BHV Marais, the Parisians' favourite department store* (2016).

Shiona Chillas is Lecturer in Management, based in the Institute for Capitalising on Creativity in the School of Management, University of St Andrews, where she has worked since gaining her PhD in the Department of Human Resource Management (HRM) at the University of Strathclyde. Her research interests include creative labour, graduate employment, and new technology at work, and she is currently working on a project examining the role of design in business start-ups. She has published in *Organization, Social Science and Medicine*, and *New Technology, Work and Employment* and has co-edited a collection entitled *The Digital Workplace* (2017). She was a team member and Principal Investigator for the Enterprise of Culture project.

Pierre-Yves Donzé is Associate Professor of Business History at Osaka University, Japan, and Visiting Professor at the University of Fribourg, Switzerland. His research interests include the business history of luxury and fashion industries, technology transfer, and the history of multinational enterprises. He is the author of numerous articles and books, including *A Business History of the Swatch Group: The Rebirth of Swiss Watchmaking and the Globalization of the Luxury Industry* (2014), *Global Luxury: Organizational Change and Emerging Markets in the Luxury Industry Since the 1970s* (with Rika Fujioka (forthcoming in 2018)), and *Industrial Development, Technology Transfer, and Global Competition: A History of the Japanese Watch Industry Since 1850* (2017). He is a member of the councils of the European Business History Association and of the Business History Society of Japan.

Rika Fujioka is Professor in Retailing and Macro-marketing at Kansai University, Japan. She is council member of both the Business History Society of Japan and the Japan Society of Marketing and Distribution. While her academic base lies in marketing, Rika's research activities have extended into business history and strategic management. She is now a Principal Investigator of a project on 'Changing Competitiveness of Japanese Retailers and Fashion Industry under Globalisation', which is supported by the Japan Society for the Promotion of Science (JSPS). Her publications include 'European luxury big business and emerging Asian markets, 1960–2010', *Business History* (2015), with Pierre-Yves Donzé, and *Comparative Responses to Globalization: Experiences of British and Japanese Enterprises*, with Maki Umemura (2013).

Ingrid Giertz-Mårtenson is a senior advisor at the Centre for Business History in Stockholm (CBHS), one of the Enterprise of Culture's partner organizations, through which she served as an interviewer for the project's pilot oral history programme. An ethnologist, trend analyst, and historian, Ingrid has had a long career in the fashion industry, having worked at French couture houses and other European fashion organizations before becoming director of the Swedish Fashion Council. Ingrid initiated the establishment of the Centre for Fashion Studies at Stockholm University and subsequently steered the documentation of H&M's corporate history in collaboration with the CBHS. Ingrid is a consultant to a range of cultural and business institutions, and has curated fashion exhibits such as the *Ten Views of Sweden* touring exhibition. She contributes to a range of publications and print media, most recently with 'No One Escapes Fashion' in Sofia Hedman's *Utopian Bodies: Fashion Looks Forward* (2015).

Melinda Grewar is a Research Assistant and PhD student in the Institute for Capitalising on Creativity at the School of Management, University of St Andrews. Her doctoral research considers audiences' practice of taste on the Internet. Prior to her academic career, she worked in local authority arts and craft development in Scotland and New Zealand, and in journalism and educational publishing in the United States. She was a researcher with the Enterprise of Culture project.

Geoffrey Jones was on the advisory board for the Enterprise of Culture. He is Isidor Straus Professor of Business History at the Harvard Business School in the United States. He holds BA and PhD degrees from Cambridge University in Britain and honorary doctorates from Copenhagen Business School and Helsinki University. His recent books include *Profits and Sustainability: A History of Green Entrepreneurship* (2017), *Entrepreneurship and Multinationals: Global Business and the Making of the Modern World* (2013), and *Beauty Imagined: A History of the Global Beauty Industry* (2010). Geoff serves as co-editor of the quarterly journal *Business History Review*, and is a Fellow of the Royal Historical Society and the Academy of International Business.

Tereza Kuldova is Researcher at the Department of Archaeology, Conservation and History, University of Oslo and a Visiting Senior Researcher at the Department of Cultural and Social Anthropology, University of Vienna. She is a trained social anthropologist specializing in India and Europe, and her projects span from a study of Indian fashion industry to her current research on outlaw motorcycle clubs and biker subculture. She is the author of *Luxury Indian Fashion: A Social Critique* (2016). She was a Postdoctoral Fellow with the Enterprise of Culture project.

Wessie Ling is a Reader at Northumbria University. A trained cultural historian and artist, she uses academic writing and visual art practice to address her work. Author of *Fusionable Cheongsam* (2007), she was a Co-Investigator for the Arts and Humanities Research Council (AHRC) project, 'Translating and Writing Modern Design Histories in East Asia for the Global World' (2012–14). She co-edited *Making Fashion in Multiple Chinas: Chinese Styles in the Transglobal Landscape* (2018) and a guest issue on 'Hyper-Text(ile)s: Transnational Networks in Fashion Exchange' (2018) in *Textile: The Journal of Cloth and Culture*. She has been granted a Research Fellowship at The Research Institute for Languages and Centres of Asia (RILACA, Mahidol University, Bangkok, 2018) and was a Visiting Scholar at The University of Hong Kong (2017). Text and installations are used in her artistic practice to address the cultural properties of fashion. Works were exhibited in Saint Dominic's Priory Church (2016, Newcastle upon Tyne), Oxfordshire Visual Arts Development Agency (OVADA) (2015, Oxford), Danson House (2013, Bexleyheath), Brunei Gallery (2012, London: SOAS), Saltram House (2012, Plymouth: National Trust), and the Victoria and Albert Museum (2011, London) among others. www.WESSIELING.com

Véronique Pouillard is Associate Professor in the History of Modern Europe at the University of Oslo, Department of Archaeology, Conservation, and History. Prior to Oslo, she held posts and fellowships at the Université Libre de Bruxelles and at Columbia University, and was a Newcomen Fellow at the Harvard Business School. Véronique has widely published on the history of international business, especially in the fields of fashion, advertising, and intellectual property. She is now the Humanities Coordinator of the Nordic Branding research project at the University of Oslo. She was a Principal Investigator with the Enterprise of Culture project.

Sonnet Stanfill is Acting Senior Curator in the Department of Furniture, Textiles and Fashion at the Victoria and Albert Museum (V&A) where she has worked since 1999. Her research focuses on twentieth and twenty-first-century fashion production and consumption and includes the evolution of the fashion industry in postwar Italy; the influence of the geography of the city on fashion design; and fashion in 1980s' London. Sonnet's exhibitions include *Ossie Clark* (2003), *New York Fashion Now* (2007), and co-curation of *Ballgowns: British Glamour Since 1950* (2012), with accompanying publications. She curated the major exhibition, *The Glamour of Italian Fashion* (2014) and edited its publication. Sonnet joined the curatorial team for *Alexander McQueen: Savage Beauty* (2015), and then served as consultant curator for the exhibition, *Balenciaga: Shaping Fashion* (2017). Sonnet holds an MA in the history of dress from the Courtauld Institute of Art. Before joining the V&A she worked as retail buyer in San Francisco and

New York. She worked with the Enterprise of Culture as the representative from the V&A, one of the project's affiliated partners.

Barbara Townley is Emeritus Professor at the Management School, University of St Andrews. After gaining her PhD at the London School of Economics, she taught at the Universities of Lancaster, Warwick, Alberta, Canada, and Edinburgh. Her research on the creative industries focuses on the role of intellectual property (IP) in creative small and mid-sized enterprises (SMEs) and micro organizations; the role of design in fledgling business start-ups; and strategies of distinction in the Scottish fashion and textile industry. She is currently writing, with Nicola Searle, *Creating Economy: Enterprise, Intellectual Property and the Valuation of Goods* for Oxford University Press. She was a Principal Investigator with the Enterprise of Culture project.

Ben Wubs was a Principal Investigator for the Enterprise of Culture in the School of History, Culture, and Communications at Erasmus University in Rotterdam. He is an associate professor at Erasmus and an appointed Project Professor at the Graduate School of Economics at Kyoto University in Japan. He is engaged in projects on multinationals, business systems, transnational economic regions, Dutch-German economic relations, and the transnational fashion industry. His books include *International Business and National War Interests: Unilever between Reich and Empire* (2008) and *Over Grenzen: Multinationals en de Nederlandse Markteconomie* (2009). Between 2008 and 2012, he was an Erasmus Fellow working on a research project on 'The Dutch Big Four in Germany: AKU, Royal Dutch Shell, Unilever and Philips, 1920–1960', and he co-supervised *Outport and Hinterland*, a large research project on Rotterdam and its German hinterland, published in 2017. Wubs is a council member of the European Business History Association.

Johanna Zanon is a PhD candidate at Institutt for Arkeologi, Konservering og Historie (IAKH), University of Oslo. She is particularly interested in business history, the history of fashion, and the history of decorative arts. Her doctoral dissertation looks at the history of the sleeping beauties of haute couture through a series of case studies, including Jean Patou, Elsa Schiaparelli, and Madeleine Vionnet. After completing her master's degree in the history of European art at Ecole Pratique des Hautes Etudes in Paris in 2011, she obtained the degree of Archivist-Paleographer at Ecole nationale des Chartes in Paris in 2012, with a research conducted on the house of Jean Patou in the interwar years. In spring 2015, she was a visiting scholar at the European Studies Centre at Columbia University, and she was also a visiting scholar at the Graduate School of Economics at Osaka University in the spring of 2016.

Foreword

This volume is a most welcome addition to the literature on the history of the fashion industry, and creative industries in general. As in so many areas of history, there has in the past been an unfortunate tendency to silo knowledge behind the far too rigid borders created by academia. This book represents a sustained interdisciplinary and global assault on such artificial constraints which have constrained much research on the fashion industry in the past.

The fashion industry has long been a particular victim of the borders between academic disciplines that have pursued their own agendas and employed their own language with minimum dialogue with outsiders. Fashion historians have provided rich studies of the creative processes of designers, but they have had little interest in the entrepreneurial and managerial dimensions of the industry. Business historians, like most management scholars, have until recently mostly avoided the creative industries altogether. Instead their professional attention was focused on capital-intensive industries, from railroads to automobiles, along with high-technology industries, such as computers. This comparative neglect of fashion and beauty reflects over-preoccupation about understanding the rise of big business in the United States and Western Europe. It may also reflect the former male dominance of business history, resulting – and perhaps encouraging – a reluctance to address industries in which women were both prominent entrepreneurs and major consumers. This book marks a big step forward in re-integrating the history of the fashion industry. It demonstrates how important it is to look at both design and management if the drivers of innovation and the creation of value are to be fully understood.

The book breaks down other borders too. Many historical studies have heavily focused on the ecosystems of Paris, Milan, New York, and other fashion hubs. This was appropriate in an era when, for example, Paris was the acknowledged capital of fashion before World War II. As this book makes clear, Paris and Europe as a whole have remained disproportionately important in the fashion world subsequently, but as we moved from Parisian hegemony to the world of fast fashion, transnational approaches and methodologies have become necessary. Here again the book breaks new grounds as the authors trace the actors involved, from the luxury conglomerate LVMH to retailers, including the iconic Swedish firm H&M. The world of retail buyers and other staff in retail stores has been more or less a black box in explaining how tastes in fashion were made and diffused, so this is really a pioneering contribution.

A final border which is broken down is the excessive focus on the West, which is still such a feature of mainstream business and economic history. This book contains rich new material on both Europe and the United States, but it pioneers by including three fascinating essays on the non-Western world. The stories of the Japanese denim and jeans industry, the Chinese "Red-White-Blue" plastic carrying bag, and ethical luxury Indian fashion, provide refreshing and provocative lenses on the world of fashion. They are especially important through their incorporation of the key social, cultural and ethical dimensions of fashion into their discussions, and their employment of an eclectic range of methodologies. In these essays and in the volume as a whole, readers can not only learn a lot about the transition from haute couture to fast fashion, but can also get a preview of the business and fashion history of the future.

Geoffrey Jones
Harvard Business School

Acknowledgements

This book was funded by HERA II: Humanities in the European Research Area, which from 2013 to 2016 sponsored our three-year collaborative research project, The Enterprise of Culture: International Structures and Connections in the Fashion Industry since 1945. We are grateful to the HERA II Research Programme, the European Science Foundation, and the national funding agencies who are part of the HERA funding network for their confidence in our exploration of the business and economic aspects of the global fashion industry, which has been most often studied from a theoretical or cultural perspective.

Over the three years of its existence, the Enterprise of Culture project sponsored more than a dozen public events and academic conferences on the business history of European fashion; produced numerous books, journal issues, and academic articles; and hopefully, laid the foundation for further research in this territory. This anthology is mainly based on research by the core team and partners of The Enterprise of Culture, with contributions by scholars who participated in some of our meetings and conferences. The title of our research project, The Enterprise of Culture, reflects our interdisciplinary approach to research on the history of the fashion industry.

The Enterprise of Culture was a collaborative endeavour, and we are grateful to our team. We warmly thank Principal Investigators Shiona Chillas and Barbara Townley at the University of St Andrews, Alan McKinlay at the University of Newcastle, Robert MacIntosh at Heriot-Watt University, and Ben Wubs at Erasmus University; Advisory Board members Geoffrey Jones at the Harvard Business School, Giorgio Riello at the University of Warwick, and Hartmut Berghoff at the University of Göttingen; and collaborators at our two Associated Partners: Alexander Husebye, Ingrid Giertz-Mårtenson, and Anders Houltz at the Centre for Business History in Stockholm, and Glenn Adamson and Sonnet Stanfill at the V&A. Thanks also go to Andrew MacLaren at Heriott-Watt University; Melinda Grewar at the University of St Andrews; Thierry Maillet at Erasmus University; Richard Coopey at Aberystwyth University; Katharine Carter and her staff at the Marks and Spencer Company Archive at the University of Leeds; and the research team at the University of Oslo, comprised of Tereza Kuldova, Mari Kirkerud Pettersen, and Johanna Zanon.

We are grateful to several individuals who helped to bring our work on the business history of fashion to fruition, including Fiona Blair in the Enterprise of Culture's home office at the University of Leeds, Graham Loud and Simon Hall at the University of Leeds; Tør Egil Forland, Erlend Haavardsholm, Henrik Olav Mathiesen, and Tarjei Solberg at the University of Oslo; David Appleyard, Emma Brennan, Paul M. Clarke, Bethan Hirst, Alun Richards, Deborah Smith, and Susan J. Womersley at Manchester University Press; and our very capable subeditors Mary Schoeser and Diane Mackay, who are blessed with talent, patience, and endurance. We are also thankful to Jon Williams and Lucas Clawson at the Hagley Museum and Library for providing us with the DuPont Company photograph on the cover of this book, which also served as the main image for The Enterprise of Culture.

Regina Lee Blaszczyk, University of Leeds
Véronique Pouillard, University of Oslo

1

Fashion as enterprise

Regina Lee Blaszczyk and Véronique Pouillard

Pierre Cardin, a young Parisian couturier born in Italy, designed the coat dress on the cover of this book (figure 1.1). In his early years, Cardin had been the director of tailoring at the house of Christian Dior, the firm that helped to orchestrate the comeback of haute couture during the postwar era. In 1948, when it became apparent that Christian Dior's designs were being leaked to mass-market garment manufacturers, the French police interrogated Cardin at length. The young designer was found innocent, but he was deeply offended by the episode. When starting his own business in the 1950s, Cardin innovated and designed fashions that embodied a hopeful future for the postwar consumer. In 1959, he was banned from the prestigious Chambre Syndicale de la Couture Parisienne – the trade association for the haute couture industry that had been established in 1868 – for having designed for All Printemps, one of the large department stores on boulevard Haussmann in Paris. Although Cardin was eventually welcomed back to the Chambre Syndicale, his eyes were fixed on a broader clientele. In the transformative times of the 1950s and 1960s, the old system of haute couture was challenged by the demands of consumer culture. Cardin licensed his brand more widely than any couturier before him, putting the name of Pierre Cardin before the masses.[1]

Our cover photo from February 1961 is more than a picture of an outfit designed by Pierre Cardin. The image embodies the complexities of the European fashion system and speaks to its place in the new global order that was in its infancy in the postwar years. At first glance, the picture looks to be a publicity photograph taken in a well-heeled Paris suburb to advertise a new collection. However, the picture is not from the archive of Pierre Cardin, but from the vast collection of business records from the American chemical giant, E. I. du Pont de Nemours and Company, of Wilmington, Delaware. As the world's largest manufacturer

1.1   DuPont photograph of a Pierre Cardin coat dress, 1961.

of synthetic fibre, the DuPont Company was one of the invisible players in the international fashion-industrial complex of the postwar era. To build consumer trust in man-made materials, DuPont routinely collaborated with French textile mills and couturiers in the Chambre Syndicale to showcase fabrics made from its synthetic fibres. The coat dress by Pierre Cardin was made from a Lesur fabric woven from lightweight Shetland wool blended with Orlon acrylic, a synthetic wool by DuPont.[2] If we took the picture at face value, we would only see yet another Parisian costume. But when we look deeper, a far more complex and interesting story emerges.

The new fashion scene

The seventy years that followed World War II witnessed the demise of the old European fashion hierarchy that dated from the mid-1800s. For more than a century, elite haute couture houses, most of them members of the Chambre Syndicale, had dominated Western fashion. In 1858, Englishman Charles Frederick Worth and his young Swedish business partner, Otto Gustaf Bobergh, set up a fashion salon on the rue de la Paix in Paris. This enterprise, Worth and Bobergh, was the first haute couture house to be run on modern principles. Previously, elite dressmakers had collaborated with wealthy clients on the design of a personalized costume. Under the system introduced by Worth, the couturier – or the couturiere (a female designer) – presented the client with an original creation that was the product of his or her imagination.[3] In the United States, extremely expensive couture outfits worn by the European social elite were described and illustrated in *Godey's Lady's Book* and emulated by fashion-conscious consumers within their budgets. The story was much the same in other Western consumer societies, from Britain to Germany.

At the turn of the twentieth century, the Norwegian-American economist Thorstein Veblen and the German sociologist Georg Simmel theorized about the global power of fashion centres. Paris ruled over women's fashion, while London was the capital of men's tailoring. Veblen observed that fashion was essential to the display of social status and to the emulation of one's social betters.[4] Simmel emphasized the trickle-down movement of fashion. No sooner were designs emulated by the lower ranks than they were abandoned by the elites for newer, more distinctive styles.[5] These theorists were fascinated by fashion because it underpinned and reflected the social hierarchy, and because 'the masses' seemed so willing to emulate fashions worn by 'the classes'. While fashion came to encompass a more diverse range of consumer products, including home furnishings, it was particularly powerful in female dress. Men's wear and children's attire, although they also followed fashion, overall changed less markedly and less quickly than women's attire.

More recently, the eminent American sociologist, Diana Crane, observed that a major shift in consumption and meaning occurred within the fashion system in the mid-twentieth century. Fashion went from being an emblem of high social status to being a commodity that could be enjoyed by nearly everyone in the West.[6] Ready-to-wear triumphed over custom-made dresses, whether the consumer was a Danish princess who was fitted for her evening gowns in a Parisian couture salon or a British schoolteacher who sewed her own clothes. The casual look, developed in response to changing lifestyles, became the new order of the day. Affordable easy-going outfits were made possible by advanced technologies such as synthetic fibres and high-speed knitting machines, by young designers concerned to create styles that embodied modernity, and eventually, by outsourcing production from Europe and North America to low-wage economies in North Africa, Eastern Europe, the Middle East, and Asia.

In 1999, Teri Agins, the senior fashion reporter at the *Wall Street Journal*, sized up the American scene in *The End of Fashion*. The American woman, who in the postwar years had been celebrated as the 'best dressed woman in the world', now drove to the mall in a velour tracksuit, trainers, and a pink baseball cap. Elegance had disappeared, a result of the casualization of everyday life.[7] More recently, the Paris-based fashion forecaster, Lidewij 'Li' Edelkoort, issued her manifesto on the state of European fashion, similarly declaring the end of an era. 'It's the end of fashion as we know it', she told *Dezeen* in March 2015. 'Fashion with a big F is no longer there … Actually the comeback of couture, which I'm predicting, could bring us a host of new ideas of how to handle the idea of clothes. And maybe from these ashes another system will be born … fashion has become a way to say "cool". And it's no longer addressing clothes.'[8] Edelkoort's predictions followed on the heels of the growing popularity of 'normcore', a unisex clothing style in part popularized by Silicon Valley entrepreneurs Mark Zuckerberg and the late Steve Jobs. Normcore aficionados have rejected sartorial rules for bland everyday clothing that is practical and anonymous: T-shirts, jeans, and sneakers. The goal is to buck the idea that fashion is a vehicle for expressing difference, and to use clothing as a form of camouflage, as a tool for blending into the crowd.[9] As historians, we are less concerned with the latest dictates circulating on the Web than with the broad historical developments that transformed the fashion business from 1945 to the present. We contend that the postwar shakeup in Paris did not result in the end of fashion, but gave birth to an ever-powerful and increasingly global fashion industry. The hegemony of Paris and prescriptive modes of dress were replaced by a global network of intermediaries and 'fashion for everyone'.

In this transformation, the old couture houses shut their doors, and the rue de la Paix lost some of its cachet. However, for most consumers, the world of fashion changed for the better. Fashion became less elitist and more democratic. In the first two decades after World War II, clothing was still expensive, and consumers thought of new apparel as an investment. It was still common for the average European woman to get fitted for her clothes by a local seamstress or to make her own dresses at home. As Europe recovered from the war, these practices gave way to the convenience of buying readymade fashion in the shops. Starting in the 1960s when the Dutch-owned chain retailer, C&A Modes, introduced an early version of 'fast fashion' to teenagers in Mod London, more and more consumers had access to clothing that was created to be worn for a season or two and then discarded.[10] One unintended consequence of the ramping up of the fashion cycle was the emergence of the used clothing trade and the recycling business, mainly but not exclusively in developing countries. Consumers in the city of Ndola on the Copperbelt of Zambia in Africa rummaged through second-hand clothing stores that stocked discarded Western clothing, while industrial workers in Italy shredded imported American rags to create recycled fibres that the Prato woollen industry would mix with virgin wool to create stylish fabrics for global export.[11] One person's discarded fashion was another person's treasure, or the fibres were reborn as a jacket available from such diverse companies as the activewear producer The North Face and the creative label Vetements, two prominent brands in the new fashion system.

This book shifts the debate on fashion from the broader culture to the internal culture of the fashion trade – and then returns to the broader culture by explaining the significance of value creation for the fashion industry. While creators and designers of fashion have been the subject of many stimulating studies, this book reconnects the two faces of the fashion system: the designer who stands in the spotlight and the manager who works in the shadows. The history of entrepreneurs, with their charge of strategies, risk, and experimentation – and their failures – complements the more visible creativity of the designer. This book emphasizes the work of fashion professionals who worked behind-the-scenes as intermediaries: trendsetters, retail buyers, stylists, art directors, advertising executives, public relations agents, brand managers, and entrepreneurs. The celebrities of postwar and contemporary fashion, from Elsa Schiaparelli to Karl Lagerfeld, have received their fair share of coverage in the fashion literature. Editors and socialites, from Diana Vreeland to Anna Wintour, are also household names among fashion bloggers and their fashionista followers. In contrast, the intermediaries who served as information brokers and negotiators within the fashion system were omnipresent but often invisible. Their names are lesser-known in the annals of fashion history: Jean d'Allens, Giovanni Battista Giorgini, Erling Persson, Maurice Rentner, Margareta van den Bosch, and Harriet Wilinsky, among others. This constellation of actors was characterized by a cosmopolitan outlook, an openness to new modes of operation, and the acknowledgement that women had something to say about fashion, not simply as consumers, but as fashion buyers, executives, and leaders. It is crucial to understand the role of these actors in order to fathom the process of value creation in the fashion industry.

Fashion, a cultural *and* economic activity

Over the course of the last seventy years, the European fashion business has moved from celebrating the craftsmanship of haute couture to revelling in ever-changing fast fashion, from everyday elegance to everyday casual (figure 1.2). This book examines the transition from the old system to the new in a series of case studies grouped around three major themes. Part I of the book deals with the transformation of Paris from a couture production centre to a creative hub for design and brand management. Part II examines the special role of retailers and retail brands in promoting European fashion, with reference to transnational exchanges between Europe, America, and the wider world. Part III explores seminal developments in a select group of global fashion hubs on the European periphery or entirely outside of Europe, and their roles in critiquing the mainstream fashion system with heritage marketing, vintage aesthetics, ethical brands, and local styles.

This anthology embodies a new approach to the study of fashion history. It is highly interdisciplinary and informed by design history, cultural anthropology, ethnography, management studies on creativity, and the 'new' business history. The book differs from most work in fashion studies because it pulls back the curtain on firms, trade associations, and government organizations to examine how value is created. Intrinsically, this value is both artistic and commercial, and it is rooted in both design and management. Some fashion history researchers emphasize the creative genius of the designer, but we contend that creativity was embodied both in the designer and in other actors within the firm, whose collective expertise formed a winning entrepreneurial combination. Furthermore, the process of value creation was transmitted from one generation to the next, and know-how was circulated geographically.

Thirty to forty years ago, the study of fashion and clothing was the purview of museum curators and costume historians who focused on object appreciation or social history. Influenced by art history, classic works such as James Laver's *A Concise History of Costume* (1969) discussed basic style changes over the longue durée.[12] Since the 1980s, fashion studies has blossomed into a field that encompasses a large literature on clothing, meaning, and cultural identity.[13] We now have a deep understanding of fashion and the body, apparel production, gender and dress, and a range of subcultural looks, from the zoot suit to Punk.[14] A slew of talented

Byrrh Advertisement by Georges Léonnec, *L'Illustration*, 16 April 1932, illustrating the interwar **1.2**
influence of Scottish tweeds in the development of casual wear for women.

researchers in cultural history, sociology, and anthropology have contributed to the growth of fashion studies as a vibrant field.

This anthology builds on the bedrock of fashion studies and takes an entirely new turn. It combines the insights of fashion studies with the new culturally oriented business history to offer a distinctive take on the European fashion system since 1945. To understand what is innovative about our approach to business history, we must take a look at what came before. For much of the late twentieth century, the historical study of modern enterprise was dominated by the work of Alfred D. Chandler Jr., a professor at the Harvard Business School who was called the 'dean' of business history because of his influence on the field. Chandler used social-science methods to explore the managerial revolution in American business and its global triumph during the Cold War. In a series of books that included his Pulitzer Prize-winning magnum opus, *The Visible Hand*, he examined the role of professional managers in major corporations in the United States and Europe, mainly manufacturers, in an effort to explain the success of the American business model. How and why did the large, multidivisional enterprise, run by professional managers, come to dominate the American economy, and how did this model come to be admired and emulated around the world? Chandler and his followers did much to advance our understanding of modern management practices in important companies such as DuPont, the General Motors Corporation (GM), and Sears, Roebuck and Company.[15] The Chandler school explained how managers in such enterprises harnessed technological innovations to redefine and reshape markets, and how they created new strategies and tactics to manage complex multidivisional companies, many of which had global influence.[16]

Although culture underpins economic activities, cultural analysis was largely absent from the Chandler paradigm. A devotion to the cult of objectivity led Chandler and his followers to adopt a certain degree of detachment, scrutinizing managers without concern for their personalities or personal lives. Reading Chandler, one would never know that Alfred P. Sloan Jr., the organizational man who headed GM for some four decades, was a dedicated follower of fashion with a taste for exquisitely tailored suits. This telling personal detail about the man at the top helps us to understand why this particular mid-century Detroit automobile manufacturer had a strong commitment to design management.[17]As consumer society unfolded, people looked to buy goods that could help them establish their place in the social hierarchy.[18] The mechanisms of ostentatious consumption studied by Thorstein Veblen did not entirely disappear. Quite the contrary: they migrated to unexpected places with the help of visionaries like Sloan. Under his leadership, GM pioneered the idea of a 'car for every purse and purpose'. The annual model change, a now-ubiquitous marketing concept, encouraged consumers to think of automobiles as fashion accessories.[19] Sloan acknowledged that fashion mattered; Chandler and most of his followers did not.

The Chandler school of business history was notable for other silences. Topics such as consumer culture, small business, women, minorities, and brands were left out, along with the strong story line that can make history readable and engaging. Starting in the 1980s, a new generation of researchers influenced by American studies, social history, and cultural history began to challenge the Chandler model. These innovators took a 'cultural turn' and created the new business history. Committed to highly readable narratives, advocates of the cultural turn homed in on the relationships among enterprise, culture, and society.[20] Working in North America and to a lesser extent in Europe, these pioneers ventured into topics such as advertising, marketing, consumer culture; material and visual culture; and product design and innovation.[21] It was only a matter of time before this new generation of researchers turned its attention to beauty products, hair salons, and colour forecasting.[22] Fashion was also a natural fit.[23]

In their recent book, *Reimagining Business History*, Philip B. Scranton and Patrick Fridenson have built on the foundation of the new business history to lobby for further developments in the field. During the heyday of the Chandler school, the entrepreneur was most often depicted as a white male in a large corporation. Scranton and Fridenson are representative of researchers who have striven to interrogate a wider range of business actors, whether they are black or white, men or women, gay or straight. The new business history also acknowledges that there is no such thing as a 'free market', and that, in addition to firms, we need to examine institutions such as national governments, city councils, and consumers' associations. Furthermore, while quantitative data is important, the new business history does not stop at the balance sheet. It is now possible to study small and medium-sized enterprises (SMEs), private companies that did not make their accounts public, and enterprises situated on the margins of the law. This more open-minded way of studying business history has informed our approach to under-researched questions and actors in the fashion system.[24]

Concurrent with the development of the new business history, an innovative group of curators began to acknowledge the importance of business enterprise to the fashion system. In North America, two exemplary curatorial works combined the study of artefacts and business records: Alexandra Palmer's book on Parisian couture in Toronto for the Royal Ontario Museum and Dilys Blum's exhibition catalogue on Elsa Schiaparelli for the Philadelphia Museum of Art. Palmer looked to department store records, while Blum examined a range of business and trade materials.[25] In Europe, Sonnet Stanfill took a similar approach in exhibitions and publications for the Victoria and Albert Museum.[26] These museum-based researchers started with the objects and then moved into trade journals, newspapers, and company archives to probe the inner workings of the firm. In contrast, the authors in this book are mainly academic researchers who begin the opposite way, posing questions about the creative process and looking to the documents for evidence. However, our approach is highly sympathetic to the work of Palmer, Blum, and Stanfill, the latter of whom has contributed to this book.

In this anthology

Fashion is a cosmopolitan field of activity that links large metropolitan centres in Europe and North America to the global periphery. For centuries, all types of manufacturing have moved to new locations in pursuit of cheap labour, better markets, and new talent. Clothing and fashion are no exceptions. As nineteenth-century Westerners looked for goods that helped them to define their place in the social hierarchy, fashion was added to the consumer identity kit.[27] In response to the demand for affordable everyday clothing, entrepreneurs such as John Barran of Leeds mechanized the European readymade clothing industry.[28] Barran and like-minded entrepreneurs adopted the sewing machine and other mechanical devices to expand the production of ready-to-wear in cities such as Leeds, Berlin, London, New York, Paris, and Philadelphia.[29] To further reduce costs, they employed labourers to work long hours in crowded factories or as outworkers in bleak tenements.

During the twentieth century, several factors exercised pressure on costs in the garments industries. The democratization of fashion emerged first and foremost in nineteenth-century United States, which was the world's largest consumer market. Department stores, chain stores, mail-order catalogues, 'specialty' stores, and countless small shops retailed fashion goods that were made in thousands of factories and workshops. Some of these workshops were subsidiaries of retailers, but most were independent entrepreneurial ventures. Pressure from the market to lower prices, as well as fierce competition among garment makers, resulted in low wages and difficult labour conditions, especially in workshops that produced goods for the lower end of the market. In the early twentieth century, some eighty per cent of garments produced in the United States were manufactured in New York City, and the rest were made in industrial cities such as Philadelphia, Chicago, and Rochester, New York.[30] Garment makers could start a workshop with a small amount of capital, often benefiting from extensive kinship networks in the trade. But the unpredictability of trends made garment manufacturing a high-risk enterprise, and bankruptcies were frequent. The fragmented and volatile industrial landscape, combined with the complexities of the supply chain, made it difficult to control the labour force. From the 1960s onward, retailers in the

United States and the United Kingdom increasingly looked off shore for cheaper sources of textiles and garments. British retailers, for example, turned to Hong Kong, Israel, and Turkey.[31] By the New Millennium, the West had virtually been stripped of its manufacturing capacity in fibres, fabrics, and fashion. The relocation of most textile and garment production to low-wage economies has made it difficult to monitor and control. The International Labour Organization, an agency of the United Nations that brings together governments, employers, and workers around the world to set labour standards, has met significant challenges in trying to implement its conventions within the global garment industry.[32]

Many researchers have examined manufacturing and labour in the garment industry. For the global era, the economist Pietra Rivoli offers the most extensive discussion of the clothing supply chain in her highly readable book about the commonplace cotton T-shirt. Rivoli also acknowledged that her project is to understand 'the virtues of markets in improving the human condition'.[33] An important group of scholars and journalists that include Naomi Klein, a Canadian social activist whose book *No Logo* denounced sweatshop labour, have pushed for further study of labour conditions in distant production sites, and have reinvigorated consumer advocacy and corporate social responsibility.[34] In the field, activist groups such as the Clean Clothes Campaign lobby to improve working conditions and empower labourers in the garment and sportswear industries around the world.[35]

Although we admire this work, our book focuses on a different set of concerns. The fascinating issue at the heart of this anthology is the inner workings of innovation in the fashion industry. We are concerned about the nature of creativity, the ways in which creators read and respond to the market, and the strategies that have been used to adapt fashion to the new global environment. That history necessarily homes in on the firms, associations, and institutions that create value and, ultimately, make fashion into one of the most desired consumer goods in the world.

Part I: Reinventing Paris fashion

The immediate postwar period – the years 1945 to 1970 – was the last golden age of haute couture.[36] The business of high-end fashion had its origins in the luxury trades of the Ancien Régime, yet it was with the House of Worth, founded in 1858, that haute couture came to embody global leadership in women's wear. As demonstrated by the art historian Nancy Troy and a recent crop of researchers, haute couture orchestrated a tour de force in marketing. The couture houses touted their creations as exclusive, authentic, and distinctively Parisian, and forbade unauthorized reproductions (figure 1.3). Everything about the creative process, the clients, and the semi-annual shows was cloaked in secrecy. At the same

1.3   Chambre Syndicale atelier, where detailed handwork such as sewing collars and cuffs on to garments was undertaken, photographed in the 1950s.

time, the couture houses promoted Paris fashion as a luxury industry with outstanding designs that the whole world should admire. In short, haute couture was a paradoxical business. It was closely guarded, but hungry for attention.[37]

In the interwar period, the Chambre Syndicale de la Couture Parisienne set up the rules for the trade. Members were only permitted to sell their products to private customers, both domestic and international, and to international corporate clients such as department stores. The Chambre refused to give French garment manufacturers and French retailers access to the Paris couture shows. French garment factories and department stores had to work the system to gain access to couture models, sometimes surreptitiously re-importing models that had been purchased by foreign buyers. These policies, implemented to maintain exclusivity, were debated throughout the interwar period and were abandoned in 1944.[38]

The book starts with a chapter by Véronique Pouillard that examines the postwar couture industry at an important transitional moment. After World War II, the couture industry began to collaborate with the French garment industry (figure 1.4). A very dynamic French fashion press and a system of government subventions nurtured haute couture and the nascent ready-to-wear industry. Haute couture experienced its final spurt of creativity during the 1950s, serving a rarefied international clientele and especially targeting a North American audience. Around this time, labour costs rose, rapidly rendering haute couture unprofitable. However, the Parisian fashion system did not disappear. As Pouillard demonstrates, it simply changed its business model.

Haute couture put on a new face and adapted to a situation wherein Paris was no longer the only fashion capital. By the late twentieth century, the world had several fashion capitals, each with a distinctive specialization: New York for ready-to-wear; London for boutique trends and for men's wear; Milan for luxury ready-to-wear, accessories, and men's wear; and Tokyo for street style.[39] The Paris cluster became more open to new ways of doing business, and haute couture morphed into luxury brands. The voracious consumer appetite for fashion gave birth to a new generation of creative professionals who fostered the development of the London boutique and introduced the designer brands that became the hallmark of the Seventh Avenue fashion district in New York.[40] One particularly important business practice that enabled the democratization of European fashion was the development of licensing regimes. The Paris couturiers acknowledged that they had to adapt to survive, and they developed a licensing system for linking their names to tie-in products such as perfumes, scarves, beachwear, cruise lines, and gift lines.[41] The proliferation of brands through licensing agreements gave more and more consumers access to upmarket designers such as Pierre Cardin, the Paris innovator who created the coat dress for DuPont and who eventually became the couturier with the greatest number of brand licences. From the 1960s onward, the Paris haute couture houses reinvented themselves as creative laboratories for luxury brands.

While the postwar period showed that haute couture was not a very profitable activity, it also demonstrated that the symbolic capital accumulated by luxury brands had enormous value for the fashion industry. Ms. Postwar Consumer would buy affordable stylist-designed clothes at Monoprix, a chain store developed by Galeries Lafayette, or at its rival Prisunic, a store opened by Au Printemps for the budget-conscious shopper who loved fashion. She could also purchase high-end perfume, accessories, and fine alcoholic beverages branded by Cardin, Christian Dior, or Moët & Chandon.[42] From the ashes of the old haute couture system, the

Tissu. BLACK and WHITE de

H. Moreau &Cie

Tailleur de
Jacques Heim

1.4   Jacques Heim advertisement, 1956, typifying his collaboration with fabric manufacturers such as
H. Moreau & Cie.

Paris fashion industry developed a new business model built around the concept of luxury for everyone.

The multinational luxury groups that emerged in the late twentieth century are now some of the most profitable businesses in Europe, but their histories are largely unexplored in fashion studies. Pierre-Yves Donzé and Ben Wubs examine the French company Moët Hennessy Louis Vuitton, SE (better known as LVMH), the largest luxury goods group in the world. Acknowledging that creativity is a major resource for LVMH, these historians consider the ways in which the creative process is socially constructed in relation to other functions within the group, such as finance, distribution, management, and corporate strategy. As Per H. Hansen, the prominent Danish historian of business and design, has argued, the stories that corporations tell about themselves are often more revealing than the products that they make.[43] Donzé and Wubs explore how LVMH has reinvented brands that date from earlier decades and even earlier centuries, and how the firm promotes these brands using stories about romance, heritage, and luxury. Continuing in this vein, Johanna Zanon examines the Parisian 'sleeping beauties', dormant couture brands that entrepreneurs have reawakened for the twenty-first century. She considers how one French father-and-son team, Guy de Lummen and Arnaud de Lummen, reinvented Madeleine Vionnet and Paul Poiret, and considers the role of heritage stories in their rebirth.

One important question that emerges from our reinterpretation of Paris fashion relates to the value of history to the fashion business. Do the genuine histories of luxury brands and their constructed narratives have as much immaterial value as the recent investment in the past seems to suggest? And does history really matter? This is a fitting topic for consideration at a time when many old haute couture firms have been folded into luxury groups or have been rebranded as modern labels, and when large conglomerates like LVMH have established nonprofit foundations to preserve their heritage and advance European art and culture.[44] Is the revisiting of old designs and brands a way to give soul to the brand, or to refresh creativity?[45] Only time will tell.

Part II: International connections and the role of retailers

Today, the global fashion industry is dominated by giant corporations, from multinational retailers such as H & M Hennes & Mauritz AB (the Swedish firm that owns H&M, COS, Cheap Monday, and other brands) and Inditex (Industria de Diseño Textil, S.A., the Spanish parent company to Bershka, Massimo Dutti, Zara, and other brands) to luxury goods conglomerates like LVMH and holding companies such as Kering. But giantism in the distribution of fashion and luxury goods is a relatively recent phenomenon, and some comparatively small privately-owned firms, such

1.5   The H&M Fifth Avenue flagship store in New York City, on the occasion of the launch event of the Comme des Garçons collection for H&M, 13 November 2008.

as Chanel, have remained extremely dynamic. Historically, family-owned department stores and (in the US) specialty stores were the most important actors in delivering fashion to the consumer.

The French novelist Émile Zola, who depicted the Bon Marché in *Au bonheur des dames* (*The Ladies' Delight* or *The Ladies' Paradise*), contributed to the mystique of the Parisian department store and the stereotype of the fashion-crazed consumer. Many elements documented in Zola's 1883 novel – profligate shoppers, aspirational counter clerks, and charity-minded entrepreneurs – have become the staples of fashion and consumer history. Generations of intellectuals and social critics chastised the penchant for fashion as morally suspect, and blamed consumer society for phenomena such as kleptomania, sexual promiscuity, debt, and personal bankruptcy.[46] Published a century after Zola's novel, Michael B. Miller's history of the

Bon Marché is an exemplary scholarly work that has inspired many rich studies.[47] But some three decades hence, we can begin to see the many dimensions of fashion retailing that have not been scrutinized.

In Part I, the focus on Paris as a creative hub helped us to understand how the birthplace of haute couture adapted to late twentieth-century trade winds that dropped licensing regimes, ready-to-wear, luxury brands, and heritage marketing on its doorstep. Part II considers the retailer's role in shaping taste, responding to consumer expectations, and disseminating fashion merchandise. This section shifts the discussion from the companies that create fashion to the companies that sell it, and explores the give-and-take among producers, distributors, and consumers.

The first generation of historians who studied modern consumer culture, including T. J. Jackson Lears, William Leach, and Richard Tedlow, demonstrated how new types of enterprise shaped consumers' expectations starting in the late nineteenth century.[48] The readymade clothing industry was in its infancy, and 'fashion' and 'fabrics' were synonymous. Some retailers that sold fabrics began to diversify their stock, and in doing so, pioneered the concept of a store with different departments that each carried a special line of merchandise. Emporia like the Bon Marché catered to the bourgeoisie and wealthier classes who could afford fashion merchandise. In Milan, the Grandi Magazzini 'Alle Città d'Italia', founded by the brothers Ferdinando and Luigi Bocconi in 1865 and renamed La Rinascente in 1921 under new ownership, is a case in point. In the physical store and by mail-order catalogue, the Bocconi brothers' emporium sold fabrics, thread, lace, and other goods needed for dressmaking; hat shapes and the ribbons and feathers for embellishing them; stockings and undergarments; and some readymade clothing, such as shawls, capes, and coats. The Bocconi store did little trade with the working classes, but reached middle-income households where the breadwinner was a physician or an engineer.[49]

As the great style capital of Europe, Paris played a seminal role in the growth of fashion retailing. In the late nineteenth and early twentieth centuries, department stores began to crop up on the grand boulevards of La Rive Droite, or the Right Bank of the river Seine, from the rue de Rivoli to boulevard Haussmann.[50] In Germany, department stores were slower to develop, but by the early twentieth century, they 'surpassed all but American stores in both number and sales volume'.[51] The Philadelphia entrepreneur John Wanamaker is often identified as the father of the American department store because of his commitment to a broad selection of merchandise, fixed prices, and other modern business practices. Large American cities such as Chicago, Houston, Los Angeles, New York, and Philadelphia, and smaller ones around the country, all had family-run department stores on the main street. Some American entrepreneurs recognized the value of specialization, and stores dedicated exclusively to fashion appeared, among them William Filene's Sons Company in Boston and Henri Bendel, Saks, Bergdorf Goodman, and Lord & Taylor in New York. Ongoing research suggests that these large fashion-only retailers may have been a distinctive American phenomenon. Writing in 1966, for example, the fashion journalist for the London *Times* noted, 'Nothing like the American fashion specialty stores exists in England.'[52] Collectively in the transatlantic world, department stores and specialty stores dominated the fashion scene until the late twentieth century, when chains garnered significant competitive advantage. In the UK, for example, local family-owned department stores mainly disappeared from the high street. They were pushed aside by chain department stores such as Debenhams and House of Fraser; by fashion multiples such as Aquascutum, Austin Reed, Burberry, C&A Modes, Country Casuals, Jaeger, Topshop, and Wallis; variety store chains such as Marks and Spencer; and eventually by international chains such as H&M, Primark, and Zara.[53]

Retailers have long performed a vital go-between function in the fashion system, acting as brokers between the companies that create the merchandise and the consumers who buy and use it. In many ways, retailers add value to the fashion system by acting as interpreters and tastemakers. They take the pulse of consumers, interact with suppliers to select the goods that will appeal to their trade, and help the merchandising staff to present the items to shoppers in an appealing setting. As Regina Lee Blaszczyk has demonstrated, retail buyers were important 'fashion intermediaries' who connected the store to the consumer, and whose merchandise choices could make or break the season's profits.[54] In the United States, the men who managed most retail enterprises soon discovered the importance of 'the woman's viewpoint' to merchandise selection and presentation. From the early twentieth century, American department stores and specialty fashion retailers employed women as fashion buyers, merchandise managers, publicists, and advertising copywriters. Store managers believed that the feminine understanding of fashion was a business asset that needed to be harnessed to produce higher sales. In turn, a job as fashion buyer provided the aspirational career woman with an avenue for upward mobility. By examining the internal workings of retailing, we can see how gender stereotypes played out in the fashion supply chain.

The chapters in this section consider four major fashion retailers – Galeries Lafayette in Paris, I. Magnin in San Francisco, William Filene's Sons Company in Boston, and H&M in Stockholm – within the context of the revival of European fashion after World War II and the global democratization of fashion in our own time. Collectively, the essays look inside the department store, the specialty fashion retailer, and the global brand to examine the retail managers, buyers, fashion directors, merchandise managers, and window display artists who have been largely absent from the annals of fashion history. In France, men tightly held the reins in retailing, but in America and Sweden, women held influential positions in retailers and at global brands. In the postwar era, they helped to disseminate and reinterpret European fashion for the prosperous American market, and in more recent times, some have shaped the design strategies and product development process in global mass-market fashion.

After World War II, European and American fashion retailers faced the challenge of determining what types of goods to stock in their stores. Italian products had cultural cachet and nicely fitted the bill. In the immediate postwar years, the French took their cues from America, where stores like R. H. Macy & Company in New York City put on popular promotions of Italian merchandise. As Florence Brachet Champsaur explains in her chapter, when Galeries Lafayette imported Italian goods, Parisians objected because they wanted to see French merchandise in their favourite high-class department store (figure 1.6). In the United States, two influential stores – I. Magnin on the West Coast and Filene's on the East Coast – looked to France, Italy, and Britain for the latest fashions. As Sonnet Stanfill shows in her discussion of I. Magnin, Italian fashion proved especially popular among California shoppers because the casual look of Italian ready-to-wear was a good fit with West Coast lifestyle. The buyers sourced Italian fashion for their store, while helping Italian designers to understand the needs of the American market.

The food hall at 'La Fleur de la production italienne', Galeries Lafayette, 1953   **1.6**

At Filene's in Boston, the subject of Regina Lee Blaszczyk's chapter, a large team of buyers, merchandise managers, publicists, and advertising copywriters collaborated to make their fashion specialty store into a one-stop shopping destination for New England fashionistas. Filene's executives dreamt of a great transatlantic entente, wherein North America and Europe would share textiles, fashion, and design sensibilities. However, this goal was never realized due to changing American tastes that rendered obsolete the formal clothes modelled after French haute couture. In the Filene's case study, we see the first signs of ageing in the major retailing institutions that had dominated the commercial landscape since the years around 1900. The women who had been hired to interpret popular taste wanted to remake the consumer in their own image, but the American shopper had a mind of her own and wanted casual styles rather than couture knock-offs. Today, department stores and large fashion specialist retailers are endangered species, lumbering giants in a forest dominated by nimble chain retailers such as H&M.

To conclude our discussion of retailing, Ingrid Giertz-Mårtenson provides an in-depth case study of H&M with reference to the firm's history and the contemporary inclination to associate the retailer with fast fashion. She goes back to the social-democratic roots of H&M, showing that the brand was animated by the desire to make fashion available to mass consumers. Giertz-Mårtenson argues that the founders of H&M were aligned with political democracy and the advent of the consumer-citizen in Sweden.[55] Some six decades after its founding, H&M's commitment to a consumer's democracy was shaping its internal culture and corporate strategy. This strong tradition stands at odds with the public image of the company as an advocate of throwaway culture and fast fashion. As creative director Margareta van den Bosch explains, it takes H&M about a year to plan a new fashion line – how 'fast' is that?

Part III: European fashion on the periphery

In recent years, the Western fashion industry has ramped up the fast fashion process to deliver new trends to the global masses in rapid fire. H&M is often associated with the fast fashion regime, which is more accurately embodied by the quick-production activities of Inditex (parent company of Zara) and the Irish retailer, Primark, which is a subsidiary of Associated British Foods. Some observers praise the advent of fashion for everyone, while critics yearn for a return to slower modes of production and to more judicious consumption habits. In the age of democratized fashion, pundits have looked to charity shops buckling under the weight of barely worn clothing and have raised questions about the environmental costs of incessant style changes.[56]

Part III of the book looks to alternative visions of the European fashion system that have bubbled up in unexpected places. Collectively, the chapters highlight the relationship between core and periphery, and bring the book to closure with discussion of the global context for value creation (figure 1.7). We shift the focus away from the major creative hubs of Europe and the consumption centres of America to a new zone: the so-called periphery and its players. Here we examine a constellation of people and places that are important to the European fashion system, even though they are at quite some distance, either geographically or symbolically, from any European fashion capital.

Fashion has always been a global trade. The twenty-first century has witnessed a new phase of globalization made possible by international trade agreements, technologies such as container ships and digital communications, and the modernization of Asian economies such as India and China. The sea change in the democratization of fashion began in the late twentieth century with the relocation of garment production to low-wage economies. Many mass-market fashion brands contract with factories or workshops to manufacture goods on their behalf. Competition between subcontractors leads to lower production costs for the retailer.[57] Pressure comes from the consumer as well, who wants more, better, and cheaper fashion. Over the last few decades, clothing has become less expensive. The design content of cheaper clothing has improved, and rapid response in production has further contributed to the democratization of fashion.

For large numbers of consumers, especially in the West, the democratization of fashion has been something to celebrate. As the fashion theorist Gilles Lipovetsky explains, fashion is a creative outlet. It allows consumers to express their individuality – even if this means that people dress to look like other members of their group – and the widespread availability of fashion goods blurs class differences.[58] Yet distinction remains. It is visible through the quality of the garment, through subtle details of the cloth and the construction, and through expensive accessories, particularly handbags which have replaced hats as the favourite fashion pick-me-up. Even in an age of casualization and democratization, distinction has not disappeared, but it has reappeared in new sartorial forms.[59]

There have always been significant human costs associated with mechanized clothing production. Tragedies such as the Triangle Shirtwaist Factory fire in New York City in 1911 and collapse of the Rana Plaza factory building in Bangladesh in 2013 have resulted in a loss of life. These events are testimony to the dark side of the fashion system. More than a hundred years ago, the Triangle Shirtwaist Factory made inexpensive button-down blouses for the 'Gibson Girl' who had to look presentable for her job as a teacher, counter clerk, or typist.[60] Today, factories in Bangladesh, India, China, and Vietnam produce casual clothing for the consumer who tries to make ends meet by shopping at Asda, H&M, Primark, or Wal-Mart.[61]

1.7   'Workshop of the Empire' by Jill Kinnear, 2008. Made in Australia from digitally printed single and triple silk georgette and silk shantung, this garment speaks of the role tartans have played in the construction of a Scottish identity and mythology. Both in its construction and pattern (called 'Steel Tartan'), the dress evokes 'empire'.

At the same time, many Asian factories produce high-end clothing and accessories for the status-conscious fashionista who can afford to shop in luxury boutiques at the Galleria Vittorio Emanuele II in Milan or on the avenue Montaigne in Paris. Some observers point to the negative side of offshoring luxury production.[62] The journalist Dana Thomas has questioned the ethics of a fashion business that uses sweatshops to produce luxury brands retailed at premium prices.[63] This research has done much to open consumers' eyes to the Janus face of the fashion industry.

Social scientists have also debated the histories of the relocation of fashion production and its side effects. Their work reveals the complexity of fashion production. While ethically conscious consumers may refuse to buy garments produced in low-wage economies, scholars have shown that diverting production from these countries might be damaging. Many countries that make cheap apparel – locations such as Bangladesh, Vietnam, Laos, but also Montenegro and Bulgaria – are undergoing what the *New York Times* journalist Adam Davidson has called the 'T-shirt phase' of the economy. Britain had the closest equivalent to a T-shirt phase in the eighteenth century when poor farmers migrated to urban factories during the First Industrial Revolution, while the United States had two T-shirt phases, one in the nineteenth century with the rise of the New England textile mills and second in the twentieth century with the industrialization of the New South.[64] Eliminating the T-shirt phase from a developing economy might result in the withdrawal of foreign direct investment. The loss of foreign capital, in turn, might encourage reinvestment in more advanced industries that pay higher wages. These arguments, however, beg the question as to where clothing would be made, and how much the merchandise would cost in the stores.

Recent media debates over fashion and textile production have advocated for partial re-shoring of the fashion industries back to the West.[65] Those who advocate for reinvestment in Western manufacturing often link their arguments to the creation of national brands with a heritage identity. In the United Kingdom, the Campaign for Wool, an effort to promote British-made wool fabrics and fashions under the royal patronage of Prince Charles, exemplifies the effort to reinvest in Western industry and heritage.[66] Here too, social scientists have shown that there is no easy solution. A more complex reality may stand behind a 'made in Europe' tag. In one scenario, some production processes – making the thread, weaving the cloth, and cutting the cloth, for example – are completed overseas, while the finishing is done in Europe.[67] Furthermore, the site of production should not make us forget that humans migrate. Factories in the West may be staffed with under-paid workers, including illegal migrants who follow factory jobs.[68]

The rise of a multipolar system of fashion capitals has entirely transformed the geographies of fashion production. Several factors need to be considered. Some cities hope to achieve the status of fashion capital in order to boost their local, regional, and national economies. Older industrials hubs, devastated by the offshoring of production, have attempted to reconvert manufacturing spaces into creative centres. This has occurred all around Europe, from Flanders to Poland.[69] Spaces that once had little or no association with the fashion system are now vested with new symbolic value by the creative class.[70] Locales that were once production centres for traditional cloth, whether Japanese cottons or Scottish woollens, have discovered value in their authenticity and heritage. In the final decades of the twentieth century, the reinvention of tradition, combined with considerable soul searching among consumers adrift in a sea of fast fashion, generated a new interest in fashion products that were earmarked by quality and durability.[71]

We have seen that although couturiers – whether from France, Italy, or elsewhere – tried to protect their original creative designs from copyists, they were rendered helpless by the accelerated pace at which fashions changed.[72] In recent decades, the increasingly rapid turning of the fashion cycle has come under scrutiny. The accelerated pace of change has created micro-seasons and confusion over what is a new style. In a very postmodern way, endless revivals of retro styles have diluted the precision that characterised the seasonal change of fashion in the early years of Cardin, Dior, and their peers. Over the past few decades, designers and consumers have complained that fashion is going so fast that there might no longer be any fashion at all. Not everything can find new life in second-hand shops or as recycled rags. Environmentalists deplore overconsumption and landfills piled high with cheap clothes that were made to be worn once, photographed in selfies, circulated on social media, and then forgotten.

Some consumers have begun to demand a slower pace of consumption. Albeit limited to cultural and economic elites, laments over disposable fashion have inspired new forms of production and have revitalized traditional industries. Chapters 9 and 10 examine the role of heritage aesthetics as a counterpoint to fast fashion through case studies of the Japanese denim industry, and Scottish tartans and tweeds, respectively. In these essays – by Rika Fujioka and Ben Wubs on Japan and by Shiona Chillas, Melinda Grewar, and Barbara Townley on Scotland – we see companies that have chosen to harness the cult of imperfection and the cult of imagined traditions, respectively, and that seek to create design statements about permanency and legacy in a throwaway world. Are these examples the beginnings of a paradigm shift, or do they simply reflect the interests of niche markets? Regardless, these examples need to be viewed through a pragmatic lens. Such enterprises will never make goods that reach the mass market unless they follow the example of the Asian denim producer Kaihara and reduce costs by relocating production to a lower-wage economy, in their case, from Japan to Thailand.

Chapters 11 and 12 are perhaps the most provocative in the book. The first of these, by Tereza Kuldova, is an anthropological study of luxury brands and elite consumers in India that questions the ethics of ethical fashion, suggesting it might be a feel-good quick fix for the environmental degradation facing India on a massive scale. The reinvention of tradition and the concomitant borrowing of cultural motifs by fashion innovators has a dark side. This case study of India explains how the rise of ethical fashion was less a response to consumer demand than a bold marketing move. More problematic, says Kuldova, is that arguments for ethical fashion were developed in tandem with the rise of philanthropic foundations designed to address, and even mask, deep social problems such as growing economic inequality.[73]

Finally, fashion also remains a powerful voice for individual expression and collective social messages. Haute couture, as an institutionalized system, developed close ties with the arts. The producers of fashion and the creators of art both use clothing and accessories as vehicles for expression. In our book's final chapter, Wessie Ling traces the Chinese Red-White-Blue carrier bag from its origins in the market stalls of Hong Kong to its dissemination and adaptation up and down the social ladder, from global migrant communities to global luxury brands (figure 1.8).

Stanley Wong, 'Investigation of a journey to the west by micro+polo: redwhiteblue', Tea and Chat installation, Venice Biennale, 2005.   **1.8**

This case study shows how one artefact travelled from the site of its invention in Asia to distant Africa where it was used by poverty-stricken refugees. Yet this ordinary object of mass consumption, with all the symbolic charge that it embodies, was also expropriated by European fashion brands and by global artists, each with different intentions. Fashion has never ceased to signify meanings, whether in its production or in its re-appropriation.

In all four chapters, the authors consider important social and cultural questions from the perspective of the company, the brand, and the larger context, always giving voice to the actors behind the scenes. This balanced perspective, which considers the voices of creators unedited by the public-relations machine, is often missing from criticisms or celebrations of the contemporary fashion scene. Collectively, the concluding chapters speak to the open-endedness of contemporary history, which necessarily raises questions but provides few solutions. We hope at least to provide food for thought.

New directions

Over the past few decades, Western consumers have significantly increased their fashion budgets and have purchased more and more fashion goods. The price of clothing has steadily declined, particularly in the New Millennium with the removal of tariffs and quotas by the World Trade Organization (WTO). Despite the proliferation of inexpensive fashion, luxury brands constitute one of most profitable sectors in today's global economy.[74] The middle ground has evaporated, and the consumer market is bifurcated into high and low.

The case studies in this book have examined the mechanisms for creating value within the fashion system. Why is fashion such a desirable commodity? What makes fashion 'hot' and saleable at all price points? What makes a Gucci bag attractive to a Middle Eastern heiress who shops at Harrods, and what makes a knock-off appealing to the shopper who frequents the flea market on Petticoat Lane? Is it accurate to think of consumers as fashion victims, or are consumers the driving force behind the fashion system? This book has explored these quandaries by stepping outside the factory and examining the activities that serve as a prelude to manufacturing. Our goal has been to trace the pathways of fashion design, management, marketing, retailing, branding, and consumption. Through this effort, we have sought to understand how consumer desires are interpreted and translated into marketable new objects by the creative class in the fashion system.

Although manufacturing is now mainly located in the East, much of the aesthetic, cultural, and financial capital of fashion has remained in the West. Whether in 1947 or today, fashion experts travel around the world, exchange knowledge, and relentlessly track new trends. This book has weighed heavily on Europe and America, exploring fashion centres and following in the footsteps of the people who generated fashion know-how. Our chapters have necessarily moved between the local and the global, assessing the transformation of local industries into global brands and codes. Case studies have ranged from Swedish-designed apparel and Scottish tweeds to Japanese denim, Indian luxury goods, and Hong-Kong carrier bags. Our story began with the fading glory of haute couture and ends with the vibrant world of fashion for everyone.

We contend that three geographical ensembles are fundamental to understanding the functions of fashion as a business. One space can be broadly defined as *European*. That space encompasses the relationships among central fashion capitals like Paris and regional manufacturing centres like Scotland. This book explores the changing relationships between those economic regions and taste cultures. The second space is *transatlantic*. Several contributions to this book consider the special fashion-industry connections between Europe and North America, notably the United States, which deserve scrutiny in order to better understand the dynamics of markets and innovation in the twentieth century. While the New York garment district manufactured the lion's share of mass-produced garments, the output of European centres offers a striking counterpoint to the postwar idea of American hegemony in the spheres of economy and consumption. The final space can be called *global*. The major European cities proved to be enduring centres of research and development and innovation in fashion design, while places in the so-called European periphery served as manufacturing centres for textiles and garments and gave birth to new creative fashion hubs. Several contributions in this book shift the focus from Europe to the new production capitals of Asia. Studies of emerging players in manufacturing and branding, notably in Japan and India, rounds out our approach to the business and economic history of fashion production.

Our research blends theoretical and critical approaches with empirical studies. Core questions point to what makes this edited volume unique. Who were the real innovators in the Western fashion system? Why did Europe remain important to fashion despite the upheavals in the global economy in the late twentieth century? What can we learn about the creation of cultural forms by looking below the surface – beneath the hype about brands – and into the ateliers of creative professionals, the design studios of textile mills, and the merchandising offices of mass-market retailers? The case-study approach combines the empirical and the theoretical, and offers lively narratives. We are pleased to pull back the curtain, peek in on fashion experts at work, and show how entrepreneurs and firms created one of the most successful business sectors in modern Europe and adapted it to the changing markets of our own time.

Notes

1 B. Polan and R. Tredre, *The Great Fashion Designers* (London: Bloomsbury, 2009), p. 101.
2 Hagley Museum and Library, Wilmington, DE, Pictorial Collections, accession 84.259: DuPont Product Information Collection, box 66, folder: 'Paris Photographs – February 1961', photograph no. 84.259.5856.
3 N. Troy, *Couture Culture: A Study in Modern Art and Fashion* (Cambridge, MA: MIT Press, 2003); A. de la Haye and A. Mendes, *The House of Worth: Portrait of an Archive* (London: V&A Publishing, 2014).
4 T. Veblen, *The Theory of the Leisure Class: An Economic Study in the Evolution of Institutions* (New York: Macmillan, 1899).
5 G. Simmel, 'Fashion', *American Journal of Sociology*, 62:6 (1957), 541–58. This article was first published in 1904.
6 D. Crane, *Fashion and Its Social Agendas: Class, Gender, and Identity in Clothing* (Chicago: University of Chicago Press, 2000).
7 T. Agins, *The End of Fashion: The Mass Marketing of the Clothing Business* (New York: Morrow, 1999).
8 M. Fairs, '"It's the end of fashion as we know it" says Li Edelkoort', *Dezeen* (March 2015), at www.dezeen.com/2015/03/01/li-edelkoort-end-of-fashion-as-we-know-it-design-indaba-2015/ (accessed 16 October 2016).
9 F. Duncan, 'Normcore: fashion for those who realize they're one in 7 billion', *New York Times Magazine* (26 February 2014), at http://nymag.com/thecut/2014/02/normcore-fashion-trend.html (accessed 24 October 2016); L. Cochrane, 'Normcore: the next big fashion movement? *Guardian* (27 February 2014), at www.theguardian.com/fashion/fashion-blog/2014/feb/27/normcore-the-next-big-fashion-movement (accessed 24 October 2016).
10 R. L. Blaszczyk, *Fashionability: Abraham Moon and the Creation of British Cloth for the Global Market* (Manchester: Manchester University Press, 2017), chap. 5.
11 K. T. Hansen, *Salaula: The World of Secondhand Clothing and Zambia* (Chicago: University of Chicago Press, 2000); Blaszczyk, *Fashionability*, chaps. 6–7.
12 J. Laver and A. de la Haye, *Costume and Fashion: A Concise History*, (London: Thames & Hudson, 4th edn 1995).
13 C. Breward, *The Culture of Fashion: A New History of Fashionable Dress* (Manchester: Manchester University Press, 1995); L. Przybyszewski, *The Lost Art of Dress: The Women Who Once Made America Stylish* (New York: Basic Books, 2014); C. Breward, *The Suit: Form, Function and Style* (London: Reaktion Books, 2016).
14 On fashion and the body, see, for example, V. Steele, *Fashion and Eroticism: Ideals of Feminine Beauty from the Victorian Era to the Jazz Age* (New York: Oxford University Press, 1985); C. Kidwell and V. Steele (eds), *Men and Women: Dressing the Part* (Washington, DC: Smithsonian Institution Press, 1989); V. Steele, *The Corset: A Cultural History* (New Haven: Yale University Press, 2001); C. Evans, *Fashion at the Edge: Spectacle, Modernity and Deathliness* (New Haven: Yale University Press, 2003). On apparel production, see N. L. Green, *Ready-to-Wear and Ready-to-Work: A Century of Industry and Immigrants in Paris and New York* (Durham, NC: Duke University Press, 1997); K. Honeyman, *Well Suited: A History of the Leeds Clothing Industry, 1850–1990* (Oxford: Oxford University Press, 2000); C. Rose, *Making, Selling and Wearing Boys' Clothes in Late-Victorian England* (Farnham: Ashgate, 2010). On gender, see L. Taylor, *Study of Dress History* (Manchester: Manchester University Press, 2002), and L. Ugolini, *Men and Menswear: Sartorial Consumption in Britain, 1880–1939* (Aldershot: Ashgate, 2007). On subcultural style, see K. L. Peiss, *Zoot Suit: The Enigmatic Career of an Extreme Style* (Philadelphia: University of Pennsylvania Press, 2011); P. Mears et al (eds), *Ivy Style: Radical Conformist* (New Haven: Yale University Press, 2012); D. Clemente, *Dress Casual: How College*

Students Redefined American Style (Chapel Hill: University of North Carolina Press, 2014); J. Potvin, *Bachelors of a Different Sort: Queer Aesthetics, Material Culture, and the Modern Interior in Britain* (Manchester: Manchester University Press, 2015).

15 A. D. Chandler Jr., *Strategy and Structure: Chapters in the History of the Industrial Enterprise* (Cambridge, MA: MIT Press, 1962); A. D. Chandler Jr., *The Visible Hand: The Managerial Revolution in American Business* (Cambridge, MA: Belknap Press of Harvard University Press, 1977); A. D. Chandler Jr. and T. Hikino, *Scale and Scope: The Dynamics of Industrial Capitalism* (Cambridge, MA: Harvard University Press, 1994).

16 R. John, 'Elaborations, revisions, dissents: Alfred D. Chandler Jr.'s *The Visible Hand* after twenty years', *Business History Review*, 71:2 (summer 1997), 151–200.

17 R. L. Blaszczyk, *The Color Revolution* (Cambridge, MA: MIT Press, 2012); S. Clarke, 'Managing design: the Art and Colour Section at General Motors, 1927–1941', *Journal of Design History*, 12:1 (1999), 65–79.

18 R. L. Blaszczyk, *American Consumer Society, 1865–2005: From Hearth to HDTV* (Hoboken, NJ: Wiley, 2009).

19 R. Tedlow, *New and Improved: The Story of Mass Marketing in America* (New York: Basic Books, 1990).

20 For early critiques of Chandler that laid the groundwork for the cultural turn, see D. B. Sicilia, 'Cochran's legacy: a cultural path not taken', *Business and Economic History*, 24:1 (fall 1995), 27–39, and K. J. Lipartito, 'Culture and the practice of business history', *Business and Economic History*, 24:1 (winter 1995), 1–41.

21 R. Marchand, *Advertising the American Dream, Making Way for Modernity, 1920–1940* (Berkeley: University of California Press, 1986); R. L. Blaszczyk, *Imagining Consumers: Design and Innovation from Wedgwood to Corning* (Baltimore: Johns Hopkins University Press, 2000); P. W. Laird, *Advertising Progress: American Business and the Rise of Consumer Marketing* (Baltimore: Johns Hopkins University Press, 2001); V. Pouillard, *La publicité en Belgique: Des courtiers aux agencies internationales, 1850–1975* (Brussels: Académie Royale de Belgique, 2005); V. Pouillard, 'American advertising agencies in Europe: J. Walter Thompson's Belgian business in the interwar years', *Business History*, 47:1 (2005), 44–58; V. Howard, *Brides, Inc.: American Weddings and the Business of Tradition* (Philadelphia: University of Pennsylvania Press, 2006); E. Brown, C. Gudis, and M. Moskowitz (eds), *Cultures of Commerce: Representation and American Business Culture, 1877–1960* (New York: Palgrave Macmillan, 2006); and M. Moskowitz, *Standard of Living: The Measure of the Middle Class in Modern America* (Baltimore: Johns Hopkins University Press, 2009).

22 S. Zdatny (ed.), *Hairstyles and Fashion: A Hairdresser's History of Paris, 1910–1920* (Oxford: Berg, 1999); K. Peiss, *Hope in a Jar: The Making of America's Beauty Culture* (New York: Metropolitan Books, 2000); T. M. Gill, *Beauty Shop Politics: African American Women's Activism in the Beauty Industry* (Urbana, IL: University of Illinois Press, 2010); G. Jones, *Beauty Imagined: A History of the Global Beauty Industry* (Oxford: Oxford University Press, 2010); Blaszczyk, *Color Revolution*; H. Berghoff and U. Spiekermann (eds), *Decoding Modern Consumer Societies* (New York: Palgrave Macmillan, 2012); H. Berghoff and T. Kühne (eds), *Globalizing Beauty: Consumerism and Body Aesthetics in the Twentieth Century* (New York: Palgrave Macmillan, 2013); R. L. Blaszczyk and U. Spiekermann (eds), *Bright Modernity: Color, Commerce, and Consumer Culture* (New York: Palgrave Macmillan, 2017).

23 'Fashion and style' special issue, *Business History Review*, 80:3 (autumn 2006), 415–528; R. L. Blaszczyk (ed.), *Producing Fashion: Commerce, Culture, and Consumers* (Philadelphia: University of Pennsylvania Press, 2008); W. A. Friedman and G. Jones (eds), 'Creative industries in history' special issue, *Business History Review*, 85:2 (summer 2011), 237–366; V. Pouillard, 'Design piracy in the fashion industries of Paris and New York in the interwar years', *Business History Review*, 85:2 (summer

2011), 319–44; F. Polese and R. L. Blaszczyk (eds), 'Fashion' special issue, *Business History*, 54 (February 2012), 6–115; V. Pouillard, 'The rise of fashion forecasting and fashion public relations: the history of Tobé and Bernays', in Berghoff and Kühne (eds), *Globalizing Beauty*, 151–69.

24 P. B. Scranton and P. Fridenson, *Reimagining Business History* (Baltimore: Johns Hopkins University Press, 2013). See also R. L. Blaszczyk and P. B. Scranton (eds), *Major Problems in American Business History: Documents and Essays* (Boston, MA: Houghton Mifflin, 2006).

25 A. Palmer, *Couture and Commerce: The Transatlantic Fashion Trade in the 1950s* (Vancouver: University of British Columbia Press, 2001); D. Blum, *Shocking! The Art and Fashion of Elsa Schiaparelli* (Philadelphia, PA: Philadelphia Museum of Art, 2003).

26 S. Stanfill, *New York Fashion* (London: V&A, 2007); S. Stanfill (ed.), *The Glamour of Italian Fashion Since 1945* (London: V&A Publishing, 2014).

27 Blaszczyk, *American Consumer Society*.

28 Honeyman, *Well Suited*.

29 Numerous studies have examined production and labour in the garment industries. See, for example, Green, *Ready-to-Wear and Ready-to-Work*; V. Pouillard, *Hirsch & Cie, Bruxelles (1869–1962)* (Brussels: Editions de l'Université Libre de Bruxelles, 2000); A. Godley, *Jewish Immigrant Entrepreneurship in New York and London, 1880–1914* (New York: Palgrave, 2001); A. Godley, 'Selling the sewing machine around the world: Singer's international marketing strategies 1850–1920', *Enterprise and Society*, 7:2 (2008), 266–314; A. D. Mendelsohn, *The Rag Race: How Jews Sewed Their Way to Success in America and the British Empire* (New York: New York University Press, 2015).

30 Green, *Ready-to-Wear and Ready-to-Work*; V. Pouillard, 'Production and distribution', in A. Palmer (ed.), *The Cultural History of Dress and Fashion. Vol. 6: The Twentieth Century* (London: Bloomsbury, 2016), pp. 43–61.

31 Blaszczyk, *Fashionability*, chaps. 6–7.

32 J.-M. Servais, *International Labor Organization* (Alphen aan de Rijn, Neth.: Wolters Kluwer, 2011); D. R. Maul, 'The International Labour Organization and the struggle against forced labour from 1919 to the present', *Labor History*, 48:4 (2007), 477–500.

33 P. Rivoli, *Travels of a T-Shirt in the Global Economy: An Economist Examines the Markets, Power and Politics of World Trade* (Hoboken, NJ: John Wiley & Sons, 2005), p. xv.

34 N. Klein, *No Logo: Taking Aim at the Brand Bullies* (Toronto: Alfred A. Knopf Canada, 1999).

35 Clean Clothes Campaign, at https://cleanclothes.org/ (accessed 20 October 2016); L. Sluiter, *Clean Clothes Campaign: A Global Movement to End Sweatshops* (London: Pluto Press, 2009).

36 C. Wilcox (ed.), *The Golden Age of Haute Couture: Paris and London, 1947–1957* (London: V&A Publishing, 2007).

37 Troy, *Couture Culture*; M. L. Stewart, *Dressing Modern Frenchwomen: Marketing Haute Couture, 1919–1939* (Baltimore: Johns Hopkins University Press, 2008); Pouillard 'Design piracy in the fashion industries of Paris and New York in the interwar years'.

38 V. Pouillard, 'Keeping designs and brands authentic: the resurgence of the post-war French fashion business under the challenge of US mass production', *European Review of History*, 20:5 (2013), 815–35.

39 C. Breward and D. Gilbert (eds), *Fashion's World Cities* (New York: Berg, 2006).

40 I. Daria, *The Fashion Cycle* (New York: Simon & Schuster, 1990).

41 T. Okawa, 'Licensing practices at Maison Dior', in Blaszczyk (ed.), *Producing Fashion*; C. Goldstein, *Creating Consumers: Home Economists in Twentieth-Century America* (Chapel Hill: University of North Carolina Press, 2012), 139–40.

42 Okawa, 'Licensing practices at Maison Dior'.

43 P. H. Hansen, 'Business history: a cultural and narrative approach', *Business History Review*, 86:4 (winter 2012), 693–717.

44 LVMH, 'The Fondation Louis Vuitton, Art and Culture', at www.lvmh.com/group/lvmh-commitments/art-culture/fondation-louis-vuitton/ (accessed 20 October 2016).

45 R. Marchand, *Creating the Corporate Soul: The Rise of Public Relations and Corporate Imagery in American Big Business* (Berkeley: University of California Press, 2001).

46 L. Tiersten, *Marianne in the Market: Envisioning Consumer Society in Fin-de-Siècle France* (Berkeley: University of California Press, 2001); E. Rappaport, *Shopping for Pleasure: Women and the Making of London's West End* (Princeton: Princeton University Press, 2000); S. Jaumain and G. Crossick (eds), *Cathedrals of Consumption: The European Department Store 1850–1939* (London: Ashgate, 1999).

47 M. B. Miller, *The Bon Marché: Bourgeois Culture and the Department Store, 1869–1920* (Princeton: Princeton University Press, 1981).

48 T. J. Jackson Lears, *Fables of Abundance: A Cultural History of Advertising in America* (New York: Basic Books, 1994); William Leach, *Land of Desire: Merchants, Power, and the Rise of a New American Culture* (New York: Pantheon Books, 1993); Tedlow, *New and Improved*.

49 E. Merlo and F. Polese, 'Turning fashion into business: the emergence of Milan as an international fashion hub', *Business History Review*, 80:3 (autumn 2006), 415–47; E. Merlo and F. Polese, 'Accessorizing, Italian style: creating a market for Milan's fashion merchandise', in Blaszczyk (ed.), *Producing Fashion*, pp. 42–61.

50 See, for example, F. Brachet, M. Allera, and S. Desvaux, *Du Grand Bazar de l'Hôtel de Ville au BHV Marais, le grand magasin préféré des parisiens* (Paris: Assouline, 2016).

51 P. Lerner, *The Consuming Temple: Jews, Department Stores, and the Consumer Revolution in Germany, 1880–1940* (Cornell, NY: Cornell University Press, 2015), p. 13.

52 Prudence Glynn, 'The multi-story clothes park', *The Times* (29 October 1968). The history of the large American specialist fashion store will be discussed in Regina Lee Blaszczyk's forthcoming book on fashion retailing.

53 Blaszczyk, *Fashionability*, chaps. 5–8.

54 On chain-store buyers and department store buyers as fashion intermediaries, see Blaszczyk, *Imagining Consumers*, pp. 89–167.

55 S. Schwarzkopf, 'The consumer as "voter", "judge", and "jury": historical origins and political consequences of a marketing myth', *Journal of Macromarketing*, 31:1 (March 2011), 8–18.

56 H. Clark and A. Palmer (eds), *Old Clothes, New Looks: Second-Hand Fashion* (London: Berg, 2004).

57 Green, *Ready-to-Wear and Ready-to-Work*, pp. 15–43; Pouillard 'Production and distribution'.

58 G. Lipovetsky, *L'empire de l'éphémère: La mode et son destin dans les sociétes modernes* (Paris: Gallimard, 1987).

59 P. Bourdieu, *La distinction: Critique sociale du jugement* (Paris: Minuit, 1979).

60 D. Von Drehle, *Triangle: The Fire that Changed America* (New York: Atlantic Monthly Press, 2003).

61 J. Kasperkevic, 'Rana Plaza collapse: workplace dangers persist three years later, report finds', *Guardian* (31 May 2016), at www.theguardian.com/business/2016/may/31/rana-plaza-bangladesh-collapse-fashion-working-conditions (accessed 4 September 2016).

62 Rivoli, *Travels of a T-Shirt in the Global Economy*.

63 D. Thomas, *Deluxe: How Luxury Lost Its Luster* (New York: Penguin, 2007). For a discussion that is more historically grounded, see P. McNeill and G. Riello, *Luxury: A Rich History* (New York: Oxford, 2016).

64 A. Davidson, 'Economic recovery, made in Bangladesh?', *New York Times Magazine* (14 May 2013).
65 S. Berger, *Making in America: From Innovation to Market* (Cambridge: MIT Press, 2015).
66 Blaszczyk, *Fashionability*, chap. 9.
67 P.-Y. Donzé, *Histoire du Swatch Group* (Neuchâtel: Alphil, 2012).
68 R. Kloosterman and J. Rath, 'Immigrant entrepreneurs in advanced economies: mixed embeddedness further explored', *Journal of Ethnic and Migration Studies*, 27:2 (2001), 189–201.
69 J. Gimeno Martinez, 'Restructuring plans for the textile and clothing sector in post-industrial Belgium and Spain', *Fashion Practice*, 3:2 (2011), 197–224.
70 R. Florida, *The Rise of the Creative Class: And How It's Transforming Work, Leisure, Community, and Everyday Life* (New York: Basic Books, 2002).
71 On the reinvention of tradition in earlier periods, see E. Hobsbawm and T. Ranger (eds), *The Invention of Tradition* (Cambridge: Cambridge University Press, 1983).
72 On the accelerators, see R. Barthes, *Système de la mode* (Paris: Seuil, 1967), p. 332.
73 T. Piketty, *La capital au XXIᵉ siècle* (Paris: Seuil, 2013).
74 Donzé, *Histoire du Swatch Group*; L. Bergeron, *Les industries du luxe en France* (Paris: Odile Jacob, 1998).

PART I

Reinventing Paris fashion

2

Recasting Paris fashion: haute couture and design management in the postwar era

Véronique Pouillard

World War II had turned the fashion world upside down. For the first time, international buyers stopped going to Paris. Under the German occupation from 14 June 1940 to 24 August 1944, the world centre of women's fashions was cut off from all Allied countries, and from a good share of its buyers. In the meanwhile, New York took the leadership. In the spring of 1940, the Germans had not yet entered Paris, but the situation was clear. Fiorello La Guardia, the mayor of New York City, was invited to speak at a luncheon of the New York Fashion Group, an influential organization of women in the fashion industry. He acknowledged that his first interest was New York City, not fashion, but that reality did not deter him from addressing this brilliant group of several hundred fashion experts.

Present at the table that day were Carmel Snow, editor of *Harper's Bazaar*, Julia Coburn of the Tobé-Coburn School for fashion careers and president of the Fashion Group, and Adam Gimbel, president of Saks Fifth Avenue and of the Uptown Retail Guild, a trade association for high-end retailers.[1] The mayor underlined that, historically, fashion had been the exclusive purview of a few social elites who could afford Paris haute couture.[2] Dressing in style was limited to the happy few. That said, American women, whether they lived on farms or in big cities, had started to demand fashionable dress. Paris was about to fall to the Nazis, and it was time, according to La Guardia, to acknowledge the huge American market and to support the work of New York designers. Up to this time, garment manufacturers in the United States had invested too little in design development. 'It is getting to be a habit to hire designers by the hour or sometimes by the day and it is simply disgraceful! You just can't expect creative work to be successful and to be beautiful if the creator is working under the stress of economic problems', La Guardia exclaimed. 'A good designer ought to be employed by the season, at least. Of course, you take a chance. It can't be helped; that is part of the risk of the trade.'[3] Designers, added the mayor, had to work on meeting the needs of their markets and adjust to economic conditions; the 'first thing that the designer must do today is to save in every possible way, count every stitch that goes into that dress, every button that must be sewed on, everything that adds to the cost of that dress'.[4] This approach to design was far removed from the methods used by Paris couturiers, who rarely counted the lengths of material and or the cost of human energy when designing a new collection. However, La Guardia had a particular agenda in mind. New York had to become the world's fashion capital.[5]

After the war, Paris fashion came back to life and haute couture experienced a new golden age in the 1950s.[6] To compete with the up-and-coming fashion capitals such as New York City, the Paris couture houses had to develop a new business model. 'For things to remain the same, everything must change', is a relevant famous line from *Il Gattopardo*, the great novel by Giuseppe Tommasi du Lampedusa, whose depiction of the nineteenth-century Italian aristocracy was published posthumously in 1958 (and translated as *The Leopard*). Parisian haute couture of the 1950s faced a comparable fate to the one that the Italian aristocracy had experienced in the previous century; both risked losing touch with the changing worlds in which they lived. Haute couture catered to exclusive clients, expecting its designs to trickle down from the top and to be imitated by the lower strata of society. This class-based system was out of touch with the postwar world.[7]

For haute couture to survive and for Paris to remain one of the world's great fashion cities, the industry had to adapt. This chapter explores the struggles of postwar couture from three focal points.[8] The first section of the chapter sheds light on the dissemination of Paris couture through the development of agreements with domestic French manufacturers to reproduce couture lines for a wider audience. The second section addresses the relationship between the couturiers and the French government, and the politics of subventions granted by the state to haute couture during the 1950s. The main association of Paris couturiers, the Chambre Syndicale de la Couture Parisienne (hereafter Chambre Syndicale) drew on a government subvention to open an office in New York, which was a dramatic break from couture's historical association with Paris. The third section examines how entrepreneurs in the couture business sought to protect their portfolios of intellectual property rights in the years around the signature of the Treaty of Rome, 1957, which created the foundation for European integration through the formation of the Common Market. These three major developments emerged against the backdrop of the development of the welfare state.[9]

Out of Paris: couture going domestic, and international

Founded in 1868 and redefined in 1910, the Chambre Syndicale played a central role in the management of Paris's haute couture cluster. During the early twentieth century, it developed and oversaw a system that limited commercial attendance at couture shows to an elite cadre of registered buyers, mainly those foreign retailers and manufacturers that were prestigious enough to reproduce and sell haute couture abroad. Before World War II, French manufacturers had been prohibited from entering haute couture shows because their mass copies of haute couture had the potential to denigrate the value of the originals in France. These restrictive policies had generated problems. They had the opposite effect of generating the piracy of haute couture in the French home market and internal disagreements between couturiers. In 1944, the Chambre Syndicale decided that the end of the war would bring the opportunity for a change, and the members of the association, which included nearly all Paris couturiers, drafted the so-called Paris-Province agreements. These agreements defined the nature of haute couture production. They also specified that Paris haute couture shows would be opened to domestic manufacturers and retailers, provided they registered, obtained a buyer's card from the Chambre Syndicale, and pledged to spend a guaranteed minimum in haute couture purchases (see 'Guarantee of purchase' in table 2.1). More importantly, these agreements meant that French domestic manufacturers would now be able to reproduce haute couture, or to design after haute couture, under the law.

Prior to 1947 when the Paris-Province agreements went into effect, the French department stores and provincial manufacturers had relied

Table 2.1 French provincial manufacturers' purchases of haute couture, 1954–60

Season	Number of contracts	Guarantee of purchase in francs	Controlled purchases in francs
1954 Spring-Summer	85	24,600,000	37,150,000
1954 Autumn-Winter	82	23,700,000	32,122,000
1955 S-S	85	24,850,000	29,064,000
1955 A-W	84	24,950,000	29,751,797
1956 S-S	83	25,900,000	–
1956 A-W	–	–	–
1957 S-S	75	22,500,000	36,331,000
1957 A-W	79	23,700,000	30,000,000
1958 S-S	75	22,500,000	35,837,000
1958 A-W	72	21,600,000	28,123,500
1959 S-S	90	23,100,000	30,214,380
1959 A-W	90	20,700,000	42,494,915
1960 S-S	82	19,200,000	31,166,063
1960 A-W	84	19,200,000	29,333,340

Source: Chambre Syndicale de la Couture Parisienne archives (CSCPA), Rapports d'activité, years 1954–61, data compiled by the author.

upon surreptitious methods to obtain access to designs.[10] In the postwar
era, the authorization for provincial manufacturers to attend Paris fashion
shows removed barriers that had prevented the French ready-to-wear
manufacturers from accessing haute couture shows. As a consequence,
the design quotient in French mass-produced clothes increased. The new
connections developed in France between haute couture and mass manufacturing created a considerable source of revenue for postwar couture,
as shown in the 'Controlled Purchases' entry in table 2.1. The new rules
also made it easier for haute couture houses to develop their own ready-
to-wear lines. Attempts to implement such a system during the interwar
period had not been successful due to cultural and structural factors.

We have seen in the address of Mayor La Guardia that the New York
garment industry had hoped, during World War II, to permanently sup-
plant Paris as the world's capital of fashion. Despite New York's heady
ambitions, several fashion cities flourished in the postwar period. Paris
returned to the front of the stage, but now among a small group of fashion
capitals that included London, Florence, Milan, Rome, Los Angeles, and
New York. The renaissance of Paris was marked by the emergence of one
especially creative designer, Christian Dior, who received the support of
Marcel Boussac, the most prominent textile manufacturer in France (see
figures 2.1 and 2.2). The couturier Dior established a limited liability company in 1946 and branched out to New York in 1948. Within a few years
the house of Dior, supported by large capital investments from Boussac
and by the excellent management of Jacques Rouët, became the paradigm
for the new business model of haute couture. The company emerged as
a new type of couture house dedicated to mapping out a global haute
couture brand – something inconceivable before World War II.[11] During
the interwar period, haute couture had remained anchored in Paris due to
both the contraction of global trade during the Great Depression and the
strong desire of the Chambre Syndicale to keep couture as a local cluster
firmly within Paris, where they could preserve its creative soul and maintain control of its ownership.

With the new business model developed by Dior and Boussac, creation
of couture lines remained in Paris, while retail branches opened all over
the postwar world, from New York and London to Cuba and Caracas.[12]
Other Paris couturiers followed in the footsteps of the house of Dior.
They developed lines bearing their name, manufactured by licensee firms
carefully selected by the couturiers for their technical ability to translate a
design into a garment and put it before the world. These strategies were
aimed at retaining control of the dissemination channels for haute couture
designs. Couturiers had always been confounded by the rampant copying of their designs. Now they hoped that the business model developed
by Dior would allow them to cash in on the benefits of their creativity.
Reinforcement policies protective of intellectual property rights were a

B. Altman & Co. advertisement of a Christian Dior dress, 1951. Photograph by Richard Avedon.

2.1

priority for couture, but this was not enough. Producing one's own ready-to-wear was a more proactive method of retaining control over innovative design.[13]

One haute couture entrepreneur who was an early postwar adapter to ready-to-wear was Pierre Balmain. He apprenticed with Dior at the

TISSU GARANTI
Boussac

le meilleur
pour son usage
et pour son prix

500 KILOMÈTRES DE TISSU PAR JOUR, MAIS SEULEMENT 10 %
DE LA PRODUCTION COTONNIÈRE FRANÇAISE. VÉRIFIEZ DONC
BIEN LA PRÉSENCE DE L'ÉCUSSON BOUSSAC SUR LES ARTICLES
QUE VOUS ACHETEZ. CHEMISES, ROBES, BLOUSES, TABLIERS,
VÊTEMENTS DE TRAVAIL ET DE SPORT, SERVICES DE
TABLE, MOUCHOIRS, LINGE ÉPONGE, TISSUS D'AMEUBLEMENT.

2.2   Boussac advertisement by the illustrator Brènot, 1953. This fabric manufacturer's brand was established in 1933.

house of Lelong and opened his limited liability firm at rue François-Ier on 24 May 1945.[14] Balmain travelled to New York in 1946 to study the American market and signed a contract for the diffusion of his designs by Californian department store I. Magnin, an important buyer for European fashion discussed by Sonnet Stanfill in Chapter 6.[15] Balmain started his first ready-to-wear line in the United States in the early 1950s in partner-ship with New York manufacturer Maria Krum.[16] In 1951, Balmain designs were purchased as follows: twenty-five per cent by international private clientele, mostly socialites with refined tastes and a full social agenda; forty per cent by American private customers; thirty-four per cent by private and corporate clients in France; and one per cent by American wholesalers.[17] The last group, although small in number, had a widespread influence on the industry because they bought models for reproduction at various price points for the American market. In 1955, Balmain received the Neiman Marcus Award for Distinguished Service in the Field of Fashion, the high-est accolade in the American fashion industry. The award acknowledged the importance of his designs to the American market; fittingly, Dior had received this award in 1947.[18]

Another Paris couturier who had an early start with ready-to-wear was Jacques Fath, who began licensing ready-to-wear in 1947 and tripled his sales between 1947 and 1949.[19] Fath set up an agreement with the American manufacturer Joseph Halpert, which brought him into competi-tion with Dior, at that time developing wholesale couture with the help of other New York garment manufacturers.[20]

Such ventures demanded an excellent understanding of the American market, a great sense of commercial adaptation, knowledge of foreign laws, and a copious supply of funds. Although Boussac had set up Dior, others did not benefit from such generous funding. One viable option for couturiers was to federate, or join forces, when launching their ready-to-wear lines, a project supported by the Chambre Syndicale. In June 1950, one such joint venture, the Couturiers Associés, comprising Fath, Marie-Louise Carven, Jean Dessès, Jeanne Paquin, and Robert Piguet, linked up with seven French ready-to-wear manufacturers for the creation of designs sold in twenty-five French provincial cities under the label of 'Couturiers Associés'. Dresses were retailed at prices varying between 25,000 and 45,000 francs, or $75 to $115.[21]

The couturiers considered the possibility of extending such ready-to-wear designed-by-couturiers operations to the United States.[22] A journal-ist in *Le Monde* pondered the pros and cons of such a business venture. What would this strategy bring to France? A major counter argument was that couture must remain entirely in Paris so as to provide the city with a source of revenue from direct taxes. In this view, the exportation of pro-duction and retailing would undermine the economy of the Paris haute couture cluster. In addition, indirect tax revenues would be threatened. Critics wanted to see American tourists in Paris. American visitors not only bought the new dresses sold under the labels of Dior and Balmain, but they also used the services of hotels, bars, and restaurants. They pur-chased souvenirs and encouraged other Americans to visit Paris. Fashion tourism attracted wealth, and it was therefore difficult for many fashion professionals and government officials to see Paris couturiers establishing branches abroad.[23]

While some Paris couturiers actively developed their ready-to-wear and wholesale lines, there was a lot of ambivalence about such a strategy. This was despite the fact that from 1911 (when the Chambre Syndicale had split from the *confection*, as the garment manufacturing profession was called in French) couturiers had opened *boutiques* where they sold branded perfumes, accessories, and small gift objects. While the boutique was a strategy that had helped haute couture houses to survive the Great Depression, the Chambre Syndicale periodically questioned the relevance of the development of this form of commerce for its members. By the mid-twentieth century, the Chambre Syndicale was still ill at ease with the idea of its members venturing into readymade garments, beachwear, and small gift articles. In 1943, haute couture finally received a legal definition, which limited the use of the word 'couture' to firms working according to the century-long principles of craftsmanship dressmaking. Traditionally, haute couture garments were conceived, realized, sewn, shown, and sold on the premises of the haute couture house. While such a definition was protective of haute couture, the law made it more difficult for haute couture to update its techniques and reduce its costs. The inherent tension between tradition and modernization experienced by the haute couture milieu was strongly felt in the postwar years. The couture system was no stranger to the rising cost of the workforce created by the development of the welfare state, which mandated a complete system of social benefits that consisted of minimum wages, maximum working hours, paid holidays, retirement funding, access to health care, and the right to unionize. It was particularly important for firms within such a creative industry as haute couture to retain the most qualified workforce. This level of stability could be guaranteed only by offering high salaries to the qualified workers, as shown in table 2.2. Couturiers however were torn between the need to modernize and the demands of their craft.

While the Chambre Syndicale worried about the likelihood that such new strategies would damage the symbolic capital of haute couture and even provoke the end of the Paris haute couture cluster, the New York fashion industry, which had its own higher-end firms like Hattie Carnegie and Maurice Rentner, had other worries. However, historian Nancy Green has underlined what united the fashion firms of both sides of the Atlantic Ocean. Even where batch production ruled and even in the lower-priced lines and in the most mechanized factories, the human hand was always needed. If we examine the New York high-end and medium-range fashion industry, however, we see that the Seventh Avenue firms had generally adopted a business model different from the approach adopted by Paris couture. The New York garment district produced lines in anonymous workshops; the goods were retailed in department stores under various

Table 2.2 The Paris haute couture cluster in 1954, listing the haute couture houses acknowledged as fitting the classification 'Couture-Création' by the French Ministry of Economy and Finances.[a]

Firm	Form of the company	Date of foundation	Number of designs per year	Are designs registered?	Workers	Top yearly salary (francs)
Alex Maguy	One-person firm	1924	160	Yes		
Amy Linker	s.a.r.l.[b]		130	Yes		
Ardanse	One-person firm	1939	80		15, of whom 9 manual	45,000 (première)
Balenciaga	s.a.r.l. Capital 30 million	24 June 1937	204	Yes	318, of whom 250 manual	119,700 (cutter)
Bernard Sagardoy	One-person firm		173	Yes	28, of whom 20 manual	40,000 (cutter)
Bruyère	s.a.r.l.	1928	250	Yes		
Calixte	s.a.r.l.					
Carven	s.a.r.l.	1 January 1937	302	Yes	138, of whom 80 manual	73,709 (première)
Charles Montaigne	S.A.[c]	January 1940	242	Yes	84, of whom 64 manual	75,000 (cutter)
Christian Dior	s.a.r.l.	8 October 1946	325	Precise conditions outlined in the form	969, of whom 530 manual	114,435 (cutter)
Edmond Courtot	s.a.r.l.	June 1931	50	Yes	19, of whom 14 manual	39,000 (première)
'Enfantillages' – Steinmuller	One person firm	2 October 1950	71	50%	14, of whom 12 manual	65,000 to 100,000 (cutter)
Georgette Renal	s.a.r.l.	1932	164	Yes	30, of whom 22 manual	40,000 (cutter and première)

Table 2.2 Continued

Firm	Form of the company	Date of foundation	Number of designs per year	Are designs registered?	Workers	Top salary (francs)
Germaine Lecomte	s.a.r.l.	17 November 1932	178	Yes	70, of whom 46 manual	55,000 (cutter)
Grès	One-person firm	1 August 1942	223	Yes	128, of whom 84 manual	74,000 (cutter)
Helen Hubert	s.a.r.l.	1925	150	Not yet	38, of whom 35 manual	60,000 (cutter)
Henry à la Pensée	s.a.r.l.	1800	195	Yes	107, of whom 51 manual	54,625 (cutter, head of workshop)
Hubert de Givenchy	S.A. Capital 2 million	20 December 1951	258	Not always	105 (71 manual)	90,000 (cutter)
Irmone	s.a.r.l.		118	Not yet		
Jacques Fath & Cie	S.A.	1937	426	Yes	420, of whom 318 manual	117,060 (cutter)
Jacques Griffe	s.a.r.l.					
Jacques Heim	S.A.	1898, S.A. since 1929	414	Yes	245, of whom 128 manual	97,000 (cutter)
Janine Germaine	s.a.r.l.	1932	72	Yes	11, of whom 10 manual	43,000 (for cutter, and première – same top salary for men and women)
Jean Dessès	s.a.r.l. Capital 1 million	1 June 1937	352	Yes	381, of whom 235 manual	100,000 (cutter)
Jean Patou	S.A.	1 June 1914	238	Yes	205, of whom 138 manual	75,000 (cutter)
Jeanne Fardeau	s.a.r.l.	July 1949	77	Some	23, of whom 21 manual	50,000 (première)
Jeanne Lanvin	S.A.	1886	275	Yes	278 (153 manual)	80,000 (cutter)
Juliette Chauvel	One-person firm	1914	71	Yes	17 (14 manual)	50,000 (cutter)
Line Carmine	One-person firm	4 March 1938	148	No (yes after visit)	33 (24 manual)	70,000 (cutter)

Name	Legal form	Date founded	No.	Export	Employees	Amount
Louis O'Rossen	S.A.	O'Rossen frères 8 February 1913	49	Yes	26 (17 manual)	86,375 (cutter)
Mad Carpentier	S.A.	30 January 1948	159	No (yes after visit)	46 (28 manual)	55,000 (première)
Madeleine De Rauch	S.A.	1927	320	Yes	145 (90 manual in workshop), plus 11 workers at home	82,000 (cutter)
Société nouvelle haute couture Maggy Rouff	s.a.r.l. (was a S.A. before 1949)	1949	136	Yes	211 (126 manual not counting apprentices)	90,000 (cutter)
Manguin	s.a.r.l.	30 October 1948 1902, became Société nouvelles des Etablissements Martial et Armand in 1951	198	No	97 (67 manual)	66,000 (première)
Martial Armand	S.A.		170	Yes	84 (51 manual)	65,000 (cutter)
Michelle Lambert	One-person enterprise	1919	130	Yes	46 (28 manual)	55,000 (cutter)
Nina Ricci	s.a.r.l. Capital 5 million. One branch in New York	1932	448	Yes	288 (178 manual)	75,000 (cutter)
Paquin	British S.A. (Ltd.)	1890, registered 1896	192	Yes	211 (103 manual)	90,000 (cutter)
Pierre Balmain	s.a.r.l. Capital 1 million	24 May 1945	129	Yes	400 (289)	113,000 (cutter)
Pierre Cardin	s.a.r.l.	6 August 1948	125	No	60 (52 manual)	50,000 (cutter)

Table 2.2 Continued

Firm	Form of the company	Date of foundation	Number of designs per year	Are designs registered?	Workers	Top salary (francs)
Pierre Clarence	s.a.r.l. Capital 2.500.000	15 April 1937	167	Yes	105 (46 manual)	80,000 (cutters)
Raphaël	One-person enterprise	30 December 1932	217	Yes	92 (57 manual)	140,000 (cutter)
Raymonde Coste	One-person enterprise	4 January 1933	128	Yes	39 (33 manual)	73,800 (cutter)
Renée-Lise	s.a.r.l.	1 January 1951	67	Yes	30 (34 manual)	50,000 (première)
Revillon	S.A.	1904	75	Yes	20 (of whom 12 in the workshops, 6 working at home). Only for couture – total of the firm is over 500 workers (fur)	65,650 (cutter)
Valentine Bourgade	One-person enterprise	19 October 1933	48	Yes	19 (14 manual)	70,000 (cutter)
Vera Boréa	S.A. capital 1 million	April 1934	125	Yes	41 (25 manual)	116,770 (cutter)
Worth	S.A.		192	Yes		

Source: CSCPA, *Rapports d'activité*, years 1952–61, data compiled by the author.
Notes: [a] AN F12 10505. The forty-eight houses above were selected from a first round of seventy-one haute couture firms that had filled an in-depth questionnaire. The following houses had been accepted in the classification couture-création in 1952–53, but did not renew their questionnaire for 1954: Agnès-Drecoll (closed), Alice Levon, Callot Soeurs (closed), Christiane Misset (closed), Grahay John (closed), Creed & Cie, Geneviève O'Rossen (closed), Jean Baillie, Madeleine Geroy, Marcel Rochas, Madeleine Chaumont (closed), Marthe Fargette, Roger Worth (closed), Hermès, Jacques Volber, Jean Dargence, Lola Prussac, Serge Kogan (closed), Madeleine Vramant (closed). Closures increased every year while the programme lasted.
[b] sarl: société à responsabilité limitée
[c] SA: Société Anonyme

trade names, often without a reference to the creative origins of the product.[24] In the first half of the twentieth century, American fashion industrialists had experienced difficulties building their brand image because the creative process and the retailing operation were disconnected. The manufacturer who made a collection of dresses did not give his name to the line. This resulted in a greater difficulty for American garment manufacturers to create a strong brand identity.[25] Even the most prominent and creative manufacturers in New York, such as Rentner, often sold their lines anonymously to department stores and specialty shops, like Lord & Taylor, where the retailer's name would be added to the label as the brand of the garment.[26] It was acknowledged that the New York garment industry suffered from rampant copying, but its biggest challenge in the early postwar years was still a deficit in brand image.

Government subventions 1951–62

The decision to include French provincial manufacturers in the Paris fashion system, and the expansion of the international business, were the first two components in the new postwar strategy for haute couture. The French government was acutely aware that these efforts might detract from the prestige of haute couture and the glamour of Paris as a fashion capital. It was imperative to preserve traditional haute couture for the sake of the wealth and status of the French nation. In this context, the French government initiated a programme of financial support for the haute couture houses. The funds came from a tax on the textile industry, which had always played a supporting role to haute couture. The new programme of public subventions was not an unusual initiative, since the French government had long been a direct supporter of industrial clusters such as the one that included state porcelain manufactory at Sèvres, just outside of Paris. Furthermore, as studied in detail by the historian Richard Kuisel, the postwar period was characterized by the development of a large programme of nationalization of companies by the French state.[27] Haute couture firms remained in private hands, but in order to give subventions to haute couture houses, the French Ministry of Economy and Finance mandated a commission called Classification Couture-Création (CCC) to investigate the operations of the Paris haute couture houses. Beginning in 1951 at the latest, members of CCC conducted in-depth personal enquiries to ensure that each haute couture firm worked within the tradition as defined by law. Only firms who operated to the letter of the 1947 Paris-Province agreements would be eligible for subventions.[28] CCC members visited each of the firms up to four or five times, sometimes without making an appointment.[29]

Jacques Heim, whose house had opened in 1930, claimed that ready-to-wear was not appropriate output for the Chambre's members. This was despite Heim's past activity as an early promoter of haute couture spin-off lines; his Jeunes Filles ('junior misses') collection of couture adapted for youthful customers was first produced in 1936.[30] His view may have been coloured by his failed attempt to license some of his designs in the United States market in 1946. In any event, in the 1950s, the Heim firm was divided into two companies: Heim SA, and a second firm called Heim Actualités, which produced ready-to-wear collections. This second firm was liquidated in 1954 and all of its operations placed under Heim SA, which was to oversee haute couture and two remaining ready-to-wear lines, called Heim Jeunes Filles and Heim Actualités (the latter now absorbed into the firm Heim SA).[31] At the end of that year, Heim underscored that his house had reverted to a focus on haute couture and abandoned all previous ready-to-wear and wholesale lines (see figure 2.3). In February 1955, the CCC visited the Heim workshops and asked to see the

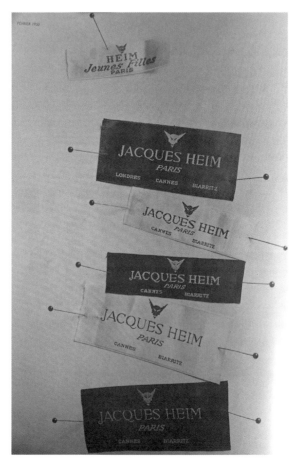

2.3   Jacques Heim labels as shown in *Vogue*, February 1950.

full collection that was hanging on the rails. The government-appointed visitors checked all the finishes to make sure that the garments were hand-made. Knowing that Heim had had, until the end of 1954, several lines of ready-to-wear to be sold to private clients and wholesale couture to be sold to corporate clients, possibly for authorized reproduction, the CCC visitors made sure to check that all of Heim's production met the demanding standards of haute couture. The assessment was positive. Heim matched the most rigorous criteria of craftsmanship and received a subvention.

The case of Heim shows the contradictions faced by the Paris couturiers. These can be examined in the light of the notion of 'creative destruction', coined by the economist Joseph Schumpeter to explain the fact that certain types and clusters of enterprise die when their production becomes obsolete.[32] Even at Dior, the most successful haute couture house of the postwar period, it was clear that catering to private clients was not very profitable. Due to the numerous private fittings necessary to adapt the handmade garment to the measurements and tastes of the client, haute couture was very costly. After four private fittings on a client, the couturier was working at a loss; in some cases, there were up to eight fittings.[33] Haute couture was on its way to becoming a rarefied craft, with little or no profitability. Yet instead of letting the industry undergo creative destruction, the French government decided to support it financially. But if haute couture firms wanted to receive this support, they had to respect strict criteria that prevented them modernizing their production methods. This dilemma was resolved in different ways by different entrepreneurs. The couturiers who had established a separate firm to produce and sell their perfumes, for example, were a bit more shielded from this difficulty; the existence of a separate company or a distinct perfume division did not prevent them from receiving the government subvention. Yet most couturiers had boutiques, or small side shops, selling lines that were under scrutiny by the CCC.

In order to make boutiques and licences viable, couturiers developed strategies for demarcating the line between couture and ready-to-wear. The Dior concern, one of the earliest and most successful movers in this new direction, hired the Manhattan-based lawyer Ellen Engel to determine how to define the firm's different lines in the American market. The problem was how to not alienate the devotees of haute couture, while attracting a wider clientele for licensed products. A balancing act in branding and managing intellectual property rights was required.[34] In so doing, haute couture proved able to tap into the unique symbolic capital that it had built over the previous generations.[35]

Other firms did not follow in the footsteps of Dior with these types of strategies. There were several reasons why: their production was too mechanized, they were too small, or they did not produce all their collections in-house. Table 2.2 lists all of the firms that received haute couture subventions in 1954. Thanks to the enquiries by the CCC, we benefit from a unique set of data mapping out the whole cluster of Paris couture during its last golden age in the 1950s. We can see from table 2.2 that the size of firms was very diverse, from roughly a thousand workers at Dior to two dozen or so workers at lesser-known firms. The typology of firms varies accordingly, with a series of public companies, limited liability companies, and private companies, the latter being peculiar to artisans working on a very small scale. This apparent diversity was not the effect of chance, but reflected the transition period that haute couture was experiencing. To continue working in an upmarket and exclusive way, the couture houses had to pay small groups of highly skilled artisans who sewed seams and did embroidery by hand. At the other end of the spectrum, companies that had very strong backers, such as Dior with Boussac or Jean Dessès (which was supported financially by the Greek shipping magnate Aristotle Onassis), could afford to maintain a larger workforce and to conduct business on a large scale.[36]

Paris couturiers benefited from government subventions for a decade, from the early 1950s to the early 1960s. The number of haute couture houses that used the Couture-Création label tended to decrease over the course of the period when the subvention programme was in effect. In 1952, the number of couture houses acknowledged by CCC was forty-five; in 1960, the number had fallen to twenty-four. There were few new houses among these firms. The notable exception was that of Gabrielle 'Coco' Chanel, who reopened her haute couture operation in 1954, after a fifteen-year absence. She received a subvention from the CCC in 1955. The goal of these subventions was to support haute couture and to reinforce the long-term links between French haute couture and the French textile industries. The money allocated was directly sourced from taxes paid by the textile industries to the government. The firms receiving subventions were required to use a minimum of ninety per cent of French textiles to make their collections. The subventions were also used to help disseminate Paris haute couture abroad. The Chambre Syndicale used part of the funds to support the establishment of its New York bureau and pay the year-round services of legal counsels in the United States.[37]

In 1957, Dior died suddenly while convalescing from illness and overwork in Italy. He had become so central to the fashion industry that his loss was deeply felt personally and professionally. Heim commented, 'Now that Dior is dead, the spotlight turns on Balenciaga. But all of us, the whole couture, must get down to business. We have to work harder and be more efficient to save the future of French high fashion.'[38] The prominent New York garment manufacturer, Rentner, who was called 'the Dean of the Garment Industry' by his peers, was asked by the American trade press who could possibly succeed Dior. He replied that it was too soon to know. Rentner was eminently well qualified to comment on Dior's passing, because he had always championed fair commercial relations between Seventh Avenue and Paris haute couture. In the absence of United States copyright laws protecting fashion design, Rentner had worked to change the system. During the interwar period, he was a founder of the Fashion Originators' Guild of America, which set up a private system for the registration of fashion design in the United States. A significant part of the Guild's activities was deemed to be in violation of anti-trust regulations and it was disbanded by Federal Trade Commission in 1941, but the Guild remained in existence and kept advocating the use of clear labels through the postwar period. Rentner added that success depended not only on the creative abilities of an individual designer, but also on the entrepreneurial skill needed to recruit talent, help it grow, and build efficient teams. Rentner himself suffered from a stroke in March 1958 and died a few months later in July.[39] Within the course of a few short months, two of the most important fashion entrepreneurs of the twentieth century had gone.

The creative influence of the designer Dior was so strong that all Paris feared a collapse of the haute couture industry without his presence. But a few months after Dior passed away, Heim noted that American buyers were flocking to Paris as they had when the great designer was alive, buying 'like mad'.[40] It was now easier and faster to travel from Paris to New York by air, bringing the two fashion capitals closer than ever – Pan American World Airways advertised commercial flights between Paris and New York taking eleven and a half hours.[41] In the Paris winter collections of 1959, the American buyers and press noticed the emergence of new talent.[42] Heim announced that the future was bright with the rise of the young Yves Saint Laurent, who designed for the Dior firm. In Heim's view, the legacy of Dior lived in two great emulators, Saint Laurent, who was known for his design genius, and Pierre Cardin, who had entrepreneurial vision.[43]

New York was now the world fashion centre, according to *New York Times* journalist Virginia Pope, writing in the early 1950s. The Europeans had a positive influence in New York; Pope believed that European inspiration had helped the city to grow 'even stronger' as a creative centre.[44] The 'foreign invasion' of New York, said Pope, had started in 1948 with Dior's New York branch. This was followed by Fath and others: Balmain, Dessès, Elsa Schiaparelli, and Antonio Castillo.[45] As noted earlier, La Guardia had hoped to see New York City become the fashion capital of the world; this ambition had grown during World War II, and was nurtured further by the foundation of the Fashion Institute of Technology at the heart of the Garment District in 1944, which linked professionalization and education.[46] In the mid-1950s, the city's new mayor, Robert F. Wagner, revisited the ambition to put New York on top of the fashion world. For several decades, top industrialists, such as Rentner as part of the Fashion Originators' Guild, had been organizing collective fashion shows that displayed clothing designed in Paris and made in New York, as well as some collections entirely created in New York. These initiatives became institutionalized in the postwar period. On 6 December 1956, Mayor Wagner made New York Fashion Week official with a public presentation at City Hall.[47] Wagner understood that the fashion industry added almost a billion dollars annually to the city's economy.[48] Paris had the advantage of symbolic capital, but economically, America led. In comparison, Paris haute couture made an estimated $13 million a year of which roughly a half was from private clients, both domestic and international. The total amount of Paris couture purchased by private American clients was $1.2 million per year. American fashion expert Bernard Roshco commented, 'Paris' receipts are like a pebble next to a boulder. Some Seventh Avenue manufacturers sell more merchandise in the United States than all the couturiers together sell to the entire world.'[49]

During these years, Heim continued to establish connections between the fashion businesses as in Paris and New York, especially during his term as the president of the Chambre Syndicale between 1958 and 1962. In 1958, the propaganda service of the Chambre Syndicale hired an Anglo-American press agent, Marjorie Dunton, and additional public-relations staff.[50] Heim proceeded to develop his ambition of establishing a New York branch of the Chambre Syndicale. This initiative must be analysed in light of the long-term policies of the Chambre Syndicale in Paris, which had previously refused to relocate, even during stressful periods of war.[51] The purpose of the New York branch was to develop connections with the American press, to get to know the United States market better, to expand networks, and to organize fashion shows for the benefit of buyers around the country.[52] The Chambre Syndicale developed similar agreements and representation in other countries that had a significant market for luxury products and designer ready-to-wear. In 1958, it signed an agreement with the German organization Imos (today the Modeverband Deutschland e.V.) with the advent of the European Common Market in mind.

Heim commissioned Gallup, Inc., a major United States consultancy, to survey the American fashion market, so that he might develop a couture business plan accordingly. The poll was conducted on a sample of 713 elite American women whose annual household income was $7,000 or higher, or who were listed in the Social Register, a directory of elite families, mainly 'old money'.[53] In a newspaper interview with the *New York Times*, Heim stressed that there had been a misunderstanding about the Paris-New York relations, and that the industries of the two cities should develop links in order to fully exploit the economic potential of Paris haute couture.[54]

The work of the Chambre Syndicale's haute couture office in New York soon yielded results. Heim hired the services of the consultant Edward Gottlieb to handle communications. The Manhattan law firm of Sylvan

Gotshal was in charge of all questions related to the protection of the intellectual property rights of the Paris couturiers in New York. Gotshal was the major expert on intellectual property in the American fashion industry. Baroness Monique de Nervo, a French society woman who had married into the industrial Louis-Dreyfus family, was hired to take care of the New York office, assisted by a secretary who was bilingual in English and French. De Nervo alternated two months in Paris with four months in New York in the service of the promotion of Paris haute couture among high society. De Nervo was a trend influencer already acting as the style ambassador to represent the interests of French glove producers in the United States. The New York office coordinated the activities of French couturiers in America, including the organization of charity events, business travel for French visitors, and meetings between fashion industrialists from both continents. Operational funds were dedicated to transatlantic travel, the costs of Gotshal's legal services, and the fees of the Gottlieb organization for public relations. For example, Heim organized a ten-day visit to the United States in 1958. His entourage included a team from the Chambre Syndicale, which further developed projects with American television, organized package trips to Paris for American personalities, and looked into the creation of special labels with regard to the royalties that would be incurred. Additional goals comprised the setting up of a 'Franco-American moral authority' against unfair competition, and the reorganization of the press and buyers' cards. The New York division of the Chambre Syndicale also encouraged the training of American fashion designers in Paris.[55]

The 1958 financial statements of the Chambre Syndicale reveal that the New York office consumed a large portion of the association's budget, but not exceedingly so, with an expense for that year equivalent to $90,000 in today's money.[56] Its investment in New York showed early evidence of a pay-off. Prominent retailers from the New York area, such as the Ohrbach's store in midtown Manhattan, were now purchasing haute couture designs instead of relying upon copies. The American press was increasingly favourable to French couture.[57] The office continued operations in 1959–60, with significant cost reductions due to lessons learned from the first year of operations.[58]

But in 1961, the French government decided to curtail the programme of subventions to haute couture. In parallel, the French government had also been funding the development of the French ready-to-wear industry, especially with regard to the mechanization of production, and this programme started showing results in the late 1950s. Through the Paris-Province agreements, haute couture had influenced the creativity of the French ready-to-wear industry. The ready-to-wear manufacturers were now in a phase of technological development that would lead to the progressive phasing out of couture.[59] Operating with a reduced budget, the Chambre Syndicale downsized the New York bureau and cancelled the contracts with Gottlieb and Gotshal.[60] The government subventions to Paris couture ended, and the couturiers were on their own.

The allocation of a subvention from the French government to haute couture from 1951 to 1962 begs the classic Schumpeterian question of whether Paris couture was maintained under the oxygen tent, artificially kept alive economically instead of letting nature take its course. If the process of creative destruction had been allowed to operate, it could have resulted in the disappearance of haute couture firms that no longer had sufficient clients to be profitable.[61] Or, perhaps, haute couture may have survived as a laboratory of style, an idea and a term often tossed around during those years by fashion professionals. The style lab option proved closer to reality. In the long term, many Paris haute couture firms were absorbed by luxury groups that are today among the most powerful fashion companies in the world. As we shall see in Chapter 3, the group Moët Hennessy Louis Vuitton (LVMH) was born from the purchase of the house of Dior haute couture firm by luggage specialist Louis Vuitton, which eventually merged with alcoholic beverage specialist Moët & Chandon. The inclusion of haute couture in such large conglomerates signified that traditional high-end fashion could survive with the support of much larger financial capital if needed, while helping to develop creative talent and nurture symbolic value in diversified groups and holdings. The two decades after World War II witnessed the remake of haute couture, often carried out at a loss. Haute couture preserved craftsmanship and realized profits from spin-off products such as perfumes, cosmetics, accessories, and ready-to-wear (see figure 2.4). Haute couture as imagined by its founding father, Charles Frederick Worth, had ended, but the cluster of activities that haute couture entrepreneurs had created eventually led to something greater. The extremely powerful symbolic capital of haute couture was absorbed by global luxury brands.[62]

Intellectual property rights in the era of European integration

How did haute couture design morph into global luxury branding? The answer is not obvious, because couturiers could very well have chosen to remain a local cluster of small, relatively secretive artisans focusing on skill, like Swiss watch-makers or Italian leather-goods craftsmen.[63] In order to understand this puzzle, it is useful to examine the history of the couturiers' approach to intellectual property rights.[64] In this legal field, France was more advanced than Germany, Belgium, Italy, Luxembourg, and the Netherlands, the other five countries in the European Economic Community (EEC), or the Common Market, created by the Treaty of Rome in 1957 and in effect from 1958.[65] In France, fashion designs benefited from the double protection of the industrial property law of 1909 and the artistic property law. The latter law, also known as the author's right law,

Balmain advertisement by the illustrator H. R. Herz, 1962, highlighting the designer's knitwear   **2.4**
made with man-made fibres.

was first passed in 1793 and was revised three times between 1902 and 1957. The overlap of protection for industry and for creators, also called the principle of the unity of art, made the French law one of the strongest systems for the protection of fashion.[66] However, Germany also had a well-established system of intellectual property rights, including laws that covered design. Belgium had a system that was close to France's, and was one of the first countries that permitted data access to French lawyers and Interpol for investigations of design piracy.[67]

Some European countries and the United States had limited fashion protection. In this context of legal asymmetry, the Chambre Syndicale developed a coordinated effort across national boundaries to repress counterfeiters.[68] In the early postwar period, the use of the term 'haute couture' became strictly regulated in the French law.[69] Over the next two decades, the association extended its surveillance effort to guard a large ensemble of Parisian phrases and symbols that were used in association with haute couture and French national identity. The couturiers managed to secure restrictions on the use of terms like 'Paris', 'Belle France', and 'Champs Elysées', and symbols like the Eiffel Tower when used on fashion products that were not made in Paris. Couturiers sued counterfeiters of the Paris brand at the global level.[70] Observers around the world took note. 'This popularization of the Paris label has brought about a revolution in Franco-American fashion relations', wrote Bernard Roshco in 1963. 'Like more serious social and economic revolutions, it is worth exploring because of what it reveals about the world in which it occurred.'[71]

Entrepreneurs in French haute couture were eager to reinforce their intellectual property rights at home and abroad. Two important goals were to make it easier to prove ownership of an original design as intellectual property, and to raise the penalties meted out to counterfeiters. The Chambre Syndicale had half a century of experience in this domain and lobbied authorities within the EEC for strong protection of fashion innovation.[72] Economic integration between the six member countries laid the foundation for a new pan-EEC law on related intellectual property rights. The French believed that the nation and the national law could provide stronger protection to an industry than could the EEC. But the international interests of European fashion entrepreneurs were also at stake, especially with the relocation of both legitimate manufacturing and illegitimate manufacturing, or counterfeiting, to Asia. The EEC law of 1962 therefore had advantages in that it unfied rules among several key European players, such as France, Italy, and Belgium. The fashion industries of these nations had previously suffered from the asymmetries in national laws related to intellectual property rights.

In the early 1960s, an EEC committee based in Brussels examined the situation regarding the protection of innovation in the fashion industries. The French delegation to this committee collected information from the haute couture houses and lobbied to obtain the best possible protection of fashion creativity within the EEC.[73] One proposed option was that the new project should rest entirely upon the registration of designs. The French haute couture entrepreneurs were not interested in this proposal. According to Dior manager Jacques Rouët, this would represent the regression of existing French laws on intellectual property rights.

The Chambre Syndicale took measures to understand how haute couture houses dealt with the registration of their designs. The Chambre sent a questionnaire to all members in February 1962, including Dior, whose response is given below. The first part of the questionnaire was dedicated to the methods used by the firm to protect creations. The house of Dior did not systematically register designs at the Prud'hommes, the designated registration board within France. The reason for this was that haute couture creations were protected by the law on author's right, which did not require registration. If Dior registered a design, the firm did so secretly to avoid putting the design in the public domain and exposing it to potential copyists. At the international level, the Dior firm usually did not register its designs at the International Registration Bureau in Geneva. International registration was meant to protect the designs in the countries that belonged to the Hague Union: Germany, Belgium, the Netherlands, Spain, Switzerland, Liechtenstein, Monaco, Morocco, Tunisia, Vietnam, Egypt, Indonesia, and Vatican City. The management at Christian Dior thought that the number of countries covered was too small for the measure to have much of an effect. The markets in North America and South America, where most of Dior's clientele were based, were not part of the agreement. This fact does much to explain the somewhat relaxed attitude of the house of Dior towards international registration. There were also fears among the couturiers of 'leaks' in the confidentiality of the registered designs. The management at Dior thought that organizing a system of design protection for the European Economic Community would be helpful, but hoped that regulations concerning the proof of counterfeiting would be made easy, fast, and efficient.[74]

Dior's questionnaire showed that couturiers were interested in unifying the laws on intellectual property rights across nations, and the Chambre Syndicale supported this transnational position in a number of international forums. In an April 1959 meeting of the United Nations Educational, Scientific, and Cultural Organization (UNESCO), French fashion entrepreneurs advocated the double protection of the author's rights law and industrial property law. The question was discussed again in several professional congresses, and after considerable lobbying, French fashion entrepreneurs managed to retain the double protection of fashion under the laws of industrial property and author's right. European integration harmonized the laws in member countries and made it easier to pursue counterfeiters. Today, fashion design is protected under French law, based on both the concepts of industrial property and the author's right.[75] But since there were important variations in the laws internationally, and given the fact that suing pirates was not always successful, fashion entrepreneurs kept developing their intellectual property rights portfolios with a strategic eye on the courts.

Within this legal context, it was not surprising that couturiers focused on developing their brand identities during the 1950s and 1960s. When going global, many of these firms capitalized on their extant reputations and systematized their use of brand names. The fact that the United States did not include fashion design in its copyright laws was one among several factors that pushed for a reinforcement of the brand in the intellectual property rights' portfolios of couturiers. The Chambre Syndicale closely examined the changes brought about by European integration in terms of the protection of the brand. Specialized studies were circulated among the Chambre's members, notably a substantial report by the lawyer Yves Saint-Gall.[76] On 31 December 1964, the French law on brands was rewritten. This new version limited protection to a ten-year horizon. After that, brand property would by nullified if it was not still being exploited. The Chambre Syndicale advised the couturiers to register their brands and to renew older brands in regard to the ten-year clause.[77]

The reign of the brand

In 1944, the Chambre Syndicale decided to open Paris haute couture shows to manufacturers from the French provinces and started applying this policy in 1947. The next year, the house of Dior branched out into the United States and developed a global company. Ten years later, the Chambre Syndicale opened an office in New York, thanks to a French government subvention. These decisions mark a change of paradigm for haute couture. It was the end of Paris as the home of an haute couture manufacturing cluster and the advent of the export of haute couture as a type of global brand. Was this the right decision?

The golden age of haute couture in the 1950s and early 1960s is considered to be the last gasp of haute couture. Sociologist Gilles Lipovetsky has conceptualized the haute couture system as the fashion of a hundred years, from Worth in the 1850s to Dior, Cardin, and Saint Laurent in the postwar era. Does this mean that Paris couture abruptly died in the 1960s, as a consequence of the opening of the Paris cluster both to domestic manufacturers and to branching out abroad, notably in the United States?[78] In the case of certain artisanal clusters, the members of the cluster are anonymous, as with some Italian glassmakers and ceramicists, for example. Paris couturiers took the opposite road, kept their names front and center, and increasingly capitalized on the brand.[79] Fashion design was not protected by copyright law in the United States, which was a major market for Paris fashion, whether accessories or evening gowns. To be classified as Couture-Création, couturiers had to develop their brands along specific lines. Dior inaugurated this model with the opening of his New York branch, by which time he had devised a system that differentiated his couture lines from his wholesale lines. Ensuring the coherence of one's name while avoiding the erosion of the brand would remain a challenge for the decades to come.

Haute couture developed brands to an unprecedented level during the postwar period and set up licensing agreements with clear financial objectives. In a context of weak intellectual property rights protection at the global level, the brand names became a useful strategy for differentiation among the Paris couturiers. This chapter has shown that American industrialists were at a disadvantage when it came to the symbolic value of the brand, even though the ownership of brands was easier to defend in the legal system of the United States compared to fashion design. It is therefore logical that the battle against brand counterfeiting eventually became a dominant concern on the agendas, first of the Common Market and then of the European Union.[80] Paris couturiers provided the missing link by increasingly developing the branding dimension of their intellectual property right portfolios, shifting from a Paris-based local cluster to global business.

Notes

1 New York Public Library, Fashion Group International Archive (hereafter NYPL FG), Box 73, folder 8, Biltmore Hotel, Madison Avenue, transcript of luncheon meeting (hereafter TLM), 20 March 1940, pp. 4–5.
2 NYPL FG, 73, 8, TLM, 20 March 1940, p. 4.
3 NYPL FG, 73, 8, TLM, 20 March 1940, pp. 8–9.
4 NYPL FG, 73, 8, TLM, 20 March 1940, p. 9.
5 'The Mayor on styles', *New York Times* (22 March 1940), 16.
6 A. Palmer, 'Inside Paris haute couture', in C. Wilcox (ed.), *The Golden Age of Haute Couture: Paris and London, 1947–1957* (London: V&A, 2007), pp. 63–80.
7 T. Judt, *Postwar: A History of Europe Since 1945* (London: Penguin, 2005).
8 Y. Kawamura, *Fashion-ology: An Introduction to Fashion Studies (Dress, Body and Culture)* (London: Bloomsbury, 2nd edn 2005); M. Porter, *The Competitive Advantage of Nations* (New York: The Free Press, 1990), pp. 33–67. There are other factors to study, but this angle results from a new business history approach and from the unpacking of little explored sources: the haute couture files of the French Ministry of Economy and Finances, the archives of the Chambre Syndicale de la Couture Parisienne, and the archives of the House of Dior. In this chapter, I consider Paris haute couture to be an industrial cluster, as in the works of Michael Porter, Annalee Saxenian, and Enrico Moretti, among others.
9 C. Omnès, *Ouvrières parisiennes: Marché du travail et trajectoires professionnelles au 20e siècle* (Paris: Editions de l'EHESS, 1997), pp. 34, 42.
10 J. Lanzmann and P. Ripert, *Cent ans de prêt-à-porter: Weill* (Paris: P.A.U, 1992); Union Centrale des Arts Décoratifs, Centre de Documentation, Paris, Sales books of the Société Madeleine Vionnet, 1923–25.
11 Attempts by Paris couturiers to branch out and launch global brands remained limited until World War II. L. M. Font, 'International couture: the opportunities and challenges of expansion 1880–1920', *Business History*, 54:1 (2012), 30–47.
12 The history of the Christian Dior firm is well known. G. Jones and V. Pouillard, *Christian Dior: A New Look for Haute Couture*, Harvard Business School Case No. 809–159 (2009, revised 2013); T. Okawa, 'Licensing practices at Maison Christian Dior', in R. L. Blaszczyk (ed.), *Producing Fashion: Commerce, Culture, and Consumers* (Philadelphia: University of Pennsylvania Press, 2008), pp. 82–107; A. Palmer, *Dior: A New Look, A New Enterprise* (London: V&A Publishing, 2009); M.-F. Pochna, *Christian Dior* (Paris: Flammarion, 2004).
13 Porter, *The Competitive Advantage of Nations*, pp. 35–40.

14 The French original name for such a firm is: Société à responsabilité limitée.

15 *Pierre Balmain, 40 années de création* (Paris: Musée Galliera, 1985), p. 45.

16 *Ibid.*

17 B. Furman, 'Paris dressmaker decries trade lag', *New York Times* (23 October 1952), 37.

18 *Pierre Balmain, 40 années de création*, p. 46.

19 D. Grumbach, *Histoires de la mode* (Paris: Editions du Regard, 2nd edn 2008), pp. 135–6; V. Guillaume, *Jacques Fath* (Paris: Adam Biro, 1993); C. R. Milbank, *Couture: The Great Designers* (New York: Stewart, Tabori & Chang, 1985), pp. 264–6.

20 Dior Archive (hereafter DA), Box USA 2, Note to the press, 25 November 1948.

21 V. Pope, 'Paris couturiers in new venture', *New York Times* (9 August 1950), 32; Grumbach, *Histoires de la mode*, pp. 228–35.

22 C. Anbert, 'Une bombe sur fond de tulle: La haute couture doit-elle se démocratiser?', *Le Monde* (14 June 1950), 6.

23 *Ibid.*

24 V. Pouillard, 'Design piracy in the fashion industries of Paris and New York in the interwar years', *Business History Review*, 85:2 (summer 2011), 319–44.

25 G. Fowler, 'Preparation of a line: 4 months from Paris trip to next week's openings', *Women's Wear Daily* (27 May 1953), 1.

26 Fashion Institute of Technology, Oral History Collections, Memoirs of Maurice Rentner Collection, Interview of Ira Rentner (1982), 92–5.

27 R. Kuisel, *Capitalism and the State in Modern France: Renovation and Economic Management in the Twentieth Century* (Cambridge: Cambridge University Press, 1981), pp. 215, 248–50.

28 For more details on the rules applied, see V. Pouillard 'Keeping designs and brands authentic: the resurgence of post-war French fashion business under the challenge of US mass production', *European Review of History*, 20:5 (2013), 815–35.

29 Archives Nationales de France (hereafter AN), F12.10505, Ministry of Economy, application files, Jacques Heim, Madeleine de Rauch.

30 Chambre Syndicale de la Couture Parisienne private archives, Paris (hereafter CSCPA), Committee Meeting Minutes, 25 October 1955, p. 8.

31 AN, F12.10505, Jacques Heim application file.

32 J. Schumpeter, 'Capitalism in the postwar world', in R. Clemence (ed.), *Essays of J. A. Schumpeter* (Cambridge, MA: Addison-Wesley, 1989), p. 185.

33 'Dior to celebrate 10th birthday', *Women's Wear Daily* section 1 (2 January 1957), 13.

34 Okawa, 'Licensing practices at Maison Christian Dior'; Palmer, *Dior.*

35 D. Thomas, *Deluxe: How Luxury Lost its Luster* (New York: Penguin, 2007).

36 I thank historian Gelina Harlaftis for sharing her knowledge on Onassis' business connections. See notably G. Harlaftis, *A History of Greek-Owned Shipping: The Making of an International Tramp Fleet, 1830 to the Present Day* (London: Routledge, 2005).

37 CSCPA, General Assembly Meeting Minutes, 3 May 1960, Activity Report for the Year 1959.

38 'Future of Paris fashions is called bright by Heim', *New York Times* (19 September 1958), 20.

39 Harvard Business School, Baker Library, Resseguie Collection, press clipping, E. Dash, 'Rentner in stormy career steered true to fashion', *Women's Wear Daily* (8 July 1958), 19.

40 'Future of Paris fashions is called bright by Heim'.

41 *Ibid.*

42 C. Donovan, 'French styles en route: Dior's skirt split critics', *New York Times* (26 August 1959), 32.

43 'Future of Paris fashions is called bright by Heim'.

44 V. Pope, 'One world of fashion', *New York Times* (7 September 1952), SMA52.

45 *Ibid.*

46 Fashion Institute of Technology, Our History, at www.fitnyc.edu/about/history.php (accessed 2 March 2016).

47 'Fashion Week announced', *New York Times* (7 December 1956), 42.

48 *Ibid.*

49 B. Roshco, *The Rag Race: How New York and Paris Run the Breakneck Business of Dressing American Women* (New York: Funk & Wagnalls, 1963), p. 135; N. L. Green, *Ready-to-Wear and Ready-to-Work: A Century of Industry and Immigrants in Paris and New York* (Durham, NC: Duke University Press, 1997).

50 CSCPA, Report on Propaganda, January–December 1958, 1.

51 P. Montégut, 'Boué Sœurs: the first haute couture establishment in America', *Dress*, 15:1 (1989), 79–86; D. Veillon, *La mode sous l'Occupation* (Paris: Payot, 1990).

52 'Couture unit to open bureau in New York', *New York Times* (6 December 1957), 35.

53 'French designers study U.S. tastes', *New York Times* (10 June 1958), 37.

54 'Paris aims to improve fashion tie', *New York Times* (4 April 1958), 14; CSCPA, Report on Propaganda, January–December 1958, p. 2.

55 CSCPA, Report on Propaganda, January–December 1958, pp. 2–5.

56 CSCPA, Accounting sheet, 1958. The original sum on French francs was 4,708,255 francs. It is converted here using the cost of living index converter for Francs into 2015 euros, themselves converted in $. www.insee.fr/fr/service/reviser/calcul-pou voir-achat.asp.

57 CSCPA, Report on Propaganda, January–December 1958, p. 3.

58 CSCPA, Statutory General Assembly, 3 May 1960, p. 4.

59 A. D. Galloway, 'Ready-to-wear trade due for gain in France', *Women's Wear Daily* section 1 (2 January 1957), 14.

60 CSCPA, General Assembly Meeting Minutes, 8 May 1962, report from Jean Manusardi, p. 15.

61 Schumpeter, 'Capitalism in the postwar world', p. 185.

62 Porter, *The Competitive Advantage of Nations*, p. 540.

63 Porter, *The Competitive Advantage of Nations*, pp. 308–31; 421–53; P.-Y. Donzé, *Les patrons horlogers de La Chaux-de-Fonds (1840–1920): Dynamique sociale d'une élite industrielle* (Neuchâtel: Alphil, 2007).

64 D. Lefranc, 'The metamorphosis of contrefaçon in French copyright law', in L. Bentley, J. Davis, and J. C. Ginsburg (eds), *Copyright and Piracy: An Interdiscplinary Critique* (Cambridge: Cambridge University Press, 2010), pp. 55–79; S. Scafidi, *Who Owns Culture? Appropriation and Authenticity in American Law* (New Brunswick, NJ: Rutgers University Press, 2005); M. L. Stewart, 'Copying and copyrighting haute couture: democratizing fashion', *French Historical Studies*, 28:1 (2005), 103–30.

65 G. Bossuat, *Faire l'Europe sans défaire la France: 60 ans de politique d'unité européenne des gouvernements et des présidents de la République française (1943–2003)* (Brussels: PIE Peter Lang, 2006); A. Milward, *The European Rescue of the Nation State* (London: Routledge, 2000).

66 V. Marchal, 'Brevets, marques, dessins et modèles: Evolution des protections de propriété industrielle au XIXe siècle en France', *Documents pour l'histoire des techniques*, 17 (2009), 8; G. Galvez-Behar, *La République des inventeurs: Propriété et organisation de l'innovation en France (1791–1922)* (Rennes: Presses Universitaires de Rennes, 2008), p. 210; H. Valabrègue, *La propriété artistique en matière de modes* (Paris: Librairie générale de Droit et de Jurisprudence, Thèse de Doctorat en Droit, 1935); M.-C. Piatti, 'Le droit de la mode', unpublished paper, Fashion History Seminar, Institut d'Histoire du Temps Présent, Paris, 28 April 2006, pp. 3–7.

67 DA, SODEMA file, document 'La propriété artistique. Les dessins et modèles. S.P.A.D.E.M., activité internationale' (Financial Year 1958–59), p. 1.

68 Grumbach, *Histoires de la mode*, p. 74; CSCPA, General Assembly Meeting Minutes, Activity Report for the Year 1959, Propriété Artistique [n.p.: folio 3].

69 On the use of norms in incomplete or nonexistent systems of intellectual property rights, see for example E. Fauchart and E. von Hippel, 'Norms-based intellectual property systems: the case of French chefs', *Organization Science*, 19:2 (2008), 187–201.

70 Such measures were ensured with the support of the Union des Fabricants. See CSCP, General Assembly, Activity Report for the Year 1959, Propriété Artistique [n.p., folio 4].

71 Roshco, *The Rag Race*, p. 154.

72 CSCPA, General Assembly Meeting Minutes, Activity Report for the Year 1959, Propriété Artistique [n.p.: folios 3 and 4]; L. Lanzalaco, 'Business interest associations', in G. Jones and J. Zeitlin (eds), *The Oxford Handbook of Business History* (Oxford: Oxford University Press, 2007), p. 294; M. Offerlé, 'L'action collective patronale en France, 19ᵉ–20ᵉ siècles: Organisations, répertoires et engagements', *Vingtième siècle. Revue d'histoire*, 114 (2012), 83–97.

73 DA, Ministère de l'Industrie. Comité National d'Etudes sur le Rapprochement des Législations de Propriété Industrielle des Pays membres de la Communauté Economique Européenne. Groupe 'Dessins et Modèles', 1 February 1962.

74 DA, SODEMA file, Questionnaire relatif à la protection des dessins et des modèles (1 February 1962), 4 pages.

75 Republic of France, Conseil supérieur de la propriété littéraire et artistique, at www.culture.gouv.fr/culture/infos-pratiques/droits/protection.htm (accessed 13 August 2016).

76 DA, SODEMA file, document 'Conseils à nos adhérents', Yves Saint-Gall, 'Aspects actuels de la notion de marque et ses rapports avec la réglementation de la concurrence, plus spécialement dans le cadre de la Communauté Economique Européenne', Université de Liège, 21 December 1962.

77 DA, SODEMA file, document 'Conseils à nos adhérents', 1962, p. 1.

78 G. Lipovetsky, *L'empire de l'éphémère: La mode et son destin dans les sociétés modernes* (Paris: Gallimard, 1988).

79 P. Duguid, 'French connections: the propagation of trade marks in the nineteenth century', *Enterprise and Society*, 10:1 (2009), 3–37.

80 Republic of France, Sénat français, compte-rendu intégral des débats (18 September 2007), at www.senat.fr/seances/s200709/s20070918/s20070918001.html (accessed 13 August 2016).

3

LVMH: storytelling and organizing creativity in luxury and fashion

Pierre-Yves Donzé and Ben Wubs

During the 1980s, the European luxury and fashion business experienced a period of radical change characterized by a shift from an industry dominated by small and medium-sized family companies to a few multinational conglomerates or groups. A conglomerate or group is here defined as a large corporation that consists of a number of seemingly unrelated smaller businesses. This organizational change was the result of luxury and fashion groups exerting centralized control over financial resources, distribution systems, and a portfolio of brands. In truth, the creative process within luxury conglomerates remained autonomous and decentralized, according to the existing literature.[1]

The French holding company Moët Hennessy Louis Vuitton (LVMH), the world's largest fashion and luxury group, is an excellent embodiment of this organizational change.[2] Today, LVMH presides over a €35 billion (approximately $39 billion) luxury and fashion empire from headquarters in the upmarket eighth arrondissement in Paris. This chapter is a case study of LVMH that explores the evolution of the fashion and luxury industries, entrepreneurship and innovation, and the management of creativity. The LVMH example is especially important because it links Paris to global markets for luxury goods, the largest of which is China.[3]

'Passionate about Creativity' is the headline that appeared on all LVMH's annual reports from 2002 to 2010. In 2011, LVMH shortened its tagline to two short words: 'creative passion'.[4] How can we define creativity and how is this linked to the concept of creative industries? Although this issue has not been addressed for the fashion and luxury industries, there are some works on creativity that help us to understand this phenomenon. According to the psychologists Mark A. Runco and Garrett J. Jaeger, standard definitions on creativity should include two elements: originality or novelty, and usefulness. Creativity that is not used in either of these two ways does not make sense. Creative work 'tends to be useful for some group', and therefore the social context of creativity matters. Surprise might be a third element of creativity.[5] The economist Montserrat Pareja-Eastaway states that human capital and talent are the main resources of the new creative economy, which includes 'creative "genius", both individual and collective, in the production of innovation in different spheres'.[6] Innovation, creativity, and creative industries are therefore closely linked concepts. Creative industries are based on creativity, skills, and talent, and 'the potential for wealth and job creation through the development of intellectual property'.[7] The geographer Richard Florida has stressed in his seminal work that the 'creative classes' gathered in cities are a major driving force of economic growth.[8] Moreover, according to Pareja-Eastaway, 'symbolism in the production of goods and the aestheticization of consumer products' represents challenges to the creative industries: 'intangible elements acquire economic value and are one of the most important assets in the creative industries'.[9] We could not agree more in the case of LVMH. The luxury and fashion conglomerate, however, does not fit into the generalized observation that the creative industries of Europe are particularly small and therefore entrepreneurial.[10] This chapter shows that the opposite is possible. LVMH is the largest luxury and fashion group in the world, but it behaves in an entrepreneurial way.

Furthermore, although luxury and fashion share many characteristics, one must emphasize that the process of creativity differs in these two businesses. In the luxury industry, unlike in the fashion industry, creativity is not so much a matter of providing novelty and usefulness, as has been stressed in Runco and Jaeger's classical definition of the concept.[11] Creativity in this business is related to the idea that luxury goods are handcrafted or 'created' by artisans rather than being designed by anonymous factory art directors and manufactured in industrial plants. This myth is largely maintained by consultants and business school professors who use the word 'creation' instead of 'production'.[12] Kapferer and Bastien argue that 'the imaginary picture of the artisan, which is not far from the artist, is also one of the embodiments of the notion of tradition'.[13] Hence, 'creativity' is a way to emphasize the historical continuity of traditional know-how and the closeness with art. As for fashion, novelty is a very important element that is understood to be part of the general context of creation by designers. The deep historical context is less important for fashion marketing than for luxury goods marketing, but the emphasis on the artistic dimension is similar to that in the luxury sector.

Although LVMH has been the object of several publications by journalists, those studies either celebrate the achievements of the company or criticize the management style and personality of Bernard Arnault, the firm's wealthy founder and CEO (figure 3.1).[14] There are very few academic publications that examine the development of LVMH and the way in which

French LVMH luxury group Chairman Bernard Arnault (R) speaks with deputy CEO Antonio   **3.1**
Belloni, 15 September 2004 in Paris, during the presentation of company's results for the first
semester 2004. Photo: Daniel Janin/AFP/Getty Images.

this conglomerate manages creation. Historians Patrick Eveno and Hubert
Bonin are among the few scholars who examine the process of creation of
LVMH group within the broader context of the industrial reorganization in
France during the 1980s and the 1990s. Eveno and Bonin consider how
a new business model – the merging of former independent family firms
with strong brands – enabled the growth of the company.[15] Bonin in particular argues that creativity was at the basis of a new corporate image.
He shows the high visibility of celebrity designers and artistic directors
such as Karl Lagerfeld, Tom Ford, and John Galliano in the French high
fashion and luxury industries since the 1980s and examines their role in
launching new products, organizing provocative shows, and making Paris
an 'event-making place'.[16] However, these studies, which emphasize the
importance of creativity in the general process of growth of the industry,
do not focus on the way companies manage creativity.

Our central question therefore is about how a conglomerate like LVMH
has organized and managed creativity and entrepreneurship over time.
What are the roots of this company's unique organizational structure,
and how did the structure evolve over the last thirty years? Blending the
study of economic and cultural factors, this chapter critically assesses the

narratives generated by the company and by the mass media about craft heritage and the 'genius' of fashion creators. Acknowledging that creativity is a major resource for LVMH, the chapter considers the ways in which the creative process is socially constructed through storytelling. Moreover, it addresses the question of how and where the LVMH group organizes the innovation process. LVMH claims that its subsidiaries are autonomous in the creative process, but it is necessary to find out which parts of the operational processes are managed centrally.

To address these issues, the chapter is divided into three parts. The first focuses on the evolution of the conglomerate as a multinational business in order to show how the management of various operating companies and brands gradually became centralized. The second explores the ways LVMH established itself as a creative enterprise and how storytelling supports this construction. The third analyses the management of creativity within the LVMH group. This chapter is mainly based on the stunning amount of information in LVMH's annual reports and so-called reference documents (official background information for investors), which are all found on the group's website.[17]

The construction of a centralized and multinational luxury and fashion group

The most important characteristic of LVMH is that this company was created from the merger of a large number of smaller enterprises, usually independent and family-owned firms. Many of the original companies had been in existence for several decades. They had strong brands, but lacked the financial resources to grow on the global market. Merging a large number of firms required knowledge in management, brand portfolio, and finance. In that sense, Bernard Arnault was, in his own words, a 'creator' who was able to build a new kind of enterprise in the luxury and fashion industries. Hence, organizational capabilities are at the core of the competitiveness of LVMH. This section investigates how LVMH group developed since its foundation in 1987.

LVMH's evolution can be divided into three phases. The first phase is the pre-history of the company. When Louis Vuitton SA and Moët Hennessy merged to form LVMH in 1987, both were family firms with strong brands that had expanded successfully since the 1960s.[18] As the potential development of their own brands and markets was limited, both of these firms started to invest in other French companies and diversified to other products.[19] Moët Hennessy had been founded in 1971 through a merger between producers of champagne (Moët & Chandon) and cognac (Hennessy). The expansion of Moët Hennessy had itself been based on takeovers of other champagne producers (Ruinart in 1962, and Mercier in 1970) and on the diversification into other goods, including takeovers of the cosmetics maker RoC and of Parfums Christian Dior (both in 1971). Louis Vuitton focused on leather goods, such as high-end luggage, until it started to diversify to accessories in 1986. In the first half of the 1980s, Louis Vuitton showed exceptional growth, with gross sales skyrocketing from the equivalent of €51.7 million in 1981 to €213.4 million in 1985, and extraordinarily high profitability (about forty per cent before taxes).[20] These retained profits were reinvested in 1986 and used for the purchase of the Veuve Clicquot group, which held several champagne brands and the company Parfums Givenchy.

The families behind both groups Moët Hennessy and Louis Vuitton needed more cash to grow and were looking to create an organization that would protect their interests as owner-managers. Moreover, a merger would allow the companies to rationalize the champagne and perfume businesses. Consequently, Moët Hennessy and Louis Vuitton merged to create LVMH in 1987, with the financial support of two major French banks, Lazard Frères and Paribas. Both groups protected themselves from a future hostile takeover through the judicious distribution of ownership rights. Thirty-seven per cent of the capital was in the hands of the families, and they still had fifty-five per cent of the voting rights. But there was conflict between Henri Racamier, the CEO of Louis Vuitton, and Alain Chevalier, the CEO of Moët Hennessy. Internal strife within the newly formed LVHM created the opportunity for a minority shareholder, Bernard Arnault, to acquire Racamier's shares with the financial support of the British beverage group Guinness, and ultimately to control LVMH through the financial company Jacques Rober.[21] A few years earlier, around 1984–85, Arnault had purchased the textile group Boussac, which had controlled the house of Christian Dior since 1946 and the classic Paris department store Le Bon Marché since 1984. Arnault had also acquired the leather goods manufacturer Céline in 1987 and in the same year funded the setup of a company by the couturier Christian Lacroix. Hence, Arnault's idea was to merge these brands and companies into one large group that would dominate the consumer goods luxury sector.[22]

Table 3.1 shows the organization of LVMH after Arnault took control. It highlights two characteristics. First, Arnault's strategic decision to purchase and control companies in the luxury and consumer goods business was typical of the French economy in the second part of the twentieth century.[23] The construction of a pyramidal organization structure, with financial companies Arnault & Associés, Financière Agache, and Jacques Rober SA, made it possible for one entrepreneur to control operating companies without holding a majority interest in every single company. A prerequisite to the success of the construction was to find suppliers of capital, such as the French banks and the British beverage group Guinness. Second, despite the creation of a new company, the organization of LVMH was still

Table 3.1 Organization of LVMH in 1987, simplified

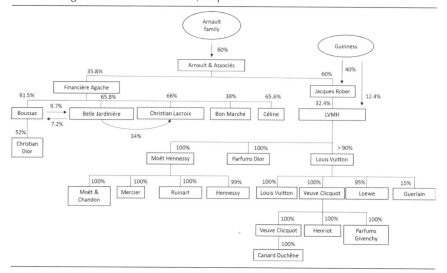

Source: drafted by the authors on the basis of Eurostaf Dafsa, *LVMH*, 1987.

decentralized. Louis Vuitton and Moët Hennessy continued to control and manage their own subsidiaries, except Parfums Dior.

The second phase in the evolution of LVMH from the late 1980s to the mid-1990s was characterized by slow growth and further rationalization of the group's organization. Sales went from €2 billion in 1987 to €4.5 billion in 1995, while profitability (operating income) was an average of twenty-six per cent of gross sales during these years (see table 3.2). The basic pyramid structure did not change – that structure is still in place today – but rationalization could be observed at the level of operating companies (see table 3.3). Louis Vuitton had oversight for the subsidiary companies that were active in fashion, while Moët Hennessy managed the subsidiaries in beverages. As late as 1997, however, the rationalization process remained incomplete. The retailer Le Bon Marché and the luxury fashion brand Christian Dior still played a role as financial intermediaries in the pyramidal structure. The first wave of acquisitions was realized within this organizational framework. For example, Louis Vuitton acquired the couturier Givenchy in 1988, the fashion company Kenzo in 1993, and perfumes Guerlain in 1994.[24] Moreover, LVMH divested from companies outside its core businesses; one was the cosmetic company RoC, which was a less prestigious brand and was sold to Johnson & Johnson in 1993.

The 1994 restructuring of relations with the British firm, Guinness PLC (renamed Diageo PLC in 1997), embodied a major change. Luxury goods offered LVMH a better profitability than beverages. The leather goods division had an operating income (profit before taxes) of 43.2 per cent in 1996,

Table 3.2 Net sales in million euro and operating income as a %, 1987–2014

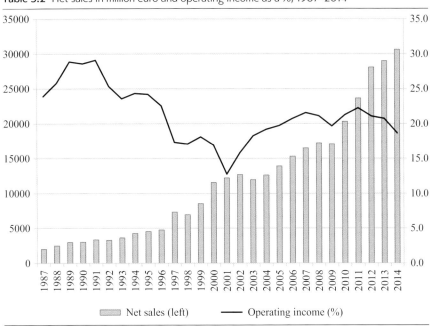

Source: LVMH, annual reports, 1987–2014.

whereas beverages had an operating income of 24.8 per cent, and had good perspectives for high growth. Moreover, LVMH was already the world market leader in champagne and cognac. It endeavoured to diversify into new fields of the luxury and fashion industry through mergers and acquisitions, but the management did not want to issue new stocks, or to get more debts from banks, in order to keep control over the group. Consequently, a new agreement was made with Guinness in 1994.[25] The British firm acquired thirty-four per cent of Moët Hennessy and continued to cooperate with LVMH for the worldwide distribution of its beverages. At the same time, Guinness withdrew from LVMH's capital, and LVMH in turn reduced its stake in Guinness from twenty-four to twenty per cent. These transactions generated nearly €3 billion cash for LVMH, which enabled the group to acquire more companies in the luxury and fashion industry.

During the third phase, which started in the mid-1990s, LVMH focused on their luxury and fashion businesses. The conglomerate divested unrelated businesses, notably the US cosmetics companies Candy and Urban Decay in 2002, and the auction house Phillips, de Pury & Luxembourg in 2003. It sold off companies that did not add value to its brand portfolio, such as the champagne makers Pommery in 2000 and Canard-Duchêne in 2003, the fashion design company Michael Kors in 2003, the cognac producer Hine in 2003, and the watchmaker Ebel in 2004. All these brands

Table 3.3 Organization of LVMH in 1997, simplified

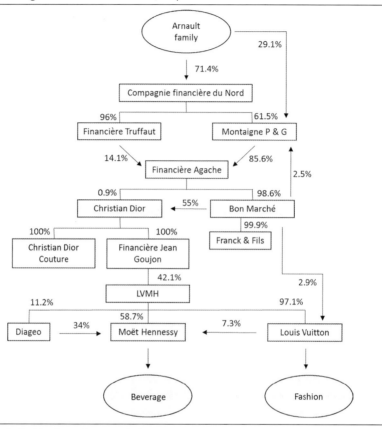

Source: drafted by the authors on the basis of Eurostaf, *LVMH*, 1999

were in competition with other LVMH's brands, so that the management decided to focus on a few of them, and strengthen their market positioning. LVMH also strengthened its position in two new directions through acquisitions.[26] The first new direction was an investment in retailing with the purchase of the French fine grocery company Franck & Fils in 1994, the cosmetics chain Sephora in 1997, and two duty-free chains, DFS in 1997 and Miami Cruiseline in 2000. The second new direction was the diversification into watches and jewellery with the takeovers of the French companies Fred (1995) and Chaumet (1999), the Swiss companies TAG Heuer (1999), Zénith (1999) and Hublot (2008), and the Italian company Bulgari (2011).[27] Moreover, at the same time, LVMH sought to expand existing divisions in fashion and beverages. Along these lines, important fashion acquisitions included the French shoemaker Berluti in 1996, the Spanish fashion and leather goods company Loewe in 1996, the British shirtmaker Thomas Pink in 1999, the US ready-to-wear brand DKNY in

2001, and the Italian luxury ready-to-wear brand Fendi in 2002, among others. New beverage assets included the champagne maker Krug in 1999 and several wine and spirits firms: Château d'Yquem of France in 1999; Millennium of America, which held a premium vodka brand, in 2004; Glenmorangie of Scotland in 2005; and in 2007, Wenjun of China, which produces traditional Chinese white spirits. These acquisitions, many of which were outside of France, transformed LVMH into a genuine multinational enterprise in luxury and fashion goods. In 1991, nearly sixty-seven per cent of the group's workforce had been employed in France. By 2014, the number of French employees had dropped to eighteen per cent.

LVMH's tremendous expansion had two major effects on the group's structure. First, vertical integration was pursued through takeovers of distribution firms. The direct control of distribution was key for developing strong control of brand management and for internalizing profits. Second, the diversification into distribution opened the possibility of what management scholars Christopher Moore and Grete Birtwistle call 'parent advantage', that is, the creation of synergies between different divisions.[28] For example, LVMH could achieve scale economies by holding joint launches of perfumes and watches. These developments were made possible through another major rationalization of LVMH's structure in 1998.[29] In that year, the group introduced a central management structure and product divisions for leather goods, perfumes and cosmetics, fashion, wine and spirits, and selective distribution. This new multidivisional organization, similar to organizational innovation realized in manufacturing firms such as the General Motors Corporation, was the basis for LVMH's staggering global expansion up to today (see table 3.4).[30]

Hence, external growth, that is, the growth through buying other companies, had been the key engine of LVMH since the second part of the 1990s. Net sales went from €4.5 billion in 1995 to €11.6 billion in 2000 and €30.6 billion in 2014. Profits were slower to grow. The operating income fell sharply during the second part of the 1990s – from just over twenty-four per cent in 1995 to seventeen per cent in 2000 – mostly due to the deterioration of the fashion and leather goods division. This decline of profitability was obviously the result of rising costs following the purchase of numerous companies, before the implementation of the rationalization policy of this division. But operating income went up to an average of nearly twenty-one per cent in the years between 2010 and 2014. Moreover, the development of LVMH within the new organization set up in 1998 relied essentially on fashion and leather goods, which constituted more than twenty-seven per cent of sales in 2000, compared to thirty-five per cent of sales in 2014, and on retailing, which constituted approximately twenty-nine per cent of sales in both years. Watches and jewellery showed promising growth, going from five to nine per cent of sales. The contribution of fashion and leather goods to LVMH's total profits has increased

Table 3.4 Organization of LVMH in 2015, simplified

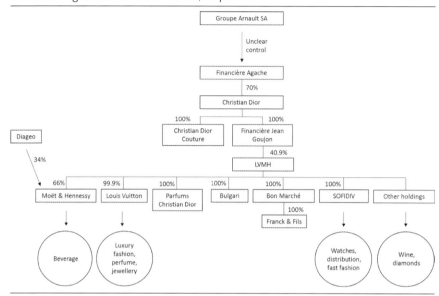

Source: drafted by the authors on the basis of LVMH, Annual Report, 2015.

tremendously since the beginning of the third millennium. For the years 2000 to 2014, fashion and leather goods represented fifty-eight per cent of the total operating income of LVMH. In contrast, wine and spirits dropped from twenty to thirteen per cent, while perfumes and cosmetics fell from eighteen to thirteen per cent.

Clearly, LVMH's decision to focus on luxury and fashion goods had been a highly profitable business strategy. The group claims that this staggering financial success is based on creativity, applied in all parts of its multidivisional organization. For example, in the 2010 annual report, Arnault explained that

> LVMH has enjoyed an uninterrupted growth, to which all our business groups have contributed … The Group's performance is also, above all, the result of the relevance and consistency of our long term strategy, [a] strategy that we pursued, unchanged, throughout the recent economic crisis. In support of the enduring values of our star brands, creativity is an absolute imperative.[31]

Let us now turn to the analysis of how storytelling contributed to LVMH's success.

Storytelling: LVMH by LVMH

A major feature of luxury and fashion goods is the discrepancy between the production cost of the merchandise and its sales price. The process of creating economic value results mostly from a marketing strategy that emphasizes the uniqueness of the goods and differentiates them from common consumer goods. Qualities such as craft processes, the high quality of the materials, and traditional know-how are evoked in marketing and advertising campaigns to stimulate consumer longing. Since the early 1990s, storytelling has become one of the major techniques to build brands and to add economic value to goods. Based on the idea that telling a story is much more profitable than having a discourse based on facts, storytelling was developed in United States politics during the 1980s and later adopted by managers in the private sector.[32] Management scholar Douglas Holt argues that a brand 'emerges' from stories told not only by the companies themselves but also by intermediaries and the brand's customers.[33] In the specific case of luxury and fashion, the importance is even higher than for common consumer goods, due to the necessity to differentiate and to add more emotional value to a brand. Something very important here is history, as heritage and tradition are at the core of the storytelling process in the luxury and fashion industry. The French gurus in luxury marketing, Jean-Noël Kapferer and Vincent Bastien, argue that 'if there is no history, it must be invented'.[34] They explain that three types of history can be used by luxury companies: true history, which makes it possible to create a myth; the re-appropriation of true historical elements by recent brands; and the creation of a new legend based on inspiration from the past.[35]

We will therefore start the analysis by the way in which LVMH tells stories about its brands with a special focus on the importance of creativity in this process. The main material for our analysis is LVMH's annual reports from 2002 to 2015.[36] One remarkable feature of these glossy reports is the high level of detail provided for each part of the company. On average each of these annual reports contains 80 to 110 pages of detailed information on corporate governance, strategy, shareholder relations, worldwide operations, and major brands and divisions. The annual reports, along with reference documents and hundreds of pages of additional information, can be found on a spectacular and extremely informative LVMH website.[37] This material has been prepared by LVMH to provide information on the company to existing and future shareholders. The main message is that LVMH shares outperform all other shares on the Paris stock exchange, showing an average annual return on investment that often amounts to ten per cent or more.

LVMH was and is a staggering financial success. It shows amazing growth figures compared to other French firms, even during periods in which other industries suffered from the effects of geopolitical conflicts and crises. Only in 2008 after the bankruptcy of Lehman Brothers, which led to a general lack of confidence in financial markets, was LVMH seriously affected. The share price, which had doubled in the previous five years, fell by forty-two per cent. LVMH's market capitalization went down from €40.5 billion at the end of 2007 to €23.4 billion one year later, making it still the eleventh-ranked company on the Paris stock exchange.[38] By 2015, however, LVMH's market capitalization was again up to €73.6 billion, outperforming all other major stocks in Paris listed on the CAC 40 index (a weighted measure of the forty most significant values on the Euronext Paris).[39] The market value was thus much higher than the book value of the group (€25.8 billion) at the end of 2015, which means that shareholders attached great importance to LVMH's intangible assets, such as its brands and the reputation of the brands. In general, companies with strong brands are valued much higher than the value of their tangible assets.[40] In 2014, the net value of brands and goodwill in LVMH's balance sheet 2014 amounted to €20.9 billion.[41]

One might argue that so far, there is not much storytelling involved in this slew of financial data. However, the argument here is that behind these staggering financial figures there is a lot of storytelling, partly based on true history, partly based on re-appropriation, and partly based on the creation of new legends. The reputations of brands are built through the careful construction and presentation of a self-image. In the case of the annual reports, LVHM's storytelling is geared primarily towards the shareholder rather than the consumer, and much of the data that we have discussed thus far is financial rather than visual or textual. Undeniably, strong brands also create important links and loyalties with consumers who identify with luxury products through the promises of quality, crafts-manship, and uniqueness. We now turn to the narratives in the annual reports.[42]

Two central themes in the annual reports are creativity and innovation, which are often tied to the concept of heritage. For example, one editorial in the 2005 annual report states:

> A coherent universe of men and women passionate about their business and driven by the desire to innovate and achieve. An unrivalled group of power-fully evocative brands and great names that are synonymous with the history of luxury. A natural alliance between art and craftsmanship where creativity, virtuosity and quality intersect.[43]

This is in a nutshell the message that LVMH wants to convey to the world. Its brands are 'synonymous with the history of luxury' (figure 3.2). However, the fact that some brands have a long history – Louis Vuitton suitcases were exported to Australia at the end of the nineteenth century, and Hennessy cognac was sold in New York as early 1794 and China since 1859 – does not mean that all LVMH brands have a long history.[44] In addition, even the old brands have been extended and have been completely changed from their original products, with the exception of cognac, which is still relatively close to its original form and taste.

The phrase 'a natural alliance between art and craftsmanship' is another example of how the LVHM group uses words to create new myths

Products of LVMH, a group bringing together seventy houses including the makers of Moët & Chandon Dom Perignon champagnes, Dior and Givenchy products, Hennessy cognac, and Louis Vuitton luggage. Photo: Brian Hagiwara/The LIFE Images Collection/Getty Images.

3.2

and legends. For some products, LVMH is using craftsmanship, but naturally many of its products are manufactured with modern machines in state-of-the-art plants in France, Switzerland, and Italy. In 2016, the group operated over one hundred manufacturing sites in France.[45] Louis Vuitton opened new and bigger factories, and by 2014, it already owned seventeen production sites. Among these manufactories, seventeen plants – twelve in France, three in Spain, and two in the United States – produce bags and accessories, while one plant based in Italy produces shoes.[46] In 2015, Guerlain opened a brand new factory for skincare products and cosmetics in the so-called Cosmetic Valley in Chartres, France.[47] As for the watch business, LVMH has invested massively in developing factories in Switzerland since the mid-2000s.[48] Moreover, for all its products, from champagne to leather goods, LVMH relies on a wide international network of suppliers of raw materials and semi-finished goods.

The last part, 'where creativity, virtuosity and quality intersect', is also telling. Here the concept of 'creativity', the absolute buzzword in LVMH's parlance, is linked to the high quality of its products. True, in 2008 Louis Vuitton closely collaborated with the American painter and photographer Richard Prince and the Japanese painter and sculptor Takashi Murakami, but this was done for two special collections by the designer Marc Jacobs.[49]

3.3   Karl Lagerfeld, who still provides artistic direction to Fendi, part of the LVMH group, is photographed for *Paris Match* at the group's headquarters in Paris, 28 May 2014; looking on are Delphine Arnault, director of Louis Vuitton, and Christopher Bagley from *W Magazine*. Photo: Alvaro Canovas/Paris Match/Contour by Getty Images.

LVMH hires top celebrity designers to create collections, but of course this is not done for every single product line. Nevertheless, the network of connections among fine artists, photographers, celebrity models, and designers is a tool for generating more brand value (figure 3.3).

Another message that LVMH endeavours to communicate is that its success can be explained by a combination of cultural heritage and tradition, on the one hand, and modern marketing techniques, industrial organization, and management techniques, on the other hand. The second part of the editorial in the 2005 annual report is enlightening:

> A remarkable economic success story with near 60,000 employees worldwide and global leadership in the manufacture and distribution of luxury goods.
>
> A unique blend of global vision and dedication to serving the needs of every customer. The successful marriage of cultures grounded in tradition and elegance with the most advanced marketing, industrial organization and management techniques. A singular mix of talent, daring and thoroughnessin the quest for excellence.A unique enterprise that stands out in its sector.
>
> Our philosophy can be summarized in two words – creative passion.[50]

This is another good example of storytelling, because indeed LVMH's success can be explained largely by a strong managerial and industrial organization, including innovative capital and brand management techniques.

In addition, the LVMH group hires the best people for its operations and divisions, including top designers. However, history and heritage do not explain the company's success. Rather, it is the clever and creative operationalization of LVMH's heritage that creates more brand value. Not least, this is creative storytelling: it is often very near to reality, but the causality is not always right.

History and heritage is present in the reference documents that support the annual reports and that are first and foremost written for LVMH's shareholders. Although the group was set up in 1987, these documents claim that the firm's roots go back to the eighteenth and nineteenth centuries and to the era of Claude Moët and Louis Vuitton. For example, one reference document dated 31 December 2014 states:

> Today, the LVMH group is the world's leading luxury goods company, the result of successive alliances among companies that, from generation to generation, have successfully combined traditions of excellence and creative passion with a cosmopolitan flair and a spirit of conquest. These companies now form a powerful, global group in which the historic companies share their expertise with the newer brands, and continue to cultivate the art of growing while transcending time, without losing their soul or their image of distinction.[51]

To prove the historic background, the founding dates of famous LVMH brands are listed, starting in year 1365 with the establishment of Domaine du Clos des Lambrays and ending in 2010 with Parfums Fendi. According to this document, most LVMH brands were established between the eighteenth century and the twentieth-first century. We will not discuss here whether it is possible to establish the exact founding date of one brand, and one definitely finds a lot of 'invention of tradition' going on here, to cite the work of historian Eric Hobsbawm.[52] The point is that the LVMH group aims to prove its historical roots and wants its shareholders and consumers to believe that the craftsmanship of its brands can transcend time 'without losing their soul' and their distinctive character. The reference document adds that 'the historic companies share their expertise with the newer brands'.[53] This is again a creative play on words, which, in turn, creates a significant amount of shareholder value.

To sum up, storytelling has become an important tool of the largest luxury and fashion group in the world. It has created invented traditions, even when there was no tradition to begin with. Some brands acquired by LVMH actually had a long history, but once they became part of the group, they were reinvented and extended, often aided by famous designers. But equally important has been the work of marketing managers and communications officers, who showed ingenuity in linking past and present. In 2007, the LVMH group's Managing Director Antonio Belloni lifted a corner of the veil:

> We often say that our designers and our artisans are the soul of our companies, but we can also state that our marketing and communications teams give

our brands their modernity, that our sales teams are the artisans of our successes in the field, that our financial and legal teams ensure good governance
and the power of the Group. I would like to insist on this point: within LVMH,
all the businesses are businesses of excellence, and it is strategic to recruit,
find and develop the best talent in each position.[54]

As Belloni shows, human resources played a major role in the LVMH's
stunning expansion over the past thirty years, finding the best people for
the organization. Moreover, LVMH is regularly mentioned as the favourite
company, and as a highly desirable employer, by the recent graduates of
French business schools.[55] The next section shows how LVMH manages
creativity, and how this strategy became the ideological basis of this highly
competitive conglomerate in luxury and fashion

Organizing and managing creativity

Despite the differences between luxury and fashion, these two businesses
share a similar idea that goods are not 'produced' but 'created', by artisans
and designers, respectively. Moreover, 'creativity' in these industries also
refers to the creation of economic value. Engaging in the manufacturing
and distribution of luxury and fashion goods can provide large profits
to companies, which obviously organize themselves in order to achieve
this goal.

This twofold dimension of creativity can be observed readily in the discourse of LVMH's founder and chief executive, Bernard Arnault. In 2000,
he published *La passion créative* (*The Creative Passion*), a book based on
interviews by the French journalist Yves Messarovitch. Arnault starts by
introducing himself as a 'real creator', as if he were the entrepreneur 'who
had invented a new industry in the world, the luxury industry'.[56] Then, he
explains what creation means to him:

> To create high quality goods, to sell them around the whole world through
> a network of boutiques in constant evolution ... But above all, creating an
> economic reality based on ideas from creators of the group is precisely the
> 'creative passion'.[57]

Arnault uses an ambiguous narrative about creativity. In his view, there
are two types of creativity, 'economic value creation' and 'artistic creation',
which operate simultaneously. Therefore, the management of creativity –
controlling the making of profits through the manufacturing of traditional
luxury goods – is a major objective for LVMH. We can emphasize the following three dimensions.

First, the LVMH headquarters in Paris control the creation and creativity of the group. The reorganization of the conglomerate after its numerous acquisitions during the 1990s led to its centralization and to a strong
hierarchical chain of command. During the second part of the 1990s,

LVMH gradually organized an executive committee to coordinate the activities of subsidiaries that were involved in a same industry. The reorganization started with champagne in 1995, was followed by perfume in 1997, and by other products soon afterwards.[58] The executive committee, which included twelve members in 2016, had a major impact on the positioning of the various brands and on product development. The committee defined strategic objectives, and coordinated their implementation.[59] Then, the management of each operational company of the LVMH group was expected to implement the creative instructions.

Major outcomes of the coordination of activities by the Paris headquarters are the synergies and scale economies realized between the different businesses within the LVMH group. LVMH owns manufacturing facilities that can make a wide array of products, and they make the same goods for each LVMH brand.[60] For example, shortly after the establishment of LVMH in 1987, Louis Vuitton signed a contract to make leather goods for Christian Lacroix, a company that belonged to Arnault.[61] Hence, Lacroix was able to use the production facilities of Louis Vuitton, another brand of LVMH, to make handbags and other products for its customers. The watch division further demonstrates the effective implementation of parent advantage. Two years after the takeover of Swiss watch companies TAG Heuer and Zénith in 1999, LVMH opened in La Chaux-de-Fonds, Switzerland, a facility to assemble watches for its subsidiaries, Christian Dior, Fred, and Louis Vuitton. In 2002, Louis Vuitton launched its first collection of watches, equipped with movements manufactured by Zénith, a company owned by LVMH.[62] A similar process can be observed for the production of perfumes. Synergies between subsidiaries made it possible for the fashion brand Kenzo to launch its own perfume in 2000. Then, in 2010, the group founded LVMH Fragrance Brands, a company expressly dedicated to making perfumes for its fashion brands.

Second, LVMH invested heavily in the procurement of luxury goods in France and in other countries where its subsidiaries are based. Since 2000, the direct control of the production of goods has been a major challenge in the luxury business. The growing competition among different luxury groups led each of them to absorb their subcontractor in order to insure their supplies materials, ingredients, and components. For example, in 2009, LVMH created a joint venture with Masure Tannery, a supplier of leather to Louis Vuitton since 1988. Three years later, in 2012, LVMH purchased another leather supplier in southern France.[63] In the watch business, LVMH took over two manufacturers of cases and dials in 2011. This strategy is not limited to large companies like LVMH but is quite common in the luxury industry; smaller companies like Chanel have implemented the same strategy.[64]

Besides such acquisitions, LVMH encouraged the preservation of traditional know-how and craft techniques on the part of independent artisans through various projects to train the next generations of craftsmen. In 2013, the LVMH Spanish subsidiary Loewe opened a school for training artisans in leather goods, calling it *Escuela de Maroquinería (Institute for Leatherwork)*. The following year, LVMH launched a new programme entitled the Institut des Métiers d'Excellence (Institute of Crafts of Excellence) to support the organization of several training programmes in concert with French vocational schools, particularly in fashion and jewellery. In this respect, LVMH follows in the footsteps of the tradition started by the Chambre Syndicale de la Couture Parisienne, which invested in education and apprenticeship to support creativity.[65] Moreover, LVMH founded an award for young designers in 1994 and a prize for young fashion creators in 2014. These activities are important ways to support creativity and preserve the craftsmanship tradition. At the same time, they are part of LVMH's public relations strategy, which emphasizes the group's role as a supporter of creation and adds value to its luxury and fashion brands.

Third, the employment of celebrity designers as artistic directors was another way to add value to LVMH brands and products. Personalities like John Galliano at Dior and Marc Jacobs at Louis Vuitton were important to the development of new products that enhanced the group's different brands. Arnault argued that Galliano realized 'what Dior would have done himself today'.[66] Yet, these designers were employed not only to create luxury goods, but also to create economic value. Galliano was hired to replace Gianfranco Ferré, who served as the artistic director at Dior between 1989 and 1996, when the latter failed to generate profitable lines. In contrast, Galliano would become a cash machine for the Dior brand. He became famous through his provocative haute couture shows on the Parisian catwalks and later used his fame to boost ready-to-wear collections and accessories. He attracted the attention of media through the introduction of male models and shocking catwalk extravaganzas, such as a fashion show inspired by the homeless and sadomasochism. In 2000, Arnault said that ready-to-wear sales grew fourfold after Galliano became head of design at Dior.[67] In 2011, Galliano was witnessed insulting patrons in a Paris bar, making racist and anti-Semitic comments. This created an immediate outcry in the fashion industry and beyond, and subsequently, Galliano was fired in 2011. According to Arnault, continuing to employ him after such a mediatized episode was too harmful for the Dior brand. Galliano then went through a period of rehabilitation and gave public excuses. After several years of hiatus, Galliano returned as a designer to the Maison Martin Margiela, part of the Only the Brave group, and designed his first collection for that brand in 2015.[68] After the exit of Galliano, the design of the Dior collections was delegated to Bill Gaytten, Galliano's former right-hand man, while LVMH searched for a new director. Belgian Raf Simons was hired to general acclaim, but after a few seasons he stepped down, allegedly due to the huge pressure of the job.[69]

In 2016, Maria Grazia Chiuri was the first woman appointed as the head designer of Dior.[70]

It is no surprise that the choice of designers matters. Another function of the designers is to strengthen the presence of the LVMH group in specific markets. The best example of this strategy is the collaboration between Louis Vuitton and the Japanese artist Takashi Murakami. The painter and sculptor designed several brightly coloured handbags and leather goods between 2002 and 2015, including colourful monograms, which first became famous in Japan before achieving success on the global market. While Louis Vuitton's products are usually brown and classical, the introduction of colourful goods helped to strengthen the brand among new generations of customers. Hence, Murakami contributed to the excellent reputation of Louis Vuitton in one of its major markets, Japan.

Hence, creativity is not the only result of actions by designers and 'creators'. It is a major resource of the company, orchestrated by the Paris headquarters in order to increase visibility of brands, sales, and profits. LVMH implemented organizational capabilities to control creativity management. Superstar designers hired by the group embody creativity for mass media and customers, and they are backed by an effective organization. The Galliano affair in 2011 shows the ambiguous relationship between the company and the creator. The importance of brand image also puts a huge pressure on the shoulders of the creator. Galliano had to provide new goods and attract the attention of mass media to promote Dior. Yet, when the creator's behaviour started to damage the brand image, the company took control and changed the creator. Creation is thus subjected to brand management and profitability.

Telling the LVMH story

LVMH is the largest luxury and fashion group in the world. As such, its history is an appropriate window onto the radical changes in the global luxury and fashion industry, which over the past three decades was transformed from a sector dominated by small family firms to one controlled by a few multinational conglomerates. Despite a general tendency towards consolidation, each conglomerate in this industry is characterized by its own particular evolution. This especially applies to LVMH, which developed a unique organizational structure that came to foster new approaches to product design and development. Moreover, the crucial role of Arnault, whose views on creativity have been applied to the whole LVMH group, makes this case illuminating.

LVMH's organizational structure was subject to constant change. At the beginning, the organization of LVMH was rather decentralized; Louis Vuitton and Moët Hennessy continued to manage their own subsidiaries. During the 1990s, the company expanded through acquisitions in France and elsewhere and further rationalized its organization. This culminated in a fundamental reorganization after the introduction of a central management team based in Paris and a multidivisional structure, which formed the basis for the continuous global expansion of LVMH in the 2000s.

According to LVMH's annual reports and reference documents, creativity is a major resource for the group. This chapter has analysed the ways in which the creative process was socially constructed. Storytelling appears to be an important tool for the luxury and fashion industries due to the necessity to differentiate the various products or brands and to add emotional value to them. Heritage and tradition were at the core of LVMH's storytelling, which created myths and legends by re-appropriating true historical elements for its new brands. We have shown through several examples how heritage and preserved or revived craftsmanship were used to give LVMH's brands and products a historical dimension. Even new luxury and fashion products and brands were imbued with this historical flavour and sense of legendary quality.

According to Arnault, creativity forms the basis of LVMH's success and is a symbiosis of economic value creation and artistic design. Managing creativity, in its multifaceted dimensions within the group, is a major strategic tool for LVMH. In the mid-1990s, a coordinating committee was set up to position the various brands and develop products. The committee defined strategic objectives and coordinated their implementation within the operational companies of the group. In that way, synergies could be realized between different businesses and brands. Furthermore, the group invested heavily in mechanisms to control its supply chain, and helped its subsidiaries to secure their materials through the takeovers of suppliers in the 2000s. The employment of top designers as creative directors was another way to add value to its luxury and fashion brands. Clearly, however, these creative minds were also made subordinate to the strategic objectives of the group. Finally, LVMH supported creativity and the preservation of craftsmanship outside the group. It encouraged the preservation of traditional crafts through various projects, supported vocational schools, and founded awards for young designers and fashion creators. In so doing, LVMH also situated its activity within the continuity of the French luxury tradition, including the activity of the Chambre Syndicale de la Couture Parisienne (see Chapter 2).[71]

Every one of these initiatives is part of LVMH's storytelling, which emphasizes its role as a significant supporter of creation and creativity. But at the end of day, the stories all add value to the firm's luxury and fashion brands and, ultimately, increase the market value of the group. Finally, LVMH's financial success in the last thirty years can largely be explained by strong managerial capabilities and industrial organization, innovative capital constructions, and clever brand management techniques.

Notes

1 P.-Y. Donzé and R. Fujioka, 'European luxury big business and emerging Asian markets, 1960–2010', *Business History*, 57:6 (2015), 822–40.

2 A. Chatriot, 'La construction récente des groupes de luxe français: mythes, discours et pratiques', *Entreprises et histoire*, 15:46 (2007), 143–56.

3 Donzé and Fujioka, 'European luxury'.

4 LVMH, *Annual Report 2011*, p. 2, at https://www.lvmh.com/investors/publications/?publications=29&pub_year=&pub_month=# (accessed 9 September 2016).

5 M. A. Runco and G. J. Jaeger, 'The standard definition of creativity', *Creativity Research Journal*, 24:1 (2012), 96.

6 M. Pareja-Eastaway, 'Creative industries', *Journal of Evolutionary Studies in Business*, 1:1 (2016), 40–2.

7 *Ibid.*

8 R. Florida, *The Rise of the Creative Class: And How It's Transforming Work, Leisure, Community, and Everyday Life* (New York: Basic Books, 2002).

9 Pareja-Eastaway, 'Creative industries', 40–2.

10 Pareja-Eastaway, 'Creative industries', 42–3.

11 Runco and Jaeger, 'The standard definition of creativity'.

12 See for example M. Chevalier and G. Mazzalovo, *Luxury Brand Management: A World of Privilege* (Singapore: John Wiley & Sons, 2012), pp. 189–214.

13 J.-N. Kapferer and V. Bastien, *The Luxury Strategy: Break the Rules of Marketing to Build Luxury Brands* (London: Kogan Page, 2nd edn 2012), p. 98.

14 N. Forestier and N. Ravai, *Bernard Arnault ou le goût du pouvoir* (Paris: Olivier Orban, 1993); B. Arnault and Y. Messarovitch, *La passion créative* (Paris: Plon, 2000); A. Routier, *L'ange exterminateur: la vraie vie de Bernard Arnault* (Paris: Albin Michel, 2003).

15 P. Eveno, 'La construction d'un groupe international, LVMH', in J. Marseille (ed.), *Le luxe en France, du siècle des Lumières à nos jours* (Paris: Association pour le développement de l'histoire économique, 1999), pp. 291–321; H. Bonin, 'A reassessment of the business history of the French luxury sector: the emergence of a new business model and renewed corporate image (from the 1970s)', in L. Segreto, H. Bonin, A. K. Kozminski, C. Manera, and M. Pohl (eds), *European Business and Brand Building* (Brussels: Peter Lang, 2012), pp. 113–35.

16 Bonin, 'A reassessment of the business history of the French luxury sector', p. 125.

17 LVHM, at https://www.lvmh.com/investors/publications/?publications=29&pub_year=&pub_month=# (accessed 9 September 2016).

18 V. Houtteville, *LVMH* (Paris: Eurostaff, 1987).

19 M. Refait, *Moët & Chandon: De Claude Moët à Bernard Arnault* (Reims: Dominique Guéniot, 1998); S. Bonvicini, *Louis Vuitton: Une saga française* (Paris: Fayard, 2004).

20 Louis Vuitton, *Rapports annuels*, 1981–85.

21 Guinness is headquartered in London, listed on the London Stock Exchange, and is less 'Irish' than most people think. C.R., 'Why Guinness is less Irish than you think', *The Economist explains*, at www.economist.com/blogs/economist-explains/2014/03/economist-explains-13 (accessed 26 April 2016); T. S. Lopes, *Global Brands: The Evolution of Multinationals in Alcoholic Beverages* (Cambridge: Cambridge University Press, 2007).

22 Houtteville, *LVMH*.

23 Bonin, 'A reassessment of the business history of the French luxury sector', pp. 117–18.

24 LVMH, *Lettre aux actionnaires*, February 1994.

25 *Ibid.*

26 LVMH, *Lettre aux actionnaires*, November 1997, and Eurostaff, *Stratégies et Performances Comparées des Groupes: LVMH*, 1996.

27 P.-Y. Donzé, *A Business History of the Swatch Group: The Rebirth of Swiss Watchmaking and the Globalization of the Luxury Industry* (Basingstoke: Palgrave Macmillan, 2014), pp. 117–20.

28 C. M. Moore and G. Birtwistle, 'The nature of parenting advantage in luxury fashion retailing: the case of Gucci group NV', *International Journal of Retail & Distribution Management*, 33:4 (2005), 256–70.

29 G. Martin, *LVMH* (Paris: Eurostaf, 1999).

30 A. D. Chandler Jr., *Strategy and Structure: Chapters in the History of the American Industrial Enterprise* (Cambridge, MA: MIT Press, 1962).

31 LVMH, *Annual report 2010*, p. 2, at https://www.lvmh.com/investors/publications/?publications=29&pub_year=&pub_month=# (accessed 9 September 2016).

32 C. Salmon, *Storytelling: La machine à fabriquer des histoires et à formater les esprits* (Paris: La Découverte, 2007), pp. 45–73.

33 D. B. Holt, *How Brands Become Icons: The Principles of Cultural Branding* (Cambridge, MA: Harvard University Press, 2004), p. 3.

34 Kapferer and Bastien, *The Luxury Strategy*, p. 93.

35 Kapferer and Bastien, *The Luxury Strategy*, p. 95.

36 LVHM, Annual reports, at https://www.lvmh.com/investors/publications/?publications=29&pub_year=&pub_month=# (accessed 9 September 2016).

37 LVMH, Publications, at https://www.lvmh.com/investors/publications/?publications=29&pub_year=&pub_month=# (accessed 9 September 2016).

38 LVMH, *Annual Report 2008*, p. 12, at https://www.lvmh.com/investors/publications/?publications=29&pub_year=&pub_month=# (accessed 9 September 2016).

39 LVMH, *Annual Report 2015*, p. 47, at https://www.lvmh.com/investors/publications/?publications=29&pub_year=&pub_month=# (accessed 9 September 2016).

40 U. Okonkwo, *Luxury Fashion Branding: Trends, Tactics, Techniques* (Basingstoke: Palgrave Macmillan, 2007), p. 104. According to Okonkwo, companies with strong brands are valued four to twenty times higher than the value of their physical assets. However, this appears to be an exaggeration if we compare it with our research into LVMH.

41 LVMH, *Translation of the French Document de référence, fiscal year ended December 31, 2014*, p. 36, at https://r.lvmh-static.com/uploads/2015/02/lvmh-2014-reference-document.pdf (accessed 27 April 2015).

42 Okonkwo, *Luxury Fashion Branding*, p. 105.

43 LVMH, *Annual Report 2005*, p. 3, at https://www.lvmh.com/investors/publications/?publications=29&pub_year=&pub_month=# (accessed 9 September 2016).

44 LVMH, *Annual Report 2007*, p. 3, at https://www.lvmh.com/investors/publications/?publications=29&pub_year=&pub_month=# (accessed 9 September 2016).

45 'LVHM will open some fifty of its sites to the public for three days in May', FashionMag.com, 16 March 2016, at http://us.fashionmag.com/news/LVMH-will-open-some-fifty-of-its-sites-to-the-public-for-three-days-in-May,670256.html#.V6tOhk3r3IU (accessed 10 August 2016).

46 LVMH, *Exercice 2015: document de référence*, p. 15, at https://r.lvmh-static.com/uploads/2016/03/lvmh-document-de-reference-2015-vf.pdf (accessed 12 August 2016).

47 LVMH, 'La Ruche, the new French production site for Guerlain', n.d., at https://www.lvmh.com/group/lvmh-commitments/economic-footprint/la-ruche-the-new-french-production-site-for-guerlain/ (accessed 10 August 2016).

48 Donzé, *A Business History of the Swatch Group*, pp. 117–20.

49 LVMH, *Annual Report 2008*, p. 3.

50 LVMH, *Annual Report 2005*, p.3.

51 LVMH, *Translation of the French Document de référence, fiscal year ended December 31, 2014*, p. 1.

52 E. Hobsbawm and T. Ranger (eds.), *The Invention of Tradition* (Cambridge: Cambridge University Press, 1983).

53 LVMH, *Translation of the French Document de référence, fiscal year ended December 31, 2014*, p. 1.
54 LVMH, *Annual Report 2007*, p. 8.
55 Universal Global, *Les employeurs qui font rêver*, at http://top100.universumglobal. com/france/ranking/ (accessed 12 April 2016).
56 Arnault and Messarovitch, *La passion créative*, p. 9.
57 Arnault and Messarovitch, *La passion créative*, p. 67.
58 *Les Echos* (20 January 1995) and (3 December 1997), at http://recherche.lesechos. fr/ (accessed 12 April 2016).
59 LVMH, *Translation of the French Document de référence, fiscal year ended December 31, 2012*, p. 109, at https://r.lvmh-static.com/uploads/2014/10/document_de_refer ence_2012_va.pdf (accessed 12 April 2016).
60 T. Okawa, 'Licensing practices at Maison Christian Dior', in R. L. Blaszczyk (ed.), *Producing Fashion: Commerce, Culture, and Consumers* (Philadelphia: University of Pennsylvania Press, 2008), p. 103.
61 LVMH, *Lettre aux actionnaires*, February 1994.
62 L. F. Trueb, *The World of Watches: History, Industry, Technology* (New York: Ebner Publishing, 2005), p. 285.
63 I. Letessier, 'LVMH s'offre un tanneur de Romans', *Le Figaro* (2 May 2012).
64 P.-Y. Donzé and R. Fujioka (eds), *Global Luxury: Organizational Change and Emerging Markets in the Luxury Industry Since the 1970s* (Basingstoke: Palgrave Macmillan, 2017).
65 V. Pouillard, 'Managing fashion creativity: the history of the Chambre Syndicale de la Couture Parisienne during the interwar period', *Investigaciones de Historia Económica – Economic History Research*, 12:2 (2016), 76–89.
66 Arnault and Messarovitch, *La passion créative*, p. 75.
67 Arnault and Messarovitch, *La passion créative*, p. 80.
68 'John Galliano set to join Maison Martin Margiela', *Business of Fashion* (6 October 2014), at www.businessoffashion.com/articles/news-analysis/john-galliano-set-join-maison-martin-margiela (accessed 9 September 2016).
69 Nicole Phelps, 'Raf Simons to step down at Christian Dior' (22 October 2015), at www.vogue.com/13363642/raf-simons-leaves-christian-dior/(accessed 9 September 2016).
70 Sarah Mower, 'It's official: Maria Grazia Chiuri is in at Christian Dior', *Vogue* (8 July 2016), at www.vogue.com/13450872/christian-dior-maria-grazia-chiuri/ (accessed 9 September 2016).
71 Pouillard, 'Managing fashion creativity'.

4

Reawakening the 'sleeping beauties' of haute couture: the case of Guy and Arnaud de Lummen

Johanna Zanon

The term 'sleeping beauty' is used to describe a Parisian haute couture brand that, once world-renowned but long dormant, has been rediscovered and reintroduced as a brand in the contemporary market. A sleeping beauty business embodies a new type of creative industry whose aim is to recover, from a prestigious past, a cultural asset for use in the future. For a company to be a sleeping beauty, it has to have gone through a disruption of its main activity and key players, including the designer and the entrepreneur. While this chapter examines sleeping beauties in the luxury fashion industry, one can also find them in other sectors, such as the automobile industry.

In the famous sleeping beauty fairy tale told in different versions by Charles Perrault, by the Grimm Brothers, and by Walt Disney, the princess was cursed by a wicked fairy godmother, who predicted that she would one day prick her finger on the spindle of a spinning wheel and die. A good fairy softened the curse into a hundred years of sleep, from which only the kiss of a king's son could awaken her.[1] While Sleeping Beauty epitomizes feminine passivity, the motif of the long magic sleep provides a seren-dipitous metaphor to explain all phenomena that include a long period of interruption, such as revivals of extinct brands. Drawing upon the classic fairy tale makes for a good brand narrative.

It is no wonder that the term 'sleeping beauty' was employed by brand managers before the media started using it more frequently in the 2000s. The media, however, has used the phrase somewhat ambiguously and applied it both to bona fide sleeping beauties, and to houses that lost their edge but did not close their doors before being rejuvenated. The term has been applied to revived businesses in the early twenty-first century, but the phenomenon of revival can be traced back to 1968, when the house of Worth in London woke from a long slumber and reintroduced a couture line.[2]

In borrowing from the fairy tale, luxury brands could mask possible failures of the brand in the past. Conveniently, a sleeping beauty brand is seen not to have failed, but just fallen asleep. The term embodies the industry's narrative of success: a sleeping beauty firm passes from an initial success to subsequent success through processes of revival. The term also translates easily in many languages such as French (*belle endormie*), Spanish (*bella durmiente*), and German (*Dornröschen*), and facilitates the introduction of the brand on international markets. More importantly, the tale is widely spread across the world. Its meaning is therefore not lost in translation, which makes it a powerful branding asset.[3]

There is more to the reawakening of a sleeping beauty than a magic kiss. Pierre Bourdieu's concept of cultural capital is particularly relevant to explain why the sleeping beauty phenomenon was possible at all. The French sociologist first elaborated the notion of cultural capital to enforce his view of culture as a currency that people use, rather than an intrinsic quality.[4] According to Bourdieu, there are three forms of cultural capital, including the 'objectified state', which consists of cultural goods that one can own such as paintings, books, and machines.[5] Bourdieu's definition concerned tangible cultural goods, but can also be applied to brands as intangible cultural goods.

A sleeping beauty brand is the repository of objectified cultural capital. The brand accumulated cultural capital from the moment it was established to the moment it shut down. That cultural capital became dormant when the house ceased operations. It has no value in a contemporary market unless it is activated strategically by its new owner. 'All those objects on which cultural value has ever been bestowed', wrote Derek Robbins in his *Bourdieu and Culture*, 'lie perpetually dormant waiting to be revived, waiting for their old value to be used to establish new value in a new market situation.'[6] In other words, objectified cultural capital is permanently stored potential, but always dependent on the choices of individuals.

Drawing upon the conceptual tool elaborated by Bourdieu, this chapter analyses the cases of two entrepreneurs, Guy de Lummen and his son Arnaud de Lummen, whose investment in dormant fashion firms exemplifies the sleeping beauty phenomenon. This chapter shows how the father-and-son team appropriated the objectified cultural capital of sleeping beauty brands, both materially and symbolically, first, by buying the legal rights to use them, and second, by acquiring the knowledge necessary to commercialize new products. For a sleeping beauty to succeed, the brand needs to be invigorated with new business skills and its managers need to harness the history of the brand, which is its biggest asset. Entrepreneurs curate the history of the brand by selecting the relevant historical elements that support their revivalist strategy.

The initial glory years of sleeping beauty firms such as Schiaparelli, Vionnet, and Worth have been researched at great length, whereas these brands' revivals have received far less scholarly attention. This chapter builds upon a wide range of unpublished sources, including interviews with Arnaud de Lummen, records of the family's firms, and material and objects held in public institutions. The chapter probes the mechanisms of the revival from Guy de Lummen's initial idea that it was possible to revive an extinct brand in the 1980s, to Arnaud de Lummen's systemization of the method in the 2000s, when he acted as an intermediary between a reservoir of extinct brands and the marketplace.

Guy de Lummen and Madeleine Vionnet (1988–2004)

The 1980s brought turmoil and change to the luxury industry. The rise of luxury conglomerates through mergers and acquisitions resulted in the disappearance of many traditional family-run couture houses, which were small and medium-sized enterprises.[7] At the same time, the luxury sector started a democratization movement, targeting a broader audience than that of the traditional elite customers, relocating production into countries with cheap labour, and betting on the all-powerful label through a vast array of licences.

One entrepreneur seemingly went against the tide. Guy de Lummen, a French entrepreneur born Guy Paries Watelin Van Marcke de Lummen, used his personal funds to revive Vionnet, a historic Parisian couture house that had been long dormant, albeit not for a hundred years. Established in 1912, the Société Madeleine Vionnet & Cie was among the most successful haute couture houses of the interwar years. The firm closed in 1939, when founder and designer Madeleine Vionnet retired. No wicked fairy godmother cursed the dressmaker, who was then sixty-three years old and decided to end her house's activities on the date of expiration of the company, which had been founded for twenty years by a deed dated 15 June 1919.[8]

But was the revival of Vionnet really against the tide? The 1980s were also a time when haute couture received new recognition from French cultural institutions, culminating in the opening in 1986 of the Musée de la Mode et du Textile in the Marsan wing of the Louvre.[9] At the same time, fashion gained new academic recognition through the work of leading authors such as Philippe Perrot and Daniel Roche.[10] The fashion industry changed as well. Many haute couture houses realized that their heritage mattered, and took steps to inaugurate in-house archives. Fashion designs on the catwalks were equally influenced by the past. The links between fashion and culture, as evidenced by the pioneering research of the historian Valerie Steele, were more visible than ever before.[11] De Lummen's apparently anachronistic venture must be understood in this context.

Born on 27 June 1945, Guy de Lummen was initially trained as a textile engineer, but widened his knowledge of production techniques to become a product manager handling about twenty licences at the Paris haute couture house Maggy Rouff.[12] In the 1980s, de Lummen established himself as a specialist of upmarket ready-to-wear and directed the ready-to-wear department of couturier Ted Lapidus before launching the ready-to-wear activity of Pierre Balmain in 1982, through a licensing agreement with the Weinberg company.[13] During that time, Paris haute couture was restructuring along the idea that haute couture would become a laboratory for creativity, while profits would be generated by deluxe ready-to-wear, in addition to the perfume and accessory lines.[14]

In 1988, Balmain terminated the licence agreement with Weinberg, and de Lummen found himself in search of a new career path. He formulated an innovative idea: he would revive one of the most prestigious prewar couture houses through the creation of licences, on which he was an expert. The idea for the new house of Vionnet therefore resulted from the creativity of an entrepreneur in search of a new business opportunity and not from a designer in search of a financial backer, since Madeleine Vionnet had died in 1975.

How did de Lummen single out Vionnet among the heavily populated fashion pantheon? Browsing through fashion books in his library, he searched for houses with a rich heritage. He cross-referenced the selected names with the availability of the intellectual property rights of these firms to a potential buyer. Paul Poiret was de Lummen's first choice, but the trademark had been registered by the jeweller Poiray, whose brand name was a tribute to the dressmaker.[15] He opted instead for the equally important Madeleine Vionnet. According to his son Arnaud, neither the exhibition *Three Women: Madeleine Vionnet, Claire McCardell, and Rei Kawakubo* at the Fashion Institute of Technology in New York in 1987, nor the 1985 auction sales of the furniture that had once belonged to Madeleine Vionnet, played a role in his father's decision.[16] Vionnet, it seems, was 'in the air', and Guy de Lummen was on the money.

Assembling a clear portfolio of intellectual property rights worldwide constituted the starting point of de Lummen's sleeping beauty business. He bought the Vionnet trademarks from a company of undisclosed name, which had registered but not used them after they fell into the public domain.[17] In July 1988, he re-trademarked the Vionnet name.[18] In the following October, he registered a new visual logo for Vionnet, consisting of the initials MV framed by a double octagon. A logo resembling the original designed in 1919 by Italian artist Thayaht (a pseudonym for Ernesto Michahelles) was re-trademarked in 1996, although de Lummen did not use it.[19] By acquiring the trademarks of the dormant Vionnet firm, he materially appropriated the objectified form of the cultural capital in Bourdieu's framework.

De Lummen was aware that reviving Vionnet, a brand of unparalleled heritage, would take time. In the meantime, he honed his skill as a brand revitalizer by focusing on Chéruit, another extinct couture house that was less renowned than Vionnet. This was long before the 2013 exhibition, *The Novel of a Wardrobe*, explored the history of Chéruit, which had been active between 1898 and 1933.[20] The idea with Chéruit was to use an old name to tap into the clientele that Guy de Lummen had built up during his six years at Balmain.[21] The entrepreneur did not focus on Chéruit's heritage, but used this venture as a vehicle for replicating his business formula. It was nevertheless a first step in the implementation of a revivalist strategy.

Chéruit succeeded to some extent, but was not a huge hit. In 1992, de Lummen therefore accepted a job at the VEV textile group, which owned the famous French textile manufacturer, Rodier, and the wool yarn manufacturer, Pingouin. He was in charge of developing a ready-to-wear line to diversify Pingouin, whose sales of yarn had declined as hand-knitting fell out of fashion. Due to a disagreement with the top management, he left the group a year later.[22] After this short and disappointing spell, he went back to his original project and worked actively to prepare the return of Vionnet. In 1993–94, through Madeleine Vionnet SA, a simplified joint-stock company whose headquarters were at 21, place Vendôme, he designed his business plan and signed licensing agreements.[23]

Licensees were open to the idea of using a historical name to sell new products. According to Guy de Lummen, they searched 'for solid values', and 'storied names'.[24] The revival of Vionnet was first announced in the trade daily *Le Journal du Textile* in August 1994. De Lummen had just signed the first licensing agreements; production had not yet started. Through this early announcement, he sought to raise brand awareness. He tried to reinstate Vionnet as a pillar of fashion history before going into the details of the brand's history. Vionnet was presented as 'a cult name' that had 'revolutionized couture', having been almost forgotten for half a century.[25]

Sleeping beauties like Vionnet require a certain degree of forgetfulness, as the son Arnaud put it.[26] Vionnet, remembered by only a few fashion experts, was virtually unknown by the average fashion consumer. 'Far from being a weakness, it is the magic Vionnet paradox: for the consumer, Vionnet is a fresh name carrying a rich story.'[27] The widespread cultural amnesia about Vionnet allowed the entrepreneur to select the most relevant characteristics of the brand for its revival, without falsifying history. As scholars Elisabetta Merlo and Mario Perugini found, returning to the past can backfire if the marketing strategy 'is not supported by an extensive knowledge of the firm's history, and by a well-documented analysis of the historical background in which the brand was originally introduced'.[28]

The purpose was not to reinvent history but curate it strategically. To this end, de Lummen released a press kit outlining the brand's history.[29]

His picture was first, preceding Vionnet's, thereby establishing two related points: that the present-day entrepreneur is the key character in a sleeping beauty business (rather than the designer of the past) and thus can choose how to present the original designer, as well as whoever he wants as a new designer. Next, the press kit defined Vionnet's life, house, and technique. Iconographic material included two famous 1931 photographs by George Hoyningen-Huene for the American edition of *Vogue* magazine, showing a model wearing flowing bias-cut crêpe pyjamas made in a Grecian style.[30] Last, a chronology presented the fashionable silhouette decade by decade, in which Vionnet embodied the 1930s. Many elements that the revived house would later develop were showcased in this early marketing tool, but they were presented in a superficial manner, lacking the profound knowledge of the brand's history.

Soon after, in February 1995, the reawakened house claimed the legacy of its founder to justify the new business orientation. It emphasized that originally Vionnet produced not only clothing, but also lingerie, bags, jewels, shoes, and furs. This wide range of products legitimized the relaunch of an accessories-based business, including products that Vionnet never commercialized such as watches.[31] Furthermore, de Lummen introduced the first men's accessory line in the history of the Vionnet brand, demonstrating the necessary balance between a reference to the past and adaptation to the current market.[32]

De Lummen hired Patrice Ewald as the artistic director for accessories.[33] The first designs made under the new Vionnet label were shown at the Salon du Prêt-à-Porter, the famous Paris ready-to-wear fair, in February 1995. The seventy-five scarves were produced by Lyon-based silk manufacturer Setb in velvet, satin, muslin, and twill cloths with designs that were plain, printed, or hand-painted.[34] Concomitantly, the Musée des Tissus, the museum of fabrics in Lyon, held the second retrospective exhibition dedicated to Vionnet – the first being the one at the newly created Musée de la Mode in Marseille back in 1991.[35] When interviewed, de Lummen mentioned that the Lyon exhibition promoted the house's collections, but neither did he finance the exhibition, nor was the revived house mentioned in the exhibition catalogue.

Many other accessories followed, all of them made in France by prestigious manufacturers. High-quality products with high price tags positioned Vionnet as a luxury brand. The house signed a licensing agreement with the manufacturer Parfums Daniel Aubusson. De Lummen hoped to relaunch Vionnet's four original perfumes, which had been called A, B, C, D when they debuted in 1925, before introducing new products.[36] Perfume was not central to Vionnet's business activities and never reached the importance of Chanel No. 5.[37] Aubusson wanted instead to release new fragrances, considering the re-edition of an old perfume too passé. Eventually, de Lummen listened to Aubusson.[38] A new fragrance, called Haute Couture, was released in 1996 at the Tax Free World Exhibition in Cannes, the largest trade fair for duty-free and air travel merchandise.[39]

The luxury aspect of the Haute Couture perfume was reflected in the bottle conceived by Thierry de Bachmakov and 'born from a fabric roll and represented a woman wearing a dress cut in the bias'.[40] Two super-imposed golden thimbles completed the silhouette. Similar bottles were used for the second new perfume launched by Vionnet in 1998, called MV, and the third in 2000, called MV Green. With three perfumes in four years, Vionnet contributed to the frenzy of perfume launches that characterized the late 1990s.[41]

In 1997, the prominent fashion journalist Janie Samet wrote the first influential press article on the revival of Vionnet in *Le Figaro*. While Samet evaluated the products favourably, she wondered whether the dress-maker would have approved of the revival, and considered the purchase of Vionnet's name an ethical problem. 'Everything is for sale', Samet sniped. 'Even names. Especially names whose renown save investors time.'[42] Madeleine Vionnet was the name of an individual before it became the name of a brand.

Vionnet's revival polarized opinions in the industry. For many people, reawakening a couture house with a pre-existing history showed a lack of imagination, not least when there were plenty of designers looking for financial backers. The strongest resistance came from the Musée de la Mode et du Textile, which held the archives donated by Vionnet herself in 1952.[43] De Lummen's company invaded the museum's turf by creating a competing historical narrative.

Criticism did not stop de Lummen, whose revival strategy material-ized in the opening of a Vionnet boutique at 12, rue de la Paix in Paris in 1999.[44] Although this was not the historical site of the house of Vionnet, the marketing materials emphasized the links to Vionnet's original loca-tion. The press kit noted: 'The interior design, which reproduces the quin-tessence of the mythic salons of 50, avenue Montaigne decorated at the time by Georges de Feure, is strikingly modern.'[45] In reality, the new bou-tique alluded only remotely to the original couture salons, which had been decorated in grey shades, frescoes, and stained glass.[46] Reawakening a sleeping beauty is an exercise in mediating both time and space – the glory years of the original house, and its couture salons in Paris.

When the accessory shop was inaugurated, de Lummen continued to reactivate the history of Vionnet. The accessories designed by Ewald referred to Vionnet's 'favourite themes', namely, Egypt, Antique Greece, and Art Deco.[47] Patterns of the silk neckties were inspired by Vionnet's original designs such as the stylized rose. Roses were to Vionnet what camellias were to Chanel. While the designs were clearly indebted to Vionnet, the marketing failed to make the connection apparent.

Several 'Small Horses'-inspired Vionnet accessories, launched in 1999.   **4.1**

The same was true with the most dramatic reinterpretation of Vionnet's legacy, a series of accessories inspired by her 'Small Horses' dress,
including items such as gloves, umbrellas, and hats (figure 4.1). The original red dress, embroidered with black small horses, was designed in 1921
after a Greek vase (figure 4.2).[48] Several copies of this famous frock of the
1920s have survived, and one was exhibited in the Vionnet retrospectives
in 1991 and in 1994. We can speculate that de Lummen and Ewald would
have visited these exhibitions or at least read the catalogues and found
inspiration.[49] The revived house of Vionnet tried to create iconic accessories in the image of the original dress, but this original creation was
not mentioned in the new marketing and advertising materials. Only con-
noisseurs could have made the connection to Madeleine Vionnet's 'Small
Horses' dress.

4.2   The 'Small Horses' dress by Madeleine Vionnet, 1921. Paris, Les Arts Décoratifs, Musée des Arts Décoratifs – collection UFAC.

Although de Lummen hinted at the cultural significance of Madeleine Vionnet, under his leadership, the commercial and cultural values were developed separately. The dots had to be connected to achieve full impact. The change came in the mid-2000s when his son Arnaud de Lummen joined the business. The younger man actively interacted with cultural and institutional agents, accumulated a more profound knowledge of the brand history, and reactivated the cultural capital encapsulated in the brand more effectively.

Arnaud de Lummen and Madeleine Vionnet (2005–8)

Born on 26 April 1977, Arnaud de Lummen first heard about the house of Vionnet as a boy when his father bought the brand. Vionnet was a topic that fascinated him, and he sometimes took part in the company's activities. Late in 2002, for example, thanks to his fluency in English, the 25-year-old entrepreneur was involved in business negotiations that took place between his father and Sheikh Majed Al-Sabah, a member of the royal Kuwaiti family nicknamed 'the Sheikh of Chic' by *Time*.[50] Al-Sabah was looking to revive an old French couture house. The consultant he had commissioned to help him find the right name shortlisted Vionnet and the negotiations started at 21, place Vendôme.[51]

It was thrilling, as Arnaud de Lummen recalled, because the Sheikh had significant financial means and high ambitions for Vionnet.[52] In February 2003, the Sheikh announced to the press that he had partnered with the de Lummen family to revive Vionnet and had pre-selected Maurizio Pecoraro to be the new designer.[53] Soon though, the deal fell through. The announcement to the press was made before any agreement was signed and any financial plan finalized. These negotiations were nonetheless a crucial moment in the realization of Vionnet's potential for the de Lummens.[54]

Arnaud de Lummen then undertook a detailed study of Vionnet's history.[55] He read every book available on the topic, and sought out the expertise of fashion historians. He met several times with Betty Kirke, a New York-based curator and the author of the first major book on Vionnet's technique, and Jéromine Savignon, who also wrote an academic account of the house, dedicated to 'the spirit of Vionnet'.[56] Following Arnaud's idea, father and son formed the Association Madeleine Vionnet.[57] Couturier Hubert de Givenchy was its honorary president, while curator Kirke presided over the scientific committee.[58] The association's goal was to establish a permanent documentation centre, to foster theoretical and experimental research, to support the publication of books and research memoirs, and to organize or participate in any event on Vionnet and her legacy.

The association planned to commemorate the thirtieth anniversary of Vionnet's death on 2 March 2005 with a tribute, in which more than twenty designers would show Vionnet-inspired dresses on the runway, followed by a museum exhibition.[59] Although the event never took place, Arnaud de Lummen continued to emphasize the influence of Madeleine Vionnet on subsequent generations of designers. He gathered statements of famous designers such as Issey Miyake, who said, 'I always considered Vionnet to be the greatest, the only one!'[60] In this way, Arnaud de Lummen tried to establish firmly the historical significance of Vionnet to pave the way for the revival of her brand.

Meanwhile, Arnaud de Lummen worked as a lawyer. After his 2000 graduation in management from ESCP Europe (the École Supérieure de Commerce in Paris), he went on to study at the Harvard Law School in the United States, thus acquiring two skill sets – as well as an international perspective.[61] Between 2003 and 2005, he was an associate of the law firm Cleary Gottlieb in Paris, where he worked for Gucci and then Tom Ford.[62] In October 2005, he resigned to become chief executive officer at Vionnet, while his father remained chairman. His personal interest in the family business had turned into professional involvement.[63] Together, father and son prepared the relaunch of Vionnet ready-to-wear.

Since the family's capital was limited, Arnaud de Lummen 'took his pilgrim's staff' and looked for partners with whom to share costs as well as risks.[64] French players were not interested in the venture, so he turned to American investors. He secured an exclusive partnership with the upmarket New York department store Barneys, first verbally in February-March 2006, then contractually in June 2006. Barneys committed to finance two Vionnet collections upfront, while obtaining in return the exclusive distribution rights for two seasons for its stores in New York, Chicago, Beverly Hills, and Dallas.[65] In early July 2006, Barneys put a deposit on the first Vionnet collection, which had to be delivered by autumn 2006.[66]

While the house of Vionnet negotiated with Barneys, it also looked for a young designer. According to Arnaud de Lummen, younger generations were 'not closed to ideas or intimidated by her legacy'.[67] It was also cheaper to hire an up-and-coming designer than an established name. Zac Posen was Arnaud de Lummen's first choice; he had met with the designer several times. In the end, Posen turned down the offer because of other commitments.[68] In March 2006, the house of Vionnet settled on Sophia Kokosalaki, a 33-year-old Greek designer who was based in London.[69] As early as 2001, Kokosalaki professed her admiration for Vionnet's couture techniques.[70] Arnaud de Lummen thought she was a great fit for the job due to parallels with Madeleine Vionnet. Both women took inspiration from Grecian draping and worked directly with the materials instead of sketching.[71]

Kokosalaki's first collection for Vionnet was scheduled to be presented at the Paris Fashion Week early in October 2006. But it was not shown, causing *Women's Wear Daily* to quip that Vionnet was 'fashionably late'.[72] In reality, the collection was ready but Vionnet opted for another public relations strategy. Following the recommendation of the public relations KCD agency, Vionnet gave the American edition of *Vogue* exclusive press coverage.[73] The whole *Vogue* team came to see the collection at Vionnet's offices at place Vendôme in early October.[74] Editor-in-chief Anna Wintour was thrilled, and *Vogue* dedicated a four-page article to Vionnet in its December 2006 issue, illustrated with photos from the 1930s as well as photos of celebrities wearing Kokosalaki's designs.[75]

Intrigued by the revival, *Vogue* made an exception to its rule by covering Vionnet's debut collection. Usually, the magazine waited a few seasons before writing about a new brand, preferring to see it established first.[76] Only a sleeping beauty could benefit from such a swift endorsement by one of the most influential tastemakers in the fashion industry. By reactivating the cultural capital of Vionnet, the de Lummens challenged Bourdieu's linear perception of the field of fashion, where 'dominants' and 'newcomers' compete for the creation of cultural value.[77] According to Bourdieu, dominants implement conservation strategies that seek to benefit from progressively accumulated capital, while newcomers use subversion strategies designed to accumulate new capital.[78] Sleeping beauties are newcomers but they refer to the capital accumulated by the original house, as dominants do: in that sense, the newcomers' subversion strategy consists precisely in borrowing the dominants' conservation strategies. They refer to the capital accumulated by the original house and repackage it for modern times.

The official launch of the spring 2007 collection took place at Barneys New York on 2 February 2007, and was celebrated with flowing champagne.[79] The whole team from American *Vogue* was there. Prominent New York curators also attended the party; among these were Valerie Steele and Betty Kirke, then retired from a career encompassing both the Metropolitan Museum of Art (1973–79) and the Fashion Institute of Technology (1979–91), as well as Harold Koda, then curator in charge of the Costume Institute at the Metropolitan Museum of Art. Koda gave a memorable speech at the dinner afterwards, during which he explained Madeleine Vionnet's famous bias cut using the restaurant's napkins.[80] For the occasion, Barneys dedicated its famous Fifth Avenue store windows to Vionnet, past and present (figure 4.3). From a 1930s-styled mannequin painted on the wall flowed a voluminous dress with a train made entirely of photos of Vionnet's designs, while dummies wore the current collection by Kokosalaki.[81] Barneys reprinted Kirke's milestone book, which was sold in the store and mailed to select customers.[82]

The marketing material issued by the house described how Vionnet had opened a branch on Fifth Avenue in New York in 1925, creating ready-to-wear designs adapted from haute couture for the United States market.[83] This historical link implicitly justified why Vionnet relaunched its collections in New York instead of Paris. While customers could order merchandise by appointment at Vionnet headquarters in Paris, the debut collection was otherwise not distributed in France.

The new line was ready-to-wear 'with a strong couture edge'. It mainly consisted of eveningwear but also included trousers, blouses, and coats, with price tags ranging from $1,800 to $14,400. The items were produced by French firms, such as the embroidery company Lesage.[84] Arnaud de Lummen positioned Vionnet as a luxury brand, keeping pace with the

4.3   Barneys shop windows as arranged for the launching of Vionnet's ready-to-wear collection by Sophia Kokosalaki, February 2007.

trends but having a long-term vision, as opposed to a designer brand, reflecting 'whatever happens to be in the wind'.[85] The best example of a luxury brand, in his view, was Chanel, whose designs supposedly lasted from season to season. Was it his ambition to equal Chanel? The *New York Times* could only speculate.[86]

For this first collection, designer Kokosalaki selectively curated the historical features that the Vionnet brand wanted to highlight. The house no longer alluded to Egyptian and Art Deco inspirations. Only the Greek influence was kept because of its links with architectural couture and textural draping. The house spotlighted its design know-how in relation to Madeleine Vionnet, 'a maverick dressmaker who invented new pattern-making techniques'.[87] The bias cut dramatically illustrated by Harold Koda at the Barneys gala had a central place in the house's mythology. *Vogue* called the Vionnet spring 2007 collection 'gorgeous' (figure 4.4), and commented on the sophisticated construction of the model gowns. A good example was 'a water-blue gown with knotted straps twisting through the bodice and criss-crossing the spine, embossed with a 3-D pattern of waves'.[88] Here was the sensuality of Madeleine Vionnet adapted for the twenty-first century.

Did Kokosalaki have access to the archives of Vionnet to design this collection? The de Lummen father-and-son team felt they were not equipped

Dress by Sophia Kokosalaki for Vionnet, spring 2007 collection.   **4.4**

to build a private historical collection; they had neither the knowledge nor the money to invest in one.[89] However, during the preparation of the first collection, they organized a visit to the Musée de la Mode et du Textile, where Kokosalaki accessed photographs and costumes donated by Madeleine Vionnet in 1952. In addition, the Greek designer collaborated with embroiderer François Lesage, who was very knowledgeable about Vionnet.[90] In August 2006, Kokosalaki told *Le Monde*: 'By exploring the archives of such a house, I have the feeling I can understand Madeleine Vionnet's approach to couture.'[91]

Arnaud de Lummen collaborated with the Kent State University Museum in Ohio to highlight the first ready-to-wear collection. Curator Anne Bissonnette selected the garments shown in an exhibition called *Vionnet 2007*. On the opening day, Arnaud de Lummen and Kirke each gave a lecture at the museum prior to a fashion show of twenty *toiles* or muslin prototypes reproduced from the original work of Madeleine Vionnet from the 1910s to the 1930s.[92] Not only did the new Vionnet designs by Kokosalaki benefit from the cultural recognition accorded by the museum exhibition, they were also shown side by side with the couturier's original designs. The curator scrutinized the designs created by Kokosalaki through the lens of Vionnet's design philosophy: 'Madeleine Vionnet's signature minimalism, grace and elegance returns in *Vionnet 2007*.'[93]

Kokosalaki created a second collection for Vionnet, the autumn 2007 collection, which also received critical acclaim. Yet, her relationship to the house was short-lived. In early 2007, Kokosalaki found an investor for her namesake label.[94] According to Arnaud, 'she was already not involved much in Vionnet, meaning that, despite her touch, her good ideas, her good temper, her energy, it really was the studio that did most of the job and created the collections'.[95] She was confident in the fact that she could handle both Vionnet and her label. Arnaud de Lummen was of a different mind. He understood that a start-up like Vionnet needed a dedicated designer and terminated the collaboration with Kokosalaki.[96]

Marc Audibet replaced Kokosalaki as the artistic adviser to Vionnet on 21 May 2007. The house focused on his career, especially at Prada where he had designed for the city-girl type in the 1990s, and analysed his compatibility with Vionnet. The press release announcing his arrival was upbeat: 'Visionary designer, inventor of the stretch, Marc Audibet, is akin to Madeleine Vionnet in her constant ability to innovate and modernize.'[97] Arnaud de Lummen recalled that Audibet was very knowledgeable about Madeleine Vionnet, having professed his admiration for her as early as 1985.[98] Additionally, he had a conceptual and intellectual approach to fashion, was based in Paris, and had a good reputation in the eyes of most influential journalists.[99]

Audibet showed his first – and only – collection for Vionnet on 6 October 2007, in a showroom presentation (figure 4.5). The press release of this spring 2008 collection emphasized the craftsmanship and sensuality of Audibet's designs. The designer said he wanted 'liquid architecture, a feeling of rain on the body'.[100] This time, the house explained the emphasis on the body by the fact that Madeleine Vionnet wanted to liberate women from corsets. According to Arnaud de Lummen, Audibet's single collection had topped Kokosalaki's two.[101] The press was unanimously positive. Influential fashion journalist Suzy Menkes at the *International Herald Tribune* wrote, 'A red ribbon criss-crossing a bared back or just a scoop at the nape proved how deeply Audibet has understood the essence of Madeleine Vionnet.'[102]

Yet, Audibet's union with Vionnet was also short-lived. After creating one collection, he asked for a drastic salary increase – just as the house was negotiating with potential investors.[103] Despite its rich history, Vionnet in the twenty-first century was similar to a start-up company in need of cash. After the agreement with Barneys, which backed the first two

Dress by Marc Audibet for Vionnet, spring 2008 collection.   **4.5**

collections, it needed to find other financing solutions. In 2006, Vionnet's sales amounted to €520,000, but the company was operating at a loss; it was €62,000 in the red (table 4.1). In 2007, sales almost tripled, reaching €1.5 million, but extraordinary expenses resulted in a loss of €285,000. Arnaud de Lummen expected the company to become profitable in 2008, and to increase its turnover steadily to reach €25 million in 2012, with a profit of €6.7 million.[104]

Arnaud de Lummen designed an ambitious strategy to grow Vionnet internationally. He envisaged stronger marketing activities such as fashion shows, advertising in major fashion magazines, and better public relations. He contemplated opening Vionnet's first retail store in Paris in 2009, followed by Beverly Hills, New York, and London; expanding wholesale operations in the United States and in Europe; and developing franchises in Japan, the Middle East, Russia, and China. The house also wished to accelerate growth by enlarging its line of accessories (handbags, scarves, and shoes) and by licensing fragrances, eyewear,

Table 4.1 2006–12 profit & loss statement at Vionnet – summary under the de Lummens' management

€ in thousands	2006a[a]	2007a	2008e	2009e	2010e	2011e	2012e
RTW Couture	520	1,473	2,353	4,052	5,940	8,810	11,405
Shoes	–	–	–	246	600	1,465	2,775
Leather goods	–	–	–	682	1,644	2,992	5,247
Scarves	–	58	141	347	872	2,075	3,553
Fragrances & Cosmetics	–	–	–	211	600	993	1,340
Eyewear	–	–	–	–	428	646	712
Total revenues[b]	520	1,532	2,495	5,538	10,083	16,981	25,032
Collection development costs	(210)	(560)	(560)	(732)	(853)	(989)	(1,142)
Production costs	(234)	(716)	(1,180)	(2,182)	(3,449)	(5,417)	(7,308)
Other	–	(31)	(88)	(122)	(162)	(184)	(209)
Gross margin	76	225	666	2,502	5,619	10,391	16,373
as a % of revenues	14.6%	14.7%	26.7%	45.2%	55.7%	61.2%	65.4%
General and administrative	(50)	(284)	(390)	(791)	(1,185)	(1,454)	(1,791)
Communication and image	(50)	(150)	(277)	(872)	(1,209)	(1,330)	(1,463)
Amortization of leaseholds and installation costs	–	–	–	(25)	(75)	(183)	(305)
Rents and personnel costs of directly operated stores	–	–	–	(515)	(1,381)	(2,930)	(4,314)
Other store expenses	–	–	–	(61)	(216)	(540)	(952)
Other costs	(38)	(75)	(98)	(122)	(292)	(534)	(814)
Total expenses	(138)	(509)	(765)	(2,387)	(4,359)	(6,970)	(9,640)
EBIT	(62)	(285)	(99)	116	1,261	3,421	6,733
as a % of revenues	nm	nm	nm	2.1%	12.5%	20.1%	26.9%

Note: [a] 2006 and 2007 actual; 2008–12 estimate.
[b] 2008 revenues forecast assumes a pre-collection in July and a collection in October.

timepieces, and jewellery. In total, Arnaud de Lummen estimated that Vionnet needed about €5 million.[105]

The potential investors, mainly foreigners, were not familiar with Audibet's work. Many simply wanted to put their favourite designer in charge of artistic direction at Vionnet. The situation was not easy for either Audibet or Arnaud de Lummen.[106] In January 2008, when Audibet resigned, he exposed alleged weaknesses at Vionnet to the Agence France Presse, describing the management's 'incapacity' to create the 'material and financial conditions' necessary to make collections.[107] His departure from Vionnet generated a buzz in the blogosphere. The *Luxe Chronicles* noted that 'the recent departure of not one but two talented young designers … is never a good sign'.[108] The Vionnet firm replied that the house was in the midst of signing a new financial partnership 'in which Audibet [had] no place'. The company shrugged off his accusation of financial troubles as groundless.[109]

The management at Vionnet thought it would be foolish to hire a third designer, especially given that the studio was coping well. So Gaëtane

Vionnet dress by in-house designer Gaëtane Maze, autumn 2008 collection.   **4.6**

Maze, who had directed the studio since 2006, designed the next collection (figure 4.6). 'Vionnet does not need to be associated with a designer's name', Arnaud de Lummen announced. 'It's an institution.'[110] The collection continued the evolution of Vionnet design codes. On 29 February 2008, the house produced its first-ever runway show at Le Crazy Horse, one of the legendary cabarets of Paris.[111] Some fashion commentators, especially bloggers who did not attend the show, perceived a mismatch between the sanctified designer and the burlesque club.[112]

In the end, this studio collection gave Guy and Arnaud de Lummen more freedom in their negotiations with potential investors. The potential backers were of two types: those who were interested in a partnership but had limited resources, and those who wanted to buy the brand entirely and had far greater, if not unlimited, resources. After some hesitation the de Lummens eventually sold all their shares. There was no 'happily ever after' ending to this fairy tale. Beyond the profits generated by the sale, Arnaud de Lummen claimed that selling the family's shares to wealthier investors would prevent protracted negotiations over limited resources and provide the means to grow Vionnet globally.[113]

Both Guy and Arnaud de Lummen believed that Matteo Marzotto, an heir to the Italian textile dynasty, had the best ideas for the Vionnet brand. After selling Valentino in 2007, Marzotto together with Gianni Castiglioni, the chief executive officer of Italian brand Marni, wanted to relaunch Vionnet. The transaction, for an undisclosed amount, took place in the summer 2008 and was announced in February 2009. Marzotto and Castiglioni managed Vionnet until 2012, when Kazakh businesswoman Goga Ashkenazi acquired a major stake through her company GoTo Enterprise SARL. After appropriating materially and symbolically the cultural capital of Vionnet, the de Lummens transferred the property of the brand and the means to use it to the new owners.

Arnaud de Lummen and Luvanis SA (2009–)

When asked whether he had planned to sell Vionnet all along, Arnaud de Lummen replied that the revival of this sleeping beauty was supposed to be his family's great adventure. If a sale had been his goal, he would have kept Kokosalaki on, nurtured the value of the brand, and then sold it. Instead, he replaced Kokosalaki with Audibet to please his team and create better working conditions.[114] His lifetime business adventure may not have lasted a lifetime, but Arnaud de Lummen had discovered a new business model.

He could replicate what he did with Vionnet with other dormant brands. He thus became a fashion intermediary as identified by historians such as Regina Lee Blaszczyk: a type of go-between actor operating between a reservoir of extinct brands and entrepreneurs keen on restoring them.[115] Instead of kissing a single sleeping beauty awake, he could stir several sleeping beauties from their slumber before introducing them to their princes. In 2009, Arnaud de Lummen founded Luvanis SA, a private investment company based in Luxembourg, to focus on long-dormant luxury brands.[116] Guy de Lummen is a shareholder of Luvanis but he retains no operative role. Through Luvanis, Arnaud de Lummen established the systematic appropriation and subsequent dissemination of cultural capital as anticipated in Bourdieu's framing. In doing so, he institutionalized the sleeping beauty business.

Arnaud de Lummen took advantage of the growing competition engendered by the sleeping beauty renaissance in the 2000s. By this time other entrepreneurs had revived the houses of Elsa Schiaparelli and Nina Ricci, creating global brands. The second wave was caused, among other things, by the increased nostalgia that followed the economic crisis of 2008 and boosted the demand for luxury products. The marketing researcher Robert Olorenshaw has defined 'escapism' as a process of entering through 'mimicry or consumption' into an imaginary world from which one is in reality excluded. It is therefore easy to understand why 'the purchase of mimetic luxury goods [would] increase rather than decrease during an economic crisis'.[117]

But sleeping beauties also became attractive because of the slowdown in the growth of megabrands owned by luxury groups. A 2015 study by the investment company Exane BNP Paribas found that megabrands were progressively shifting 'from stars into cash cows'.[118] After over-democratizing, some brands had lost their luxury status and elite dimensions.[119] The power of their labels eroded. Some commentators even feared 'the end of fashion'.[120] Niche brands banked on the appeal of long-lasting goods made by skilled artisans. In this context, the sleeping beauties had great appeal to the new luxury players.

Arnaud de Lummen has evolved his business model to follow three steps: identification, protection, and incubation. First, he identifies brands with an inner potential.[121] As long-dormant brands get snatched up by competitors, this stage has become increasingly difficult. There remains only 'a limited supply and scope of brands with resurrection potential', he explained in 2012.[122] The European Union Intellectual Property Office counted forty-one brands belonging to Luvanis in 2015, and fifty-five in 2016, including important names in fashion history such as Jacques Doucet.[123] Arnaud de Lummen did not plan to revive every brand in his portfolio, only the 'prime brands'. He acquired less-desirable brands as a defensive measure, preventing his competitors from buying them and thereby protecting his leadership position in the sleeping beauty market.[124]

Second, as Arnaud de Lummen assembled a worldwide intellectual property rights portfolio, he materially appropriated the cultural capital of the sleeping beauties. This is a long and often complicated process. 'When he finds a revival-ready brand', his financial partner explained, Arnaud scours 'the globe for every last scrap of intellectual property'.[125] From the intensifying competition stem legal battles. For instance, with regard to the brand of the Anglo-American couturier Charles James, Arnaud de Lummen battled the Weinstein Company (TWC) for control over a period of two years.[126] In 2016, Luvanis and TWC finally agreed to collaborate when relaunching the James brand.[127]

Arnaud de Lummen's job does not end with the acquisition of a portfolio. Through Luvanis, he 'incubates sleeping beauties before proposing them to luxury players'.[128] There is a maturation phase during which he collects historical material, researches publications and exhibitions, and establishes the genealogy of the brand's influence over time. He also creates several prototype business plans to show potential investors what they could accomplish with the brand, and in the process, he symbolically appropriates the cultural capital of the sleeping beauty. Then he sells the brand for an undisclosed amount. In so doing, Arnaud de Lummen gives

Table 4.2 Sleeping beauty brands reawakened by Guy and Arnaud de Lummen, 1988–2016

Brand name	Established in	Closed in	Reawakened by de Lummen in	Sold on to
Chéruit (haute couture)	1898	1933	1988–92	(Still in de Lummens' brands portfolio)
Madeleine Vionnet (haute couture)	1912	1939	1988–2008	Matteo Marzotto and Gianni Castiglioni
Moynat (leather goods)	1849	1976	2008–10	Arnault group
Belber (leather goods)	1891	c. 1975	2010–12	Fashionista China Holdings Limited
Paul Poiret (haute couture)	1903	1929	2012–15	Shinsegae International

his clients unfettered access to the defunct couture house's embodied cultural capital by proxy. On top of the right to use the brand, he passes his knowledge on to them. Ultimately, the new owner decides how to proceed and must develop a vision for the brand.

Between 2008 and 2016, Arnaud de Lummen fully revived three sleeping beauty brands: Moynat, Belber, and Poiret (table 4.2). The detailed story of those brand revivals is beyond the scope of this chapter, but a few observations can be made. These reawakenings follow the same pattern as the Vionnet revival. Entrepreneurs reactivated the brand name's history to suit the needs of the company in the contemporary market, while constantly rewriting this history as needs evolve. Additionally, each of these revivals contributed to shaping Arnaud de Lummen's business model.

With the trunk maker Moynat, Arnaud de Lummen left the realm of haute couture for that of luxury accessories, and applied his method to another product category. Then, in 2010, Bernard Arnault bought the brand via the Arnault group (and not via LVMH, the luxury conglomerate whose strategies are examined in detail in Chapter 3) and the revival was officially announced a year later in tandem with the opening of the first shop (figure 4.7). After this, Arnaud de Lummen continued in a consultancy role for Moynat. Originally established in 1849, Moynat in the twenty-first century went through a revival based on the model devised by Louis Vuitton and Goyard, both traditional luxury leather goods companies.[129] Interestingly, Arnault invested in both Vuitton and Moynat, illustrating the need for higher-end brands in the same sector.

Arnaud de Lummen remarked that Arnault had distanced himself from the strategy of most sleeping beauty owners. Instead of claiming that he had heroically revived the luggage maker, he created the illusion that Moynat had continuously been in business since its founding.[130] According to the French edition of the magazine *Elle*, a sleeping beauty is successful 'when the revival is so carefully crafted that one has the impression' that the brand 'never disappeared'.[131] In acquiring Moynat, Arnault, who at the

Interior of the Moynat boutique, Paris, 2011.   **4.7**

helm of LVHM can rightfully be called the 'king of luxury', validated the
sleeping beauty trade within the field of fashion.[132]

    After Moynat, Arnaud de Lummen worked on the revival of the American
leather goods manufacturer Belber. This project expanded the geographic

and market reach of Luvanis to the United States and to 'affordable luxury'. Belber had been a Philadelphia-based trunk maker selling travel accessories and baggage under the slogan 'as modern as tomorrow'.[133] Founded in a basement by two brothers of modest background, it represented the American dream of rags-to-riches. Belber declined after the Second World War, when air travel developed, and went dormant in the mid-1970s. The revival of Belber was modelled after that of Coach, an American brand that reinvented itself around the concept of affordable luxury after spending too many years in the mass market. In February 2014, Luvanis officially announced it had sold Belber to Fashionista China Holdings Limited, a Francophone-owned company based in Hong Kong.

The Belber brand was relaunched in January 2016 through a digital strategy evoking the concept of 'urban nomadism'. The Belber website conjured up a vision of urban nomadism for the global digerati: 'Travel isn't about the destination anymore. It's not even about the journey. It's about the connection. And we're all very connected.'[134] Belber has profiles across social media, and focuses on the unisex trend.[135] However, Luvanis and Belber parted ways before the official relaunch in 2016 because Arnaud de Lummen believed it was a mistake to revive the brand in Hong Kong rather than in the United States. From his perspective, a single New York showroom was not in line with the American image the brand needed have to tap a large clientele, including in Asia.[136] Arnaud de Lummen's experience at Vionnet showed him the importance of the brand's country of origin. As an intermediary, though, he could propose options, but the owner of the brand had the final say.

With Poiret, Arnaud de Lummen went back to reawakening haute couture brands. This time, however, he used a somewhat unusual way to reach potential investors, organizing a public online auction of Poiret global trademarks in late October 2014.[137] Savigny Partners assisted him in selecting the appropriate investor.[138] The idea was to reach out to people with a possible interest in the Poiret brand, but who would not have heard about the sale because they did not belong to the same network. In this way, Arnaud de Lummen broadened the geographic reach of Luvanis and became more visible internationally.[139]

Unlike Moynat and Belber, the name of Paul Poiret still enjoyed a strong reputation. A press release reminded potential buyers that this couturier had been known as the 'King of Fashion' in America and 'Le Magnifique' in Paris.[140] Luvanis prepared a luxurious illustrated brochure to make those claims explicit. A novel addition to the tactics at Vionnet, the brochure showed contemporary reinterpretations of Poiret's designs by famous houses, including Christian Dior.[141] Arnaud de Lummen hinted that Poiret had a unique legacy that combined art and fashion, which the right investor could harness for commercial gain.[142] In the early twenty-first century, the fashion industry indeed emphasized its links with art through diverse strategies such as capsule collections by notable artists as shown in the discussion of LVMH in Chapter 3.[143]

However, this was not what caught the attention of Shinsegae International Company Ltd, the South Korean conglomerate that purchased Poiret in August 2015. This move, which followed on the heels of the acquisition of Belber by a Hong-Kong company, confirmed the Asian interest in sleeping beauties.[144] Savigny Partners assisted Shinsegae in its development strategy and made the connection with Luvanis. As a premium luxury brand retailer, Shinsegae had been looking to invest in a luxury cosmetics and perfume brand, and found real appeal in Parfums de Rosine, which Paul Poiret had famously launched in 1911.[145] The future will tell us what the revivalist path chosen by the new owners will be.

Conclusion

In combining the resources of business history and fashion history, this chapter has shed light on the methods used in the reawakening of sleeping beauty brands. In 1988, Guy de Lummen had the innovative idea of reviving the long-dormant house of Vionnet. In doing so, he exemplified Bourdieu's concept of cultural capital, which explains how the objectified capital of cultural goods – here a brand – can lie dormant until an entrepreneur or intermediary reactivates it both materially and symbolically. Guy de Lummen strategically selected elements from the history of Vionnet that were relevant to his business in accessories licensing in terms of product, range, and design.

Guy de Lummen hinted at the importance of history and culture in revival strategies, but it was his son, Arnaud, who fully developed their potential from the mid-2000s onwards. With increased knowledge of the brand's history, father and son successfully launched an upmarket line of ready-to-wear labelled Vionnet. They recrafted the identity of Vionnet through elements chosen from its past, such as drapery, architecture, and Greek motifs. Through greater interaction with fashion gatekeepers, especially museum curators, they contributed to shaping the heritage value of Vionnet, thus strengthening the legitimacy of the brand. Facing the financial challenges that often plague start-ups, in 2008 the de Lummens handed Vionnet over to other entrepreneurs keen on continuing the restoration of its bygone glory.

Arnaud de Lummen then went on to found Luvanis, an enterprise marking the institutionalization of the sleeping beauty business. He became an important intermediary in the sleeping beauty trade, transferring both the right of ownership and the cultural capital on to new owners. His experience at Vionnet proved invaluable, allowing him to replicate the revival model with brands such as Moynat, Belber, and Poiret. These investments have proved successful so far, and while the revival of several brands is still in the making, the business model does have its limitations. The stock of haute couture brands, albeit vast, is not infinite. A saturation of the market might prevent further revivals.

Notes

1 See notably *Old-Time Stories told by Master Charles Perrault*, trans. A. E. Johnson (New York: Dodd, Mead, 1921); J. and W. Grimm, *The Original Folk and Fairy Tales of the Brothers Grimm: The Complete First Edition*, trans. J. Zipes (Princeton and Oxford: Princeton University Press, 2014); Walt Disney Studios, *Sleeping Beauty* (1959, 1:15:00).

2 I do not consider Chanel a sleeping beauty brand. True, Chanel stopped her haute couture activity between 1939 and 1954. Yet, the story of Chanel unfolds differently from that of the sleeping beauties of haute couture. When the house of Chanel resumed haute couture, 'Coco' Chanel was the one heading the collections, and she was financially backed by the same entrepreneurs that supported her house before the Second World War. In other words, there was no disruption of the main players. As a result, Chanel does not fulfil the fundamental paradox of using a brand that bears the name of an individual without that individual being involved in the business.

3 On fairy tale branding see F. Cochoy, 'A brief theory of the "Captation" of publics: understanding the market with Little Red Riding Hood', *Theory, Culture & Society*, 24:7–8 (2007), 203–23.

4 See A. Rocamora, 'Pierre Bourdieu: the field of fashion', in A. Rocamora and A. Smelik (eds), *Thinking Through Fashion* (London: I. B. Tauris, 2016), 233–50; B. Townley, 'Exploring different forms of capitals: researching capitals in the field of cultural and creative industries', in A. Tatli, M. Özbilgin, and M. Karatas-Özkan (eds), *Pierre Bourdieu, Organisation, and Management* (New York and London: Routledge, 2015), pp. 187–206; B. Townley and N. Beech, *Managing Creativity: Exploring the Paradox* (Cambridge and New York: Cambridge University Press, 2010).

5 P. Bourdieu, 'Les trois états du capital culturel', *Actes de la recherche en sciences sociales*, 30 (1979), 3–6.

6 D. Robbins, *Bourdieu and Culture* (London and Thousand Oaks, CA: Sage Publications, 2000), p. 35.

7 See A. Chatriot, 'La construction récente des groupes de luxe français: mythes, discours et pratiques', *Entreprises et histoire*, 46:1 (2007), 143–56.

8 Archives of Paris, D32U3 105, Registration of the deed of incorporation of Madeleine Vionnet & Cie. See F. Brachet Champsaur, 'Madeleine Vionnet and Galeries Lafayette: the unlikely marriage of a Parisian couture house and a French department store, 1922–40', *Business History*, 54:1 (2012), 48–66.

9 M. Jan, 'Culture couture: la reconnaissance patrimoniale du vêtement de couturier-créateur en France, de la fin du XIXe siècle à nos jours' (PhD dissertation, Université Paris I, 2011), 169–209. This phenomenon is explained by the arrival of the left wing to power in 1981. The French President (François Mitterrand) and the Ministry of Culture (Jack Lang) recognized fashion, and especially haute couture, as a major art. They established the 'oscars of fashion', allowed the fashion shows of haute couture houses to take place in the 'cour carrée' of the Louvre, and opened the museum of fashion.

10 See P. Perrot, *Les dessus et les dessous de la bourgeoisie: Une histoire du vêtement au XIXe siècle* (Paris: Fayard, 1981); D. Roche, *La culture des apparences: Une histoire du vêtement, XVIIe–XVIIIe siècle* (Paris: Fayard, 1989).

11 V. Steele, *Paris Fashion: A Cultural History* (Oxford: Berg, 1998).

12 Arnaud de Lummen, interview by author, Paris, 6 October 2014.

13 Arnaud de Lummen, interview by author, Paris, 18 July 2016.

14 See V. Pouillard, 'Keeping designs and brands authentic: the resurgence of the post-war French fashion business under the challenge of US mass production', *European Review of History*, 20:5 (2013), 815–35.

15 C. de Vincenti, 'Cultissimo: Poiray, la jeune fille de la place Vendôme', *W the Journal* (1 February 2012), at www.thejournal.com/news/print/14208 (accessed 10 April 2016, link now defunct).

16 Arnaud de Lummen, interview by author, Paris, 24 September 2014. See *Three Women: Madeleine Vionnet, Claire McCardell, and Rei Kawakubo* (New York: Fashion Institute of Technology, 1987); and 'Mobilier Art Déco Madeleine Vionnet, Souvenirs de Jacques Doucet', *Nouveau Drouot* (31 May 1985).

17 Arnaud de Lummen interview, 24 September 2014.

18 Madeleine Vionnet (marque française), no. 1524211, 11 July 1988, *Bulletin officiel de la propriété industrielle marques*, 39 (1989), 47.

19 MV Madeleine Vionnet (marque française), no.1495021, 4 October 1988, *Bulletin officiel de la propriété industrielle marques*, 14 (1989), 203; Madeleine Vionnet (marque semi-figurative), no. 96610182, 12 February 1996, *Bulletin officiel de la propriété industrielle marques*, 47 (1996), 32. On Vionnet and Thayaht see A. Fiorentini, 'The collaboration between Thayaht and Madeleine Vionnet (1919–1925)', *Dresstudy*, 56 (2009), n.p.

20 See S. Grossiord (ed.), *Roman d'une garde-robe: Le chic d'une Parisienne, de la Belle Époque aux années 30* (Paris: Paris-musées, 2013).

21 Arnaud de Lummen interview, 18 July 2016.

22 Arnaud de Lummen interview, 18 July 2016.

23 On 1 September 1989, Société Anonyme Madeleine Vionnet had been established (RCS 351 777 685). The company was founded before any commercial activity was envisaged, because consultancies in intellectual property rights advised their clients regarding how to establish a company with the trade name of the brand they wanted to protect. The initial company was liquidated as early as 27 June 1991, and the Vionnet trademarks were managed thereafter by the newly established Société par actions simplifiées Chéruit. Greffe du tribunal de Commerce, Paris, Extrait Kbis, SA Madeleine Vionnet, RCS B 403 946 916.

24 M. Valmont, 'La griffe mythique de Madeleine Vionnet renaît', *Le Journal du Textile* (31 August 1994), 109.

25 *Ibid.*

26 Arnaud de Lummen interview, 24 September 2014.

27 Archives of Arnaud de Lummen, Luxembourg (hereafter ADL Archive), Vionnet, 'Vionnet Information Memorandum', n.d. [2008].

28 E. Merlo and M. Perugini, 'The revival of fashion brands between marketing and history', *Journal of Historical Research in Marketing*, 7:1 (2015), 93.

29 Musée des Arts Décoratifs, Centre de Documentation, Paris (hereafter AD-CD), Madeleine Vionnet files, Press kit, n.d. [1990–95].

30 'Bas Relief by Vionnet', *Vogue* (15 November 1931), 44–5.

31 Valmont, 'La griffe mythique'.

32 AD-CD, Vionnet files, L. Martin, 'Madeleine Vionnet ressuscité', *Le Journal du Textile* (20 February 1995), n.p.

33 *Ibid.*

34 *Ibid.*

35 *Madeleine Vionnet : Les années d'innovation, 1919–1929* (Lyon: Musée des Tissus, 1994); *Madeleine Vionnet (1876–1975): L'art de la couture* (Marseilles: Direction des Musées, 1991).

36 D. Saurat, 'Chronologie', in P. Golbin (ed.), *Madeleine Vionnet, puriste de la mode* (Paris: Les Arts Décoratifs, 2009), p. 296.

37 On Vionnet A, B, C, D, see J. Demornex, 'Un parfum discret', *Madeleine Vionnet* (Paris: Éditions du Regard, 1990), p. 131; on Chanel No. 5, see E. Briot, 'Le 5 de Chanel, numéro gagnant de la parfumerie française (1973–2012)', *Entreprises et histoire*, 2:79 (2015), 117–34.

38 Arnaud de Lummen interview, 6 October 2014.

39 On duty-free and travel retail see G. Jones, 'The global and the local in the beauty industry: a historical perspective', in H. Berghoff and T. Kühne (eds), *Globalizing Beauty. Consumerism and Body Aesthetics in the Twentieth Century* (New York: Palgrave Macmillan, 2013), p. 30; G. Jones, *Beauty Imagined: A History of the Global Beauty Industry* (Oxford: Oxford University Press, 2010), pp. 209–10.

40 AD-CD, Vionnet files. See 'Madeleine Vionnet: Traüme in Glas', *Parfum, Die exclusive Welt der schönsten Düfte*, 41 (1998), 681; A list of perfumes (June 2015) is preserved at the Osmothèque, Versailles; Arnaud de Lummen interview, 6 October 2014.

41 See E. de Feydeau, *Les parfums: Histoire, anthologie, dictionnaire* (Paris: Laffont, 2011), p. 372.

42 AD-CD, Vionnet files, J. Samet, 'Madeleine Vionnet: Son nom ressuscité!', *Le Figaro* (26 June 1997).

43 Arnaud de Lummen interview, 24 September 2014.

44 P. Cabasset, 'Repères boutiques', *L'Officiel* (December 1999), 34.

45 AD-CD, Vionnet files, Press kit of Vionnet, n.d. [1999].

46 See I. Millman, 'Georges de Feure et la maison de couture Madeleine Vionnet', *Bulletin de la société de l'histoire de l'art français* (1989), 312–13.

47 AD-CD, Vionnet files, Press kit of Vionnet, [1999].

48 R. Arnold, 'Vionnet and Classicism', *Madeleine Vionnet: 15 Dresses from the Collection of Martin Kramer* (London: Judith Clark Costume Centre, 2001), [p. 5].

49 See dress no. 43, *Madeleine Vionnet (1876–1975): L'art de la couture*, p. 60; and drawing no. 99, *Madeleine Vionnet: Les années d'innovation (1919–1929)*, p. 81.

50 L. Goldstein, 'The Sheikh of Chic', *Time* (10 February 2003), atcontent.time.com/time/magazine/article/0,9171,419752,00.html (accessed 10 July 2016).

51 Arnaud de Lummen interview, 18 July 2016.

52 Arnaud de Lummen interview, 18 July 2016.

53 G. Baudo, 'Maurizio Pecoraro rilancerà Vionnet', *Milano Finanza Fashion* (28 February 2003), at www.mffashion.com/it/archivio/2003/02/28/maurizio-pecoraro-rilancera-vionnet (accessed 10 July 2016).

54 Arnaud de Lummen interview, 18 July 2016.

55 Arnaud de Lummen interview, 24 September 2014.

56 B. Kirke, *Madeleine Vionnet*, trans. H. Tokai (Tokyo: Kyuryudo Art Publishing, 1991); B. Kirke, *Madeleine Vionnet* (San Francisco: Chronicle Books, 1998); J. Savignon, *L'esprit Vionnet et ses influences de la fin des années vingt à nos jours* (Lyon: Association pour l'Université de la mode, 2009).

57 ADL Archive, Letter from the Association Madeleine Vionnet to the Préfet de Police de Paris, 8 November 2004.

58 On Kirke see A. Bissonnette, 'Doing history with objects: Betty Kirke and Madeleine Vionnet', *Fashion Theory*, 19:3 (2015), 281–314.

59 'Fashion scoops: high art', *Women's Wear Daily* (23 November 2004), 19.

60 ADL Archive, Tribute', n.d.

61 ADL Archive, Curriculum vitae of Arnaud de Lummen.

62 See S. G. Forden, *The House of Gucci: A Sensational Story of Murder, Madness, Glamour, and Greed* (New York: Morrow, 2000).

63 Arnaud de Lummen interview, 24 September 2014.

64 Arnaud de Lummen interview, 24 September 2014.

65 'Fashion scoops: revival game', *Women's Wear Daily* (2 March 2006), 11.

66 Arnaud de Lummen interview, 18 July 2016.

67 AD-CD, Vionnet files, E. Napier and M. Kessler, 'Master class', *Autore Magazine* (2005/06), 94.
68 Arnaud de Lummen interview, 18 July 2016.
69 'Fashion scoops: revival game', 11.
70 L. Beurdeley, 'Ruffo, l'alternance des talents', *L'Officiel* (February 2001), 100.
71 Arnaud de Lummen interview, 6 October 2014.
72 'Fashion scoops: fashionably late', *Women's Wear Daily* (12 September 2006), 14.
73 Arnaud de Lummen interview, 18 July 2016.
74 Arnaud de Lummen interview, 18 July 2016.
75 S. Mower, 'Goddess worship', *Vogue* (December 2006), 182–90.
76 Arnaud de Lummen interviews, 24 September 2014 and 18 July 2016.
77 P. Bourdieu, 'Haute couture et haute culture', *Questions de sociologie* (Paris: Éditions de Minuit, 2002), pp. 196–8.
78 Bourdieu, 'Haute couture et haute culture', p. 198.
79 ADL Archive, Vionnet, invitation card, 2 February 2007.
80 Arnaud de Lummen interview, 18 July 2016.
81 ADL Archive, Vionnet, photos of the opening at Barneys, 2 February 2007.
82 ADL Archive, 'Vionnet's Revival', *Wall Street Journal* (2 February 2007).
83 ADL Archive, 'Vionnet Information Memorandum'.
84 *Ibid.*
85 AD-CD, Vionnet files, Napier and Kessler, 'Master class', 94.
86 ADL Archive, G. Diliberto, 'Revival of the fittest', *New York Times Style Magazine* (27 August 2006).
87 ADL Archive, 'Vionnet Information Memorandum'.
88 Mower, 'Goddess worship', 184.
89 Arnaud de Lummen interview, 24 September 2014.
90 Arnaud de Lummen interview, 18 July 2016.
91 ADL Archive, V. Lorelle, 'Sophia Kokosalaki ressuscite la griffe Vionnet', *Le Monde* (29 August 2006).
92 ADL Archive, press release of Vionnet, 'Kent State University Museum Features the New House of Vionnet', 27 August 2007.
93 *Ibid.*
94 L. Zargani, 'Rosso adds to Diesel brand stable', *Women's Wear Daily* (9 January 2007), 5.
95 Arnaud de Lummen interview, 24 September 2014.
96 Arnaud de Lummen interview, 24 September 2014.
97 ADL Archive, press release of Vionnet, 'Vionnet announces new creative leadership', 21 May 2007.
98 AD-CD, Marc Audibet files, M. Molyneux, 'Marc Audibet: En finir avec les coutures', *Libération* (25 March 1985).
99 Arnaud de Lummen interview, 24 September 2014.
100 ADL Archive, Vionnet press release for spring-summer 2008, 6 October 2007.
101 Arnaud de Lummen interview, 24 September 2014.
102 ADL Archive, S. Menkes, 'Turnaround begins at Vionnet', *International Herald Tribune* (8 October 2007).
103 Arnaud de Lummen interview, 24 September 2014.
104 ADL Archive, 'Vionnet Information Memorandum'.
105 *Ibid*.
106 Arnaud de Lummen interview, 24 September 2014.
107 R. Murphy, 'Audibet leaves after one season', *Women's Wear Daily* (14 January 2008), 3.
108 'Vionnet: when bad things happen to a good brand', *Luxe Chronicles* (25 February 2008) at www.theluxechronicles.com/the_luxe_chronicles/2008/02/vionnet-when-ba.html (accessed 20 October 2016).

109 Murphy, 'Audibet leaves after one season'.
110 R. Murphy, 'Vionnet brand setting stage for expansion', *Women's Wear Daily* (20 February 2008), 25.
111 ADL Archive, Vionnet press release for fall-winter 2008, 29 February 2008.
112 'Vionnet: when bad things happen to a good brand'.
113 Arnaud de Lummen interview, 6 October 2014.
114 Arnaud de Lummen interview, 24 September 2014.
115 R. L. Blaszczyk (ed.), *Producing Fashion: Commerce, Culture, and Consumers* (Philadelphia: University of Pennsylvania Press, 2008); R. L. Blaszczyk, *Imagining Consumers: Design and Innovation from Wedgwood to Corning* (Baltimore: John Hopkins University Press, 2000).
116 Luvanis, press release, 'Paul Poiret global trademarks for sale for the first time in 80 years', 28 October 2014, at www.paulpoiret.com (accessed on 14 November 2014, link now defunct).
117 R. Olorenshaw, 'Luxury and the recent economy crisis', *Vie & sciences de l'entreprise*, 188:2 (2011), 78.
118 ADL Archive, L. Solca, P. Bertini, and H. Fan, in collaboration with Luvanis SA, 'The growth relay: Cinderellas, Snow Whites and Sleeping Beauties', Exane BNP Paribas (9 April 2015), 1.
119 J.-C. Daumas and M. Ferrière le Vayer (eds), 'Les métamorphoses du luxe vues d'Europe', *Entreprises et Histoire*, 46:1 (2007), 6–16; B. Heilbrunn, 'Comment penser la marque de luxe à l'âge de la démocratisation du luxe?', in O. Assouly (ed.), *Le luxe. Essais sur la fabrique de l'ostentation* (Paris: IFM, 2011), pp. 423–43.
120 T. Agins, *The End of Fashion: How Marketing Changed the Clothing Business Forever* (New York: William Morrow Paperbacks, 2nd edn 2000).
121 ADL Archive, D. Kalt, 'Ein Wecker für Dornröschen', *Schaufenster, Die Presse* (24 October 2012).
122 M. Socha, 'De Lummen's revival model', *Women's Wear Daily* (2 May 2012), 1, 12.
123 'Luvanis S.A.', European Union Intellectual Property Office (EUIPO) at euipo.europa.eu/eSearch/#details/owners/359172 (accessed 10 June 2015 and 20 July 2016).
124 Arnaud de Lummen interview, 18 July 2016.
125 Socha, 'De Lummen's revival model'.
126 The Fashion Law, 'The Charles James Revival, An Exclusive Look at the Behind-the-Scenes War', 12 April 2015, at www.thefashionlaw.com/why-the-charles-james-revival-never-happened-the-behind-the-scenes-war (accessed 17 August 2016).
127 Arnaud de Lummen interview, 18 July 2016.
128 ADL Archive, Solca, Bertini, and Fan, 'The growth relay'.
129 ADL Archive, 'Moynat Malletier', Moynat Executive Summary circulated by Luvanis on April 2010.
130 Arnaud de Lummen interview, 24 September 2014.
131 S. Gachet, 'Actes de renaissance', *Elle* (16 November 2012), 168.
132 S. Daneshkhu, 'King of luxury upsets France's Socialists', *Financial Times* (14 September 2012) at www.ft.com/cms/s/0/78878222-fd93–11e1–8fc3–00144fe abdc0.html#axzz4IodvBhOW (accessed 30 August 2016).
133 Belber, 'Our story', at www.belber.com/our-story.html (accessed 30 March 2016).
134 Belber, 'Brand values: Belber's Spirit, Urban Nomadism', at www.belber.com/brand-values.html (accessed 17 August 2016).
135 Press release of Belber, 'The revival of Belber 1891', 15 January 2016, at www.belber.com (accessed in 10 April 2016, link now defunct).
136 Arnaud de Lummen interview, 18 July 2016.
137 M. Socha, 'Poiret Trademarks Up for Auction Online', *Women's Wear Daily* (28 October 2014), 6.

138 'Paul Poiret – How to Bid', 28 October 2014, at www.paulpoiret.com (accessed 14 November 2014, link now defunct).
139 Arnaud de Lummen interview, 18 July 2016.
140 Luvanis, press release, 'Paul Poiret global trademarks for sale'.
141 'Paul Poiret Presentation'. The reinterpretations of Paul Poiret's designs were taken from the May 2007 issue of American *Vogue*.
142 Luvanis, press release, 'Paul Poiret global trademarks for sale'.
143 See for instance M. O. Smith and A. Kubler, *Art/Fashion in the Twenty-first Century* (London: Thames & Hudson, 2013).
144 See M. Socha, 'Paul Poiret trademarks acquired by Shinsegae International', *Women's Wear Daily* online (10 August 2015), at http://wwd.com/fashion-news/designer-luxury/paul-poiret-acquired-shinsegae-designer10198971–10198971/ (accessed 24 August 2016). On the Asian market, see P.-Y. Donzé and R. Fujioka, 'European luxury big business and emerging Asian markets, 1960–2010', *Business History*, 57:6 (2015), 822–40.
145 See C. Parpoil (ed.), *Paul Poiret, couturier-perfumer* (Paris: Somogy, 2013).

PART II

International connections and the role of retailers

5

Buying abroad, selling in Paris: the 1953 Italian fair at Galeries Lafayette

Florence Brachet Champsaur

Incorporated in 1893 as a novelty shop, Aux Galeries Lafayette was the last department store to be opened in Paris. The Alsatian founders, Theophile Bader and Alphonse Kahn, had trained in the garment district of Paris and chose to set up their trade on a busy crossing near Gare Saint-Lazare, the Opera, and the couture houses of rue de la Paix. Well-established competitors included the Bon Marché and their next-door neighbour on Boulevard Hausmann, Au Printemps, founded in 1852 and 1865, respectively. Despite the seniority of its rivals, Galeries Lafayette expanded rapidly: from the time of its transformation into a limited liability company in 1899 to the start of World War I in 1914, the company's annual turnover increased twenty-two fold.[1] The theatrical cupola and the shop extension inaugurated in 1912 demonstrated the success of the department store.

When World War I broke out, Galeries Lafayette was a pre-eminent player in the retail industry. In 1916, the company opened a branch in Nice and invested in manufacturing with the creation of an industrial subsidiary, the Société Parisienne de Confection (SPC). Faced with the monopoly of the Parisian couture houses as the only recognized fashion trendsetters, the SPC manufactured models inspired by couture and sold under the Galeries Lafayette private label. Its vertical integration strategy allowed Galeries Lafayette to challenge the fashion system: with quantity-production capacity, the department store became a leading intermediary between fashion design and broad segments of the consumer market.

During the interwar period, Galeries Lafayette, following a European trend, developed a price-point store chain at national level under the Monoprix brand. Thanks to competitive distribution costs, the new retail format appealed to a working and middle-class clientele. After World

War II, this new way of buying and selling constituted a first step in the process of the modernization of retail in Western Europe. The rise of consumer society in Western Europe resulted in a fundamental change in the patterns of consumption, while the French fashion industry underwent major transformations. The 'invention' of ready-to-wear in France after 1945 and the reorientation of haute couture (Chapter 2) were to directly impact the strategy of Galeries Lafayette and required a new production and distribution paradigm. In this disrupted context, the department store had to find a way to reinvent itself.

Engaged in a process of modernization and transformation, Galeries Lafayette took an active part in the geographical reconfiguration of the fashion industry and the emergence of new fashion territories that challenged Paris after World Word II. This important Parisian department store also played an active and critical role in the transatlantic managerial, marketing, and technical transfers that accelerated after 1945. In addition, the company owners, convinced of the value of free trade, supported the building of a European Common Market. In 1953, Galeries Lafayette was one of the founding members of a European trade association of department stores in charge of setting up a supplier network at international level.

Drawing on the archives of the Galeries Lafayette, this chapter presents a case study of the 1953 Italian fair, a commercial event offering Parisian customers the very best Italian imports, from food to textiles (figure 5.1). The Italian fair, called 'La fleur de la production italienne' (The Best of Italian Production), was held in the flagship store of Galeries Lafayette in Paris and highlights the transformation of the buying policy of the firm. The case study allows us to assess the extent of influence on the French department store of American management practices on the one hand and the building of a new European commercial network on the other. The organisation of this promotional event is indicative as much of the European free trade commitment of Galeries Lafayette as of the impact of American ideas on the company – the Italian fair was inspired by an event previously held at R. H. Macy & Company in New York in 1951.

This case study of the 1953 Galeries Lafayette Italian fair is a suitable starting-point for the historical study of those fashion professionals working behind the scenes. While fashion history research more often has privileged the figure of the designer or couturier, given emphasis here are those key intermediaries central to the fashion system.In addition, the chapter covers the post 1945 period, a less thoroughly researched moment in the historiography of retailing. It offers an opportunity to respond to the call of Victoria de Grazia, who underlined that 'the evolution of modern systems of distribution is astonishingly understudied'.[2]

'La fleur de la production italienne', the store-wide display at GL flagship, Galeries Lafayette, 1953.   **5.1**

'America can't be explained, it has to be seen'

The dramatic transformation of retailing in postwar Europe put department stores under pressure.[3] They had to face the implementation of self-service, the establishment of supermarkets and their expansion in the 1950s and 1960s, and the invention of the suburban shopping mall.[4] Department stores were not in a strong position with regard to the competitive prices of the newcomers, and needed to focus on a differentiation strategy.

In the changing commercial environment of the postwar era, Galeries Lafayette decided to seek solutions internationally. Although the store's directors had been visiting the United States since the 1920s, the number of company representatives crossing the Atlantic Ocean dramatically increased from 1946 onwards. Like other actors sent on missions for the European Recovery Program, also known as the Marshall Plan, they wanted to study American productivity first hand with a view to importing new ideas in order to modernize Galeries Lafayette.[5] The influence of America was profound for Max Heilbronn, the chief executive and longest-serving head of the enterprise. As he later explained, 'Had I not known the US, my whole life in the department store business would have been different.'[6]

The minutes of committee meetings mention some twenty trips by Galeries Lafayette executives to the United States between 1947 and 1969. Company representatives from Galeries Lafayette visited stores on the East and West coasts and in Texas. The stores most frequently cited in the reports of these trips are R. H. Macy & Company, Saks Fifth Avenue, Bloomingdale's, Gimbels, Bonwit Teller, and Ohrbach's, with special attention paid to Lord & Taylor. Some of these retailers, such as Macy's and Gimbels, were fully-fledged department stores, while others followed the Filene's model discussed in Chapter 8 and were large specialty stores that focused on fashion.

However, American influence on France's postwar modernization and the significant advances in productivity which began in 1949 must be put in perspective. During the interwar period, French industrialists had imported American productivity methods from the United States, many of which fell under the rubric of Taylorism (from the name of the inventor and early promoter of scientific management, Frederick Winslow Taylor). Closer to home, they had also been inspired by the work of Taylor's French counterpart, Henri Fayol.[7] Also active were consulting agencies such as French management consultant Paul Planus, who advised Galeries Lafayette in the adoption of innovative methods, facilitated technology transfers, and introduced scientific management.[8] The spectacular economic growth of the United States during World War II set off a second wave of Americanization after 1945 in which productivity took on an ideological dimension.[9]

Private sector initiatives were more significant than government-led measures in bringing the retail practices observed in the United States to France. From 1957, the National Cash Register Company held training classes taught by Bernardo Trujillo at the company headquarters in Dayton, Ohio.[10] A world-renowned distribution expert, Trujillo also led the well-known Modern Merchandizing Methods (MMM) seminars in which he lectured international executives on the most recent marketing methods in retail.[11] He strongly influenced the retail trade and helped to pave the way for the introduction of discount stores, stating that 'Mass distribution should be the counterpart of mass production.'[12] While clearly advocating mass distribution as a universal model, Trujillo also saw a place for 'the artists', a market segment dominated by 'department stores specializing in luxury products and high fashion. As it expands and becomes even more elegant and lovely, this store will offer its clients not only more than 300,000 items but all sorts of excellent services'.[13] No mention of Trujillo's seminars have been found in the Galeries Lafayette archives, but both Heilbronn of Galeries Lafayette and Etienne Moulin of the SCA (Monoprix's buying organization) are mentioned in one of his publications, thus confirming they were aware of each other's ideas.[14]

Others also facilitated the transfer of new American methods to France. Galeries Lafayette consulted American fashion forecasters, particularly Tobé, publishers of the famous *Tobé Report*.[15] In the early 1950s, the company was also in regular communication with an American correspondent, one Madame Lord, based in New York and undoubtedly a stylist, who provided information on the American scene for Galeries Lafayette. Her main task was to send samples, as well as brochures and various documents about the local market.[16] She also worked with company representatives who were visiting from Paris.

Convinced of the superiority of the American merchandizing model, Galeries Lafayette invested in the establishment of a central purchasing organization in the United States. Speaking to the board of directors in 1956, Heilbronn argued that the American-based buying office should become a permanent fixture, as an 'essential source of vital information on both merchandise and business organization'.[17]

In 1952, back from another transatlantic visit, the two top executives of Galeries Lafayette, Raoul Meyer and Max Heilbronn, noted that there had been no big changes and few innovations since the last trip. 'On the contrary [economic and business development in the United States] seems to have come to a standstill everywhere, even with Lord & Taylor. There is a generalized apathy, with less enthusiasm and dynamism than a few years ago.'[18] Their travels became less frequent after this

In 1956, the management at Galeries Lafayette drew up a strategic document, the 'Ten Year Plan for the Modernization and Expansion of Sales and Services' for 1960–70.[19] The strategic plan was informed by presentations made by Galeries Lafayette executives after visiting the United States, where they met with the chairman of Bullock's and two Bloomingdale's executives, as well as the F. & R. Lazarus and Company team in Columbus, Ohio. References to the American model are omnipresent in the Ten Year Plan. In developing it, however, executives were also inspired by French sources, such as the ideas advocated in *Prospective*. Founded in 1957, this magazine was dedicated to studies on economic, social, and cultural forecasting. Galeries Lafayette executives were equally influenced by their contacts with the modernizer Marcel Demonque, a leading industrialist then chairman of one of the largest French multinationals, the cement company Lafarge.[20] Thus the Ten Year Plan exhibited a certain distance from the American model and was critical of it. 'If we do not yield to the discipline of long term planning in ten or twenty years', noted the Plan, 'the anarchic expansion and modernization of the store will turn it into a Macy's.'[21]

The store executives' fascination with the American model was tempered by their awareness that it was not entirely translatable into the French context. 'We must not forget the profound difference between the American and French mentalities and temperaments', noted the executive committee in 1954.[22] As a consequence, Galeries Lafayette looked elsewhere for additional inspiration.

New international suppliers: the finest European products

As shown by the historian Laurence Badel, the commitment to free trade on the continental level by major French retailers was already strong in the 1920s.[23] World War II was followed by three decades of ever-closer ties between European department stores in the context of the construction of the European Community. A few organizations played a crucial role in this process, including the Association Internationale des Grands Magasins (AIGM), established in 1928, and the Comité d'Action Economique et Douanière (CAED), established in 1925. The latter was to be one of the rare pro-European organizations to survive World War II. Founded by Jacques Lacour-Gayet, a spokesperson for the interests of the department store trade, the CAED was successful in building public opinion through publication campaigns in favour of a European market built on liberal tariff policies.[24]

Strongly committed to the construction of a European economic community and to a unified market, Galeries Lafayette saw the build up of a continental business network as source of growth. Jean d'Allens (1909–70) played a decisive role with regard to this openness towards foreign suppliers and the development of a new purchasing policy, in his position ashead of Galeries Lafayette's central purchasing bureau, the Société Parisienne d'Achats et de Manutention (SPAM). D'Allens joined the company in 1930, initially working as an assistant buyer and then as a buyer at SPAM, which had been set up in 1929. At the suggestion of Max Heilbronn, Galeries Lafayette's chief executive, he was hired by the SCA, the central purchasing unit of Monoprix, the price-point chain store founded in 1932. On 2 August 1949, d'Allens became a member of the Galeries Lafayette executive committee and successively served as Purchasing Director and as Deputy General Director.

During an executive meeting held on 23 August 1949, d'Allens called for an exchange of information with department stores in Belgium, Italy, the Netherlands, Sweden, Switzerland, the United Kingdom, and the United States. He emphasized the need for a nexus that would bring department stores together, rather than working through intermediaries.[25] As part of this strategy, in October of the same year, he met with Israel Sieff, vice president of Marks and Spencer (M&S), a limited company in London, to negotiate purchases at cost and without commission from this leading British high-street retailer whose eyes were fixed on overseas expansion.[26]

The relationship between Galeries Lafayette and M&S predated this commercial agreement. Earlier in 1949, M&S had suggested the establishment of a joint design office for printing textiles that would be run by Galeries Lafayette.[27] Hans Schneider, the design chief at M&S from 1949 to 1970, put together attractive collections that won the admiration of the fashion world. During these years, the M&S fashion department expanded from fifteen employees to more than a hundred.[28] Confirming the close relations between the two companies, a 1950 contract called for the exchange of clothing styles and textile patterns between M&S and Galeries Lafayette.[29]

To broaden the number of partners in this international cooperation, in January 1950 d'Allens looked to find possible suppliers in Belgium, the Netherlands, and Denmark.[30] That same year, Galeries Lafayette buyers went to Italy in search of cotton items, summer shoes, and Murano glass. They also attended Swiss Fair Basel, a major venue for staple and luxury foodstuffs, household goods, sports articles, toys, furnishings and fittings for the home, not to mention watches and jewellery, and graphic design.[31] The store negotiated partnerships with the leading department stores in Belgium and the Netherlands, L'Innovation and De Bijenkorf, respectively.[32] These rapidly implemented initiatives led to a spectacular increase in foreign purchases, which went from 30 million francs in 1949 to 61 million francs in 1950.[33]

After the formation of the General Agreement on Tariffs and Trade (GATT) in 1946, new customs regulations lowered duties, with effect from 1948, further boosting initiatives. Galeries Lafayette hoped to take advantage of this to buy woollen goods for haute couture, silk for evening gowns, and plaid blankets from the United Kingdom.[34] In 1952, d'Allens asked the executive committee to authorize an extra 50 million francs for foreign purchases. In the end he was allocated an additional 25 million francs to import merchandise mainly from Italy and the United Kingdom, for a total budget of 150 million, more than double that of 1950.[35] D'Allens was an outstanding buyer whose colleagues described him as 'quick to make decisions, dynamic, creative, enthusiastic and deeply nonconformist'.[36] D'Allens provided a decisive push to the new international purchasing orientation of Galeries Lafayette.

The free market views held by the management at Galeries Lafayette and other European department stores led to the founding of a new trade association, the Association Commerciale Internationale (ACI). Galeries Lafayette organized a preparatory meeting in Paris, early in May 1953. Its representatives were Heilbronn and d'Allens. Galeries Lafayette was one of the nine founding members of ACI along with De Bijenkorf in the Netherlands, Globus in Switzerland, L'Innovation in Belgium, Magasin du Nord in Denmark, Nordiska Kompaniet in Sweden, Steen & Strøm in Norway, Stockmann in Finland, and Westdeutsche Kaufhof in West Germany. The mission of the ACI was 'to step up exchanges of information about merchandise'.[37] Four years before the signature of the Treaty of Rome on 25 March 1957 – the agreement establishing the European Economic Community – the members of this new association expressed their belief that free markets would raise consumer living standards in their countries.[38] With 'the overall interests of consumers as their primary concern', the association's founders were driven by the conviction that international exchanges of business information would lower distribution costs.[39] The solemn declaration in the preamble to the ACI's articles signalled the humanist intentions of the association.

The ACI's active stance allowed SPAM, the buying organization of Galeries Lafayette, to access purchasing networks in Belgium, Germany, Denmark, Finland, the Netherlands, Norway, Sweden, and Switzerland, along with intermediaries in Spain, Italy, Japan, the United Kingdom, and the United States.[40] ACI's member department stores shared documentation about their suppliers while maintaining their independence in purchasing. Department stores would introduce foreign buyers to suppliers in their respective countries. Suppliers took the existence of a purchasing network into account, and the high volume of purchases increased the department stores' buying power, which led in turn to better sales conditions and exclusive rights for some items.[41] This presupposed that only one department store per country could belong to ACI and that members would not communicate information about suppliers to non-member stores. Members were free to organize a joint purchasing office abroad or to remain independent. In any event, ACI had the great advantage of eliminating sales commissions in all transactions between member stores.[42] A coordinating body was established to collect reports submitted by

Galeries Lafayette fashion show for ACI members, 1958.   **5.2**

members. The members assigned a liaison officer, usually a person with buying experience, to be in charge of the communication with the coordinating office. Twice a year, SPAM presented the new Galeries Lafayette collections to ACI's top management and buyers as well as to its own branch managers (see figure 5.2).[43]

While looking forward to the construction of an eagerly awaited unified European market, representatives of major retailers thereby demonstrated their conviction to free trade on the Continent with the formation of the ACI. Following the ratification of the Treaty of Rome, the ACI's Secretary General Valère Wolfcarius gave members a detailed presentation about 'the extremely significant impact the Common Market will have on our businesses'.[44] Extolling the Common Market as 'a great achievement', Wolfcarius expressed the European convictions of the founding department store companies. These convictions were concretely demonstrated by trade initiatives such as 'La fleur de la production italienne', a promotion sponsored by Galeries Lafayette in 1953. Such promotional shows constituted trial runs for manufacturers and distributors, and at the same time, provided a glimpse of the impact that free trade would have on consumers. The 1953 show reveals both the obstacles and the advantages of increased relations with foreign suppliers.

'La fleur de la production italienne': the challenges of opening up

Opening at the flagship store on boulevard Haussmann on 27 April 1953, 'La fleur de la production italienne' was one in a series of thematic promotions mounted by Galeries Lafayette from the 1950s to the 1990s to

5.3   'La fleur de la production italienne' display at Galeries Lafayette, 1953.

spotlight the culture and products of foreign nations (figure 5.3). The choice of Italy for 1953 stemmed from the influence of American department and specialty stores, which as shown in Chapters 6 and 7, were enthusiastic about Italian fashion, and from Galeries Lafayette's desire to stock merchandise from around the world. Moreover, it reflected Galeries Lafayette's close attention to fashion trends and the store's constant scouting in places where the new styles emerged. Galeries Lafayette's increased openness should be considered in the context of new entrants challenging the leadership of Paris as the world's fashion capital.[45] Indeed New York, London, and the Italian cities of Florence, Rome, and Milan emerged from the 1950s as credible contenders to the title of 'fashion capital'. [46]

The interest of professional fashion buyers from major American stores in Italian styling was pivotal to the spectacular emergence of Italy as a fashion leader in the postwar period. On 12 February 1951, the fashion promoter Giovanni Battista Giorgini held a fashion show in his Florence home, Villa Torrigiani, bringing together the main Italian houses, with haute couture from Carosa, Fabiani, Simonetta Visconti, Emilio Schuberth, Sorelle Fontana, Jole Veneziani, Vanna, Noberasko, and Germana Marucelli. In addition, ready-to-wear came from Emilio Pucci, Avolio, La Tessitrice dell'Isola and Mirsa. Together, there were a total of 180 designs.[47] The date was carefully chosen to take advantage of the fact that American journalists and buyers usually came to Europe in February and August to see the haute couture collections in Paris.

The show marked a symbolic turning point in what has been called the 'invention' of postwar Italian fashion.[48] Italy's garment and textile industries (silk, leather, knitwear, and straw) were ancient and did not originate in the 1950s. Giorgini had worked for the American market since the 1920s as a consultant to purchasers of ceramics, glasswork, lace, embroidery, and straw goods from Italy. He had also opened a gift shop for allied soldiers in Florence.[49]

To build a brand image that could promote and legitimize Italian fashion, Giorgini followed the couturier Rosa Genoni (1867–1954) whose work associated fashion with art by evoking the Italian Renaissance, the heyday of the Italian influence on Western culture. The association of modern Italian fashion with the Renaissance 'period of excellence' successfully produced a new image for the industry. While immediately after World War II the Italian garment industry remained trapped in the pre-industrial era, a 'second Renaissance' was made possible by the modernization of textile factories under the aegis of the European Recovery Program.[50] This stimulated the modernization of the garment industry and the clothing distribution sector as shown by the trade journal *Quaderni*.[51] As a consequence, major vertically-integrated enterprises dedicated to clothing production and distribution emerged in Italy in the 1950s and 1960s in the context of the Italian economic 'miracle'.[52]

Giorgini's genius lay on one hand in the way he was able to activate his network of professional contacts to attract American buyers, and on the other hand in his skills at inducing the major Italian fashion houses to converge on Florence, the cradle of the Italian Renaissance. When he invited the press and international buyers in 1951 to his home in Florence, Giorgini reinforced the already-existing historical connection in the minds of American journalists. They were ready to label Italy's postwar economic recovery a 'second Renaissance'.[53] One character would embody the whole idea for them: Emilio Pucci. He was the first Italian designer to achieve a breakthrough in America with his designs of tight trousers and printed silks.[54] The perfect symbol of the Italian aristocrat, Pucci claimed the link between the Renaissance and the city of Florence as his source of inspiration: 'a mysterious and timeless feeling of beauty, creativity and harmony traceable in Florence'.[55]

Giorgini, who spoke English fluently, began by nailing down the participation of the Bergdorf Goodman (New York) representative with whom he had worked for years. Then he emphasized this accomplishment in a letter to his colleagues and competitors: 'Bergdorf Goodman is going to be present and also such other stores'.[56] American department stores and fashion specialty stores were as attracted by the success of the catwalk show and the reasonable prices – less than half the price of the clothing presented in Paris – as they were by the designs themselves.[57] At his second show, held at Grand Hôtel in July 1951, Carmel Snow, the influential fashion editor of *Harper's Bazaar*, sat in the front row. From 1952 onwards, what had become twice annual affairs took place in the renowned Sala Bianca in the Palazzo Pitti in Florence. In January 1953, d'Allens and buyers from Galeries Lafayette attended the fashion show.[58]

American department stores, the pioneers of the Italian fashion renaissance

It was mainly the American press and major American retailers – department stores and specialty stores – that brought international recognition for Italian fashion.[59] In the early 1950s, the United States was the leading international market for apparel. On 10–22 September 1951, in the wake of Giorgini's first Italian fashion show in Florence in 1951, Macy's held a Italian promotion on the fifth floor of its New York flagship store. Its title refers directly to the narrative set up to promote Italian fashion: 'Italy-in-Macy's, U.S.A: How Italy's "Second Renaissance" Came to Macy's' (figure 5.4).[60] The theme was picked up by *Women's Wear Daily*, which wrote of this 'Second Renaissance in Italian Craftsmanship'.[61] The

HOW ITALY'S "SECOND RENAISSANCE" CAME TO MACY'S

5.4   Poster for the exhibition, Italy-in-Macy's, U.S.A., New York City, 1951.

spectacular themed promotion occupied more than 12,000 square metres of floor space. It took Macy's buyer eighteen months to select the 1,028 items of specialty merchandise on display.[62]

The Italian promotion was sponsored by the Italian government and took on a political dimension whose implications went far beyond the retail trade. As Macy's president Richard Weil said, 'The exposition itself, of more than a thousand different new types of merchandise, will be a vivid and realistic application, by American and Italian private enterprise, of efforts "beyond the Marshall Plan" to strengthen the economy of the free world.' In light of these political stakes, George C. Marshall, the advocate of the European Recovery Program (ERP) and the outgoing United States Secretary of Defense, lent Macy's a basket given to him by the Sicilians for his contribution to the economic recovery of Italy through the ERP after World War II. [63] In a letter to the store management, Marshall said, 'I think your efforts will strengthen the already strong cooperation between Italy and this great country of ours.'[64]

Macy's promotional materials printed for the occasion described the show as an initiative from the Italian government and Italian industrialists looking for an American partner to promote as much trade as possible between the two countries. For Macy's president, the story behind 'Italy-in-Macy's' proved that a country with a strong manufacturing base could durably and significantly increase the volume of its dollar-denominated exports if it adapted itself to 'the special demands of the US market'.[65] Such an adaption to the American market was the precondition for any discussion.

Once the Italian government defined the qualifications that it sought in a US partner, Macy's identified itself as matching its three criteria:, 'consumer-contact, scope and buying-power, [and] promotional leadership'. By virtue of being America's largest department store, Macy's could claim to be 'the world's largest store' and was the best-placed retailer to become the intermediary between Italian industry and American consumers. Its buyers were better able to advise potential suppliers than diplomats with no marketing expertise. At the time of the show, Macy's network with its central foreign purchasing unit yielded $775 million in annual turnover, a potential volume capable of inciting the exporting country to orient its production towards that market.[66] Finally, due to an aggressive sales policy, Macy's had acquired a solid reputation for organizing, staging, and promoting sales events. For these reasons, the famous New York department store constituted an ideal showcase in the eyes of Italian authorities, who hoped that this first show would also galvanize Macy's competitors.

From Macy's to Galeries Lafayette

The success of Macy's Italian promotion had a powerful impact on Galeries Lafayette. The store archives document the Macy's event in the papers of

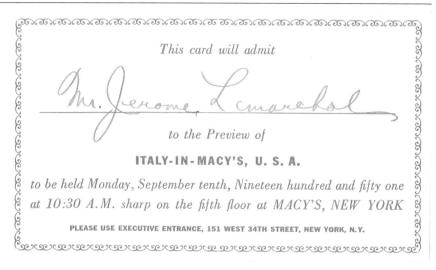

This card will admit

Mr. Jerome Lemaréchal

to the Preview of

ITALY-IN-MACY'S, U. S. A.

*to be held Monday, September tenth, Nineteen hundred and fifty one
at 10:30 A.M. sharp on the fifth floor at MACY'S, NEW YORK*

PLEASE USE EXECUTIVE ENTRANCE, 151 WEST 34TH STREET, NEW YORK, N.Y.

5.5   Gérôme Lemaréchal's invitation card for the private preview of the exhibition, Italy-in-Macy's, U.S.A., arranged in co-sponsorship with the Italian Government.

director Gérôme Lemaréchal, who visited the United States on this occasion.[67] Macy's president invited Lemaréchal to a preview and the official opening of the exposition on 10 September 1951 (figure 5.5).[68] In the wake of this visit, the Galeries Lafayette management team began envisioning an Italian show in Paris.

The French were spurred on by a similar show at the Brussels department store L'Innovation in 1952, as attested in a report on a visit to Belgium. 'The ambience is created not only by the merchandise but also many related events', noted the report on the Belgian store. 'On the third floor, an Italian Museum features artworks lent by Italy, with paintings, sculptures, furniture, etc.'[69] Here, too, we can see the role of the Italian authorities and the government itself in the 'invention' of Italian fashion and the construction of a 'Made in Italy' brand legitimized by its association with art. At the beginning of the Belgian show, Henry Weill, director of L'Innovation and a member of ACI along with representatives from Galeries Lafayette, wrote to Raoul Meyer, a top executive officer of Galeries Lafayette. The point was to inform Meyer that the Italian Embassy in Belgium, and several Italian ministers and mayors, as well as representatives of the Italian National Press Agency (ANSA), all of whom had come for the opening of the Italian show at L'Innovation, intended to contact French department stores to hold a similar exposition in the French capital.[70] Upon receiving the letter, d'Allens immediately contacted the Italian Embassy in Paris to officially request diplomatic support for an Italian show at Galeries Lafayette.[71] The advance information provided to Galeries Lafayette by L'Innovation shows the strategic importance of the network that Galeries Lafayette had developed with its foreign counterparts. The director of L'Innovation also sent d'Allens a letter with 'the complete list of lines of items we have selected in Italy'.[72]

When d'Allens went to Florence in January 1953 for the Sala Bianca fashion show, he carried along with him a letter of introduction from the Italian Embassy in Paris. The letter confirmed the agreement to organize an Italian promotional event in Paris and asked Italian industrialists and other manufacturers to collaborate in what the ambassador called 'una ottima propaganda commerciale per l'Italia' ('an excellent trade propaganda for Italy').[73] During this 1953 buying trip, d'Allens and his team also researched prospective suppliers, as indicated by a report written by a SPAM associate who visited several manufacturers – Turrifor for furniture and mirrors, Magnoni & Tedeschi for furniture coverings, Manspugna for terrycloth, and Venini for deluxe Murano glassware. The associate remarked on the high quality of merchandise at La Rinascente, the leading Milanese department store, particularly the glassware and its 'plates covered with stripes'.[74] As soon as he got back to Paris, d'Allens sketched out a work plan for each purchasing group.[75]

A miracle at Galeries Lafayette?

Following the buying trip to Florence, Galeries Lafayette had to complete the paperwork necessary to obtain the authorization for importing selected goods from Italy to France. This illustrates the complexity of international trade between European countries in the period. In the years before the Common Market, business encountered all sorts of market barriers and bureaucratic hurdles if they wanted to ship goods from one European country to another.

The signature of the European Coal and Steel Community Treaty in Paris on 18 April 1951 was the first step towards the elimination of trade barriers, but it extended to only one industry. A draft treaty on the status of the European Community, presented on 10 March 1953 in Strasbourg, envisioned the expansion of the scope of a common market. Yet in 1952, confronted with a rising balance of payments deficit, France had backpedalled on unfettered exchange and abandoned the free trade movement led by the European Organization for Economic Cooperation (EOEC). The Italian situation was comparable, with a significant important trade deficit from 1951.[76]

Thus the Italian show at Galeries Lafayette took place amid a protectionist climate. A front-page article in La voce d'Italia even described the Italian promotional show at Galeries Lafayette as kind of a miracle, 'una specie di miracolo'.[77] A translation of the newspaper article in the Galeries Lafayette archive states, 'The EOEC has been seeking free trade for several years now but for one reason or another the restrictions are always

maintained, if not increased.'[78] Franco-Italian trade agreements had provided for special quotas to allow Italian exhibitors to import goods for
French trade fairs. The French government had set the quota for these
purposes at one and a half billion francs' worth of merchandise for 1953.
The Italian government, in charge of apportioning these quotas, made the
Galeries Lafayette sales exhibition possible by allocating the department
store ten per cent of this quota, that is, 150 million francs.[79]

The detailed chronology of the measures undertaken by Galeries
Lafayette to organize 'La fleur de la production italienne' demonstrates
the proactivity of the SPAM buyers and the complexity of the era's trade
regulations. It took four months to put together the Italian promotion.
D'Allens wrote to the Italian Embassy asking for aid on 13 December
1952, and the show was opened by His Excellency Pietro Quaroni, Italy's
ambassador to France, on 27 April 1953.[80] Between these two dates a
number of intermediaries had to be brought in. They had to be paid,
which affected the price of the merchandise. Thus on 8 February 1953,
acting for SPAM, d'Allens asked the accounting department at Galeries
Lafayette to send a payment to the Italian Foreign Trade Institute (Istituto
nazionale per il Commercio Estero, or the ICE) in Rome, which charged a
half per cent commission on the factory price for the merchandise.[81] The
Italian department store chain Standa[82] also acted as an intermediary –
probably centralizing Galeries Lafayette's purchases – and was remu-
nerated according to the volume of the transactions. [83] Galeries Lafayette
applied for import licences between 23 February and 11 March 1953.
The company received its first import licences on 3 April, and the first
shipments reached French customs five days later.[84] Three days later, the
display team began installing the show on the ground floor for the public
opening scheduled on 28 April.

The opening of 'La fleur de la production italienne' received such
an 'unexpectedly successful start' that the following day d'Allens once
again asked the Italian Embassy for supplementary credits to restock
shelves left bare after a single day of sales.[85] The exhibition's layout was
designed by the Italian architect Erberto Carboni, who had also done the
1951 show at Macy's and had been recommended to Galeries Lafayette
by the Italian Embassy.[86] Carboni conceived the design in collaboration
with Jean Adnet, the display director at Galeries Lafayette (figure 5.6).
The store's art director, Peter Knapp, commissioned Carboni to design
the show's logo, a tricoloured trefoil with the words 'La fleur de la production italienne', in celebration of Italy's finest industries and creativity
(see figure 5.7).[87]

The Galeries Lafayette show offered a broad range of products,
displayed amidst a 'piazzetta and streets of Capri' stage set. The merchandise included fabrics (cotton, wool, rayon, silk, and nylon), scarves,
linen, women's ready-to-wear, sweaters, straw goods (bags, hats, etc.),

Shop windows at Galeries Lafayette, as dressed for their 1953 exhibition 'La fleur de la   **5.6**
production italienne'.

shoes, furniture, and other whitewood goods. There was also a selection
of the newest appliances, such as Vespa scooters, Olivetti typewriters,
and so on. Italian specialities such as pasta and Cittrio salami were on
sale in the food department (see figure 5.8). Shoppers could eat Italian
dishes in the tearoom and pasta at the quick service bar, and drink coffee
made by a Gaggia espresso machine. While the shelves held Panzani
factory-made pasta, real Italian artisans made pasta by hand in the display
windows.[88]

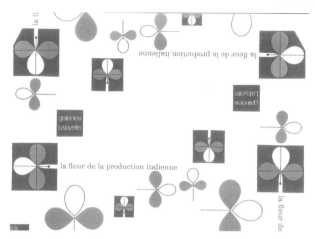

5.7   *Papier cadeaux* (wrapping paper) commissioned by Peter Knapp, designed by Carboni, and employing the 'La fleur de la production italienne' logo.

5.8   *Charcuterie et Fromage* display in the food hall, at 'La fleur de la production italienne', Galeries Lafayette, 1953.

A warning shot?

To assemble such a mix of merchandise was truly an achievement. 'How did it happen, people ask, at a time when crossing the Franco-Italian border with a slightly heavier than usual suitcase is a perilous adventure, when a kilo of Sicilian oranges, a single pair of Varese shoes or even a few crumbs of gorgonzola can not be found in Paris, how could a city-centre department store offer up such a variety of good things for sale from Italy?'[89]

Despite, or perhaps because of, its commercial success, 'La fleur de la production italienne' sparked a debate in Paris. Galeries Lafayette received protest letters expressing the 'very disagreeable surprise' of some customers shocked by the store's advertisements for Italian products and 'all too obvious position in favour of a very wide range of foreign products'.[90]

These expressions of protest reflected the high stakes posed by the Italian promotion. Two days after the event's opening, the newspaper *Les Echos* noted that 'a legitimate emotion aroused among many professions on learning that a Parisian department store was mounting a major display of products imported from Italy'.[91] To calm the waters *Les Echos* explained, in very precise and educational terms, the legal mechanism that had made the exhibition possible through the use of a portion of the quotas allotted to Italy for its participation in French trade fairs. It argued that the Galeries Lafayette event did not increase the overall amount of imports from Italy. The journalist concluded that the event's success should be taken as a 'warning shot' addressed to French manufacturers who might 'doze off at home, thinking themselves protected by comfortable customs duties'.[92]

It should be remembered that *Les Echos*, originally called *Echos de l'Exportation*, founded in 1908 by the brothers Robert and Emile Schreiber, was a fervent supporter of the lifting of trade barriers.[93] This newspaper was favourable to exporters. Published daily starting in 1928, it expanded to become the newspaper of record for economic matters. After ceasing publication during the war, it reappeared in 1945 under the management of the Servan-Schreiber heirs. Under pressure from its readership, *Les Echos* felt compelled to explain the origins of the cotton goods on display in 'La fleur de la production italienne' at Galeries Lafayette.[94]

> In response to questions from several subscribers, we confirm that no cotton fabric items were specially imported for this event … The only cotton goods for sale were imported previously, as part of normal Franco-Italian trade, with the appropriate import licences. They were moved from the store's usual shelves for this exposition and placed alongside other products on display.[95]

This clarification shows the political character of the Italian show, which had implications that extended far beyond the Paris department store itself. In fact the French cotton textile industry, mostly based in northern France, was eager to protect its domestic market and kept an eye on any foreign threat.

On 13 May 1953, *Les Echos* director Emile Servan-Schreiber published his thoughts about the Galeries Lafayette event with the headline 'Warning Shot'.[96] The editorial analysed the store's initiative in the context of the economic and political construction of Europe and the idea of free trade with reference to the role of department stores. Servan-Schreiber at first seemed to give reassurance to his readers, who were mainly French manufacturers threatened by foreign competition and who were opposed to lowering tariffs. But further on, the journalist stated his convictions and used the success of the Galeries Lafayette fair as a warning to French manufacturers who were less competitive than their Italian rivals:

> Of course, like many other people I am actively in favour of the lowering and even elimination of customs barriers. But suddenly, this unforeseen vision of a sanctuary of French taste entirely occupied by the competition (and what competition!) from the other side of the Alps makes the concrete reality tangible ... What good does it do to imagine that we have a monopoly when, actually, we do not anymore? For a long time now our car shows have brought us, alongside our own automobiles, models that are often better and cheaper than those made by our major manufacturers.[97]

The editor pointed to Galeries Lafayette's management, who now felt driven to awaken French manufacturers and exporters to the need to 'produce for the masses and democratize our goods by means of mass production'.[98]

As a token of his commitment and good relations with the business world, Servan-Schreiber noted that Galeries Lafayette had a right to respond. In fact, he wrote the response himself. In a letter dated 12 May 1953, he had submitted this text to the company's management for its approval – an opinion piece scheduled to appear the following day.[99] The article took the form of an interview with the store's chief executive, Gérôme Lemaréchal, who affirmed that the Italian initiative had brought Galeries Lafayette 'many criticisms, but also innumerable encouragements'.[100] Anxious to appease all sides, Lemaréchal announced consequently the 'Festival of French Design''where [we will] put on sale and advertise, through all channels at our disposal, new products created by French manufacturers and craftsmen'.[101]

The French festival, set for March 1954, was of course a response to the criticisms of some customers and suppliers upset by the store's Italian initiative. The idea was to spotlight French manufacturers and above all to give them access to the international network developed by Galeries Lafayette, since this new sales exposition could be imitated by department stores in other European countries. The French festival included a competition opened to French designers in order to connect them with industrialists. The winners were to have their projects produced by French manufacturers.

Retail as a key actor in the fashion system

William Wyler's movie, *Roman Holiday*, released in France a few months after the Galeries Lafayette Italian show, was a commercial success.[102] The two endeavours seem to have shared a common objective, a desire to promote European integration while emphasizing the competitive advantages enjoyed by Italy. By shooting the film at the fabled Cinecitta studios in Rome, Paramount studios was targeting the European market and particularly the country where growth in theatre attendance was most robust.[103] The American producers carefully chose a picturesque backdrop and a European-born actress, Audrey Hepburn, to ensure box office results at a period when movie-going was rising in France, Germany, and Italy, and declining in the United States and Great Britain due to the rise of television. Hollywood studios and department stores, both engaged in the creative industries, had an interest in an expanded market wherein goods could freely circulate. The film's opening credits stated that it was entirely shot in Rome. There wages for film crews were less costly than in Hollywood and this was another factor in favour of making movies in Europe for European audiences.

The resistance to 'La fleur de la production italienne' was real but the commercial success of the show demonstrated the prescriptive powers of Galeries Lafayette. At the beginning of the 1950s, Galeries Lafayette was facing the relative decline of Paris as the world's only fashion capital. This power shift created opportunities for new entrants such as the Italian fashion industry. For what one might call 'legacy players' such as Galeries Lafayette, these changes served as an inducement to self-transformation. In broadening its supply strategy, Galeries Lafayette clearly demonstrated an ability to adapt its business model to changing times. From the consumers' perspective, Galeries Lafayette was able to legitimize fashion, which was no longer the exclusive purview of Paris. The new foreign suppliers were not constrained by the traditional Parisian elitist haute couture model that emphasized costly one-of-a-kind production at the expense of ready-to-wear. Galeries Lafayette seized this opportunity to reinforce its strategy in connecting designers with manufacturers. Through initiatives such as the 1954 Festival of French Design, Galeries Lafayette aimed to stock mass-market goods and to democratize design for the consumer.

While the sociologist Yuniya Kawamura describes fashion as an 'institutionalized, systematic change produced by those who are authorized to implement it', the commercial and media success of the Italian fair reinforced the legitimacy of Galeries Lafayette as a privileged intermediary between the fashion world and consumers.[104] Finally, this case study of the 1953 Italian show at Galeries Lafayette in Paris spotlights the ensemble of fashion professionals who, along with designers, make fashion a 'collective activity'.[105]

Notes

1 F. Brachet Champsaur, *Aux Galeries Lafayette, 1893–1919: Naissance d'un leader de la distribution dans le secteur de la mode* (Master's thesis dissertation, École des hautes études en sciences sociales, Paris, 2005).

2 R. Jessen and L. Langer, 'Introduction: transformations of retailing in Europe after 1945', in R. Jessen and L. Langer (eds), *Transformations of Retailing in Europe after 1945* (Farnham: Ashgate, 2016), pp. 6–7; V. de Grazia, 'Changing consumption regimes in Europe, 1930–1970: comparative perspectives on the distribution problem', in S. Strasser, C. McGovern, and M. Judt (eds), *Getting and Spending: European and American Consumer Societies in the Twentieth Century* (Cambridge: Cambridge University Press, 1998), p. 59.

3 Galeries Lafayette Archive, Paris (hereafter GLA, Paris), Management Committee Minutes, 28 and 30 September 1954. 'L'Amérique ça ne s'explique pas, ça se voit.'

4 See E. Thil, *Combat pour la distribution: D'Édouard Leclerc aux supermarchés* (Paris: Arthaud, 1964); E. Thil, *Les inventeurs du commerce moderne: Des grands magasins aux bébés-requins* (Paris : Arthaud, 1966); C. Lhermie, *Carrefour ou l'invention de l'hypermarché* (Paris: Vuibert, 2001); A. Chatriot and M.-E. Chessel, 'L'histoire de la distribution: Un chantier inachevé', *Histoire, economie & société*, 1 (2006), 67–82; and C. Brosselin and C. Sordet, *La grande histoire des regroupements dans la distribution* (Paris: L'Harmattan, 2011). GLA mentions the first appearance of a new form of distribution in France: 'The first supermarket has just opened in Bagneux with highly sophisticated sales procedures.' See GLA Paris, Board Meeting Minutes, 20 March 1959.

5 On the European Recovery Program and its influence on France see R. F. Kuisel, *Seducing the French: The Dilemma of Americanization* (Berkeley: University of California Press, 1993).

6 'Si je n'avais pas connu les États-Unis, toute ma vie "Grands Magasins" se serait passée autrement', from M. Heilbronn and J. Varin, *Galeries Lafayette, Buchenwald, Galeries Lafayette* (Paris: Economica, 1989), p. 157.

7 On American influence and technology transfers before the establishment of the European Recovery Program and its production drive, see L. Cailluet, 'Selective adaptation of American management models: the long-term relationship of Pechiney with the United States', in M. Kipping and O. Bjarnar (eds), *The Americanization of European Business: The Marshall Plan and the Transfer of US Management Models* (London and New York: Routledge Studies in Business History, 1998), pp. 190–207.

8 In 1921, Galeries Lafayette built a garment factory in Paris inspired by scientific management and American productivity methods. In 1931, Paul Planus was assigned to oversee the garage and the organization of deliveries and supplies at Galeries Lafayette. See F. Brachet Champsaur and L. Cailluet, 'The Great Depression? Challenging the periodization of French business history in the interwar period', *Business and Economic History*, 8 (2010), 16–17. On rationalization in France and consulting agencies during the interwar period see A. Moutet, *Les logiques de l'entreprise: La rationalisation dans l'industrie francaise de l'entre-deux-guerres* (Paris: Editions de l'Ecole des hautes études en sciences sociales, 1997); G. Galvez-Behar, 'Les lieux de la conception: histoire et théorie', *Entreprises et histoire*, 58 (2010), 5–10; M. Kipping, 'Consultancies, institutions and the diffusion of Taylorism in Britain, Germany and France', *Business History*, 39:4 (1997), 67–83; A. Weexsteen, 'Le conseil aux entreprises et à l'État en France: Le rôle de Jean Milhaud (1898–1991) dans le CEGOS et dans l'ITAP' (Doctoral thesis, École des hautes études en sciences sociales, Paris, 1999).

9 Kipping and Bjarnar (eds), *The Americanization of European Business*.

10 National Cash Register (NCR), founded in 1884 by John H. Patterson, was the first company to manufacture these business tools. It set up its first sales school in 1893. See W. A. Friedman, *Birth of a Salesman: The Transformation of Selling in America* (Cambridge, MA: Harvard University Press, 2005); and J. Cortada, *Before the Computer: IBM, NCR, Burroughs, and Remington Rand and the Industry They Created, 1865–1956* (Princeton: Princeton University Press, 1993).

11 V. de Grazia, *Irresistible Empire: America's Advance through Twentieth-Century Europe* (Cambridge, MA: Harvard University Press, 2009), p. 399.

12 B. Trujillo, 'Postface', in Thil, *Les inventeurs du commerce moderne*, p. 263.

13 Trujillo, 'Postface', p. 257.

14 Trujillo, 'Postface', p. 267.

15 GLA, Paris, Executive Committee Minutes, 14 December 1949. In 1927 Tobé Coller Davis founded a fashion consulting firm and published the first issue of *The Fashion Report from Tobé*, later better known as the *Tobé Report*. See V. Pouillard, 'The rise of fashion forecasting and fashion Public Relations, 1920–1940: the history of Tobé and Bernays', in H. Berghoff and T. Kühne (eds), *Globalizing Beauty: Consumerism and Body Aesthetics in the Twentieth Century* (New York: Palgrave Macmillan, 2013), pp. 151–69.

16 GLA, Paris, Executive Committee Minutes, 24 October 1951.

17 'source d'informations précieuses tant sur le plan "marchandises" que sur le plan "organisation"'. See GLA, Paris, Board Meeting Minutes, 7 December 1956.

18 'au contraire, elle [l'évolution économique et commerciale aux Etats-Unis] marquerait plutôt un arrêt en ce sens que, partout – et même chez Lord and Taylor – on peut constater une certaine apathie: moins d'enthousiasme, moins de dynamique qu'il y a quelques années et cela sur toute l'échelle'. See GLA, Paris, Executive Committee Minutes, 12 October 1952.

19 GLA, Paris, Lemaréchal collection, 'Plan décennal de modernisation de la vente et des services', 1956. This Ten Year Plan followed an initial five-year plan adopted 1 September 1955 at Heilbronn's initiative.

20 See A. Marchal, 'Prospective par Gaston Berger, Louis Armand, François Bloch-Lainé, Pierre Chouard, Marcel Demonque, Jacques Parisot et Pierre Racine', *Revue économique*, 11 (1960), 973–5. See S. Cordobes and P. Durance, *Attitudes prospectives: Eléments d'une histoire de la prospective en France après 1945* (Paris: L'Harmattan, 2007), p. 91.

21 'Si nous ne nous résignons pas à cette discipline dans 10 ans ou dans 20, le Magasin agrandi et modernisé dans l'anarchie, sera un Macy's.' See GLA, Paris, 'Plan décennal', p. 36 ('Overall conclusion').

22 'il ne faut pas oublier la différence profonde entre la mentalité et le tempérament américain et français'. See GLA, Paris, Executive Committee Minutes, 28 and 30 September 1954. On the need to adopt the lessons of the American experience, see H. G. Schröter, 'The Americanization of distribution and its limits: the case of the German retail-system, 1950–1975', *European Review of History*, 15:4 (2008), 445. Also see M.-L. Djelic, *Exporting the American Model: The Post-War Transformation of European Business* (Oxford: Oxford University Press, 1998).

23 L. Badel, *Un milieu libéral et européen: Le grand commerce français 1925–1948* (Paris: Comité pour l'histoire économique et financière de la France, 1999).

24 On CAED, see Badel, *Un milieu libéral*, pp. 136–7.

25 GLA, Paris, Executive Committee Minutes, 16 September 1949.

26 A childhood friend of Simon Marks, Israel Sieff became vice president of Marks and Spencer in 1926, and then president after the former's death in 1964, a post he held until 1967. See R. Worth, *Fashion For the People: A History of Clothing at Marks & Spencer* (Oxford: Berg, 2007), p. 16.

27 GLA, Paris, Executive Committee Minutes, 5 and 19 April 1949.

28 Worth, *Fashion For the People*.

29 GLA, Paris, Executive Committee Minutes, 22 August 1950. Three dress and three blouse patterns had been purchased from Marks and Spencer in 1948; see GLA, Paris, Executive Committee Minutes, 7 December 1948.

30 GLA, Paris, Executive Committee Minutes, 24 January 1950.

31 GLA, Paris, Executive Committee Minutes, 25 April 1950.

32 GLA, Paris, Executive Committee Minutes, 6 July 1950.

33 GLA, Paris, Executive Committee Minutes, 5 September 1950.

34 GLA, Paris, Executive Committee Minutes, 7 November 1950.

35 GLA, Paris, Executive Committee Minutes, 29 January 1952.

36 'D'une grande rapidité de décision, créateur dynamique, enthousiaste et essentiellement anti-conformiste'. See GLA, Paris, *Information cadres*, no. 22, November–December 1970.

37 'Effort d'intensification des échanges d'informations relatives aux marchandises'. See Association Commerciale Internationale (ACI) archives (hereafter ACI archives), Paris, 'Constitution de l'Association Commerciale Internationale. Compte rendu du meeting du 27 juin 1953', p. 2.

38 ACI archives, Paris, Annex 1, 'Constitution'.

39 *Ibid.* 'Plaçant au premier rang de leurs préoccupations l'intérêt général des consommateurs'. The aims of the ACI were different from those of the Association Internationale des Grands Magasins pour l'étude des méthodes d'organisation (AIGM) founded in 1928, whose mission was the study and transfer of American organizational methods.

40 GLA, Paris, 'La S.P.A.M une organisation dynamique', *Lafayette nous voici* (March 1959), 6.

41 ACI archives, Paris, 'Constitution', p. 8. Further, Article 8 stipulates that two or more members may constitute a common purchasing unit.

42 ACI archives, Paris, Article 11, 'Constitution', p. 3.

43 GLA, Paris, J. Gerboin, ACI liaison for Galeries Lafayette, 'Présentation de collection ACI', *Lafayette nous voici* (October 1958), 23.

44 ACI archives, Paris, V. Wolfcarius, 'Exposé sur la communauté économique européenne', 1957.

45 V. Steele, *Paris Fashion: A Cultural History* (Oxford: Berg, 1998); Y. Kawamura, *Fashion-ology: An Introduction to Fashion Studies* (Oxford: Berg, 2004).

46 The idea of an American fashion free of Parisian tutelage flourished during the war, partly because of the breakdown in transatlantic trade (see Chapter 2). The New York garment industry, the press, and Mayor Fiorello La Guardia aspired to make their city an international fashion centre and denigrated their French rivals. The 1944 opening of the Fashion Institute of Technology (FIT) on Seventh Avenue was meant to facilitate the development of American fashion and connect designers and manufacturers. See Fashion Institute of Technology, 'Our History', at www.fitnyc.edu/about/history.php (accessed 7 August 2016); N. Green, *Du Sentier à la Septième Avenue: La confection et les immigrés, Paris-New York, 1880–1980*, trans. P. Ndiaye (Paris: Editions du Seuil, 1998), pp. 250–1; V. Pouillard, 'Keeping designs and brand authentic: the resurgence of the post-war French fashion business under the challenge of US mass production', *European Review of History*, 20:5 (2013), 818. On London's rise, see C. Breward, *Fashioning London: Clothing and the Modern Metropolis* (Oxford: Berg, 2000). On Italy see E. Merlo and F. Polese, 'Turning fashion into business: the emergence of Milan as an international fashion hub', *Business History Review*, 80:3 (autumn 2006), 415–47.

47 M. Belfanti, 'Renaissance et made in Italy: L'invention d'une identité culturelle pour l'industrie de la mode', *Mode de recherche*, 18 (June 2012), 10.

48 On the construction of representations and historical continuity, see E. J. Hobsbawm and T. Ranger (eds), *The Invention of Tradition* (Cambridge: Cambridge University Press, 1983).

49 Belfanti, 'Renaissance et made in Italy', 10.

50 See E. Merlo, 'Le origini del sistema moda', in M. Belfanti and F. Giusberti (eds), *La Moda, Storia d'Italia, Annali*, 19 (Turin: Einaudi, 2003), pp. 667–97.

51 Merlo and Polese, 'Turning fashion into business', 417; N. White, *Reconstructing Italian Fashion: America and the Development of the Italian Fashion Industry* (Oxford: Bloomsbury, 2000).

52 A. Colli and E. Merlo, 'Family business and luxury business in Italy (1950–2000)', *Entreprises et histoire*, 46 (April 2007), 116–17. After World War II, Italy experienced a period of strong economic growth with a doubling of its GDP between 1950 and 1962. See V. Zamagni, *The Economic History of Italy 1860–1990*, (Oxford: Clarendon Press, 2nd edn 2003), p. 337.

53 Colli and Merlo, 'Family business and luxury', 116.

54 After first appearing in the pages of *Harper's Bazaar* in 1948, Emilio Pucci's line of clothing was manufactured by the sportswear company, White Stag, for the American speciality store, Lord & Taylor. See Belfanti, 'Renaissance et made in Italy', 16.

55 K. Shirley, *Pucci: A Renaissance in Fashion* (New York: Abbeville Press, 1991), pp. 14–15.

56 Letter from Giovanni Battista Giorgini to H. Morgan (Henry *Morgan* & Company department store, Montréal, Canada), 15 January 1951, Giorgini Archives (Rezidenza Il Villino, Florence, Italy), cited by Sonnet Stanfill, 'Incorporating business history into a fashion exhibition', paper presented at the seminar on The Business of Fashion, Italian Style, Victoria and Albert Museum, London, 7 February 2014.

57 Belfanti, 'Renaissance et made in Italy', 11.

58 GLA, Paris, Italy exhibition file, Lemaréchal collection, Invitation for 'The Fifth Italian High Fashion Show', Florence, 24–27 January 1953, and report from a sales trip, 1953.

59 Merlo and Polese, 'Turning fashion into business'.

60 'Italy-in-Macy's, U.S.A.': How Italy's "Second Renaissance" came to Macy's', GLA, Paris, Italy exhibition file, Lemaréchal collection.

61 'Second Renaissance Italian craftsmanship', *Women's Wear Daily* (11 September 1951).

62 GLA, Paris, Italy exhibition file, Lemaréchal collection, *Italy-In-Macy's* brochure.

63 GLA, Paris, Italy exhibition file, Lemaréchal collection, R. Weil, New York, to G. Lemaréchal, Paris, 31 August 1951.

64 GLA, Paris, Italy exhibition file, Lemaréchal collection, G. C. Marshall cited by R. Weil, letter to G. Lemaréchal, 31 August 1951.

65 GLA, Paris, Italy exhibition file, Lemaréchal collection, R. Weil, Jr., *A Project in the Expansion of Commerce between America and Europe*, brochure c. 1951.

66 *Ibid.*

67 GLA, Paris, Italy exhibition file, Lemaréchal collection.

68 GLA, Paris, Italy exhibition file, Lemaréchal collection, Letter from R.Weil to G. Lemaréchal, 31 August 1951.

69 GLA, Paris, Italy exhibition file, Lemaréchal collection, 'Visite de l'Innovation Bruxelles, 15 décembre 1952'.

70 GLA, Paris, Italy exhibition file, Lemaréchal collection, Letter from H. Weill to R. Meyer, 11 December 1952.

71 GLA, Paris, Italy exhibition file, Lemaréchal collection, 'Rapports avec les autorités italiennes', J. d'Allens to R. Giancolla, attaché at the Italian Embassy, Paris, 13 December 1952,.

72 GLA, Paris, EVE/GL 1953, Letter from assistant director L. Evrard to J. d'Allens, 'Achats', 18 December 1952.

73 GLA, Paris, EVE/GL 1953, 'Voyage Italie', January 1953.

74 *Ibid.* Founded by Luigi and Ferdinando Bocconi in 1877, Città d'Italia is considered to be the first department store to open in Italy. After Ferdiando Bocconi's death in 1908, senator Borletti stepped in to save the company, acquiring it in 1917. Following numerous hardships and a fire, the Milanese store reopened its doors under the name Rinascente, so called in tribute to the poet Gabriele D'Annunzio. For the history of the Rinascente, see F. Amatori, *Propriet. e direzione: La Rinascente,*

1919–1969 (Milan: Franco Angeli, 1989); 'Alle origini della grande distribuzione in Italia', *Commercio*, 10 (1982); V. Zamagni, *La distribuzione commerciale in Italia fra le due guerre* (Milan: Franco Angeli, 1981).

75 GLA, Paris, Italy exhibition file, Lemaréchal collection, 'Exposition italienne. Programme de travail pour les 3ème et 6ème groupes à la suite du voyage de Monsieur d'Allens', SPAM, 31 January 1953.

76 M. Levi, 'L'évolution et la structure des échanges commerciaux de la France avec l'étranger de 1951 à 1955', *Politique étrangère*, 5 (1956), 567–86.

77 'Il fior del prodotto italiana trionfa ai magazzini Lafayette', *La voce d'Italia/La voix d'Italie* (4 May 1953).

78 GLA, Paris, EVE/GL 1953, 'La fine fleur des produits italiens triomphe aux Galeries Lafayette', translation of an article in *La voce d'Italia* (4 May 1953).

79 'Que signifie la vente massive de produits italiens dans un grand magasin parisien?', *Les Echos* (29 April 1953).

80 GLA, Paris, EVE/GL 1953, Italy exhibition file, J. d'Allens, 'Note à Monsieur Adnet', 29 April 1953.

81 This Italian public institution was called the Istituto Nazionale per la Esportazione (INE) when it was founded in 1926. It was attached to the Foreign Trade Ministry in 1947. From the beginning its mission was to support and expand Italian exports. See Treccani, La Cultura Italiana, at www.treccani.it/enciclopedia/ice (accessed 2 August 2016).

82 Standa was founded in 1931 by an executive from the UPIM (Unico Prezzo Italiano Milano) chain, who called it Magazzini Standard; the name was Italianized as Standa in 1932. With some hundred outlets after World War II, it became the second largest retailer in Italy, after the group comprising La Rinascente and UPIM. See J. Morris, 'Contesting retail space in Italy: competition and corporatism 1915–60', *International Review of Retail, Distribution and Consumer Research*, 9:3 (1999), 291–306; D. Carson, 'Marketing in Italy today', *Journal of Marketing*, 30:1 (1966), 10–16; and E. Scarpellini, 'The long way to the supermarket: entrepreneurial innovation and adaptation in 1950s–1960s Italy', in Jessen and Langer (eds), *Transformations of Retailing in Europe after 1945*, p. 62.

83 GLA, Paris, EVE/GL 1953, Italy exhibition file, J. d'Allens, 'Note à Monsieur Le Hir', 18 February 1953. In exchange, Standa agreed to lower its commission by 0.5% on all orders linked to the 150 million francs credit.

84 GLA, Paris, EVE/GL 1953, Italy exhibition file, 'Rapports avec les autorités italiennes'.

85 GLA, Paris, EVE/GL 1953, Italy exhibition file, 'Rapports avec les autorités italiennes', J. d'Allens to the Italian Embassy, 29 April 1953.

86 GLA, Paris, EVE/GL 1953, Italy exhibition file, R. Meyer to E. Carboni, 29 April 1953.

87 P. Knapp, interview by Florence Brachet Champsaur, Paris, 1 August 2008.

88 GLA, Paris, EVE/GL 1953, Italy exposition file, 'Dans un grand magasin de la rive droite des ouvrières italiennes (exposées en vitrine) vont fabriquer des pâtes', undated press clipping.

89 GLA, Paris, EVE/GL 1953, 'La fine fleur des produits italiens triomphe aux Galeries Lafayette'.

90 GLA, Paris, EVE/GL 1953, Italy exposition file, letter addressed to Galeries Lafayette management dated 5 May 1953. On receiving this letter, management initiated an investigation into the sender, P. M. Smith.

91 'Que signifie la vente massive de produits italiens dans un grand magasin parisien?'

92 *Ibid.*

93 Source: L'obs, 'L'historique des Echos', 10 July 2007, at tempsreel.nouvelobs. com/medias-pouvoirs/20070622.OBS3418/l-historique-des-echos.html (accessed 1 August 2016).

94 Starting in 1952, after a halt in steps towards free exchange with the EOEC, the French government established import quotas to protect French industry from competition, especially in the textile industry. This led to a fall in cotton textile imports, from 13.6 billion francs in 1952 to 2.4 billion francs in 1953, the year of the Galeries Lafayette exposition. This drop-off reached a 1.7 billion low in 1955. Levi, 'L'évolution et la structure des échanges commerciaux', 577.

95 'L'exposition-vente à Paris d'articles italiens', *Les Echos* (30 April 1953).

96 E. Servan-Schreiber, 'Coup de semonce', *Les Echos* (13 May 1953).

97 *Ibid.*

98 *Ibid.*

99 GLA, Paris, Italy exhibition file, Lemaréchal collection, E. Servan-Schreiber to G. Lemaréchal, 12 May 1953, along with the editorial 'Coup de semonce' and a draft reply.

100 'Un festival de la création française', *Les Echos* (14 May 1953).

101 *Ibid.*

102 Hollywood director William Wyler's movie *Roman Holiday*, starring Audrey Hepburn and Gregory Peck, was released in the United States in September 1953. See P. Kramer, 'Faith in relations between people: Audrey Hepburn, *Roman Holiday* and European Integration, in D. Holmes and A. Smith (eds), *100 Years of European Cinema: Entertainment or Ideology?* (Manchester: Manchester University Press, 2000), pp. 195–206.

103 G. Vincendeau, 'Issues in European cinema', in J. Hill and P. Church-Gibson (eds), *World Cinema: Critical Approaches* (Oxford: Oxford University Press, 1995), p. 466.

104 Y. Kawamura, *Fashion-ology*, p. 51 and on the role of intermediaries, C. Bessy and P.-M. Chauvin, 'Market intermediaries: their role in matching and valuation', paper at the international conference on Intermediaries, Brokers, Gatekeepers and Prescribers: Key Actors of Artistic Creation, Strasbourg, France, 20–22 June 2012; R. L. Blaszczyk (ed.), *Producing Fashion: Commerce, Culture, and Consumers* (Philadelphia: University of Pennsylvania Press, 2008).

105 On art as a collective activity, see H. S. Becker, *Art Worlds* (Berkeley and Los Angeles: University of California Press, 1982), pp. 1–39.

6

Anonymous tastemakers: the role of American buyers in establishing an Italian fashion industry, 1950–55

Sonnet Stanfill

At the close of World War II, the United States served as an important engine of economic recovery for Europe, in part because of the direct investment of the European Recovery Program, also known as the Marshall Plan, and due to North America's function as an expanding market for European goods, including fashionable clothing. First for European couture designers and then for its ready-to-wear producers, American department stores in cities from Boston to Houston and from Montreal to San Francisco were crucial conduits to well-heeled clients seeking the latest in continental style. As art historian Nancy Troy has written about French couturiers, 'Traditionally, they made their most lucrative sales in America.'[1]

Many North American department stores and fashion specialty stores prided themselves on their in-house couture salons, which sold the European couture originals their buyers had selected as well as the models they had paid for permission to copy. These same buyers would also consider a designer's boutique or sportswear lines and negotiate licensing agreements to manufacture lower-priced merchandise with the designer's name attached.[2] While this process of transcontinental trade is well understood, less studied is the role played by the fashion buyer. Responsible for assessing, selecting, and promoting each season's clothing, through their choices of designers and seasonal styles, as well as textiles and colours, the buyer acted as an important filter of taste for a growing market of consumers eager for the newest European fashions.

Despite functioning as instrumental tastemakers, these individuals were often behind-the-scenes figures who typically served their employers uncredited and had few occasions to step into the public eye. With the passing decades, the buyers who once wielded significant commercial influence have become nearly anonymous, their names remembered by few, their impact on an industry largely forgotten. In contrast, their counterparts in the press, the fashion editors of important newspapers and magazines, became household names which even today retain certain legendary status: Carmel Snow of *Vogue* and later of *Harper's Bazaar*; Bettina Ballard of *Vogue*; and Diana Vreeland of *Harper's Bazaar* and *Vogue*. Fashion editors and retail buyers attended the same fashion shows and endured the same ambitious travel itineraries in order to follow and pass judgment on the season's clothing. While some editors became well known personalities with published autobiographies and still-quoted fashion diktats, the buyers of that era have faded into obscurity. An examination of the working lives of these anonymous tastemakers suggests their larger cultural impact. As fashion historian Alexandra Palmer has written, 'Linking documentary data to material culture is an underused and rich academic tool.'[3]

The period in focus encompasses the years 1950–55, when the Italian fashion industry first emerged onto the international stage. Within this half decade, Italy caused immense excitement in fashion circles as a new source of leading fashion. As the following pages will show, during the early 1950s, retail buyers had their first opportunity to efficiently view, select, and import a multitude of Italian designers' seasonal collections. By focusing on the role of the fashion buyer, this chapter confirms that, as had been the case for postwar Paris, the custom of North American buyers helped to develop Italy's nascent fashion system and place it firmly on the fashion map.

The garments selected and sold within the physical spaces of the typical American department store and specialty fashion store are recognised as key cultural signifiers in the postwar period. Because a buyer's merchandise selections were the prism through which many North American women perceived European fashions and European style, this chapter places some emphasis on buyers' choices from the Italian seasonal offerings for the stores they worked for. The logistics of the retail trade are also emphasized: a buyer's day-to-day responsibilities and their experiences of conducting business abroad, as well as the complexities of the international travel their jobs required.

This research builds on Regina Lee Blaszczyk's work on fashion intermediaries: the buyers, directors, and store managers who peopled the commercial side of fashion history, which is further extended in Chapter 7.[4]

I draw heavily upon the papers of Giovanni Battista Giorgini, held in the Archivio di Stato in Florence. These papers include unpublished correspondence between the buying staff of North American department stores and Giorgini, the entrepreneur responsible for bringing widespread international attention to Italian fashion for the first time. This chapter also draws from the archives of the American department store chain I. Magnin, now held in the San Francisco Public Library. Headquartered in

California, I. Magnin was one of the first elite department stores to carry Italian couture and sportswear in the United States. Also referenced are British, Italian, and American press and magazine articles of the period.[5]

While the Italian fashion system began by following the Paris market model of an emphasis on haute couture and the attendant sales of copying permissions, it would evolve to become the leader in designer ready-to-wear. In the early 2000s, this topic has received brief mention in a variety of publications, including the usual designer monographs but also more thoughtful works investigating material culture and consumption in Italian life, fashion production during the Fascist regime, and the subject of Italy's emergence as source of leading fashion design.[6] An early exponent of this work is the historian Nicola White with her research into the role of American investment in the postwar Italian textile and fashion industries.[7]

Despite these investigations, there is much left to uncover about the dynamics in place during a period of dramatic and rapid change within the Italian fashion industry. Requiring further study are the differing experiences between the Roman, Milanese, and Florentine fashion houses, particularly since, despite the best efforts of Florence, which continued to compete with the other two Italian cities for the attentions of North American retailers, it eventually lost its once prominent position. In addition, this chapter references only one department store archive in relation to this history; a wider examination is necessary to establish a fuller picture. Finally, it will be of interest to fashion historians to understand in detail the tasks and fee structures of the buying agents, whose services many department stores relied upon to navigate the challenges of language and cultural differences, and the complexities of international importation.

Giovanni Battista Giorgini: entrepreneur and impresario

At the end of World War II, in physical and economic ruin, Italy seemed an unlikely source of leading fashion design. During the war, Benito Mussolini had placed a premium on uniformity and self-sufficiency in fashion production. Autarky was valued over creativity. From 1935, the country's national fashion authority, the Ente Nazionale della Moda, had attempted to regulate Italian fashion and textile manufacturing and promote its independence from Paris. While the war interrupted commerce for all of Europe, including fashion production and export, Italy was especially disadvantaged by its lack of a clear fashion capital. Although the Fascist regime had designated Turin as the official capital during the war, Italian cities each had their own fashion traditions and regional specialities: Florence was known for quality leather goods and straw work, Rome and Milan for couture, and Naples for fine tailoring. As in Paris, each city's designers and better dressmakers usually presented their collections within their own ateliers. As a result, tracking a large number of fashion designers across Italy's sprawling geography was challenging for foreign visitors. Compounding these logistical difficulties was the fact that the Italian designers presented their collections in October and March, rather than timing them around the Paris and London showings in February and August.[8] As postwar Europe rebuilt and trading resumed, these factors initially deprived foreign buyers of an easy means of following, selecting, and importing Italian fashion.

The emergence of an organized and coordinated Italian fashion system began in 1950. That year saw the planning of Italy's first fashion show staged expressly for the convenience of international buyers and journalists. The show was the idea of Florentine entrepreneur Giovanni Battista Giorgini (1898–1971), a buying agent before the war who had worked closely with North American department stores to help them select and import Italian handicrafts. Giorgini descended from an old Florentine family: a Giorgini family tomb purportedly sits within Florence's Santa Croce church, and ancestor General Giuseppe Giorgini supplied arms for Garibaldi's historic 1860 *mille* campaign.[9] After serving as a volunteer in World War I, Giovanni Battista Giorgini left the Tuscan city of Massa, where his family were marble quarry owners, and relocated to Florence.[10] Giorgini taught himself English, and in 1923 founded an import-export business specializing in Tuscan handicrafts such as leather goods, embroidered textiles, and ceramics. Operating from offices on via Calzaiuoli and from a store, Le Tre Stanze, on the Arno's riverfront, throughout the 1920s and 1930s Giorgini demonstrated a canny, driven entrepreneurial flair.

In this period the young businessman travelled widely across North America to cities including New York, Chicago, Cleveland, St. Louis, and Denver, where he networked tirelessly with department store representatives and secured orders for his wares. After the war, Giorgini's work resumed with the liberation of Florence in August 1944, when he established a bazaar in Florence's via Calzaiuoli selling Italian craft products to British and American soldiers. The shop's popularity encouraged Giorgini to open a store in the late 1940s, La Bottega del Ridotto, in Milan's via Montenapoleone, another in New York's East Forty-Ninth Street, and to host an exhibition of Florentine crafts at the showroom of Chicago interior designer Watson & Boaler.[11] Giorgini's American projects eventually linked him to an American museum exhibition, which would channel the Italian entrepreneur's main focus onto fashion.

In the summer of 1950, a group of American museum experts went to Italy seeking objects to include in the important travelling exhibition, *Italy at Work*. The exhibition, a joint Italian and American government-supported promotion of Italian decorative arts, was to open first at the Brooklyn Museum, and then progress on a twelve-city American museum tour. The Italian scouting trip included Meyric Rogers, the curator of decorative arts at the Art Institute of Chicago. Rogers and his colleagues chose products from a number of the artisans Giorgini represented.[12] In the autumn of 1950, Giorgini and Rogers began exploring the possibility of staging a live presentation of Italian fashions inside the Art Institute, to coincide with the exhibition. Giorgini wrote to Rogers on 15 September 1950, 'Following upon my letter of August 29th, I am glad to be able to report to you that I have spoken with all the best dressmakers in Italy and that the response about the idea of the Fashion Show in America has been enthusiastic from all of them.'[13]

Although lack of funding meant that the fashion show project did not materialize, Giorgini's efforts were not wasted. Giorgini laid his own plans. Harnessing his network of Italian fashion designers in the winter of 1950, drawing upon his existing North American department store contacts and a winning, gentlemanly charm, Giorgini produced the first fashion show in Italy intended to attract an international audience. Its success eventually led to the establishment of twice-yearly fashion showings in a single location, thus creating one prototype of the modern 'fashion week'. For his first event, not only did Giorgini secure the participation of designers from across Italy, he also banked on the attendance of some of America's most important buyers. Billed as both a fashion show and a ball, the events took place on 12–14 February 1951, in the Giorgini family's apartment in Florence's Villa Torregiani on via dei Serragli. Each of the eleven participating designers contributed eighteen original ensembles. As a convenience to buyers, all the Italian designers presented their collections in the same room. The show was scheduled the week after the Paris collections, in order to take advantage of buyers' existing European travel plans.[14] With the exhibition, *Italy at Work*, touring the United States, the Marshall Plan winding down its successful efforts in Italy, and the restless fashion world hungry for a new discovery four years after Christian Dior launched his New Look, Giorgini's first show of Italian fashion was perfectly timed.

The audience of several dozen fashion professionals who attended Giorgini's first event was small in number but highly influential, including the powerful triumvirate of American fashion, Julia Trissel of Bergdorf Goodman, Gertrude Ziminsky of B. Altman, and retailer Hannah Troy. Also present were a handful of other buyers as well as *Women's Wear Daily* reporter Matilda Taylor. For the harried buyers, whose European itineraries typically involved rushing from one designer salon to another, Giorgini's presentation must have seemed a calm, beautifully organized affair. When the guests arrived at Giorgini's apartment, they were greeted by their host, given refreshments, and invited to view the couture evening gowns and cocktail dresses, as well as informal sportswear, by the most important fashion houses from across Italy. These included Roman designers Simonetta Visconti and the Fontana sisters (Sorelle Fontana), Milanese houses such as Germana Marucelli, and the Florentine Emilio Pucci. The models paraded around Giorgini's living room to the accompaniment of a pianist. In addition to being well organized, the event was also typically Italian: elegant, yet not stuffy; relaxed and informal. At the close of the presentations, guests were treated to what would become a Florence fashion show tradition: a grand ball on the final evening, for which guests were invited to 'please wear gowns purely Italian in inspiration'.[15] Confronted with leisurely fashion presentations and glamorous parties, with Renaissance Florence as the picturesque backdrop, even jaded fashion professionals would have found it difficult to resist the seduction of this wholly different kind of buying trip.

Buyers place their orders

The openness of the early Italian fashion presentations contrasted significantly with the exclusiveness of the Parisian haute couture firms, known for strictly regulating the entrance to their shows, with support from the Chambre Syndicale de la Couture Parisienne. Italy's additional appeal came from the fact that its early high fashion exports cost roughly one-third less than their French couture equivalents.[16] Furthermore, for the North American buyers, Italy represented an exciting new source of freshly discovered fashion talent. Stores competed fiercely with one another to be the first to showcase the new Italian designer names. James Keillor, President of B. Altman, wrote to Giorgini on 20 January 1951, on the eve of Giorgini's first fashion show, 'After careful consideration, we have decided to send Mrs. Gertrude Ziminsky to Italy to attend the Italian High Fashion Show … Under the circumstances, we would prefer that you not extend invitations to Saks nor Lord & Taylor.'[17] Bergdorf Goodman of New York sent two buyers to that event, while Henry Morgan & Company of Montreal instructed their buyer John Nixon, who was already in Europe, to drop everything and head to Florence. A minor fashion drama ensued, with Nixon cabling Giorgini just days before the show to ask if his attendance was important, warning that if he were to change his itinerary in order to attend, he had no funds to make purchases that season.[18] Giorgini replied with great insistence, 'Your attendance most important … would love to have you if possible also for gala evening'.[19] Unlike the cash-strapped Nixon, Gertrude Ziminsky from B. Altman was able to place orders at the February 1951 event, which seemed to please her employer greatly. The store wrote to Giorgini after the February showings, 'This morning Mrs. Ziminsky returned from her trip full of enthusiasm about the Italian collections. We trust that you will get the things she has bought off by air with all possible effort.'[20]

Word of Italy's fashion success spread. Attendance soared to three hundred buyers and journalists for the second Florence showing, which ran from 19 to 21 July 1951 (see figure 6.1).[21] *Women's Wear Daily* reported

Department store buyers John Nixon of Henry Morgan (wearing bow tie) and Julia Trissel of Bergdorf Goodman (to his right) view a Pucci beach ensemble on the catwalk of Florence's Grand Hotel, July 1951.

breathlessly, 'Florence is seething with excitement over the unexpected influx of American trade, retailers and press representatives for the second High Fashion Show.'[22] Anticipating a larger attendance for this second event, Giorgini secured the use of Florence's Grand Hotel. His gamble paid off, with buyers from New York and San Francisco joined by those from Chicago, Dallas, New Orleans, Philadelphia, Montreal, Zurich, and Johannesburg. With fashions shown over three days by Italy's prominent houses and attendance more than quadruple that of the February showings, the event exceeded expectations. The presence of so many American and mostly female members of the industry must have caused something of a stir in the sleepy city of Florence. An Italian newspaper described their sudden arrival thus: 'very beautiful buyers, dressed *all'Americana*, with corsages, full skirts, embroidered blouses and bare shoulders already tanned from the sun. All beautifully coiffured and made-up, exhaling the faint scent of cologne'.[23] One account declared Bergdorf Goodman's buyer, Julia Trissel, 'the most beautiful American present'.[24]

Not only did the buyers come in greater numbers; from the second Florence show, they also began to place significant orders. In September 1951, the upmarket American magazine *Town and Country* reported on the new Italian designs that were just arriving in stores. Buyers Julia Trissel of Bergdorf Goodman and John Nixon of Henry Morgan both placed a bet on the same Visconti short evening dress; Holt Renfrew of Canada stocked an Alberto Fabiani opera coat; New York's Henri Bendel along with Henry Morgan of Montreal both sold a chic Emilio Schuberth dinner dress; and customers could order Ferragamo shoes through Lord & Taylor.[25] John Nixon chose particularly well that season. Henry Morgan's president, Bartlett Morgan, wrote to Giorgini on 6 September 1951, 'You will be pleased to hear that we started our Fall Fashion Shows yesterday, and they have been a great success. The Italian fashions were well received and continued to make the shows the best we have had so far.'[26]

Building on his success, for the fourth Florentine fashion event, launched on 22 July 1952, Giorgini secured the use of the Sala Bianca (White Hall) in Palazzo Pitti. This former Medici family residence, with its high ceilings bedecked with Murano-glass chandeliers, provided an appropriately dramatic setting for the latest Italian couture and stylish sportswear. For Giorgini – a marketing-minded impresario who printed his invitations with Botticelli portraits, held grand balls in historic locations, and impressed his North American guests by including a dazzling mix of titled Florentine nobility – the Sala Bianca infused his fashion events with just the right dose of Renaissance glamour. This was an association that Giorgini habitually emphasized in promoting the Florentine shows.[27]

Such strategic marketing proved effective

For the spring 1954 season, Bergdorf Goodman invested significantly in Italian fashion goods, in addition to offering its usual French imports and its own made-to-measure collection. The store imported a total of seventy-five European looks from French designers such as Cristobal Balenciaga and Pierre Balmain and their Italian counterparts Simonetta and Fabiani, all 'hand-picked by their buyers Ethel Frankau and Julia Trissel'.[28] Simonetta quickly became a popular designer with high-end retailers in the United States. That season, Bergdorf buyers, along with those from Henri Bendel, B. Altman, and Hattie Carnegie in New York, John Wanamaker in Philadelphia, William Filene's Sons Company in Boston, Marshall Field & Company in Chicago, and I. Magnin in California, all selected and imported her designs.[29] Another designer popular with North American customers was Maria Antonelli, whose spring 1953 gown of tiered white silk organdie with appliquéd pink silk roses received a favourable reception on both coasts. Titled 'Paradise Lost', the gown was for sale in Boston, selected by Carro Krug, the buyer for the Jordan Marsh Company. I. Magnin chose the same gown, which was worn by one guest to the March 1953 fashion ball held at the San Francisco Museum of Art.[30]

Conducting business

A North American buyer of European fashion in the postwar period was a sophisticated professional, often female, who oversaw the selection and importation of hundreds of thousands of dollars worth of merchandise and travelled widely across Europe. As these buyers began to add Italy to their travel schedules in the early 1950s, they found that conducting business in Florence differed from that in other European capitals. In Paris, after a designer presented a collection in her or his own couture salon, stores would place their orders for couture gowns and approved copies. This ritual was repeated by each designer.

When the same buyers arrived in Florence, they found a centralized system, with the fashion show schedule and a corresponding series of parties and entertainments organized and overseen by Giorgini's office. By the January 1953 showings, the process had evolved to include checking in upon arrival in Florence at a central bookings desk, located at the Grand Hotel, which dispensed pre-ordered admission cards to the visiting guests.[31] These guests then attended several days of fashion showings presented on the same catwalk, with one designer's work shown after another. Buyers assessed and committed to memory large quantities of designs, which they then had to recall so that they could submit their orders. From 1952, after a designer had shown their collection on the catwalk, he or she then decamped to the nearby Palazzo Strozzi, which became a kind of fashion bazaar, with dress rails laden with the clothes just presented. Buyers would converge on Palazzo Strozzi to review the clothes once more, discuss quantities and delivery dates, and place orders. Stated one report, 'After the show, buyers wish to review the styles that particularly caught their attention. The models, always smiling, are required to try on the same dresses dozens of times.'[32]

In addition to a centralized presentation format, in Italy buyers found a surprisingly swift production schedule. French fashion houses often required lead times of several months for their orders. In contrast, the Italians could typically deliver within four weeks. With Italian couture prices consistently less than those of Paris models, buyers sensed an efficient bargain. One report of early 1952 stated, 'In Italy, clothes cost approximately half the price of clothes in France ... The stuff of Italian models is duty free. Italian labour is cheap. Artisans still work with love and imagination and they work so fast that an Italian model is ready in a few days, sometimes overnight, whereas in Paris and London you might wait weeks, sometimes months.'[33] This claim of a speedy turnaround of a month or less was echoed in press reports for the following season. *Women's Wear Daily* asserted in July 1952, 'Delivery will be made by mid-August except for some of the complicated evening gowns.'[34]

In addition to Italy's notably competitive prices and swift delivery, buyers also appreciated the Italian approach to hospitality, particularly compared to the 'high prices and high-handedness' of Paris.[35] Faye Hammond, fashion editor of the *Los Angeles Times* and an enthusiastic promoter of Italian fashion, wrote in a letter of 2 August 1954 of 'my beloved Italy' and 'the nicest people in the world' and then continued with disdain, 'The Paris collections are over – Thank God! … One smiles at people here and the result is an icy stare. There must be some nice French people in Paris – but the Haute Couture is sadly lacking in them.'[36] Elizabeth Appenzellar, a Gimbels buyer, credited the Italian houses with a leisurely business attitude and notably courteous personal attention. Appenzellar recalled, 'The luncheon hour lasts from one o'clock to 4 p.m. When once again the doors are unlocked for business and the designers themselves greet their guests, they remember names and are charming hosts.'[37]

It seems probable that the buyers and other guests, who until the third show did not pay an entrance charge to attend the Florentine presentations, paid Giorgini a commission, placing their faith in his connections and on-the-ground ability to expedite their purchases in exchange for a fee.[38] While the author has not yet found evidence of Giorgini's precise role in facilitating transactions, or details of his fees, a five per cent sales commission for his services was referenced in the press of the day.[39] He was occasionally referred to as a 'commissionaire' for department stores, an agent who introduces the purchaser to suppliers and oversees the shipment of merchandise.[40] Giorgini was identified as such in 1951 for the Houston, Texas, store Sakowitz Bros, and credited with 'the responsibility of collecting the Houston orders in his office where he and his daughter (Matilde) inspect and pass on the correctness of the shipment before it is sent out through the port of New York City, or directly through the port of Houston'.[41] A 1953 article also referred to Giorgini as serving this role for I. Magnin. That season, the Florentine was responsible for handling I. Magnin's shipment of Antonelli, Carosa, Schuberth, Simonetta, and Fabiani. These he arranged to be flown to Hollywood, in order to 'give the cinema set a look at Italian high styles for this season'.[42] It is possible that a number of fashion retailers relied on Giorgini in this way.

Just as the Italian fashion presentations were becoming established and buyers had begun to add Florence to their itineraries, they encountered complications: a Roman revolt. By the third Florence show, in January 1952, the Romans Fabiani, Fontana, and Simonetta defected, refusing to come to Florence and electing to show in their own couture salons. Sorelle Fontana was also absent at the following show, in July 1952. While Fabiani and Simonetta occasionally returned to show in Florence, the influential and highly successful Sorelle Fontana never returned.[43] Some stores, if they had enough staff, dealt with the split between Florence and Rome by a 'divide and conquer' approach. For the July 1953 shows, *Women's Wear Daily* reported on I. Magnin's buying staff, 'Mrs. Henrietta Moon, custom salon manager for I. Magnin & Co's San Francisco store, and Miss Stella Hanania, manager of the Beverly Hills unit custom salon, will be in Paris July 26. Miss Hanania will remain in Paris until August 14, but Mrs. Moon accompanied by I. Magnin's Paris representative Mme Odette Tedesco, will be in Rome July 21 and 22, Florence July 23 and 24 and then in London

August 17 and 18.'[44] As this split itinerary suggests, the Roman mutiny forced those department stores that aimed to secure the best choice of merchandise, to send buyers to both cities, causing general irritation.

Adding a new fashion capital on to already busy transcontinental schedules tested stamina as well as patience. The press commented on the physical strain of continuous travel around Europe for buyers who tried to cram viewings of hundreds of models plus quantities of other merchandise within the short four weeks of the main fashion calendar.[45] Italy's complex internal travel logistics meant that Giorgini from the outset had frequently found himself in the role of travel agent, with his office arranging a variety of transport and hotel details for fashion show guests. Because the Florence airport could not accommodate large planes, thus limiting available flight options, for the July 1951 showings, Giorgini even chartered a flight from Florence to Rome for a group of guests who needed to catch a connection to Paris. The transportation was free of charge.[46] The Associated Press assured readers that, 'Dr. Giorgini has made arrangements for small planes to ferry the visitors from Rome's Ciampino airport to Florence the day before the show opens. On the same day he will also have a special express coach on the Rapido (express) train from Rome to Florence for them.'[47] Both the featured designers and retailers took advantage of this service. *Women's Wear Daily* published a photograph of Roman fashion designer Micol Fontana and retailer Hannah Troy alighting from Giorgini's chartered train. For the July 1952 shows, Giorgini again provided rail and air transportation to buyers.[48] By some measure, the lengthy itineraries of a fashion industry professional in the early 1950s mirrored the month-long circus of European and North American fashion weeks today. What differed was that in the 1950s, while air travel was becoming more common, many a buyer still made the transatlantic journey by ship, with a rough 50:50 split in numbers between air and sea. For the fashion industry, always aiming to get ideas to market as quickly as possible, speed is essential. *Women's Wear Daily*, reporting on a common compromise, stated: 'Members of the trade took ships over and flew back to incorporate style ideas in their lines as soon as possible.'[49]

There were other challenges associated with travel to this new fashion city and discomforts were not uncommon. When Giorgini secured the use of the Sala Bianca in Palazzo Pitti for his events, it seemed that he had found a suitably glamorous setting for his twice-yearly fashion presentations. But the grandeur of this elegant room was somewhat deceptive. The audience suffered inside, whether from the heat of summer or the chill of winter. For North American buyers, accustomed to air conditioning and central heating, it was often physically uncomfortable. *Women's Wear Daily* reported from the July 1952 showings, 'Because of the humid heat here, buyers are attending showings in beachwear; many men are coatless and tieless.'[50] At the January 1953 presentation the buyers shivered in the

cold of a fog-bound Palazzo Pitti, at least until the temporary heating appa-
ratus partly functioned.[51] A press release issued in early 1953 promised an
improved experience, declaring, 'You will be interested to hear that they
are working right now to install air-conditioning in Palazzo Pitti.'[52] Lack
of accommodation was another source of concern. In the early 1950s, the
influx of industry representatives into the small and somewhat unprepared
city of Florence resulted in an accommodation shortage, solved only by
'arranging with Florentines to take the overflow into their private villas and
lovely old *palazzo* homes'.[53]

Giorgini must have sensed that these world-weary travellers needed to be
properly fêted. To smooth any feathers ruffled by tiresome logistics, guests
were plied with elaborate entertainments. In the first few years of the Florence
showings these included formal suppers in the gardens of Giorgini's villa, a
cocktail party hosted by the American Consul General of Florence, a grand
ball in the Boboli Gardens, a performance of the Verdi opera Il Trovatore at
the Florence opera house, and a re-enactment of the 1784 wedding reception
for Princess Eleonora de' Medici, complete with actors in historical costume.
These entertainments remained an effective tool in courting contacts and
good press. Miriam Lippincott, the buyer for Carson Pirie Scott in Chicago,
wrote to thank Giorgini in January 1952 for 'the opportunity of going to the
receptions and especially the ball that you gave'.[54] In August 1952, the *Los
Angeles Times* fashion editor Fay Hammond wrote:

> Looking back on a summer in Europe ... the Boboli Ball seems even less real
> now than it did on that magic night in Italy when the international fashion
> press, buyers from all parts of the world and Florentine society mingled in the
> moonlit gardens of the Pitti Palace ... No royal entertainment has surpassed
> this unforgettable scene.[55]

The North American buyers and their counterparts in the press took great
delight in mixing work and pleasure in their business trips to Italy. Sally
Kirkland, a journalist for *Time* and *Life*, wrote, 'As a matter of fact, we had
quite a gay time in Portofino, as well as a successful one professionally.'[56]
For foreign visitors to Italy, there was no shortage of amusements.

When the fashion pack arrived in Italy, they found that the Italian
designers differed from their French counterparts in not only how they
presented their collections and received their guests but also how they
regarded and defined categories of fashion. While the French Chambre
Syndicale de la Couture Parisienne operated a rigorous system of defining couture or made-to-measure designs, monitoring its presentations,
regulating its production, and protecting its copyright, the Italians had a
less hierarchical approach.[57] At the first Florence show in February 1951,
buyers viewed couture cocktail dresses and eveningwear shown alongside shorts and beachwear designs. The invitation to the second Florence
show of July 1951 neatly divided the designs that were to be shown into

two categories: 'High Fashion' and 'Sportswear and Boutique', with some designers, such as Simonetta, showing both.[58]

Stores that were at first importing Italian couture gowns for their clients, were soon also importing large quantities of Italian sportswear and so-called 'boutique' clothing, terms that were used interchangeably to refer to informal yet stylish, semi-industrially-produced, lower-priced designs. The *New York Times* reported in 1953, 'Italian boutique designs, one of the most widely copied and exported items of the Italian fashion industry, continued to be inventive this year. Many buyers ... felt that boutique and sportswear should have received foremost place in the exhibition, surpassing "alta moda".'[59] The previous year, *Time* stated, 'As usual, the Italians were at their best in sportswear and plain clothes ... Said one California department store buyer, "The entire American sports world should be here!"'[60] Within a few years, press reports confirmed sportswear as Italy's most important fashion category. In 1956, the *Chicago Daily Tribune* declared, 'Season after season, the real strength of Italian fashion comes from the sports and casualwear market. The great number of export sales are made in this field, where inspiration comes from Italy's sunny atmosphere.'[61]

By the middle of the decade, Italian ready-to-wear clothing seemed the ideal solution to the American consumer's increasingly casual lifestyle. A *Women's Wear Daily* 1956 headline declared, 'Italy Boutique Items Termed High Fashion', and stated:

> Italian boutique collections are now high fashion, American retailers say as they wind up their work at the 11th Florence fashion showings and push on to Paris. Boutique merchandise, including coats, suits, dresses, skirts and sweaters were big favorites of United States retailers and Seventh Avenue coat, suit and sportswear manufacturers.[62]

Five years after Giorgini's first show, the popularity of these less formal clothes, produced in quantity, had eclipsed the demand for Italian couture originals.

I. Magnin: a case study

A leading importer of both Italian couture and sportswear was I. Magnin, the West Coast's premier department store chain. In 1950 I. Magnin's seven stores and net sales of $31 million made it the leading purveyor of high fashion in California and neighbouring states. The company was founded in San Francisco in 1876 by Dutch émigré Mary Ann Magnin. It evolved from a 'notions' store selling sewing supplies into a purveyor of fashionable clothing. In 1904, the company placed its first orders for European imports.[63] By the early 1950s, I. Magnin's purchasing power was sizeable; its orders could make or break a designer's career. In the first half of the 1950s, its branch with the highest net sales – the elegant store on San Francisco's Union Square – had months when sales totalled well over a million dollars (see figure 6.2).[64] It is not surprising that I. Magnin buyers were always warmly welcomed in Europe.

Oval millinery salon in San Francisco's I. Magnin and Co. store, c. 1948.   **6.2**

I. Magnin prided itself on the buying acumen of its staff. A surviving document, in the form of a television documentary transcript, explains I. Magnin's business approach. Though the transcript dates from a decade later than the period of focus here, it provides a window into the unusual career of the department store buyer, which typically could not be prepared for through academic study, but relied upon on-the-job training, a personable manner, and a strong work ethic. The document describes I. Magnin's 'through the chairs' path to promotion. A buyer would usually start in sales, graduating from selling assistant to full time assistant and would then be assigned to a branch store as a manager for a group of departments. 'The next job', it states, 'could be a buyer's job.' In 1969, a top I. Magnin buyer made a salary of $35,000 per year, and was responsible for annual merchandise purchases totalling between $300,000 and $5 million. The document cites an I. Magnin buyer's key responsibilities as 'selling of merchandise profitably', 'purchasing stock for each store', and also undertaking market trips, both domestic and European.[65]

Chapter 7 in this volume identifies key individuals within the Boston specialty store, Filene's, which was particularly influential. A similarly influential member of I. Magnin's staff during the 1950s was its director Hector Escobosa, who, at age forty-three, took over from the last member of the Magnin family, when Grover Magnin retired in 1951 (see figure 6.3).[66]

Hector Escobosa, President of I. Magnin, 1951.

The Arizona-born Escobosa's career trajectory indicates a common path in the retail profession. Beginning as a window dresser for the San Francisco store Emporium, Escobosa then worked in sales promotion and dress buying at the California four-store chain Hale Brothers, while studying at the University of California. He then served as a vice president for The Jones Store Company in Kansas City and left to head the Seattle department store Frederick & Nelson. Acknowledging his dual role as both merchant and financial watchman, upon his I. Magnin appointment, Escobosa declared, 'I'm not just interested in chiffons and brocades. I'm here to build up a strong sales policy.'[67]

Escobosa arrived at I. Magnin just in time to respond to Giorgini's invitation to send a company representative to the first Florence fashion show. In January 1951, Escobosa, responding to the invitation to attend the Florence showings, wrote to Giorgini, 'Of all the cities in the world which we visited, yours is our favorite one. We hope that before 1951 is over we shall have the pleasure of visiting with you.'[68] This letter inaugurated I. Magnin's determined pursuit of Italian fashion imports and solidified what would become one of Giorgini's most fruitful and enduring department store relationships.[69] Escobosa chose I. Magnin's influential and long serving fashion staffer, Stella Hanania, affectionately known to clients and colleagues as 'Miss Stella', to attend Giorgini's first show. In I. Magnin's employ from 1940 until her retirement in 1976, Hanania ran the Custom-Made Department in the Los Angeles store, presiding over a cadre of trained seamstresses, who realized Hanania's own designs for key clients and also produced I. Magnin's authorized copies of couture originals (see figure 6.4). Hanania's first Italian buying trip seems to have been an enjoyable success. She wrote to Giorgini on 12 March 1951 in reference to the Florence event, 'I want you to know how very much I enjoyed meeting you and your wonderful family ... thank you for all your kindness to me during my stay in your beautiful city – I regret very much that my visit was short.' She continued:

> I am very happy with the result – the trunks arrived in time to be shown with the French collection. They [couture designs] looked very beautiful and were very well received by everyone. I know you will be pleased to hear that. So will the 'Four Ladies' that were responsible for making them. Please thank them for me and give them my kindest regards.[70]

The 'Four Ladies' that Hanania referred to were Simonetta Visconti, the Fontana sisters, Jole Veneziani, and the house of Vanna. Hanania's first Italian selections proved that she understood the market she served, justifying her boss's faith in her to represent I. Magnin in Florence. *Women's Wear Daily* reported in March 1951 that the clothes were presented in an I. Magnin trunk show at the Los Angeles store in March 1951 as part of a 'well-edited spring collection ... made up of Paris originals, I. Magnin's

6.4   Christian Dior (centre) with I. Magnin buyer Stella Hanania (to his left) and director Hector Escobosa (to Hanania's left). Undated photograph, probably 1957.

own designer originals ... and of a group of Italian models included in this store's collection now for the first time'.[71] It is notable that the Italian designs were described as being included 'for the first time', clearly an important element in marketing them.

Hanania's first Italian imports included a Fontana red silk taffeta sleeveless evening dress; a Veneziani checked wool dress with half peplum; and Vanna's long evening gown of mauve-pink silk jersey. The same *Women's Wear Daily* article highlighted a standout design by

Simonetta, describing it as a 'lounging ensemble, with black satin boxy jacket embroidered in pearls and gold worn over tight black trousers in mid-calf length and a sleeveless top with embroidered deeply cuffed décolleté'. Since trousers for women were then often worn for casual or resort wear, their selection by I. Magnin would have been in keeping with California's less-formal dress code, the so-called 'California casual' approach that favoured informal clothing suited to a warmer climate, and to sport and outdoor pursuits.

After Hanania's first Florence foray, I. Magnin continued to invest heavily in the Italian collections. At the fourth Florence show of July 1952, they purchased forty-five Italian models and arranged a fashion show to celebrate the shipment's arrival in California.[72] The *Los Angeles Times* reported,

> The most exciting and important fashions of the French and Italian collections are in LA today, just a matter of weeks after the first model stepped out on the runway in Florence ... I. Magnin & Co. will unveil their beautiful imports this noontime at Perino's and their astonishing selection, screened from literally hundreds of styles and designers, is a tribute to the unerring taste of the firm's buyers.[73]

A separate *Los Angeles Times* article suggested the excitement of I. Magnin buyers about their Italian fashion imports. The article quoted store vice president Russel Carpenter's views that 'The Italians ... are not style creators like the French – nor (as has been claimed) are they French copyists either. Sticking to simple lines, they expend their creative energies on superb fabrics and beautiful ornamentation.'[74]

That season, I. Magnin would carry a dress by Schuberth of oyster satin, graduating to gray, overlaid with black lace appliqués. Its price of $895 was on the high end for Italian couture that season, though, according to the same *Los Angeles Times* article, the dress was 'cheap at the price believe it or not, when you consider the fantastic amount and quality of needlework that have gone into it'.[75] Automobile heiress Thelma Chrysler Foy purchased this Schuberth design but in a bolder colour palette of fuchsia pink shading to rose with the same black lace appliqué; the gown is now in the permanent collection of the Metropolitan Museum of Art (see figure 6.5). The British edition of *Harper's Bazaar* published a photograph of a similar dress from that same collection in November 1952. The magazine described the dress as featuring, 'the pinks of wine from rosé to deep claret, seen through grilles of black lace ... a really remarkable sight on the dance floor'.[76]

A highly experienced fashion professional, Hanania was a skilled couture technician with a buyer's sure sense of her customer's needs. Born in Beirut, Hanania learned to sew at the age of six, while living at a convent. From there she went to Paris, and then travelled to New York

6.5   Silk satin evening gown with cotton lace, autumn–winter 1952–53, designed by Emilio Schuberth.

where she worked in Bergdorf Goodman's couture salon from 1936 to 1940.[77] She subsequently moved to Los Angeles and began working at I. Magnin. As the head of I. Magnin's Custom-Made Department, Hanania was in firm control of the custom workroom. In addition to travelling to the European collections, she also completed her own seasonal designs and oversaw the authorized reproduction of 'the highest ranking' European designer originals. I. Magnin often showed Hanania's Custom Originals

Models inside I. Magnin's San Francisco store wearing couture evening gowns, c. 1950.   **6.6**

alongside the imported European haute couture designs at invitation-only fashion presentations within the Los Angeles and San Francisco stores (see figure 6.6). At these events, the customer would select her designs and fabrics. Then a series of fittings would be completed on the customer's individual dressmaker's form, with one fitting in person, and after a typical eight to ten-week timescale, the workroom staff completed the finished garment.[78]

Hanania was by all accounts devoted to her work. Because of her talent and decades of service she enjoyed longstanding customer loyalty and a higher profile than many of her colleagues. Hanania's reputation was such that her retirement in the 1970s prompted a front-page article in the *Los Angeles Times*. This nostalgic honouring of the buyer's thirty-five years at I. Magnin described Hanania as the last employee of a major department store to 'make clothes to order in the style of couture'and announced that her departure would occasion the permanent closure of the company's Custom-Made Department.[79]

As the 1950s American consumer began to demand, with increasing insistence, a varied wardrobe of stylish yet practical clothes, skilled buyers like Stella Hanania understood immediately the appeal of Italy's inventive and less formal high fashion and sportswear. For the spring 1955 season, I. Magnin ordered $40,000 in Italian knitwear alone.[80] Hector Escobosa summed up this market shift when commenting on one Italian designer's sportswear collection: 'I can visualize them on American women in the mountains on long automobile trips, at home on chilly evenings and even in the street for walking the dog or the baby.'[81] This kind of enthusiastic praise from North American merchants, along with their custom, spurred Italian designers and manufacturers to further develop their readymade clothes offerings in the subsequent decade. A seemingly routine observation by *Women's Wear Daily* in 1955 confirmed the seismic shift that was already underway: 'Buying office representatives for international accounts opine that the development of the Italian market has developed all European markets because Italy was the first to demonstrate quantity business was possible.'[82] Italian designer ready-to-wear was becoming the new fashion language.

Conclusion

By 1955, the Italian ready-to-wear industry and the Made in Italy campaign that would help to promote it were just visible on the horizon, thanks in large part to the merchandise choices of North American department store buyers. As this chapter has shown, these historically anonymous tastemakers were important agents of commerce within the history of fashion. By peopling the story of mid-century American retailing with identified, named figures; by illuminating the details of their semi-obscured work lives; by recording their buying selections and chronicling how they conducted business in Italy in the early 1950s, we can conclude that these buyers influenced directly not just the wardrobes of their customers, but also the development of one European country's nascent fashion industry.

Notes

1 N. Troy, *Couture Culture: A Study in Modern Art and Fashion* (Cambridge, MA: MIT Press, 2003), p. 248.
2 A. Palmer, *Couture and Commerce: The Transatlantic Fashion Trade in the 1950s* (Vancouver, BC: University of British Columbia Press, 2001), p. 18.
3 Palmer, *Couture and Commerce*, p. 8.
4 See R. L. Blaszczyk, *Imagining Consumers: Design and Innovation from Wedgwood to Corning* (Baltimore: Johns Hopkins University Press, 2000).
5 Virtually all of the press and magazine articles cited in this chapter were accessed in the Giovanni Battista Giorgini Archive (hereafter GBGA), itself in the Archivio di Stato in Florence, Italy. I would like to thank the archive's helpful staff, and acknowledge the importance and usefulness of this resource.
6 E. Scarpellini, *Material Nation: A Consumer's History of Modern Italy* (Oxford: Oxford University Press, 2011); E. Paulicelli, *Fashion Under Fascism: Beyond the Black Shirt* (Oxford and New York: Berg, 2004); and M. Lupano and A. Vaccari, *Fashion at the Time of Fascism* (Bologna: Damiani, 2009).
7 N. White, *Reconstructing Italian Fashion: America and the Development of the Fashion Industry* (Oxford: Bloomsbury, 2000).
8 GBGA, ALB 2/12, Giorgini to B. Altman, 9 January 1951.
9 GBGA, ALB 3/1, Introduction, souvenir notebook produced by Giorgini, *Second Italian High Fashion Show Organized and Sponsored by G.B. Giorgini for Foreign Firms Presented in Florence on the 19th, 20th and 21st of July 1951*. The notebook's introduction describes Giovanni Battista Giorgini's ancestors thus: 'Senator Giorgini, friend and counsellor of Cavour, son-in-law of Alessandro Manzoni and brother-in-

law of Massimo d'Azeglio, was one of the deputies of the first legation and the author of the laws for the Independence of Italy. His brother, Colonel Giorgini, Commander of the Fort of Talamone, supplied Garibaldi with the arms he required for launching of his famous 'Mille' expedition for the freedom of Sicily and Southern Italy. The third brother Carlo, grandfather of Signor Giorgini, was a volunteer in the glorious Tuscan University Battalion during the Italian War of Independence in 1848.

10 *Ibid.*

11 L. Pagliai, *La Firenze di Giovanni Battista Giorgini* (Florence: OMA, 2011), chap. 2.

12 The items selected included glassware from Empoli, ceramics by Guido Gambone and Zaccagnini, linen and embroideries by Emilia Paoli, and textiles by Tessitura di Rovezzano di Maria Antonietta. Pagliai, *La Firenze di Giovanni Battista Giorgini*, p. 60.

13 GBGA, ALB 2/7, Giorgini to Rogers, 15 September 1950.

14 According to fashion editor Eugenia Sheppard, Paris designers subsequently gave the Florence spring/summer 1951 showings the 'official pat on the back' by allowing Italian designers to show their collections before the French. 'Fine Italian fashions to make bid for fame', *New York Herald Tribune* (28 March 1951).

15 G. Malossi (ed.), *The Sala Bianca: The Birth of Italian Fashion* (Milan: Electa, 1992), p. 14.

16 According to *Harper's Bazaar* fashion editor Carmel Snow, 'a frock in Italy costs about a third of the French pieces'. 'Italian fashion special report', *New York Journal American* (16 February 1953).

17 GBGA, ALB 2/15, B. Altman to Giorgini, 20 January 1951.

18 GBGA, ALB 2/18, Nixon to Giorgini, 6 February 1951.

19 GBGA, ALB 2/19, undated draft, Giorgini to Nixon.

20 GBGA, ALB 2/36, B. Altman to Giorgini, February 1951.

21 'L'esposizione della moda a Firenze', *Il Globo* (28 July 1951).

22 'First arrivals at Italian fashion openings', *Women's Wear Daily* (19 July 1951).

23 'La Moda Italiana Va in America', *Settimo Giorno* (2 August 1951).

24 GBGA, ALB 2/41A, unattributed newspaper article.

25 'Florence in Fashion', *Town and Country* (September 1951).

26 GBGA, ALB 3/13D, Morgan to Giorgini, 6 September 1951.

27 C. M. Belfanti, 'History as an intangible asset for the Italian fashion business (1950–1954)', *Journal of Historical Research in Marketing*, 7:1 (2015), 74–90.

28 Untitled, *New York Herald Tribune* (19 March 1953).

29 GBGA, ALB 10 press release no. 4, undated (probably November 1952).

30 Untitled, *Women's Wear Daily* (3 March 1953).

31 GBGA, ALB 10, undated press release issued by Giorgini's office (probably November 1952).

32 GBGA, ALB 9/443, untitled article *Le Ore* (Milan) (6 February 1954).

33 'Report on Italian fashion', *Picture Post* (1 March 1952).

34 'Italian showings in Florence open', *Women's Wear Daily* (22 July 1952).

35 'Italy's Renaissance', *Time* (4 February 1952).

36 GBGA, ALB 11/84, Hammond to Giorgini, 2 August 1954.

37 Untitled, *New York Mirror* (3 May 1953).

38 GBGA, ALB 4/1, The invitation to the third Florence showing stated, 'Admission fee $100.00 per Firm'.

39 'Italy's Renaissance'.

40 V. Pouillard, 'Design piracy in the fashion industries of Paris and New York in the interwar years', *Business History Review*, 85:2 (summer 2001), 323.

41 'Italian fashion organizer visits Houston', *Houston Chronicle* (16 November 1951).

42 'Flying in the face of Dior', *Daily American* (14 August 1953).

43 For a summary of which designers showed in Florence from 1951 to 1957, see Pagliai, *La Firenze di Giovanni Battista Giorgini*, p. 106.

44 'The fourth Italian high fashion show', *Women's Wear Daily* (15 July 1953).

45 'European couturiers ready: openings of spring styles', *Women's Wear Daily* (28 October 1952).

46 'G.B. Giorgini welcomes all to Florence show', *Daily American* (21 July 1951).

47 'The Third Italian high fashion show, Grand Hotel', *Associated Press* (31 December 1951).

48 Untitled, *Women's Wear Daily* (1 June 1952).

49 'Heavy attendance for couture showing', *Women's Wear Daily* (16 July 1951).

50 'Italian showings in Florence open', *Women's Wear Daily* (22 July 1952).

51 Untitled, *Women's Wear Daily* (25 January 1953).

52 GBGA, ALB 10, press release no. 2, undated (probably January 1953).

53 'Fashion buyers flocking to Florence, pack hotels and villas', *Women's Wear Daily* (19 July 1952).

54 GBGA, ALB 4/176, Lippincott to Giorgini, 27 January 1952.

55 Untitled, *Los Angeles Times* (4 August 1952).

56 GBGA, ALB 11/60, Kirkland to Giorgini, 27 August 1954.

57 For a summary of this process, see Palmer, *Couture and Commerce*.

58 GBGA, ALB 3/2, Fashion show invitation, July 1951.

59 'Many buyers at Florence show put boutique and sportswear ahead of the "Alta Moda"', *New York Times* (6 August 1953).

60 'Italy's Renaissance'.

61 'Italians again provide chic in sports wear', *Chicago Daily Tribune* (27 January 1956).

62 'Italy boutique items termed high fashion', *Women's Wear Daily* (26 January 1956).

63 San Francisco Public Library, San Francisco History Center (hereafter SFHC), I. Magnin & Co. Records (SFH 2), box 1, folder 3, 'I. Magnin and Company: A Brief History', 1949.

64 SFHC, I. Magnin & Co. Records (SFH 2), box 2, folder 3, Sales Records, 1950–53.

65 SFHC, I. Magnin & Co. Records (SFH 2), box 1, folder 3, 1969 Transcript.

66 SFHC, I. Magnin & Co. Records (SFH 2), box 1, folder 22, Minutes of I. Magnin Board Meeting, 2 January 1951. Hector Escobosa was appointed as I. Magnin's director and elected as president.

67 'Retail trade: short haired merchant', *Time* (15 January 1951).

68 GBGA, ALB 2/16, Escobosa to Giorgini (probably January 1951).

69 I. Magnin first worked with Giorgini in the late 1940s, buying from his Milan shop, La Bottega del Ridotto, which specialized in furniture, arts and crafts, ceramics, and also some clothing and accessories. It is not clear what merchandise I. Magnin purchased from the store, or in what quantity. Pagliai, *La Firenze de Giovanni Battista Giorgini*, p. 64.

70 GBGA, ALB 2/37, Hanania to Giorgini, 12 March 1951.

71 'Imports from Italy at I. Magnin', *Women's Wear Daily* (7 March 1951).

72 'Italian showings in Florence open', *Women's Wear Daily* (22 July 1952).

73 'I. Magnin's present exciting French & Italian fashions today', *Los Angeles Times* (8 September 1952).

74 'In colors and workmanship the Italians can't be surpassed', *Los Angeles Times* (5 September 1952).

75 *Ibid*.

76 'Italian evenings', *Harper's Bazaar* (November 1952), 55.

77 'Miss Stella on fashion and style', *Women's Wear Daily/California* (16 August 1983).

78 'The custom-made workroom', *Magnin Newscast* (June 1944).

79 'Miss Stella steps down at the top', *Los Angeles Times* (21 November 1976).
80 GBGA, ALB 13/4, Memo, Il Centro Firenze della moda Italiana (probably January 1955).
81 'I. Magnin president Hector Escobosa writes a column from Florence shows', *Los Angeles Examiner* (27 January 1955).
82 'Buyers arrive in Florence for openings', *Women's Wear Daily* (21 July 1955).

7

The rise and fall of European fashion at Filene's in Boston

Regina Lee Blaszczyk

For three weeks in the early autumn of 1953, the store of William Filene's Sons Company in downtown Boston put on the largest fashion promotion in its history. Sponsored in collaboration with partners such as Pan American World Airways, the International Fashionations Fair displayed imported clothing for men, women, and children from thirty-one countries around the world, including Belgium, Canada, France, Great Britain, Ireland, Israel, Italy, Spain, and Switzerland, alongside American merchandise. The promotion publicized a $5 million, two-year store expansion undertaken in 1951, the new role of air cargo in international commerce, and Filene's longstanding commitment to global style. Filene's was America's largest specialty store for fashion, and Pan Am was the Miami-based airline that pioneered commercial flight across the Atlantic Ocean. Fashionations was a collaboration made in international fashion heaven.[1]

The fair celebrated the role of fashion in the revival of trade among nations after World War II by dramatizing the theme of 'fashion time around the world'. The event was launched at Grand Central Station in New York City, from whence a special train, the Filene Fashionations Flyer, transported an assemblage of diplomats, European and American designers, business leaders, and journalists to Boston for a day of red-carpet events.[2] The main attraction was the Pan American International Fashion Collection, selected by Filene's sales promotion manager Harriet Wilinsky during her visit to the European couture openings and flown across the Atlantic Ocean by Pan Am. The collection was comprised of ball gowns by five 'fashion ambassadors' from the world's fashion capitals: Pierre Balmain of Paris, Norman Hartnell of London, Sybil Connolly of Dublin, Pedro Rodriguez of Barcelona, and Alberto Fabiani of Rome. Pan Am later displayed these couture originals in its Fifth Avenue showroom and flew them to other American cities to be used in fashion and travel promotions by the local upmarket retailer.[3]

Fashionations was designed to whet consumers' appetites for European style. Many Bostonians were proud of their Puritan heritage, but New England was also home to many hyphenated Americans who traced their roots to Southern, Central, and Eastern Europe. The Italian-American shopper from Boston's North End could celebrate her Old World heritage by purchasing a ready-to-wear outfit for Sunday best from Filene's 'special "Fashionations" merchandise – made in America and reflecting foreign influence in inspiration or in use of imported fabric'.[4] In collaboration with Filene's, the 'ingenious makers of American fashions' had combined their 'great mass-producing skills' with 'rich inspiration from the whole world' to produce merchandise at 'moderate prices'.[5] 'Volume-priced' fashions designed after original European couture models brought profits to the store and satisfied consumers who wanted affordable apparel that had been 'inspired abroad'.[6]

However, American consumers were a feisty lot who decided on styles for themselves and made it difficult for retailers to keep up. From Filene's early days, Boston shoppers exhibited a taste for edgy looks that sent the buyers scampering around the world's fashion capitals in search of novelty. Evidence in the Filene's marketing archive shows postwar consumers turning their backs on European fashion dictates in favour of practical, comfortable apparel. The archive also illuminates the cultural gap between store managers like Wilinsky, who revered the European fashion system, and the realities of American consumer society, where the individual set her own style based on attitude, lifestyle, and price. In the end, European imports lost their cachet with Filene's customers, particularly with the career woman who wanted affordable easy-going styles for work and play.

In the twenty-first century, a small group of curators have examined the reception of European haute couture in North America, with reference to retailers, elite consumers, and the materiality of the garments. Alexandra Palmer considers how taste and prestige figured into the dress choices of wealthy women in Toronto, Canada, and the high-end stores that catered to them.[7] The research in this chapter builds on the object-driven scholarship of curators such as Palmer, Dilys Blum, Timothy A. Long, Sonnet Stanfill, and Valerie Steele to offer another viewpoint and illuminate a different set of questions.[8]

This case study examines how America's largest fashion retailer integrated European imports into store promotions aimed to reach consumers at all price points. It focuses on the retail professionals who brought European fashion merchandise to the United States and created mechanisms for the dissemination of European style. Elsewhere, I have analysed the important role of 'fashion intermediaries' as the vital links between producers and consumers.[9] Here that cultural analysis is extended to the

activities of retail buying, fashion merchandising, and fashion promotion. The focus is on a key group of intermediaries – the buyers, stylists,
fashion directors, merchandisers, and managers at Filene's – who harnessed European prestige to sell fashion merchandise made at home and
abroad to American consumers. These efforts produced successes such as
Fashionations – until major social and cultural shifts upset the apple cart.

Filene's machine-made frocks and other fashion firsts

William Filene's Sons Company was incorporated on 20 August 1912,
by the brothers Edward A. Filene and A. Lincoln Filene, along with a
small number of investors, including the merchandizing wizard Louis E.
Kirstein.[10] The siblings had learned the dry-goods and clothing trade from
their father, William Filene, the former Wilhelm Katz, a Jewish immigrant
from Posen, Germany. Upon the elder's retirement in 1890, the brothers
took charge of the family business, William Filene and Company, whose
upmarket Washington Street store sold 'Fancy Goods and Women's Ready-
to-Wear' to the carriage trade. The business was eventually renamed
William Filene's Sons Company. The rapid growth of the garment industry
in Boston and New York led the brothers to make the strategic decision to
expand their profits through quick turnover, and no merchandise promised
to move faster than ladies' fashion. But if it were to sell fashion in volume,
Filene's had to overcome the cultural bias against machine-made apparel.
To allay customers' anxieties, the store capitalized on its upmarket reputation and promoted ready-to-wear as a quality product. Filene's shook up
Boston's conservative retailing scene when it became the first store in the
city to sell machine-made dresses, alongside the usual American dry goods
and more exotic European style merchandise selected by Edward Filene
on his annual overseas buying trip.[11] In September 1912, the firm opened
a stupendous showcase store on Washington Street, which due to the competition Filene's had spurred, had become a bustling shopping district.[12]
Women's Wear, the New York-based daily newspaper for the American
apparel trade, took note of Filene's impressive eight-storey edifice with
access to the Boston subway line (see figure 7.1). The Renaissance Revival
building was designed by the distinguished Chicago architectural firm
of Daniel H. Burnham, which had recently created a stunning palace of
consumption for John Wanamaker, an upmarket retailer in Philadelphia.[13]

   In 1910, Boston had a population of 687,000 people and was the fifth
largest city in the United States after New York, Chicago, Philadelphia, and
St. Louis.[14] Long known as 'The Hub of the Universe', it was the financial,
commercial, cultural, and educational centre for the six New England
states: Connecticut, New Hampshire, Maine, Massachusetts, Rhode
Island, and Vermont. The regional economy was based on manufacturing,
and some of America's most important textile mills were located in cities

THE NEW FILENE STORE,
BOSTON, U. S. A.

In September 1912, William Filene's Sons Company opened a stupendous new store designed by   **7.1**
the architect Daniel H. Burnham, who created similar palaces of consumption for Marshall Field &
Company in Chicago and John Wanamaker in Philadelphia. Note the show windows filled with
fashion at street level. Filene's sometimes put fashion in the upper storeys and illuminated all the
windows for stunning night-time effects.

such as Chicopee, Lawrence, Lowell, and Manchester. Fortunes made in finance, international trade, manufacturing, and transportation benefited Boston-area institutions such as Harvard University, the Massachusetts Institute of Technology, the Museum of Fine Arts, Symphony Hall, and Trinity Church. Besides being a commercial and cultural hub, Boston was also the shopping mecca for New England. The city's many newspapers stimulated readers' appetites for fashion by regaling them with Parisian highlights: the gowns worn by actresses and princesses, the new furs and millinery, and Americans browsing at the famous Bon Marché department store.[15] Consumers from upmarket neighbourhoods such as Beacon Hill and the Back Bay and middle-class streetcar suburbs such as Brookline and Chestnut Hill flocked downtown to shop. An extensive railroad network connected Boston to the rest of New England. Local stores met consumers' everyday needs, but a major wardrobe purchase, such as a winter coat or an Easter outfit, necessitated a special trip to Boston.

Today, Boston has several retail hot spots, including the enclosed mall at the Prudential Center, the Newbury Street luxury zone, and the Downtown Crossing shopping district on Washington Street. In the early twentieth century, the first two of these retail destinations did not exist, and Washington Street was the go-to place for browsing or buying. Filene's rivals included the Jordan Marsh Company, a fully-fledged department store that sold a wide variety of goods: fashion, dry goods, wall coverings, toys, books, umbrellas, clocks and watches, household goods, and more (see figure 7.2).[16] At the start of each season, Jordan's windows tempted

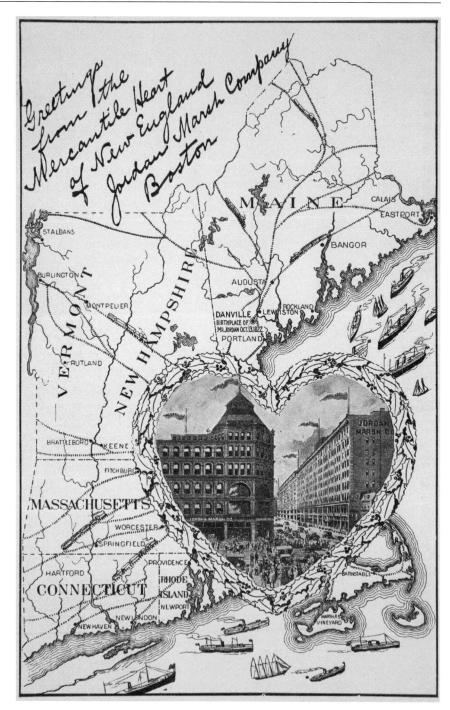

Filene's great rival, the Jordan Marsh Company, was a fully-fledged department store that stocked a wide selection of merchandise meant to attract shoppers from around New England.

shoppers with life-sized mannequins wearing the latest gowns from Berlin, Paris, and London, along with 'the proper shoes, stockings, gloves, and neckwear'.[17] A smaller competitor was the E. T. Slattery Company, founded by a dressmaker in 1867. Slattery's was a fashion emporium that sold apparel from little specialty shops, or boutiques, within the store.[18] Filene's expropriated and refined the shops-in-store concept – using a decentralized organizational structure to set up each individual shop as a self-contained financial unit that was responsible for its own turnover and profits – to create a sensational fashion paradise that was more ambitious than anything Boston had ever seen.[19]

Filene's was entirely dedicated to fashion merchandise, and when the new Burnham Building opened in 1912, the company was reported to be the greatest apparel retailer in the world with 900 employees and annual sales of $5 million.[20] The focus on fashion set Filene's apart from the department stores that have been the subject of much historical research. *Women's Wear* explained: 'The new Filene store is big enough to be called a department store, and it will probably be so generally described … The new store is a development of the department store idea along specialty lines … In this advanced class there are very few as yet.'[21] In one customer booklet, Filene's explained why it was different. 'Filene's is NOT a Department Store. Filene's sells almost entirely wearing apparel and accessories, grouped in small specialty shops. It is probably the largest store in America devoted to the personal outfitting of women, children and men.'[22] Filene's was the model for other specialty fashion retailers that are still in operation in New York City today: Lord & Taylor, which moved from Ladies' Mile on Broadway to Fifth Avenue in 1914; Bergdorf Goodman, which operated in different Fifth Avenue locations from 1914; and Saks Fifth Avenue, established in 1924. Filene's differed from these elite Manhattan retailers because it catered to consumers up and down the social ladder. Filene's inclusive merchandising strategy helped to democratize fashion in Boston and, because of the city's role as a regional shopping destination, to extend fashion's reach to consumers throughout New England.

From the start, the new Filene's store tried to capture and tame the elusive animal that was its lifeblood: fashion. In 1913, the head of the women's cloak and suit department described the challenges to the buyers. In his opinion, 'the American woman cares more for style than for any other one thing in buying clothes'. In response, the buyers had to prioritize fashion over other factors: 'style first, then quality, and next price'. Long before Zara and Primark 'invented' fast fashion, American women pressed American retailers for more styles and better styles. These early fashionistas did not give 'a second thought to whether a garment will wear two seasons'; they wanted things in the 'very latest mode'. American ready-to-wear, including Filene's machine-made dresses, answered this

The Filene Machine=Made Wash Dresses for 1908

Styles for Women—1.00 to 7.50, No Higher. Styles changed constantly

7.50

New Wm. Anderson gingham dresses—the newest circular skirt, with fold giving the fashionable tunic effect—trimming is entirely new—this dress is a novelty shown for the first time, blue and white, and pink and white, piped with bias folds of dotted percale, sizes 32, 34 and 36, with 35, 27 and 39 inch skirts.

At 7.50—A dress similar to above, in D & J. Anderson ginghams, patterns seen for the first time, and just received from Scotland by us, in stripes and plaids.

7.50

A novelty dress of "Grecian" striped lawn, showing a new idea in the butterfly sleeve, new skirt — made in princess style with new torchon lace trimming, blue and white, brown and white and pink and white. Sizes 32 to 40.

3.95

New design in two piece chambray dress—waist is trimmed with tucking and bands of self material, piped with contrasting color and outlined with French knots. Full seven-gored tucked skirt, with one fold at bottom —this model is made in light blue, pink, tan, and green. Sizes 32 to 42.

Many Other Styles in Machine=Made Dresses not advertised here

7.3   Filene's helped to democratize fashion among New England consumers by introducing washable ready-to-wear dresses. These affordable outfits were created by 'designers of the highest type dresses', 'cut out with long knives by electricity', and 'made by the thousands and all by machine'. The cloth was 'brought from the mills in bolts, saving many cents on every dress', and the 'styles and materials' were 'changed constantly, so that the dresses do not become common'. *Annual Advance Sale of Spring Novelties in Filene Machine-Made Wash Dresses* (Boston: William Filene's Sons Company, 1908).

demand – to a degree (see figure 7.3). Although affordable, American designs lacked *je ne sais quoi*, the 'indefinable touch' that gave 'individuality to garments produced abroad'.[23]

One way to get the fashion edge was to go style-hunting in the streets and showrooms of Berlin, London, New York, and Paris. In 1911, Jordan's had thirty-four buyers who went to Berlin, London, and Paris every season.[24] By 1915, Filene's upstaged Jordan's by employing more than a hundred fashion buyers to source fashion merchandise in the major markets of North America and Europe.[25] In Paris, one Filene's buyer noted that 'the Gallerie [sic] Lafayette copies styles so quickly that they have the newest things almost as quickly as the creators bring them out'.[26] Galeries Lafayette (the subject of Chapter 5) studied Parisian haute couture and, at its own production facilities, reinterpreted these costly handmade designs for mass consumption.[27] In turn, Filene's contracted to import the latest Galeries Lafayette styles from Paris. 'We have made an arrangement with them to send us the newest things as fast as they are brought out.'[28] Filene's took a similar approach to trend-scouting in New York, where the store also maintained a buying office. 'The main Filene millinery workroom is now in operation in New York City', reported *Filene Fashionisms*, the store's internal newsletter. 'This will give us hats fresh from the source of fashions every day – like having our millinery buyer on 5th Avenue continuously. We are the only store in Boston with this style service.'[29]

With an eye to the future, Lincoln Filene (who, by the start of WWI had to all intents and purposes taken over the running of the store) had helped to pioneer modern practices in retail management to gain competitive advantage for the store. As American retailing expanded during World War I, he realized that like-minded entrepreneurs might pool their resources to achieve scale economies when buying merchandise from suppliers. A buying pool would give the stores an edge against giant mail-order houses such as Sears, Roebuck & Company, which could bargain for lower prices based on volume.[30] In 1918, Lincoln Filene helped to establish the Associated Merchandising Corporation (AMC), which consolidated purchasing activities on behalf of some nineteen member stores from a central office in New York and, eventually, through resident buying offices in major cities in Europe and Asia.[31] Strife between the Filene brothers, combined with the competitive business environment of the 1920s, led to major administrative changes at Filene's after 1928, when the legal agreements of 1912 that undergirded the company expired. Edward Filene left the business, and Filene's went on the stock market as a public company.[32] Soon thereafter in 1929, Lincoln Filene, Louis Kirstein, and others incorporated the Federated Department Stores as a Delaware holding company with seven subsidiary stores based in Boston, Brooklyn, and Cincinnati.[33] Federated executives assumed responsibility for the strategic direction of the holding company, but each subsidiary, including Filene's, retained its own name and was run by a local management team. The retention of local talent was important, as each subsidiary catered to a regional market that had distinctive peculiarities and tastes. The stores relied on AMC to source some merchandise but also retained their own staff of buyers.

In the interwar years, Filene's took measures to cement its reputation as New England's one-stop destination for fashion. Throughout the 1920s, the store cooperated with other retailers to sponsor Boston Style Week, one of the earliest fashion weeks anywhere.[34] Filene's Clothing Information Bureau tutored customers on practical wardrobe matters, such as budgeting for yearly apparel purchases.[35] Early niche markets were also developed. Wealthy shoppers were the target audience for Filene's French Shops, despite its name a single in-store boutique that showed Parisian couture and sold American copies (see figures 7.4 and 7.5).[36] Female students at Hillary Clinton's alma mater, Wellesley College, could buy collegiate ready-to-wear at a small Filene's branch near the suburban campus.[37] The famous Filene's Automatic Bargain Basement, which opened in 1909 as the brainchild of Edward Filene, produced extraordinary profits under an imaginative young manager named Harold D. Hodgkinson, a Yale graduate who started as a stock boy in 1912 and rose through the

7.4   The fashion magazine *Clothes* was published quarterly for Filene's customers; shown here is the cover of the Christmas edition of December 1927.

ranks to transform the basement operation in the interwar years. A steady stream of cash-and-carry customers prowled through the discount racks for last season's merchandise culled from Filene's, Bergdorf Goodman, Henri Bendel, Lord & Taylor, and Saks Fifth Avenue.[38] To keep abreast of what consumers wanted, Filene's had set up sophisticated mechanisms to track their preferences. Daily inventories counted sales, and the clerks in the various boutiques were required to make a note of every customer who did not make a purchase and why. Every day, the buyers had fresh reports at their fingertips in an early version of fast merchandising – if not fast fashion.[39]

Filene's entered World War II on a sound financial footing. Federated had turned a profit throughout the Great Depression, with an upswing in the late 1930s. In 1941, net sales of the combined Federated stores amounted to $131 million and net profits totalled $2.6 million.[40] By this time, Federated had sixteen stores and branches in the Northeast and Midwest, from Boston to Cincinnati. All of these units were department stores, with the exception of Filene's, which was 'the world's largest specialty store', 'primarily devoted to the sale of clothing and accessories for men, women, and children'. Filene's and the R. H. White Company, a Boston store that had been its subsidiary since 1928, accounted for one-third of total sales for Federated in 1942–43: $50 million of $155 million.[41] Clearly, there was something special about specializing in fashion.

The war was a boon to Filene's. The store's cadre of fashion professionals, mainly women, took advantage of the unusual social and economic conditions to develop new niche markets. Stylist Dorothy Kelley

December, 1927

9

Moulded-to-the-head brown camel's-hair hat with little gold buckles. $25. French Shops

Beige kasha frock — reproduced from the French — with simulated lizard belt. $55. French Shops

Brown suede oxfords with a bit of open work and brown kid. $15. Fifth Floor

Individual printed velvet dress in royal blue, black and white. The ciré ti. are held in place with two silver rings. $75. French Shops

Black felt hat, moulded to the head. Can be had in any other color you might select. $20. French Shops

Four tones of gold and silver lamé are combined very subtly with black velvet. An individual model. $150. French Shops

Luxurious golden brown caracul coat with an away-from-the-face shawl collar and cuffs of baum marten. $1650. Fifth Floor

Ʃuggested holiday wardrobe for the woman whose social standing makes extreme chic essential

ℱASHION is not always a matter of choice. Sometimes one's position in the social limelight makes it quite essential that all her clothes be selected with a thorough knowledge of the mode. This takes time, and time is not always available. CLOTHES has presumed to the extent of selecting a small wardrobe for the Christmas holidays in town. It includes a beige kasha "little" frock with its accompanying coat and hat for traveling, a printed velvet dress, an afternoon gown of gold lamé and velvet, and an evening ensemble of transparent velvet gown and velvet wrap. With them all, but too numerous to picture, go the countless jewels, bags, gloves, stockings, slippers, lingerie and teatime pajamas that are needed, for even a short trip. Amber choker and bracelets, brownish nude hose, brown suede discus bag, brown suede oxfords, brown camel's-hair hat, and beige gloves for the beige kasha frock. Black felt hat with a silver pin, wide silver and gold bracelets, beige hose and gloves, and black suede bag and afternoon slippers for the velvet dress and for the gold lamé. Quantities of pearls with crystal for the peach velvet evening gown and nude stockings with peach satin slippers

Exquisite peach-colored evening gown of transparent velvet has fashion's two chief requisites — the deep back decolletage and the daringly uneven hem. Few-of-a-kind gown. $125
A furless pearl gray velvet evening wrap with large sections of exquisite French beading is chosen to accompany it. An individual piece from France. $225. French Shops

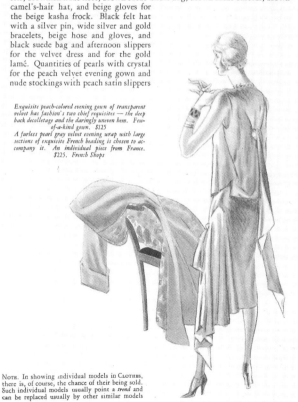

NOTE. In showing individual models in CLOTHES, there is, of course, the chance of their being sold. Such individual models usually point a *trend* and can be replaced usually by other similar models

The Christmas 1927 issue of *Clothes* included illustrations of the upmarket holiday ready-to-wear available at Filene's French Shops.   **7.5** recognized the demand for suitable campus attire among the swelling ranks of female college students who filled classrooms that had been vacated by enlisted men. Filene's not only catered to students at the small branch in Wellesley, but also did so at two boutiques in the downtown store: the Young Bostonian Shop, and Filene's College Shop, which had been created in 1941. Emulating the practical focus of Filene's Clothing Information Bureau, the College Shop hosted fashion 'clinics', wherein college-age shoppers met with the merchandising staff to discuss student needs and fashion trends. Filene's was slowly but surely learning how to pick consumers' brains and channel their ideas into the store.[42]

High-school students emerged as another niche market. Jordan's was first on the teen uptake by establishing Jordan's New Fashion Center, which offered age-appropriate fashion shows, beauty advice, and the Marsha Jordan beauty contest. Each year, the newly crowned winner received a fresh wardrobe and a seat on the store's teen fashion advisory council, which helped Jordan's buyers and merchandisers understand high-school tastes and trends.[43] In 1945, Filene's launched a comparable programme. The girls on Filene's High School Fashion Board participated in the Annual High School Fashion Show and Coke Party, sipping Coca-Cola while modelling clothes that had been pictured in the recently launched *Seventeen* magazine.[44] As with the College Shop, Filene's hoped to develop face-to-face relationships with a new consumer group to fathom their expectations.

During World War II, Filene's also promoted the work of the first generation of American fashion designers who emerged from the shadow of the European couture industry to gain some degree of name recognition. Unlike the British authorities, the United States government did not treat clothing as a commodity to be rationed. However, when the United States joined the Allies after the Japanese attack on Pearl Harbor on 7 December 1941, the federal government issued General Limitation Order L-85, which regulated the amount and type of material that could be used in civilian clothing.[45] American designers worked within the constraints of L-85 to create apparel that was simple and practical, adapting the American Look, discussed below, to wartime exigencies. Filene's star designer was the New York-based Nettie Rosenstein, who was the focus of the store's annual fashion show at Copley Plaza Hotel, the most sumptuous ballroom in Boston.[46] Claire McCardell was another Filene's favourite. Often associated with the development of sportswear, she was known for designs that combined versatility, frugality, and elegance.[47] The new market segments – particularly the new casual approach to styling – pointed to an exciting postwar world.

Going international

When peace returned, the managers at each Federated subsidiary outlined their postwar plans. Filene's kept its eyes on fashion. Anticipating the population shift from city to periphery, the store enlarged its suburban branches and expanded its regional presence with new branches. The aim was to preserve Filene's 'position as the unquestioned leader of the fashion clothes field in New England'.[48]

A new generation of fashion professionals steered Filene's through the postwar boom and the creative revival of Europe. The prime mover behind the international push was Harriet Wilinsky, whose high-profile position at Filene's made her into one of Boston's most respected businesswomen. She was the daughter of the Jewish physician Charles F. Wilinsky, himself the director of Beth Israel Hospital where Louis Kirstein, one of the store's founders, had been a benefactor until his death in 1942.[49] While connections to the Jewish community may have been an advantage, Wilinsky came to Filene's as a proven go-getter in Boston retail circles.

Wilinsky established a reputation for fashion promotion at a moment when retail management was deemed an appropriate career for women. After graduating from Barnard College in New York, she worked as a copywriter and advertising director at two Boston stores: R. H. White and E. T. Slattery. Wilinsky learned about market segmentation at Slattery's, where she researched the apparel preferences of college students and career women.[50] After a brief wartime stint in Washington, in 1943 Wilinsky joined the advertising department at Filene's (see figure 7.6).[51] She advanced to fashion director, and in 1947, she became the sales promotion manager with oversight for advertising, displays, radio, fashion promotion, publicity, and public relations.[52]

Wilinksy is one of countless career women in fashion retailing whose history has yet to be written. Most notable among these fashion retail pioneers was Dorothy Shaver, the president of Lord & Taylor from 1945 to 1959. Back in 1932, she championed native design talent with a promotion called the American Look, and by the mid-1950s, Shaver and Lord & Taylor were synonymous with practical, easy-going apparel that was designed and made in the United States.[53] Wilinsky did not run Filene's, but she was the only woman in the top echelons. She sat on the management board and reported to Harold Hodgkinson, who had been promoted to vice president and general manager.[54] Wilinsky supervised fashion promotion at Filene's for more than two decades. She became a vice president in 1968 and retired in 1970.[55]

Wilinksy put her money on the revitalized European fashion industry. The postwar years were an exciting time for the vivacious executive. In May 1945, the Fashion Group of Boston – a branch of the Fashion Group of New York, a network of female fashion professionals that germinated in 1928 – welcomed a visit from Carmel Snow, the editor of the fashion magazine *Harper's Bazaar*. Snow reported on the state of Parisian haute couture following the city's liberation from the Nazis in August 1944. Couturiers

Filene's
the world's largest
specialty store

JUNIOR SHOP FURLOUGH GLAMOUR
A CHEMISE SILHOUETTE
DINNER DRESS $25
Sizes 9 to 15

WHEN YOU THINK
OF FASHION IN NEW ENGLAND
IT'S FILENE'S

BOSTON · FALMOUTH
SOUTH HADLEY · NORTHAMPTON
WORCESTER · WELLESLEY · WINCHESTE
BELMONT · PORTLAND

7.6   In this *Vogue* magazine advertisement of 1 November 1943, Filene's was described as the 'world's largest specialty store' and a one-stop shopping destination for New England fashionistas.

such as Cristobal Balenciaga, Mad Carpentier, Lucian Lelong, and Elsa Schiaparelli were creating 'exquisite styles', but they had to use inferior textiles because the European mills had been ravaged by the war.[56] Wilinsky's ears perked up, and Filene's was soon on the case.

The textile woes of haute couture suggested endless possibilities to Wilinsky and Hodgkinson, who had New England industry at their fingertips. Hodgkinson envisioned tremendous opportunities for the textile manufacturers that supplied the New York garment makers with cotton, wool, and silk fabrics. Why couldn't the New England mills make cloth for the French couture houses?[57] Wilinsky was soon on her way to Paris for a reconnaissance mission. In early 1946, the *Daily Boston Globe* reported that she was the first fashion representative from an American retailer to fly across the Atlantic Ocean after World War II to the City of Light, as Paris was known at the time. She spent three weeks visiting the salons, studying couture designs, sizing up women on the street, and tutoring the French brides of GIs on American customs. She returned to Boston to great fanfare, honoured by Filene's at a Fashion Group meeting at the Ritz Carlton.[58] In April 1946, Filene's upstaged Jordan's and other Boston retailers by filling its show windows with the couture models that Wilinsky had selected at the Paris salons – designs by Balenciaga, Pierre Balmain, Lelong, Schiaparelli, and others.[59] Adaptions of Paris designs were sold in Filene's boutiques such as the Oxford Shop and the French Shops. That year, Filene's had 4,000 employees and sales of $60 million, an impressive figure that surpassed that of any other apparel and soft goods retailer in the world.[60]

In early 1947, Wilinsky was again on her way to Europe, this time crossing the Atlantic Ocean by the steamship *America* to collect fashion intelligence and to promote New England textiles. Her departure was dramatic. Wilinsky had packed fabric samples to show around Paris, but one particular bolt of silk was not ready when she left Boston. In a last-minute rush, Filene's flew the fabric to LaGuardia Field in New York where it was picked up by a helicopter that sped to the Manhattan docks. The silk, destined for the couturier Balmain, arrived at the ship at the eleventh hour, just as the steamer was about to leave port.[61] The *New York Times* published a picture of Wilinsky reaching up from the deck of the *America* to receive the package from a helicopter crewman.[62] The chopper was the newest commercial aviation technology, a novelty at which to marvel. In the days before overnight deliveries by FedEx and DHS, the helicopter drop-off impressed onlookers with Filene's determination. We can just imagine the chatter during the Atlantic crossing, and Wilinsky basking in her fifteen minutes of fame.

Wilinsky, exhilarated by the chopper caper, made the rounds in London and Paris. In London, she viewed the collections of top British couturiers such as Hardy Amies, Hartnell, Digby Morton, and Peter Russell. She then flew to Paris to attend the spring 1947 openings of couturiers and milliners including Balenciaga, Balmain, Madame Grès, Lelong, Maud et Nano, Robert Piguet, and Schiaparelli.[63] Upon her return, Wilinksy met the Fashion Group of New York to share her impressions of the London and Paris silhouettes, including the 'inverted tulip' shape shown by Christian Dior and famously dubbed 'the New Look' by Carmel Snow.[64] A new era of Paris fashion had begun, and Filene's could boast that Wilinsky had been present at its genesis.

Filene's French Shops

The merchandising staff at Filene's worked flat out to prepare the store for the new era of French glamour. After years of wartime simplicity, American women hungered for luxury. The North American market for couture originals was minuscule, but upmarket retailers imagined good profits in ready-to-wear adaptations of French designs. Couture did not pay the bills, but it provided an aura of exclusiveness that enhanced the store's prestige. The French Shops was the ideal space for showcasing couture trends, launching major themed promotions, and selling high-end adaptations.

To build cultural capital around European fashion, Filene's managers enlarged the French Shops to include an elegant salon, spacious fitting rooms, a private powder room, and an express elevator. The renovated boutique reopened in September 1947 stocked with high-end apparel and accessories by top-ranking American designers and ready-to-wear manufacturers, such as Adrian (the professional name for Adrian Adolph Greenburg), Maurice Rentner, Harry Rosenfeld, Rosenstein, Adele Simpson, and Pauline Trigère.[65] The stage was set for the arrival of the real fashion celebrities, the European couturiers.

In October 1947, Filene's managers rolled out the red carpet for Christian Dior, who was in Boston as their guest. As we saw in Chapter 2, by this time the celebrity couturier was looking to establish a New York branch, which would open in 1948.[66] From his luxurious suite at the Ritz Carlton, he was ushered downtown to Filene's French Shops, which was one of the first retail spaces in the United States to show his revolutionary romantic designs. Fittingly, a photograph in the *Daily Boston Globe* pictured the beaming Wilinsky flanked by the famous designer and her boss, Hodgkinson.[67] Later that month, as president of the Fashion Group of Boston, Wilinsky presided over a lecture by Balmain, the Paris couturier of the silk-by-helicopter escapade.[68] Filene's was building international connections with esteemed French couturiers to solidify its role as a fashion authority in the new postwar order.

Filene's French Shops were the responsibility of Orville Collins, who had been the boutique's buyer since the late 1930s.[69] In 1952, she expanded the offerings of the French Shops with designs from the spring couture openings in Paris and Rome. As discussed in Chapter 6, American retail buyers who flocked to Italy found much to admire. We can see Collins's enthusiasm in her handwritten letters to Wilinsky, scribbled from her hotel in Rome. She was excited about everything European, especially the personal flair and unique vision of the Italian designers. 'Schuberth has a most beautiful salon ... Very different from a New York show-room ... His casual clothes were original and young – in design.' 'The Fontana sisters also had beautiful evening clothes – I bought the one called Soap Bubbles – and the embroidery has that illusion.' 'I also bought an iridescent fabric in a cock-tail dress from Simonetta Visconti … a very attractive woman – titled – as so many are – and quite Americanized'.[70] Frequent buying expeditions to London, Paris, Barcelona, Rome, and Milan helped to strengthen Filene's reputation as a fashion leader. Excerpts from buyers' letters were published in special 'roving reporter' newspaper advertisements, which trumpeted Filene's ties to European fashion capitals.[71] Unusual designs also made for good press. In March 1952, Italian imports were the focus of a special Filene's style show that marked the debut of Italian fashion in Boston. Organized by Collins and Virginia Harris (who joined Filene's as fashion director in 1949), the event featured samples from Visconti and the Fontana sisters, whose frothy pink 'bubble' gown, covered with sequins and tiny pearls, stole the show.[72]

Filene's French Shops showcased French and Italian originals and retailed high-end American ready-to-wear selected by Harris and Collins (see figure 7.7).[73] The boutique also stocked American adaptations of European originals, sometimes relying on the AMC for group deals on Seventh Avenue reproductions. By 1952, the AMC had a European Model Buying Committee, which consisted of an AMC staff member and fashion representatives from three member stores. In August 1952, the committee had a coat by Visconti reproduced on Seventh Avenue at a cost of $49.75 to $99.75 each, depending on the fabric, for sale in the various European-themed boutiques (such as Filene's prestigious French Shops) within some of the AMC stores. In 1953, the committee expanded the reproduction programme to other departments in AMC stores 'because the markets below Frenchroom are in need of stimulation'. This referred to the realization that some of the lower-priced fashion departments within various AMC stores might benefit from an influx of innovative new styles. The committee selected six designs – suits, coats, and dresses from Dior, Russell, Visconti, Balenciaga, Jacques Griffe, and Jacques Fath – to be sewn on Seventh Avenue. 'The AMC has worked with excellent manufacturers who have kept in the adaptations the French spirit', explained *AMC Fashion News*, 'but have made clothes exciting as well as wearable for the American woman.'[74]

By this time, Filene's French Shops was at the top of its game. Harris, Collins, and Wilinsky were a tastemaking triumvirate working behind closed doors to bring Continental taste to New England. No expense was spared to promote European designs, which were equated with modernity through the association with transatlantic air travel, and no skimping occurred when collaborating with Seventh Avenue to adapt European glamour to middle-class budgets. However, the Filene's team would soon learn that modernity was a slippery slope. While the American press admired the frothy 'Soap Bubbles' dress, the modern American consumer proved to have had a mind of her own.

7.7   Got a big night on the town? This Filene's advertisement in *Vogue* (1 April 1949) suggested Roux haircolour treatments in the Beauty Salon and New York ready-to-wear from the French Shops. The gown by Ceil Chapman, a Seventh Avenue designer, was made from nylon, a high-tech material invented for ladies' stockings during the Great Depression and used for parachutes during World War II.

Trending the leisure market

For much of the 1950s, Filene's was Boston's leading fashion retailer. The emphasis on fashion continued to distinguish Filene's from other Federated subsidiaries and from Boston department stores such as Jordan's and Gilchrist's. 'We are fundamentally a fashion business', reiterated the Filene's business policy of 1953, 'concerned primarily with the merchandising of clothing and accessories for the whole family.' Different parts of the store catered to different audiences, earmarked by income or special tastes. The main store, the men's store, and the new suburban branches catered to middle-income consumers, while Filene's French Shops targeted wealthier shoppers. These consumers constituted the 'greatest sales and profit producing groups', while the famous discount basement catered to shoppers of all social classes who loved a bargain.[75]

This worldview was challenged by demographic upheavals at mid-decade. In 1954, *Life* magazine, the large-format photographic weekly published by media magnate Henry Luce, documented seismic social shifts in a film called *The Changing American Market*. Hodgkinson saw the film, which alerted him to the 'tremendous increase in the middle income group of consumers, the new pattern of working and leisure hours, the two-day week-end, the larger family, the outdoor living, the do-it-yourself revolution'. Under his direction, a Filene's sales extravaganza, 'This Is the Life', sought to address these new market opportunities. The promotion included apparel for almost every activity by every type of consumer: hobbyists, outdoor sports' enthusiasts, tourists, homebodies, and partygoers. The effort to widen Filene's customer base was prescient, but the eclecticism hinted at a certain lack of direction. None of this boded well for the future of fashion at Filene's.[76]

Filene's had been chasing new demographic segments since World War II, when it had created fashion boutiques for high school and college students.[77] After the war, the most promising new customer was the middle-class 'working girl', or 'career woman'.[78] Postwar television portrayals of the suburban housewife, epitomized by June Cleaver in the sitcom *Leave It to Beaver* (1957–63), ignored the fact that countless women worked for pay.[79] Recently, the acclaimed *Mad Men* series (2007–13) immortalized the postwar career woman in characters who worked as office manager, copywriter, consumer researcher, and retail executive. Career women such as these constituted a large enough market to have their own fashion magazine, *Charm*, which started in 1950 and was eventually absorbed by *Glamour*.[80] By mid-decade, one in every three American women had a job outside of the home. In the Boston area alone, there were 278,000 women who worked. Just as *Mademoiselle* helped retailers understand teen tastes, *Charm* provided stores with research reports and fashion promotions to help them sell office attire to the lucrative career girl market.[81]

Filene's raced neck and neck against Jordan's to win the fashion dollars of the Boston career woman. At Filene's, the primary responsibility for capturing the career market fell to Harris, an experienced publicist who had worked on radio advertising and on promotions for the Miss America beauty pageant.[82] In 1950, Harris organized the first annual Filene's extravaganza for 'working girls who have their eyes keyed to flattering fashions as well as their typewriters'. Filene's career girl fashion shows, held at downtown venues, filled a void and initially were a great success. In 1950, more than a thousand 'girls with jobs' attended the inaugural event; in 1951 Filene's made the Career Girl Fashion Show a regular part of the fashion calendar.[83] Eight years later, the career girl shows had morphed into an invitational supper at the flagship store for employees of the major corporations in the Boston area.[84]

By 1954, Filene's had established a Career Girl Cabinet that was comparable to its High School Fashion Board; members attended special fashion openings and provided feedback on the samples.[85] They emphasized the need for fashions that were practical and moderately priced. By the mid-1950s, the simple aesthetic that was the signature of American designers like Rosenstein and McCardell had meshed with the availability of new man-made 'miracle fibres' such as nylon, acrylic, and polyester. Fabrics made from stretchable nylon yarns replaced knitted woollens in active gear for sports such as skiing. Skirts made from wool-acrylic blends were durable, moth resistant, and hand washable. Sweaters knitted in nylon or acrylic yarn were far less expensive than comparable wool sweaters in merino or cashmere. In Boston as elsewhere, career women, college girls, and teenagers embraced the 'sweater girl' look popularized by the buxom Hollywood starlet Jayne Mansfield (see figure 7.8). The sweater girl look was a major move away from structured clothing and a step forward in the advancement of informal everyday attire.[86]

The growing American preference for practical easy-care clothing synergized with the informal elegance of Italian fashion (see Chapter 6). The Italians seemed to understand the American lifestyle and pocketbook. Based in Florence, the AMC accessories scout could barely contain his enthusiasm for the 1952 Italian lines: 'ITALY – so far it looks terrific.'[87] Writing from Rome in 1953, Wilinksy discussed the relevance of Italy: 'In the good old days a girl just had to go to Paris and get home ... Today, it is quite a different note ... If you think Rome cleans up the Italian situation, you're missing a lot. The next vital stop is Florence.'[88] The weather had an impact on Italian styling, inspiring designs that were cool, washable, and stylish. Italian summers were hot and steamy, much like the East Coast of the United States. 'Rome is very torrid right now, and this fact sets the fashion', Wilinsky wrote. 'Everyone dresses as comfortably as possible.'[89]

Collins, the buyer for the French Shops, caught the Italian bug and shared her enthusiasm with career women. Every year, she travelled to Italy

The sexy sweater girl came to exemplify the casual American lifestyle of the postwar era. As this **7.8**
E. I. du Pont de Nemours and Company advertisement from *Life* magazine (1948), suggests,
modern fibres like nylon transformed many aspects of the material world. Nylon was used to
create sweaters and other apparel that was affordable, washable, mothproof, durable, and
easy-going.

with the manager of the Junior Sports Shop to select ready-to-wear that was a good fit with casual American trends. In 1955, Collins returned with multicoloured slack sets, blue jeans in satiny cotton by Maria Antonelli, red shorts paired with a short striped pullover by the knitwear manufac-turer Mirsa, and hostess dinner pyjamas from Emilio Capri. After the sam-ples arrived, the store presented the merchandise to journalists, Filene's buyers, and the Career Girl Cabinet for preliminary feedback.[90]

Career women had mixed reactions to European imports and the spin-offs by American ready-to-wear factories. In 1953, one middle-class con-sumer from Lowell, a major textile centre north of Boston, was elated. 'The opportunity to see the original models when we have read of them in fashion magazines was indeed a treat', she wrote. 'I liked being brought back to our prices too when the adaptations were shown.'[91] But other career women were not impressed. The 1955 remarks of one Boston social worker pointed to a disjuncture between the tastes of Filene's fashion mer-chandisers and the career girls who shopped at the store:

> When the working girl shows were begun, the emphasis was on the average budget, the average American girl. We think you would probably agree with us that last night's clothes were beyond the budgets of most working girls and the majority were too extreme. We strive for individuality in clothes, but that does not necessarily mean we must adopt the rash extremes set by designers each season.[92]

This Boston career girl watched her pennies and shopped for practical fash-ion. In contrast to the wealthy socialite or doctor's wife, this middle-class consumer saw clothing as a vehicle for personal expression and as a meas-ure of her 'individuality'. Some career women felt that stores and design-ers who tried to reshape their tastes were just plain impertinent.

The plucky attitude of career women startled the fashion intermediar-ies at Filene's, who had been weaned on the idea that haute couture was the pinnacle of style. An emerging American psychology of fashion was apparent to astute trend watchers such as Tobé Coller Davis in New York.[93] In June 1957, Harris read some alarming statistics in a report from Tobé's fashion forecasting service. The vast majority of American consumers – seventy-seven per cent – now relied on the 'fashion pages of national magazines as their prime source of fashion news', while thirty-six per cent looked to the 'women's pages of local newspapers'. Only fourteen per cent of consumers followed fashion on television, and most troubling to Harris, a mere nine per cent turned 'to retail stores for fashion news and fashion education'.[94]

Any wide-awake fashion retailer would have been rattled by this report. 'These are saddening and deflating statistics taken at face value', Harris told the merchandising staff at Filene's, adding 'we can throw up our hands to them and decide not to bother'. But rather than heed the news,

Harris was determined not to turn her back on good taste. She boldly stated: 'OR we can look [at the statistics] as a real challenge to give the customer fashion excitement, news and education this season so that we truly enhance our leadership and authority'.[95] In an indirect way, the Tobé report had identified a sea change: the postwar European fashion bubble had popped. Filene's had spent the last decade building a massive promotion machine around the couture-driven European fashion system, which was now in decline. The store's fashion specialists did not know how to cope – and they simply carried on, doing business as usual.

Triumph of the individualist

Federated was ebullient at the start of the 1960s. Ten years earlier in 1950, it had twelve retail divisions that collectively operated fifty major stores in thirteen states. Sales for 1950 totalled $389 million with a net profit of $18 million, or 4.6 per cent of sales. Sales for 1960 had nearly doubled at $785 million, and profits totalled $32 million, or 4.2 per cent of sales. Filene's was still the only Federated subsidiary that specialized in fashion.[96]

By 1961, Filene's had nine branch stores, mainly in upmarket Boston suburbs. The retailer's major investment in suburbia coincided with the downward spiral of Boston's central business district. For decades, the city's high commercial taxes had discouraged new business development and burdened older enterprises. By the 1960s, Washington Street was still a shopping magnet, but the magnificent Burnham Building looked tired, despite the major renovation and modernisation programme of 1951–53 that had been celebrated with the Fashionations Fair of autumn 1953. The retailing superstars of Washington Street – Filene's and Jordan's – were directing resources into suburban locations that were closer to the customers. Like other businesses, they took advantage of tax policies that encouraged suburban construction. None of this helped the downtown retail district on Washington Street.

Filene's continued to promote European fashion at its flagship store, even as the allure of downtown Boston faded. The retailer's fashion scouts were upbeat about changes afoot in Paris, but new trends among ordinary consumers were undercutting the status quo. In the summer of 1959, Harris noted the proliferation of 'individualism' in the fashions worn by the Parisienne on the street.[97] A year later in 1960, she documented a new attitude. 'Women all over the world apparently want the same things from their wardrobes, whether they're Doris Duke', the American tobacco heiress, or 'Daisy-Do-It-Now, private secretary'. The practical woman of the 1960s demanded clothes that were soft, glamorous, and wearable.[98] Harris was right about the casual note, but she was mistaken in her assumption that all Americans wanted the same styles. Doris Duke and Daisy-Do-It-

Now were worlds apart in their tastes. The heiress still followed haute couture, while the secretary watched readymade trends – and then did her own thing. Like the Parisienne who draped her scarf with a distinctive flair, the average American woman, epitomized by Daisy-Do-It-Now, was coming into her own as an individualist who created her own style.

The French Shops' promotion of New York ready-to-wear designed by the Paris couture house of Nina Ricci illustrates the lack of synchrony between the store and the American market. In April 1962, *Vogue* magazine announced the Total Look by the house of Ricci, listing Filene's as the Ricci headquarters in Boston. The Total Look was a ready-to-wear collection by Jules-François Crahay, a Belgian designer who worked for the house from 1954 to 1963.[99] Conceived by Crahay in Paris, the collection was cut and sewn by Mr. Mort, a leading apparel manufacturer on Seventh Avenue. Whereas a single piece of haute couture might retail for thousands of dollars, the readymade coats, suits, dresses, costumes, and cocktail outfits in this collection each sold for around $70 to $150. Crahay achieved the Total Look with specially made French accessories – a group of hats, and a line of jewellery – and the Ricci signature fragrance, L'Air du Temps, a scent launched in 1948. For a week in late April, Filene's promoted the Total Look with newspaper advertising, window displays, and fashion shows in the French Shops.[100]

The nature of routine is that it is like an old shoe, comfortable but uninspiring. By the early 1960s, fashion promotion at Filene's was stale, and mainly in decline. Such was the case with spin generated around the Total Look. The store's fashion promoters – Wilinsky, Collins, and Harris – continued to do what they did best, oblivious to major cultural changes that swirled around them. Although more and more Americans marched to their own fashion drummers, Filene's chose a safe, familiar path. The store continued to put consumers into little boxes, using well-established categories. The idea of market segments was good, but the store overlooked key consumer groups. There were teens, misses, career women, matrons, and men, but no beatniks, country girls, or pre-teens. Innovations such as men's style shows and suburban fashion shows were added to the calendar, but there was a predictable sameness to the programmes. The repetitiveness of Filene's style promotions ran contrary to the idea of constant change, which is the essence of fashion.

Back in the 1950s, Fashionations had strengthened Filene's reputation for 'leadership and authority' in style matters, linking the store to European glamour and modern transatlantic flight. But even if the flame of the Fashionations had been rekindled, the fire would have burned out quickly. American consumers no longer looked to retailers like Filene's for fashion guidance. They read fashion magazines like *Glamour*, *Seventeen*, and *Vogue* and then looked in the mirror and asked themselves, 'How do I want to look?' and 'Who do I want to be?'

Adieu, European fashion

In the spring of 1970, *Time* magazine and the Celanese Fibers Marketing Company published the results of a fashion survey among female college students. The Celanese report documented major transitions that had been underway for some fifteen years. Whereas the wartime college girl happily donned a wool sweater and plaid skirt that marked her as a student, her counterpart in the 1970s dressed to differentiate herself from her classmates. She typically spent fifty per cent more on clothing than other Americans, often selecting better-quality merchandise at a higher price. She read the fashion magazines – and did not hesitate to critique them. 'The clothes are modeled by extremely beautiful young girls', one student said. 'No doubt a potato sack would look attractive on such a person. Perhaps advertisers should become more realistic.' As Tobé had reported, magazines rather than retailers had become the main source of style guidance and fashion inspiration. Sixty-nine per cent of the young women in the Celanese survey looked to magazines for tips on beauty and style trends.[101]

Filene's postwar investment in European fashion – haute couture, ready-to-wear, millinery, and accessories – was driven by the strategic 1912 decision to lead New England in clothing sales. Into the mid-twentieth century, the store relied on Europe to provide that special something that was missing in America. The Old World was seductive, transatlantic flights were novel, and the couture salons knew how to impress. A visit to Balmain's showroom was a dream come true for Wilinsky, who had been weaned on tales of Parisian fashion supremacy. In the United States, formal attire had been in decline for decades, but women from the upper classes – the wives of executives, attorneys, and physicians – still wore white gloves and still needed little bouclé suits for club luncheons, cocktail dresses for business events, and glittery gowns for charity balls. Wilinksy made sure that Filene's French Shops carried the correct merchandise for this status-conscious well-off clientele. The elite boutique added prestige to the store and stimulated the desire for affordable American reproductions and adaptations.

In the years after the war, Filene's general manager, Hodgkinson (who became the store's president in 1957), had envisioned a great transatlantic entente, as did earlier generations of creative professionals with European connections.[102] He hoped to connect Old World designers and New World textile mills, but there is no evidence to indicate if his aspirations materialized. European couture houses did use American materials, but the big success was in the high-tech world of synthetic fibres. The American fibre giant E. I. du Pont de Nemours and Company had arranged for members of the Chambre Syndicale de la Couture Parisienne to use French fabrics made with DuPont nylon, polyester, acrylic, and spandex. The use of test-tube fibres by couture houses linked Americans to Paris in an entirely unexpected way. The triumph of miracle fibres, in turn, advanced the rise of casual styling and hastened the decline of the formal dress customs that sustained couture.[103] By the 1960s, easy-going clothing, made from washable crease-resistant synthetics, was just one of many factors that rendered couture obsolete. Stores like Filene's, which retained some level of commitment to formal European dress, were swimming upstream.

For many years, Wilinksy, Collins, and Harris were among the most innovative retailing professionals in America. But these highly accomplished women imagined the New England consumer in their own image and believed she would appreciate European elegance. The Eiffel Tower and the Colosseum had left them breathless, and they wanted Filene's customers to absorb the European zeitgeist by admiring imported models and buying American copies. This formula proved effective just after the war, but suppertime fashion shows of form-fitting dresses seemed just plain stodgy as the standard-of-living improved for much of the population and as growing numbers of middle-class consumers shopped at Filene's. Independent-minded customers like the career girls did not much care for Paris dictates and preferred to decide for themselves what to wear. By the mid-1960s, some American department stores and specialty fashion retailers began to take the hint, and looked elsewhere in Europe for creative inspiration. The new wave of fashion imports came largely from Great Britain, where a coterie of young designers and an advanced ready-to-wear industry had pioneered the London Look. This easy-going British clothing style captured the imaginations of clothes-conscious Baby Boomers because it fed into the growing casualization of American style and the penchant for 'doing your own thing'. The international fashion baton, in short, had been handed over to a new generation of consumers and retail buyers who appreciated the versatility of sportswear rather than the novelty of an evening gown decorated with pink bubbles.[104]

Back in 1953, Fashionations had acknowledged the synergies between fashion and nations. This study of Filene's has demonstrated the value of writing fashion history from a comparative, transnational, and holistic perspective. Building on Palmer's work about couture in Toronto, it extends the discussion to new market segments such as students and career women and to the retail professionals who targeted these customers.[105] This chapter has also opened the doors onto the internal workings of the world's largest fashion retailer of the early to mid-twentieth century, and, in turn, onto a deeper understanding of how American fashion culture, with its emphasis on informality, gained currency. Fashion intermediaries like Wilinsky made a difference to the dissemination of European taste, at least for a while. Letters from Filene's customers and reports from the Tobé forecasting service show that Americans did not always accept the fashion mandates of elite French and Italian designers. By the 1960s, the differences between generational tastes had become pronounced and market segmentation increasingly important. The Filene's intermediaries discussed in this chapter stood at the intersection of 'fashion' and 'nations', for better or worse. They were part of an older generation who thought women should dress in ladylike attire; they worshipped Paris, not London, and appreciated window displays more than glossy magazines. They thought nothing of creating themed extravaganzas like Fashionations, which not only trumpeted American prosperity but also built bridges to war-torn Europe. They did important cultural work, and were just as much a part of the fashion system as were the creators of the French New Look and the British Youth Quake. The little-known stories of these retailing fashion intermediaries help us to understanding the dissemination, interpretation, and reception of European designs in distant places like the United States, and that context is essential to writing a comprehensive cultural history of the European fashion system around the world.

Notes

1 This chapter draws on the Filene's Marketing Archive at the Boston Public Library, Boston (hereafter BPL–FA) As this publication was going to press, I learned that the archive had been temporarily moved off-site and was unavailable to researchers, making it impossible for me to obtain photographs of the store, its merchandise, and displays. I hope to use these resources in future publications when the archive is again accessible to researchers. 'Filene's to present imported collection', *Women's Wear Daily* (10 August 1953); 'Fashionations Fair of Filene's biggest promotion', *Women's Wear Daily* (28 August 1953); 'Filene's announces block-wide building modernization plans', *Daily Boston Globe* (23 September 1951).

2 BPL–FA, folder: Misc. HW Fashionations 1953, press release, 'Filene's Fashionations Flyer with Diplomats, Designers, Business Leaders and Fashion Press Scheduled for September 22nd'.

3 'Filene's to present imported collection'; 'Fashionations Fair of Filene's biggest promotion'; P. Porter, 'Best from six nations', *Boston Herald* (24 September 1953); 'Top designers show creations at Boston', *New York Times* (24 September 1953); BPL–FA, folder: Miscellaneous – HW Fashionations, I. Bender to H. Wilinsky, 20 October 1953; BPL–FA, folder: Fashionations Plans and Graphics, press release, 'Pan American shows fashion collection at Filene's Fashionations Fair' [1953].

4 BPL–FA, folder: Fashionations working folder, H. Wilinsky, 'Filene's International Fashions Fair', 5 September 1953.

5 BPL–FA, folder: Fashionations working folder, H. Wilinsky, typescript on Fashionations promotion, n.d. [September 1953].

6 BPL–FA, folder: Fashionations working folder, H. Wilinsky, 'Filene's International Fashions Fair', 5 September 1953; BPL–FA, folder: Misc. HW Fashionations 1953, V. Harris to H. Wilinsky, 'Fashionations Merchandise', 29 August 1953.

7 A. Palmer, *Couture and Commerce: The Transatlantic Fashion Trade in the 1950s* (Vancouver, BC: University of British Columbia Press, 2001).

8 A. Palmer, *Dior: A New Look, A New Enterprise* (London: V&A Publishing, 2009); D. Blum, *Shocking! The Art and Fashion of Elsa Schiaparelli* (Philadelphia, PA: Philadelphia Museum of Art, 2003); S. Stanfill (ed.), *The Glamour of Italian Fashion Since 1945* (London: V&A Publishing, 2014); V. Steele and T. A. Long, *Chic*

Chicago: Couture Treasures from the Chicago History Museum (New York: Museum at FIT, 2007); and C. Wilcox (ed.), *The Golden Age of Haute Couture: Paris and London, 1947–1957* (London: V&A, 2007).

9   R. L. Blaszczyk, *Imagining Consumers: Design and Innovation from Wedgwood to Corning* (Baltimore: Johns Hopkins University Press, 2000); R. L. Blaszczyk (ed.), *Producing Fashion: Commerce, Culture, and Consumers* (Philadelphia: University of Pennsylvania Press, 2008); R. L. Blaszczyk, *The Color Revolution* (Cambridge, MA: MIT Press, 2012).

10   S. Engelbourg, 'Edward A. Filene: merchant, civic leader, and Jew', *American Jewish Historical Quarterly*, 66 (1976), 108; G. E. Berkley, *The Filenes* (Boston: International Pocket Library, 1998), pp. 109, 160.

11   Berkley, *The Filenes*, pp. 9, 37–8, 41, 49–50; R. Hendrickson, *The Grand Emporiums: The Illustrated History of America's Great Department Stores* (New York: Stein and Day, 1979); W. Leach, *Land of Desire: Merchants, Power, and the Rise of a New American Culture* (New York: Pantheon Books, 1993); and M. J. Lisicky, *Filene's: Boston's Great Specialty Store* (Charleston, SC: Arcadia, 2012).

12   'The specialty shops: Boston – William Filene's Sons Co. incorporated with capital of $4,000,000', *Women's Wear* (21 August 1912); 'Filene's opening', *Women's Wear* (3 September 1912).

13   *Women's Wear* provided extensive coverage of the new store. See, for example, 'Filene's new building', *Women's Wear* (30 July 1912), and 'Filene's new building', *Women's Wear* (2 August 1912).

14   U.S. Bureau of the Census, Population of the 100 Largest Urban Places, 1910, at www.census.gov/population/www/documentation/twps0027/tab14.txt (accessed 13 March 2016).

15   'Marie Jonreau's latest Paris fashions in gowns, garments and millinery', *Boston Daily Globe* (6 October 1895); I. de Viliers, 'The latest fashions from gay Paris', *Boston Daily Globe* (11 November 1906).

16   'Counters filled', *Boston Daily Globe* (7 December 1906).

17   'Fall fashions here', *Boston Daily Globe* (1 August 1911).

18   'How stores are selling ready to wear', *Women's Wear Daily* (20 July 1938).

19   Berkley, *The Filenes*, pp. 50–1, 122.

20   Berkley, *The Filenes*, p. 121.

21   'Filene's opening', *Women's Wear* (3 September 1912).

22   Author's collection, William Filene's Sons Company, *What Is Personal Service?* ([Boston, n.d.]).

23   'Coats and suits', *Women's Wear* (27 February 1913).

24   'Fall fashions here', *Boston Daily Globe* (1 August 1911).

25   BPL–FA, folder: Historical File – Europe, *Filene Fashionisms*, 1 (13 April 1915).

26   BPL–FA, folder: Historical File – Europe, 'Mr. Clark's Notes on Paris Styles', [1914–15].

27   Galeries Lafayette, 'About Us: Culture and Heritage', at haussmann.galerieslafayette.com/en/culture-and-heritage/ (accessed 30 December 2015).

28   BPL–FA, folder: Historical File – Europe, 'Mr. Clark's Notes on Paris Styles'.

29   *Filene Fashionisms*, 1 (13 April 1915).

30   V. Howard, *From Main Street to Mall: The Rise and Fall of the American Department Store* (Philadelphia: University of Pennsylvania Press, 2015), chap. 3.

31   Harvard Business School, Boston, Baker Library, Special Collections, Louis E. Kirstein Papers, box 82, folder: 'AMC Story', Philip J. Reilly, *Story of the Retail Research Association and the Associated Merchandising Corporation, 1916–1939* (New York: Associated Merchandising Corporation, 1939), pp. 2–3.

32   Engelbourg, 'Edward A. Filene', 111; Berkley, *The Filenes*, 229–41.

33   Federated Department Stores, *Annual Report for the Fiscal Year Ending January 31, 1930*.

34 'Style week for Boston women', *Boston Daily Globe* (21 September 1919); '"Fashion Week"', *Boston Daily Globe* (9 April 1927).

35 'Visiting lecturer advises women on correct dressing', *Women's Wear* (4 March 1922); 'Filene's prepare apparel budgets to aid shoppers', *Women's Wear* (26 July 1922); 'Clothing Information Bureau gains friends for store', *Women's Wear* (9 January 1926); 'Filene's issue new guide for apparel purchasers', *Women's Wear* (11 September 1922).

36 'Enlarging Filene French Room', *Women's Wear* (8 October 1924); 'Replicas of Paris frocks shown with originals at Filene's revue', *Women's Wear Daily* (1 April 1936); 'Privacy, individuality of service, distinguish Filene French Shops', *Women's Wear Daily* (19 August 1936).

37 'College graduates at Filene's assemble directory listing student's apparel needs for fall', *Women's Wear Daily* (26 August 1935).

38 'Filene's Automatic Bargain Basement to celebrate its 30th anniversary', *Daily Boston Globe* (4 September 1938); Hendrickson, *Grand Emporiums*, p. 130; Berkley, *The Filenes*, pp. 123–5, 164–7, 193–4, 263–4.

39 Berkley, *The Filenes*, p. 194.

40 Federated Department Stores, *Annual Report, Year Ended January 31, 1942*.

41 Federated Department Stores, *Annual Report, July 31, 1943*; Berkley, *The Filenes*, pp. 192–3.

42 'Here's success to costume fashions for college, career, or social whirl', *Daily Boston Globe* (18 August 1940); 'Filene's new "College Center" offers girls newest in campus fashions', *Daily Boston Globe* (12 August 1941).

43 'Belmont girl chosen sponsor of Jordan's teen age shop', *Daily Boston Globe* (21 August 1942).

44 'Filene's holds fashion show for "Teen-Agers"', *Daily Boston Globe* (8 August 1945); 'Filene's gives party, teen age style show', *Daily Boston Globe* (23 March 1946).

45 'Carmel Snow talks on June 15, before Fashion Group here', *Daily Boston Globe* (8 June 1942); 'New styles neater, more feminine, Carmel Snow tells Fashion Group', *Daily Boston Globe* (16 June 1942).

46 'Large audience views Rosenstein styles at Filene-sponsored show', *Daily Boston Globe* (25 September 1942); 'Little black dress is highlight of Nettie Rosenstein fashion tea', *Daily Boston Globe* (22 September 1944).

47 'Commuter cottons by McCardell', *Daily Boston Globe* (18 May 1944); C. R. Milbank, *New York Fashion: The Evolution of American Style* (New York: Harry N. Abrams, 1996).

48 Federated Department Stores, *Annual Report Fiscal Year Ended August 4 1945*.

49 'Dr. Wilinsky, Boston's silver-haired dynamo', *Daily Boston Globe* (7 November 1948); 'L. E. Kirstein Dies; Boston merchant', *New York Times* (11 December 1942).

50 'Matched jacket and skirt lead in college clinic', *Women's Wear Daily* (16 July 1941); 'Slattery in move to meet "career girls" shopping problems', *Women's Wear Daily* (30 March 1939).

51 Wilinsky accompanied her husband, the attorney Sylvan A. Goodman, to Washington, where he had a wartime position; see 'Miss Wilinsky, Slattery's ad head, to resign', *Women's Wear Daily* (15 December 1942); 'Jean Rosenblatt leaving Filene's', *Women's Wear Daily* (10 December 1943).

52 'Filene's Promotes Harriet Wilinsky to sales manager', *Daily Boston Globe* (29 October 1947).

53 [R. L. Blaszczyk], 'Dorothy Shaver (1893–1959)', 2002, at amhistory.si.edu/archives/WIB-tour/dorothy_shaver.pdf (accessed 12 March 2016).

54 'Filene's adds five to board', *Women's Wear Daily* (30 October 1947).

55 'Filene's V-P post to Miss Wilinsky', *Women's Wear Daily* (11 June 1968); 'Harriet Wilinsky plans to retire', *Women's Wear Daily* (19 November 1970); 'Retiring Harriet Wilinsky to keep active', *Women's Wear Daily* (31 March 1971).

56 The Boston branch of the Fashion Group was established in 1936. 'Few Paris clothes sold to Nazis, says speaker', *Daily Boston Globe* (12 May 1945).

57 'Filene's "N. E. Revelation" to show area's major role in U.S. economy', *Daily Boston Globe* (2 May 1946).

58 Sally Stuart, 'Filene fashion head, back from Paris, honored at Luncheon', *Daily Boston Globe* (3 September 1946); 'Filene fashion expert in Paris to instruct French brides of G.I.'s', *Daily Boston Globe* (24 February 1946); 'GI brides in Paris see couture fashions', *Women's Wear Daily* (26 February 1946); 'Back-dipping line at Lelong praised', *Women's Wear Daily* (1 March 1946).

59 'Paris originals in Filene's windows', *Women's Wear Daily* (26 April 1946); 'Filene's windows display Paris couture fashions', *Women's Wear Daily* (2 May 1946).

60 Berkley, *The Filenes*, pp. 270, 273.

61 'Helicopter rushes fabric to Filene's fashion director', *Daily Boston Globe* (17 January 1947).

62 'A modern touch is added to the sailing of the America', *New York Times* (17 January 1947).

63 'Tea party in Paris planned by Filene's', *Daily Boston Globe* (8 January 1947); 'Filene's stylist to visit London, Paris modistes', *Daily Boston Globe* (15 January 1947).

64 'N.Y. Fashion Group hears Filene expert's style report', *Daily Boston Globe* (26 February 1947); '2 New silhouettes in Paris described', *New York Times* (26 February 1947).

65 'Filene's moves to coordinate high-style fashion sections', *Women's Wear Daily* (29 July 1947); 'Customer conveniences highlight Filene's enlarged French Shops', *Daily Boston Globe* (4 September 1947); 'Filene's opens grand gala French Shops tomorrow', *Daily Boston Globe* (7 September 1947).

66 T. Okawa, 'Licensing practices at Maison Christian Dior', in Blaszczyk (ed.), *Producing Fashion*, pp. 85–6.

67 'Girls to keep "New Look" 10 years more, Dior says', *Daily Boston Globe* (13 October 1947).

68 'French designer pays Boston visit Monday', *Daily Boston Globe* (22 October 1947).

69 'Personnel changes of the week', *Women's Wear Daily* (27 October 1939); 'Boston women soon to wear styles by Irene, designer for film stars', *Daily Boston Globe* (14 January 1948); 'Orville Hewitt to retire from Filene's', *Women's Wear Daily* (2 January 1971). Orville Hewitt was previously known by her maiden name, Orville Collins.

70 BPL–FA, folder: 'Roving Reporter' Ads, 1952–53, O. Collins to Mr. Gross [February 1952].

71 BPL–FA, folder: 'Roving Reporter' Ads, 1952–53.

72 'Filene's shows spring fashions from abroad', *Daily Boston Globe* (2 March 1952).

73 E. Bernkopf, 'Filene's French Shops preview things to come', *Daily Boston Globe* (1 March 1955); 'Virginia Harris is promoted at Filene's', *Women's Wear Daily* (15 December 1949).

74 BPL–FA, folder: Europe 1953 – Source Materials and Photos, *AMC Fashion News from Paris, from Rome, from Florence* (21 August 1953), 33.

75 BPL–FA, folder: Filene's Business Policies, 1953, 'Business Policies, Wm. Filene's Sons Company', July 1953.

76 'Filene's "This Is the Life"', *Daily Boston Globe* (3 October 1954); BPL–FA, folder: "This is the Life" Promotion – Beginning Sunday, October 3, 1954, document entitled 'This is the Life', [1954]; BPL–FA, folder: 'N.Y. party, H.D.H. acknowledgement to *LIFE* and to Heiskell', typescript of document by the same title, 27 September 1954.

77 'Quincy teen-ager will fly to Paris as Filene's buyer', *Daily Boston Globe* (17 October 1948); Elizabeth Watts, 'French girl thinks U.S. teen-agers "Womanly"', *Daily Boston Globe* (27 February 1949).

78 'Jordan's scholarship in fashion careers school', *Daily Boston Globe* (15 June 1937); 'Jordan fashion careers contest opens Monday', *Daily Boston Globe* (20 June 1937).

79 J. Meyerowitz (ed.), *Not June Cleaver: Women and Gender in Postwar America, 1945–1960* (Philadelphia, PA: Temple University Press, 1994).

80 BPL–FA, folder: *Charm* 100th, H. Valentine, '100 Years of Women in Business', 16 January 1956.

81 Washington, DC, Smithsonian National Museum of American History, Archives Center, Estelle Ellis Papers, acc. 423, box 6, folder 2, *Best Dressed Woman in the World*, booklet, c. 1953.

82 BPL–FA, folder: Virginia Harris – Personal, 'Virginia Harris – Biographical Notes', 18 March 1963.

83 G. Gavin, 'Filene's career show banishes "poor working girl" to the past', *Daily Boston Globe* (10 October 1950); G. Gavin, 'Fashions for career girls shown to 3000 by Jordan's', *Daily Boston Globe* (27 September 1951); BPL–FA, folder: Fall 1959 – Career Girl Supper Show Series, H. Wilinsky, 'Plan: Fall, 1959, Career Girl Supper Show Series', 10 October 1959.

84 BPL–FA, folder: Spring 1959 Career Girl Supper Show, V. Harris to P. Bell, Fashion Coordinator, The Emporium, San Francisco, 19 August 1959.

85 R. Blake, 'Fashions: Cruise shop styles highlighted Filene's fashion show', *Daily Boston Globe* (28 December 1954).

86 R. L. Blaszczyk, 'Styling synthetics: DuPont's marketing of fabrics and fashions in postwar America', *Business History Review*, 80:3 (autumn 2006), 485–538; R. L. Blaszczyk, *American Consumer Society, 1865–2005: From Hearth to HDTV* (Hoboken, NJ: Wiley, 2009).

87 BPL–FA, folder: 'Roving Reporter' Ads, 1952–53, George from the AMC Florence Office to S. Matthews, 7 February 1952.

88 BPL–FA, folder: 'Roving Reporter' Ads, 1952–53, 'Miss Wilinsky's Report from Rome', 27 July 1953.

89 *Ibid.*

90 E. Bernkopf, 'Exciting collection of Italian fashion', *Daily Boston Globe* (20 March 1955).

91 BPL–FA, folder: Fall 1953 – Career Show, H. Cronin to V. Harris, 19 October 1953.

92 BPL–FA, folder: Career Show Supper Series, 1955, J. Parsons to Fashion Promotion, Filene's, 22 March 1955.

93 V. Pouillard, 'The rise of fashion forecasting and fashion public relations, 1920–1940: the history of Tobé and Bernays', in H. Berghoff and T. Kühne (eds), *Globalizing Beauty: Consumerism and Body Aesthetics in the Twentieth Century* (New York: Palgrave Macmillan, 2013), 151–69; V. Pouillard and K. J. Trivette, 'The career of Tobé Coller Davis: fashion forecasting in America', in R. L. Blaszczyk and B. Wubs (eds), *The Fashion Forecasters: A Hidden History of Color and Trend Prediction* (London: Bloomsbury Academic, 2018).

94 BPL–FA, folder: 'Thirty ways to win a prince', [V. Harris], 'Fall Summary, 1957', 26 June 1957.

95 *Ibid.*

96 For sales figures dating from 1950 to 1960, see Federated Department Stores, *1960 Annual Report, Fiscal Year Ended January 28, 1961*.

97 BPL–FA, folder: European Fashion Reports to February 1962, H. Wilinsky to All Concerned, 'Miss Harris' Report on the Paris Collections', 7 August 1959.

98 BPL–FA, folder: Historical File – Europe, H. Wilinsky to All Interested, 'Virginia Harris' Summary of Paris Collections and Influences', 9 August 1960.

99 V. Pouillard, 'Création, stylisme, contre-cultures: La mode des années 1970', *Cahiers d'histoire du temps présent*, 18 (fall 2007), 131–62.

100 BPL–FA, folder: Mlle. Ricci Introduction, 1962, H. Wilinsky, 'Plan: Mlle. Ricci Introduction', 26 March 1962; 'Jules-Francois Crahay, designer', *New York Times* (8 January 1988).

101 BBL–FA, folder: Celanese/*Time* Magazine Survey, 1970, Celanese Fibers Marketing Company and *Time*, 'College Women's Apparel Survey'.

102 Blaszczyk, *Color Revolution*.

103 Blaszczyk, 'Styling synthetics'.

104 R. L. Blaszczyk, 'What do Baby Boomers want? How the swinging sixties became the trending seventies', in R. L. Blaszczyk and B. Wubs (eds), *The Fashion Forecasters: A Hidden History of Color and Trend Prediction* (London: Bloomsbury Academic, 2018).

105 Palmer, *Couture and Commerce*, p. 292.

8

H&M: how Swedish entrepreneurial culture and social values created fashion for everyone

Ingrid Giertz-Mårtenson

The evolution of international fashion has consisted of different phases. These have lasted for longer or shorter periods, but have also taken the form of different expressions and played out in different arenas. The rise of fast fashion, that is, rapidly changing, easily accessible fashion, has been an integral part of the international scene since the late twentieth century. Consumers have become accustomed to constant style shifts, but at the same time also to affordable pricing, all in line with the global trends that dominate at the moment.

The Swedish clothing company H&M is one of the key players in the creation of accessible fashion for an international clientele. The company has, since its launch in 1947, grown into a global retail chain. In 2015, H&M had an annual turnover of around 210 billion Swedish crowns (approximately $26 billion) and almost 150,000 employees worldwide. As of early 2016, it was operating some 4,000 stores on six continents and in sixty-one markets. A wide mix of different collections or 'concepts' means that H&M has created a diversity in its range and managed to attract customers of different ages and with varying preferences. Women's, men's and children's collections vie with accessories and beauty products in H&M stores worldwide and through a growing e-commerce offering.[1] The business concept is summarized as 'Fashion and quality at the best price in a sustainable way'.[2] Today's H&M Group also includes a number of other fashion brands (including COS, Monki, Weekday, Cheap Monday, and & Other Stories, home furnishings from H&M Home and H&M e-commerce, as well as H&M Beauty and H&M Shoes) in a growing number of markets.[3]

Much has been written about H&M, and many of the issues that affect H&M's approach to fashion, its business strategy and history, have been discussed in various contexts. But to fully understand this global company, one needs to go back to the beginning and to the founder Erling Persson.

8.1   Erling Persson, the founder of H&M and, in the background, his son the now Chairman of the company, Stefan Persson, c. 1985.

What was his personal approach to business, and how did this entrepreneur grasp the opportunity to sell clothes? From where did he draw his motivation, and how did he formulate his ideas about how a business should be run and developed?

H&M was from the beginning, and still is, a Swedish company. Several researchers have tried to define what constitutes 'Swedish' thinking and leadership. One account of how these attributes have emerged in the last century appears in Bengt Andersson's *Swedishness*.[4] Andersson claims, among other things, that Swedish managers see themselves less as commanders than as coaches who want staff at all levels to participate in the decisions that affect them. Was Erling Persson (figure 8.1) influenced by such tendencies and by the Swedish social and political climate? These issues are discussed in this chapter, which tries to place the success of a global company in a national perspective, and to understand what a business with Swedish values is. This chapter is also about fashion's relationship to society and culture, seen through the development of a Swedish company that has become a global giant. The word 'culture' is used here as a descriptive term for the values shared by a group of people, but which always needs to be seen in its social context. Culture, and therefore fashion as an expression of culture, is a reflection of society and may to some extent explain the world and the changes that surround us.[5] Fashion can be seen as a filter through which we create our image of reality. It is 'a symbolic product that anchors cultural dreams and social aspirations'.[6] It is a creative outlet for the consumer 'to valorize oneself, to please, astonish, disturb and look youthful'.[7]

H&M, in recent years and in various contexts, has been singled out as a successful representative of the fast fashion business model in the international fashion industry. This chapter examines the reality behind this idea, and investigates whether the company's core values and production realities support or contradict this concept.

Studying the development of the postwar international fashion industry is a new opportunity to understand what fashion has meant from a geographical, social, cultural, and economic perspective – and how fashion's role as interpreter of historical and market developments in society is often underestimated. The radical changes in Europe during the second half of the twentieth century profoundly affected what we call fashion – as an industry, as a trade, and as an expression of culture, in different ways in different countries. In Sweden, this development can clearly be seen in the fashion industry's rapid transformation, in large part due to the innovative ideas of a successful entrepreneur who laid the foundations for an entirely new way of selling clothes to the consumer.

Three generations build a global business

On 31 March 2000, there was a buzz of activity on Fifth Avenue in New York. Long lines snaked around the block where H&M's new flagship store – its first location in the United States – was about to open. The tension was rising inside the giant multi-floor retail space, with its magnificent windows overlooking Fifth Avenue. Most excited were three men named Persson: Erling, Stefan, and Karl-Johan. These men are the embodiment of the three generations of the family that still holds a controlling stake in H&M and remains its biggest shareholder. Erling Persson, the founding entrepreneur, was eighty-three years old. For the previous few years he had not been active within the company, but he had travelled to New York this day to be alongside his son, Stefan Persson, Chairman and former CEO, and his grandson Karl-Johan Persson, who had already begun his career in the company and later became CEO in 2009.[8]

One can only imagine the thoughts and feelings of these three men when their business in the United States was finally about to launch. It was probably Erling Persson who was most affected. Almost fifty years earlier, he had made his first trip to the United States. After World War II, with new hopes and prospects, he went out to explore new and exciting business ideas across the Atlantic Ocean. He was already an established and successful businessman, thanks to his keen entrepreneurial sense. And it was precisely this internal compass that led him in the right direction. In New York, he discovered something different: Lerner Shops, a retail chain established in 1918 to sell women's clothes that were inexpensive but stylish.[9] The new chain tapped into the rising demand for fashionable ready-to-wear made in New York's burgeoning garment district. The Lerner business was based on low prices, wearability, high volume, and quick turnover – a completely different concept from the dominant contemporary clothing retail model in Sweden, which consisted of individual private shops.

'I will start in Västerås because if it goes badly here nobody will know.' So said Erling Persson, who was born in 1917 in the small town of Västerås, about 100 kilometres from the capital, Stockholm.[10] His father owned a butcher's shop, and Erling Persson helped with the business from an early age. At the same time he received a basic business education in the evenings.[11] But the boy had bigger hopes than to take over his father's business. He left for Stockholm and began his entrepreneurial activities on a small scale; he sold cheese in the mid-1930s, made cases for the storage of wartime rationing coupons, and, with a good friend, eventually entered the pen industry with the new company Penn-Specialisten (The Pen Specialist).[12] Another popular product in Sweden at end of World War II was the so-called Christmas star, a paper star with electric lights that soon hung in a large number of Swedish homes during the dark winter season. In March 1947, Erling Persson brought this Christmas star with him on his first visit to the United States, where he wanted to explore new business ideas. The Christmas star was not a huge success, but Erling Persson's encounter with the American retail sector opened his eyes to new possibilities. Here was a Swedish entrepreneur discovering the ideas of mass-market pioneer Frank Winfield Woolworth, who built one of America's earliest chain-store empires beginning in the 1870s. And in Lerner's apparel chain, he found a new approach to selling clothes: low-priced products with rapid sales at identical shops.[13]

Hennes – the beginning of H&M

The idea of selling low-cost garments on a large scale appealed to Erling Persson's business sense, and this is where H&M's history begins. Erling Persson opened a small shop for women's clothing in his native town, Västerås, in 1947 (figure 8.2). He called it Hennes (which means 'hers'). His sister Eivor Björkstedt, a strong and enterprising woman, became the manager of the store, which from the very beginning met with great success. The Swedish clothing market of the 1940s was dominated by garments made in Sweden, and sold in small, privately owned clothing stores. Erling Persson had bigger plans – he wanted to create a clothing retailer that sold inexpensive clothes with rapid turnover and low mark-ups to a large clientele. The original vision, 'fashion that suits everyone at the best price' is still the basis for the business concept that the company has evolved over the years – but with some important additions that will be discussed later in this chapter.[14]

Capitalizing on his early success, soon Erling Persson owned stores throughout Sweden, selling clothing from Swedish ready-to-wear

This is where the H&M story began – the Hennes Store in the small Swedish town of Västerås in 1947.   **8.2**

manufacturers as well as imported goods from other Europeans countries for women, men, and children.[15] These were followed by stores in Nordic countries, with Norway first in 1964. During the 1980s and 1990s H&M (or Hennes & Mauritz, as the company had been renamed) expanded to a dozen European countries[16] 'Mauritz' was added to the company's name when Persson bought hunting and fishing store Mauritz Widforss, next door to a Hennes shop in Stockholm, in 1968. Erling Persson, who had taken up the sale of men's wear, liked the store's name and kept it. This can be seen as an example of the founder's sense of cost-consciousness. To use the old name, Mauritz, saved Erling Persson some extra costs. No new name was needed. The company has become well known through its red 'H&M' logo.[17] Many have come to believe, since the company's Initial Public Offering (IPO) in 1974, that it has been the most successful company on the Swedish stock exchange.[18]

Postwar Sweden

Towards the end of World War II, the Swedish fashion retail market was dominated by garments sold by a healthy Swedish clothing industry. Political neutrality had kept Sweden out of war and allowed the retail sector, consisting of large and small private clothing merchants, to flourish despite wartime rationing and international isolation. The domestic textile industry also helped to supply the market with goods.[19]

Carina Gråbacke, in her book *Clothes, Shopping and Flair*, discusses how the Swedish clothing retail sector after 1945 transitioned from traditional private clothing stores to retail chains, which were first launched in big cities. Chain stores expanded in the 1950s and 1960s, and offered a completely new way of selling clothes. The emphasis was high volume, low prices, rapid turnover, and fewer Swedish-made goods. An increased reliance on imported garments led to the decline of the Swedish clothing industry over the course of several decades. In 1959, there were 115,000 people employed in this industry, but from the 1960s to the late 1970s nearly 70,000 of these jobs disappeared.[20] Furthermore, the consumption of apparel per individual went up by sixty per cent between the 1950s and the late 1970s and low-priced imports from Asia paved the way for the transformation of the retail sector and the rise of vertically integrated enterprises such as H&M.[21] In Sweden, H&M was the first and most successful player in mass-market fashion, and later led the charge towards the global transformation that contributed to a 'faster' fashion. H&M's most significant international growth, however, came only in the early 2000s. Before the New Millennium, H&M had a presence in approximately ten foreign countries, whereas the current count is sixty-one countries.[22] The ability to grow rapidly was based on Erling Persson's foresight and entrepreneurship; H&M's fundamental values can be traced to his ideas and leadership and live on in the company's model, or 'DNA', a term often used in the fashion industry.

'The Swedish Model'

Is being a successful entrepreneur an innate talent or the result of heritage, environment, and education? Much has been written about Erling Persson, his character and his personality.[23] At the same time, he remains a rather secretive individual. Erling Persson rarely gives interviews and has not been particularly interested in discussing the sorts of issues that are the concern of the worlds of media and business. But his professional collaborators tell powerful stories about him, his vision and his leadership. Was this leadership rooted in Sweden, Swedish culture, and Swedish social values? H&M has throughout its history been a Swedish company. The head office has been in Stockholm, and its corporate and creative leadership has been Swedish. At launches in other countries, Swedish representatives have been sent out to introduce the company to the new markets. Were Swedish values embedded in the company's evolution from the beginning, and in the concept and the philosophy that Erling Persson instilled in the company? To answer these questions, we need to try to understand whether there is a 'Swedish model' and what it means in this case. How did Sweden look in the mid-twentieth century and what beliefs and traditions guided Swedish society?

In their study 'Hennes & Mauritz (H&M): the Swedish Model, corporate social responsibility and fashion', Ulrika Berglund and Knut-Erland Berglund discuss the globalization of H&M against the background of Swedish values.[24] The Berglunds suggest that Sweden has become internationally known for, among other things, its model of social welfare, known widely as 'The Swedish Model'. Strongly linked to the country's leading political party, the Social Democrats, this 'social model' was established in Sweden during the latter half of the 1930s. The model was intended to build a state with room for everyone in order to overcome class prejudice. A middle way between capitalism and socialism was sought. Sweden succeeded, thanks to this model, in creating an image and a kind of utopia of a perfect society. Social stability could also be attributed to the fact that peace had prevailed in the country for hundreds of years. The Swedish people's home (Folkhemmet) was later to become another expression of the Swedish social-democratic view of society. Swedish values also were said to include the so-called 'Jante law' (Jantelagen), that is, the idea that everyone is equal and that no one is better than anyone else, and that one must never boast of personal success.[25] These aspects of 'The Swedish Model' may have influenced Erling Persson's entrepreneurial vision. While H&M has rarely been known to emphasize its Swedish geographical, historical, or cultural background in corporate marketing and communications, behind its international image is a link to a national mindset and to Swedish values of equality and democracy. From the very beginning, Erling Persson's attitude to fashion was that 'Fashion should not cost so much that some people cannot afford it.'[26]

An interesting comparison can be made with Sweden's other internationally renowned company, IKEA. This company was founded in 1943, about the same time as H&M. Ingvar Kamprad, the founder of IKEA, today remains its public face. His entrepreneurial approach has often been compared to Erling Persson's – and the two men were reportedly friends.[27] IKEA's relationship to Sweden and Swedish values is well known, from the blue and yellow exteriors at IKEA stores worldwide to the Swedish names of all IKEA products. In this way, the company has chosen to communicate and to market an image that is closely linked to Sweden. In the book *Design by IKEA: A Cultural History*, Sara Kristoffersson describes how IKEA's ties to Sweden over the years have been communicated in the form of different stories, an ongoing and lively narrative which can be summarized as corporate storytelling: companies tell stories to convey an attractive image of themselves and their culture.[28] In IKEA's case, these narratives or stories primarily involve the founder Ingvar Kamprad. They become a marketing tool that can be called 'history marketing'.[29] This type of engagement with history and narrative has never occurred at H&M. On the contrary, the company has always been very low-key when it comes to telling its own story. H&M's website has brief details about where, when, and by whom the company was founded, but little else.[30] IKEA's way of connecting its enterprise to Sweden, Swedish nature, and Swedish ideals is not reflected in H&M's marketing strategy.

Oral history interviews with various H&M executives from the retail sector, however, underline the importance of Swedish values in H&M's way of working. Jörgen Andersson, who spent twenty-five years at H&M (including as the director of global marketing, overseeing brand development, and new business), describes his view of H&M's connection to Sweden and Swedish thinking:

> Neither Erling Persson nor Stefan Persson saw any upside in being a Swedish company; they wanted to be an international company, a global company … You don't have to do the marketing around the yellow and the blue of the Swedish flag and the colour around it. We say we are a global company; in India we are an Indian company, in China we are a Chinese company because we are part of the planet, the earth. But I do think that Swedish values – the H&M values – are part of our [H&M] values, such as that we honour the group, when we go to school we do everything in a group, we work in a group, we are basically trained to work as a team … You don't want to be standing up as a representative for a group, you want the whole group to be there … And [at H&M], we believe in people, there is lots of 'space' for everyone and that, I guess, is a part of the social democratic politics that we have been raised with in our society.[31]

H&M insists that it views global fashion (and not Swedish fashion) as the driving idea behind the company. 'It is difficult to communicate fashion as being Swedish. If we did not market our own interpretation of international fashion, we could not exist', said Margareta van den Bosch, head of design of H&M for some twenty years, and today, the firm's creative director (figure 8.3).[32] This means that H&M has never focused on Swedish fashion in the same way that, for example, IKEA has sold Swedish style. The Swedish influence within H&M is demonstrated more in Swedish values such as teamwork, equality and sustainability in the construction of its businesses – values that also guide the entry into new markets. The same idea can be discerned in H&M's strategy of never highlighting the names of any of its hundreds of in-house designers. 'I do think that our company culture can be said to be Swedish', explained van den Bosch. 'First of all it is not hierarchical … At H&M everyone talks to everyone … Everyone is accessible to everyone.'[33] 'There is strong teamwork in the way we work', she continued. 'We are a team working together – that's our strength.'[34] This also means that H&M only has one spokesperson to communicate its new fashions from season to season. During her years as head designer at H&M, van den Bosch was entrusted with this role. Design historian Lasse Brunnström believes that promoting the individual designer

Margareta van den Bosch was Head Designer of H&M for more than twenty years. Today she   **8.3**
serves as Creative Advisor for the company.

can be seen as unfair and un-Swedish. This attitude can be traced back to the basic values of the Swedish model, which advocates an egalitarian and classless society.[35]

The international positioning of fashion at H&M is also underlined by the fact that the company currently has about 250 designers, representing around twenty-five different nationalities. New designers are selected through close contacts with renowned European fashion design schools, and from a pool of experienced designers who apply directly to H&M. At the start of their employment, the designers all undergo a training programme to learn 'the H&M way of working'.[36]

H&M – a corporate culture, going back to values, not manuals

As mentioned above, H&M founder Erling Persson rarely gave interviews, but in one of the extant few interviews, he pointed out some fundamental business ideas behind the success of his company. He discovered one of these during his travels around the United States in 1947: 'I realized the value of being spot-on. In everything. You've got to find the right timing and you have to look for the perfect location where the customers are. You can't be on a side street.'[37] He also put it this way: 'Business should be where the money is, and where the bags go.'[38] Like Frank W. Woolworth, Erling Persson accepted only the best possible store location – a strategy that H&M still uses today. When the company enters a new market, it never accepts second-best locations, and it would rather wait, for a long time if necessary, to establish itself in the best spots for shopping. The stores in Oxford Circus in London (figure 8.4), opened in 1979, and Fifth Avenue in New York, are cases in point.[39]

At an early stage in H&M's history, certain other basic values were also established, which are still seen as essential for everyone in the firm. During the company's evolution, they have been refined into five 'commandments' for H&M, which were later supplemented with two more. They were expressed as follows in H&M's annual report for 2015:

1 We believe in people
2 We are one team
3 Straightforward and open-minded
4 Keep it simple
5 Entrepreneurial spirit
6 Constant improvement
7 Cost-consciousness[40]

8.4   When expanding internationally H&M is always looking for the best locations; one example is their London store, centrally located in Oxford Circus and opened in 1979.

These values are attributed to the founder Erling Persson and to his way of doing business. Because he was a man with a rather unconventional management style, these points were not written down until long after he officially left the company. Erling Persson himself never wrote down any guidelines or rules, but trusted that his view of the business would be conveyed by his way of acting and managing the company – and the values live on from founder to son and grandson. A former H&M human relations manager summarizes the core of H&M values as follows:

> We are a family-run business, the Persson family has run this company from the very start … [The company's values] are the same old simple values that we constantly refine, and what are they all about? Well, there is simplicity in what we do, we work a lot with common sense and if you don't know what to do then you try to think what would seem reasonable. Another thing is internal recruitment, something that is very important for us – that we pick those who have the right kind of thinking so we'll get the culture, walk the talk, where you can see the culture through people's actions. Taking initiative is another one, to do something, to think! … We have a high tempo and we make improvements as often as we can … Teamwork is another element. I would say those values are H&M.[41]

Many of Erling Persson's employees have talked about his 'management by walking around'.[42] H&M's founder rarely sat still in his office, but constantly moved among his employees, discussing current problems on the hoof, and loathed long meetings. Bureaucracy was minimized. It was about 'keeping it simple', having direct contact with employees and, wherever possible, avoiding a heavy, overworked bureaucracy. Erling Persson also kept himself updated about the sales situation in the shops. Each day, he tried to have enough time to take a trip to the H&M stores in Stockholm, where he talked with the staff (whose names he usually knew during the early years) and in that way followed the performance of the business. His businessman's sense told him that he must constantly listen to the voice of the consumer, to acquire, in a timely way, a large as possible information base, on which to ground the growth of the business. Jörgen Andersson likens this to the information tools available via the Internet today. But while the Internet revolution allows fashion companies to engage the consumer, Andersson says that very few companies actually do this.

> They pick up on social media, pick up what is said about the company … but if they were to engage the consumer … to co-create … Why don't they post ten dresses on the Web and ask consumers to pick the five that are most popular, to be co-created? That's what Erling Persson did – he went around the stores and asked people [what they liked] … Today it's possible to get so close to the consumer – and fashion is about newness.[43]

The team spirit that has constantly permeated H&M's management is also well known. Erling Persson believed in the abilities of his colleagues and sought individuals who could 'grow' and move on to other positions within the company. His management style was unconventional.[44] This is also evident in H&M's corporate values today. Believing in people was just as important for Erling Persson's son and successor, Stefan. Jörgen Andersson saw a clear example of this during his career at H&M. Andersson was asked by Stefan Persson (who had assumed the leadership of H&M in 1982) to relocate to Switzerland in 1998 to become CEO of H&M's Swiss subsidiary, located in Geneva. Andersson replied that he knew nothing about how a CEO works, and was told 'Then why don't you talk to some other of our other CEOs and learn from them?' Andersson replied, 'But I can't speak a word of French', whereupon Stefan Persson said, 'Just take a crash course!'[45]

H&M designer collections – always looking for constant improvement

A guiding principle in H&M's development has been to constantly look ahead. It's about never being satisfied, never leaning back, but about always seeing new opportunities. Designer van den Bosch puts it this way: 'It is very important with the entrepreneurial spirit ... We always have to try to improve everything.'[46] The desire to surprise and to 'think new' has been a recurring feature in H&M's policy. Innovative advertising campaigns have always been an important tool for the company. Erling Persson was inspired by the advertising he saw in the United States during his 1947 visit. He was impressed by the long, narrow ads along the edges of newspaper pages for the fashion specialty store Lord & Taylor.

H&M's annual ad campaigns are an example of this focus on innovation. From the end of the 1990s, the company featured large lingerie ads in major global campaigns. World-famous models showed off H&M's sexy lingerie in huge images on outdoor billboards which were sometimes so attention-grabbing that they were even said to cause traffic accidents. But there was another side to these ads. H&M's female employees reacted negatively and within a few years they let the management know that they were not happy with this kind of exposure of women's bodies. It was simply too much.[47] Jörgen Andersson, at the time head of marketing for the H&M Group, recalls:

> The year was 2004, and the lingerie ads were beginning to feel old. They were more and more about the supermodels used in the advertising and less and less about the clothes they were wearing. What could we do instead to get back to H&M's business concept of 'Fashion and quality at the best price'? What idea – and who – could help us with this? The answer was simple – Karl Lagerfeld, the individual that perhaps best symbolizes Paris and the fashion world, both by his name and by his looks. We approached him and met with him after proposing our brief on a planned collaboration. He said yes within two minutes. 'I love it – let's get started.'[48]

Lagerfeld, who is known for being innovative and always wanting to push forward, was quick to reply when Andersson suggested that H&M, which sells 'fashion at a cheap price', wanted to work with him: 'No, it's not cheap, I would prefer to call it affordable.'[49] Van den Bosch says that the first collaboration with Lagerfeld was a fun idea and a test. The goal was to surprise the customers and do something different. And it quickly proved successful, both with consumers and commercially. Customers queued for hours before stores opened and the clothes sold out the first day. Since the first collaboration with Lagerfeld in 2004, the same story has been repeated every year when H&M invites an innovative, higher-end designer to create a new collection for the company's global markets. The idea was for a famous designer to bring his prestige to the masses, creating an effect known as 'massclusivity', or 'masstige', combining mass distribution with prestige and exclusivity (figure 8.5).[50]

Through these collaborations, H&M was able to build a new value into its brand, an aura or halo effect, to use the words of the influential philosopher and critical theorist Walter Benjamin.[51] The connection with major fashion brands enabled the creation of a new status. The interaction between brands broadened the public perception of H&M – the company's diverse range was the basis for making this possible. Jörgen Andersson has the following comments on the outcome of the

The H&M designer collections started with the collaboration with Karl Lagerfeld in 2004. Since then many of the world's most famous designers have created memorable fashion looks for H&M.   **8.5**

collaborations, underlining that there was a win-win situation between these 'high-and-low' brands:

> [The designers we collaborated with] had never worked in an H&M store so they thought it was cheap … but were very impressed by H&M's control in the factories. They also learned that price does not necessarily go with quality, the secret [of the low price] is also partly about distribution … Not only what H&M does, but how they do it: in a leaner way, in a smoother way, in a more efficient way … I think that [the designers we worked with] learned how they could build their variety from H&M, because we could teach them what the majority want – take away certain details, make it less complicated, so it will be cheaper in production. [Also that] the commercial side of H&M interested them very, very much. And again I think that what they were most impressed by was the communication of the outcome of the collection and the presentation of the windows, the closed universe that we created together with them.[52]

All the garments from the designer collections have been saved and are now kept in H&M's archives at the Centre for Business History (CfN) in Stockholm. However, H&M have never saved any pieces from their standard lines. This indicates that design collaborations are considered 'high-status' for the company. These garments must be preserved while H&M's in-house designs were never considered of any interest for the future.

Nor has any real interest in the history of the company been shown through the years. In a company where the focus is on always looking forward, there seems to be no room for 'contemplative retrospection … H&M is not a company that writes and reflects'.[53] However, a number of years ago, H&M decided to document its history.[54] The project was awarded to the Centre for Business History in Stockholm. H&M's archive, which today is stored at the Centre, is unique of its kind because it includes not only accessible historical material from H&M starting in 1947 (in the form of media, movies, digital materials, sketches, and other materials), but also some hundred interviews with H&M employees, from those who were there from the start and have long since left the company, to current managers from all parts of the business as well as representatives of the Persson family. With this endeavour, H&M must be seen as a pioneer, being the first Swedish fashion-related company to understand the importance of securing its history for the future.

H&M fast fashion and sustainability – a possible mix?

Constant change is in the nature of fashion – it would not be fashion if it stagnated and stood still. Cultural sociologist Elizabeth Wilson notes that fashion cannot exist without change. At its core is mutability and perpetual renewal. 'The next style is always hovering in the wings, while the very arbitrariness of the next latest thing – inviting yet refusing a plausible explanation – defeats the sense of an ending.'[55] Fashion has also been perceived as an expression and tangible manifestation of modernity. In the latter half of the twentieth century, fashion's fluctuations were affected not least by society's technological development. Increasingly rapid change is a key part of the fashion image we currently see in the West.

These rapid changes and the constantly renewed range of fashion have been called fast fashion. However, the fast fashion concept is used today in a somewhat undefined and generic way.

H&M is sometimes cited as an example of a company that represents this phenomenon, and has been called the 'legendary Scandinavian company, which is the fastest of them all. New products are churned out every day.'[56] H&M has thus become synonymous with fast fashion, a giant within its field. Companies like Zara and H&M have built multi-billion dollar businesses that are said to reproduce the latest catwalk creations at a fraction of their original price. Global marketing and high-speed production are key factors in this part of the fashion industry. In their study, the Berglunds claim that H&M has, in many ways, contributed to a change in the dissemination of fashion. New H&M collections are frequently introduced, a drastic change from the classic French fashion system created with the establishment of the Chambre Syndicale de la Couture Parisienne in 1868.[57]

But van den Bosch is unhappy with the idea of fast fashion in relation to H&M. She explains, 'We work with a lead time of about a year – just like other brands in the fashion industry. We interpret international fashion in our own way and we don't "copy the catwalk" as it's sometimes alleged.'[58] She emphasizes that while the company's hundreds of in-house designers are obviously inspired by the evolution of global fashion, 'we're careful to focus on our own interpretation' of fashion'.[59] Going back to the founder, it is interesting to note that Erling Persson's original business concept was not to create fashion, but rather to take inspiration from current trends.

In her classic article on fast fashion published in *Fashion Theory*, Simona Segre Reinach discusses the different systems or production models of fashion that have evolved over time. She claims there are three models: first, 'couture, the concept of luxury', and second, prêt-à-porter, or ready-to-wear, which pivots around the concepts of modernity and 'lifestyles'. The third model, fast fashion, focuses on versatility and on immediate gratification in the form of opportunities to rapidly change one's identity thanks to new fashion expressions. 'Each belongs to a different age', Segre explained, 'but all three coexist in different "doses" and layers that still influence the imaginary by which fashion is communicated and experienced.'[60]

Drawing on the case of H&M, I would argue that a fourth model is emerging, a different system or production of fashion that can be called 'the sustainable model'. This model is based on an evolution towards a more circular and inclusive fashion industry, and is part of the growing design philosophy with its notion of sustainability. H&M is working its way towards this fourth model. A few years ago, H&M adopted a new business concept that had evolved over the years: 'Fashion and quality at the best price in a sustainable way.'[61] More recently, H&M has put a lot of effort into its social and environmental work as well as issues dealing with sustainability that are considered to be essential to the company's long-term success. Creating conditions for sustainable cotton production, promoting fair living wages for textile workers, using renewable electricity sources, and recycling old clothing are just some of H&M's initiatives towards continuous improvement throughout the value chain.[62] The H&M Conscious collection, which uses organic fabrics and recycled materials, is an example of how design and sustainability can be combined.[63]

Conclusion

This study has focused on how a small Swedish company has developed into one of the world's largest fashion retailers. By passing on values that date back to its founder Erling Persson, H&M has managed to maintain strong cohesion and a strong forward-looking strategy. Many of the company's traits can be traced back to Swedish traditions, despite the fact that H&M has never actively sought to be perceived as Swedish. In a world where the fashion industry is increasingly accused of using fast fashion collections and low-priced products to drive short-term consumption at the expense of quality, H&M has tried to gradually adopt a philosophy that focuses on durability and sustainability. Whether this approach can continue to satisfy the market's demand for growth and ever-increasing profits, only time will tell. But the history of H&M is not just about fashion and retail. It is also the story of how founder Erling Persson's entrepreneurship and strong values have survived to this day. And it is about 'one man's vision – or rather [his] intractable stubbornness, determination and knowledge of human nature'.[64]

Notes

1 No figure on the proportion of e-commerce is officially known.
2 H&M, 'Our business concept', at http://about.hm.com/en/About/facts-about-hm/about-hm/business-concept.html#cm-men (accessed 3 August 2016).
3 H&M, *Annual Report 2015*, at http://about.hm.com/content/dam/hm/about/documents/en/Annual%20Report/Annual%20Report%202015_en.pdf (accessed 3 August 2016).
4 B. Andersson, *Swedishness* (Stockholm: Positive Sweden, 1993), p. 75.

5 J. Frykman and O. Löfgren, *Den kultiverade människan* [*The Cultured Man*] (Malmö: Gleerups Utbildnings AB, 1979).

6 R. L. Blaszczyk, 'Rethinking fashion', in R. L. Blaszczyk (ed.), *Producing Fashion: Commerce, Culture, and Consumers* (Philadelphia: University of Pennsylvania Press, 2008), p. 9.

7 G. Lipovetsky, *The Empire of Fashion* (Princeton: Princeton University Press, 1994), p. 101.

8 I. Giertz-Mårtenson, 'Sveriges modegigant mot nya mål' ['Sweden's fashion giant – toward new heights'], *Företagshistoria* (January 2014), 13.

9 B. Pettersson, *Handelsmännen* [*The Businessmen*] (Stockholm: Ekerlids Förlag, 2003), p. 43. Here Pettersson relates the following: 'On Thirty-Seventh Street in Manhattan Persson noticed a clothing store named Lerner, a name that had cropped up along his drive across the country. This, according to Persson, sparked the first impulse to start a similar chain in Sweden.'

10 For the quotation, see Pettersson, *Handelsmännen*, p. 15.

11 Pettersson, *Handelsmännen*, p. 28. Pettersson here also highlights Erling Persson's lack of interest in academic studies and quotes him as saying, 'I later realized that I'm actually dyslexic.'

12 Pettersson, *Handelsmännen*, pp. 32–3.

13 Lerner Shops was founded in 1918 by Samuel A. Lerner and Harold M. Lane in New York City. In 1995, the name was changed to New York & Company. See New York & Company, 'About Us', at www.nyandcompany.com/nyco/static/about/aboutus (accessed 3 April 2016).

14 Pettersson, *Handelsmännen*, p. 51.

15 The most important countries of import of clothes were Germany and Switzerland. See Pettersson, *Handelsmännen*, p. 56.

16 See http://about.hm.com/en/about-us/history.html (accessed 15 October 2016).

17 Giertz-Mårtenson, 'Sveriges modegigant mot nya mål', 15.

18 Otto Gustav Bobergh was another Swedish entrepreneur who started a well-known international fashion company. This relatively unknown man was a business partner of Charles Fredrick Worth. Starting in 1858, together they created one of Paris's first haute couture houses at 7, rue de la Paix under the name Worth & Bobergh. This company, with the renowned designer Worth at its helm, embodied the start of haute couture in Paris and, during its most successful period, employed more than 1,200 staff producing more than 5,000 garments per year. Otto Gustav Bobergh later returned to Sweden and opened a fashion house in Stockholm with the entrepreneur Augusta Lundin. See U. Berglund, 'Medelvägens lyx', in *Det Svenska Begäret* (Stockholm: Carlssons Bokförlag, 2015).

19 I. Giertz-Mårtenson, 'Modeurop: using color to unify the European shoe and leather industry', in R. L. Blaszczyk and U. Spiekermann (eds), *Bright Modernity: Color, Commerce, and Consumer Culture* (New York: Palgrave Macmillan, 2017), pp. 227–49.

20 There were several causes of the textile crisis, including the high costs of manufacturing in Sweden, combined with fierce foreign competition and a liberal trade policy. Clothing imports grew on the Swedish market, not only through H&M. To a large extent, domestic production moved abroad, especially to the newly developed textile and clothing factories in Asia, with their lower labour costs. See Peter Sandberg 'Näringsliv och stat i nya roller', in M. Larsson (ed.), *Det svenska näringslivets historia 1864 – 2014* (Stockholm: Dialogos förlag / Centrum för Näringslivshistoria, 2014), p. 512.

21 M. Dahlén, 'Copy or copyright fashion? Swedish design protection law in historical and comparative perspective', *Business History*, 54:1 (2012), 96.

22 C. Gråbacke, *Kläder, shopping och flärd* [*Clothes, Shopping and Flair*] (Stockholm: Stockholmia Förlag, 2015); see http://about.hm.com/en/about-us/history.html (accessed 15 October 2016).

23 The personality of Erling Persson is interpreted in different ways both in Pettersson, *Handelsmännen* and in C. Steinwall and Å. Crona, *Moderouletten* [*The Fashion Roulette*] (Stockholm: Bonniers, 1989).

24 U. Berglund and K.-E. Berglund, 'Hennes & Mauritz (H&M): the Swedish Model, corporate social responsibility and fashion', paper presented at the European Business History Association-Business History Society of Japan (EBHA-BHSJ) conference, Paris, 2012.

25 A. Sandemose, *En flykting korsar sitt spår: Espen Arnakkes kommentarer till Jantelagen* (Stockholm: Forum, 1968).

26 Pettersson, *Handelsmännen*, p. 278.

27 Ingvar Kamprad has expressed his admiration for Erling Persson thus: 'Erling is much stronger than I am – he has retired and doesn't run around and meddle.' Kamprad refers here to Erling Persson's early transferral of control of the business to his son Stefan Persson in 1982. In contrast, Kamprad has still not fully stepped down from IKEA in favour of his sons. Pettersson, *Handelsmännen*, p. 305.

28 S. Kristoffersson, *IKEA: En kulturhistoria* (Stockholm: Bokförlaget Atlantis AB, 2015).

29 I. Giertz-Mårtenson, 'Så rullas svenskheten ut i världen' ['Rolling out Swedishness into the world'], *SvD* (27 October 2015), 19.

30 H&M, 'Our History', at http://about.hm.com/en/About/facts-about-hm/people-and-history/history.html (accessed 4 August 2016).

31 J. Andersson, interview by author, Stockholm, 14 March 2016.

32 M. van den Bosch, interview by author, Stockholm, 23 February 2016.

33 Van den Bosch interview. The non-hierarchical attitude, shown in this quotation, corresponds to the following explanation by B. Andersson of Swedish management style and its way of bypassing the hierarchy: 'Swedes believe that if they want to tell somebody something, or if they need information, they should make things as simple as possible. Anyone should be able to talk to anyone else without having to ask for permission. Accordingly, Swedes go directly to the source, even if this means bypassing one or more layers of bosses.'Andersson, *Swedishness*, p. 79.

34 Van den Bosch interview.

35 L. Brunnström, *Svensk Industridesign: En 1900-talshistoria* (Stockholm: Prisma, 1997).

36 Van den Bosch interview.

37 B. Edsta, 'Intervju med H&Ms grundare Erling Persson' (Interview with the founder of H&M, Erling Persson), *H&M Oral History Project* (Stockholm: Centre for Business History, 2008), pp. 6–11. The original of this interview is deposited in the archive of Svensk Handel, Stockholm.

38 Handelns Historia, 'H&M:s grundare Erling Persson – från ostbud till imperieskapare', at www.handelnshistoria.se/profiler/kopman-och-entreprenorer/hms-grundare-erling-persson-fran-ostbud-till-imperieskapare/ (accessed 3 August 2016).

39 H&M does not own any real estate, but rents the premises for its stores in order to be as flexible as possible. J. Andersson underlines that it is easier to move clothes than houses. 'Retail is about three things: location, location and location.' Andersson interview.

40 H&M, *Annual Report 2015*.

41 M. Bengtsson, *The Art of Replicating* (Linköping: Department of Management and Engineering, Linköping University, 2008), p. 95. The comment was made by an HR Manager at the H&M Head Office.

42 Steinwall and Crona, *Moderouletten*, p. 205.

43 Andersson interview.

44 Carin Steinwall, who started at H&M in 1969 and served as head of marketing for many years, highlighted the importance of internal recruitment in the company: 'Just about all in the senior staff were promoted from below. Just about all of them came from within the company. It was obvious for us to recruit internally.' Steinwall and Crona, *Moderouletten*, p. 91.

45 Andersson interview.
46 Van den Bosch interview.
47 I. Giertz-Mårtenson, 'From fast fashion to luxury in the fashion business: the history of the H&M Designer Collections (2004–2013)', paper presented at the Business History Conference, Frankfurt am Main, Germany, 13–15 March 2014.
48 Andersson interview.
49 Giertz-Mårtenson, 'From fast fashion to luxury in the fashion business'.
50 D. Thomas, *Deluxe: How Luxury Lost its Luster* (New York: Penguin, 2007), p. 318.
51 See 'Walter Benjamin', *Stanford Encyclopedia of Philosophy*, at http://plato.stanford.edu/entries/benjamin/ (accessed 29 August 2016).
52 Andersson interview.
53 Pettersson, *Handelsmännen*, p. 19.
54 Giertz-Mårtenson, 'H&M: documenting the story of one of the world's largest fashion retailers', *Business History*, 54:1 (2012), 108–15.
55 E. Wilson, *Adorned in Dreams* (London: I. B. Tauris, 2003), p. 276.
56 S. S. Reinach, 'China and Italy: fast fashion versus prêt-à-porter, towards a new culture of fashion', *Fashion Theory*, 9:1 (2005), 43–56.
57 Berglund and Berglund, 'Hennes & Mauritz (H&M)'. See also D. Grumbach, *Histoires de la mode* (Paris: Editions du Seuil, 1993).
58 Van den Bosch interview.
59 Van den Bosch interview.
60 Reinach, 'China and Italy', 47–8.
61 H&M, 'Our business concept'.
62 Since H&M launched their garment collecting initiative in 2013, they have gathered more that 22,000 tonnes of garments to give them a new life. H&M, 'Garment Collecting', at http://about.hm.com/en/About/sustainability/commitments/reduce-waste/garment-collecting.html (accessed 7 September 2016).
63 H&M, 'About H&M Conscious', at http://about.hm.com/en/About/sustainability/hm-conscious/conscious.html (accessed 16 August 2016).
64 Pettersson, *Handelsmännen*, p. 21.

PART III

European fashion on the periphery

9

Competitiveness of the Japanese denim and jeans industry: the cases of Kaihara and Japan Blue, 1970–2015

Rika Fujioka and Ben Wubs

In the 1950s and 1960s, blue jeans became a symbol of youth protests against the conformity of their parents. As a garment, jeans appealed to the emerging youth culture in the United States. Denim was seen as a classless fabric, and the rejection of traditional fashion was a way to make a statement against intolerance and injustice during the Civil Rights era.[1] Jeans and denim spread rapidly across the Western world during the 1960s and 1970s as a symbol of liberty and non-conformity. By the 1980s, however, the manufacturing of denim and jeans had largely relocated from the United States to China, Brazil, North Africa, Turkey, and Japan. In this highly competitive market for denim and jeans, Japanese manufacturers have survived against the odds.

Anti-establishment street fashion also spread throughout Japan in the 1960s. As the demand for traditional cotton kimonos fell, many manufacturers switched to the production of denim and jeans. In the early 1970s, local manufacturers like Kaihara moved from producing traditional fabrics to making denim. Kaihara was established in 1893 by Sukejiro Kaihara as a weaver of indigo fabrics for 'Kasuri', in what is now Fukuyama City in the Hiroshima Prefecture. Today, this family-controlled company is Japan's largest denim manufacturer, operating four integrated denim mills in Japan and one in Thailand, and serving more than fifty per cent of the Japanese denim market.

During the 1970s and 1980s, designer and vintage jeans appeared on the catwalk when Vivienne Westwood, Karl Lagerfeld, and Giorgio Armani, among others, pushed these garments to the forefront of the high-end fashion market.[2] Vintage and designer denim became an important part of the global fashion system. One Japanese company that entered this new market was Japan Blue, which was set up in 1992 by indigo fan Hisao Manabe in Kojima, which is part of Kurashiki City in the Okayama

Prefecture. Japan Blue introduced four brands of premium denim jeans. The company is much smaller than the textile manufacturer Kaihara. It does not operate integrated textile mills, but collaborates with different small manufacturers whose businesses range from textiles and sewing to washing and finishing, in different manufacturing clusters in and outside the prefecture.

The two case studies in this chapter draw on interviews with the CEOs of Kaihara and Japan Blue and documents from both companies. The examples fit perfectly within a comparative, historical study of Japanese premium denim and jeans. On the one hand, the case studies demonstrate that producing denim, the fabric, is a different story and needs a different strategy from producing jeans, the garment. On the other, the two stories are also closely related because of interdependence between the two industries; Kaihara, for example, dyes Japan Blue's woven cotton. Furthermore, producing for the high-end market (Japan Blue) requires a totally different strategy from doing so for its lower-end counterpart (Kaihara). An in-depth historical analysis of these two cases will thus provide valuable insight into the historical competitiveness of denim and jeans manufacturing in Japan over the last five decades.

The history of Japanese denim is also a great example of cultural encounters. Western style became a symbol of a new, modern life and the democratization of Japanese society. Denim was one of the symbolic products of democracy. American GIs at the General Headquarters (GHQ) of the Allied forces, who all wore jeans, made a huge impression on Japanese youths. Then the Americanization, or Westernization, of Japanese youth and the rise of street culture took place in the 1960s. Denim was street fashion; it was classless, anonymous, and symbolized a lifestyle revolution wherein clothes no longer represented one's position in the social hierarchy but were an expression of one's individuality.[3]

In 1904, the German sociologist Georg Simmel published his seminal article 'Fashion', in which he argued that the individual is able to pursue desires for group identity and personal expression through clothing.[4] This meant that private values could be expressed while still following the norms of the group. People communicated through fashion, but the elite dictated what was fashionable and the lower strata followed in its wake. Simmel famously wrote:

> Social forms, apparel, aesthetic judgment, the whole style of human expression, are constantly transformed by fashion, in such a way, however, that fashion – i.e., the latest fashion – in all these things affects only the upper class. Just as soon as the lower classes begin to copy their style, thereby crossing the line of demarcation the upper classes have drawn and destroying the uniformity of their coherence, the upper classes turn away from this style and adopt a new one, which in its turn differentiates them from the masses; and thus the game goes merrily on.[5]

Half a century later, according to Robert Ross, a specialist in African studies who has written about the globalization of the clothing industry, jeans were probably the first piece of clothing to become fashionable from below, moving from the working to the upper classes, thereby turning the trickle-down fashion system described by Georg Simmel on its head.[6] However, the designer and vintage jeans that gained currency in the 1980s and 1990s did not symbolize a classless society. To the contrary, they represented class and taste, and wholesale prices increased enormously. Japanese manufacturers, with their traditional focus on quality and craftsmanship, began to play a role in this global market for premium denim and jeans.

Japanese denim is often praised for its exceptional quality, and is rumoured to be produced on vintage Toyoda looms. Is this myth or reality? The chapter aims to provide answers to a multitude of questions. How have the Japanese companies that produce denim and jeans become the leaders in the field over the last five decades, and how have they survived in a global industry that has always relocated manufacturing to low-cost nations? Is it the exceptional quality of Japanese denim and jeans which makes these manufacturers so competitive in the global market? What is the importance of economies of scale? What is the role of new technology in Japanese denim production, and why did the Okayama and Hiroshima prefectures become the centres of denim and jeans manufacturing?

Japanese fashion tradition and the introduction of Western-style fashion

A kimono is a traditional Japanese robe that is tied at the waist by a wide cotton belt called an obi. It has no buttons, zips, or any other kind of fastening (see figure 9.1). The shape of the garment is very simple and has only one pattern; traditionally the collar and sleeves are consistent in form and people adjust the garment to their own size with the obi at the waist. It makes enjoyment of the style very limited. Therefore kimono fashion trends are based on the textiles used to produce the garment, which sometimes have very modern designs and sometimes more traditional ones.[7] A kimono is made from many different types of fabric, including silk, cotton, linen, and mixed yarns. The type of fabric defines the kimono's suitability for different occasions, such as high-quality silk for ceremonial events, cotton for casual wear and work clothes, and a mixed yarn of cotton and wool for more fashionable styles. Manufacturers strive to develop new fabrics, stitching techniques, and textiles, and kimono fashion is very different from fashion in the West.

At the time of the Meiji Restoration in 1868, however, Japan started to turn its back on the kimono as part of a general movement towards Westernization. The nation began to emulate Western practices in

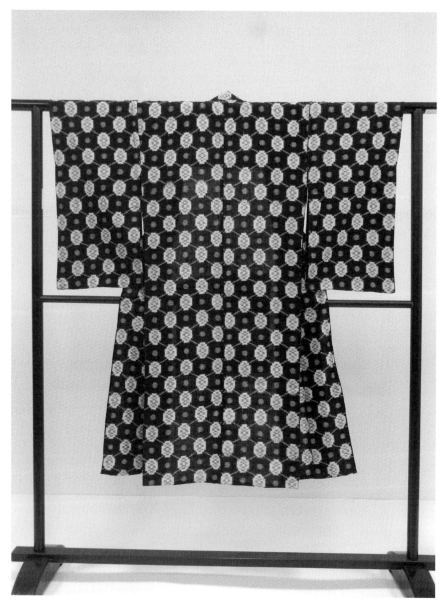

9.1   Luxury Kasuri (cotton kimono) worn on special occasions in the Taishō period (1912–26).

education, land tax systems, and conscription. In 1872, the Japanese government announced that the royal family and government officers should wear Western-style, formal regal attire at ceremonies. From then on, the Emperor wore Western-style clothes for his official duties and kimonos in private. Other royal family members, some politicians, and high-ranked officers also wore European-style clothes. Rokumeikan, the

Japanese government's first European-style guest house, was built in 1884, and politicians wearing Western clothes welcomed guests from Western countries there. The army also dressed in Western style military clothes and then Western clothes spread across Japan; these were adopted by the police, and railway and postal workers.[8]

The government strategy of catching up with the West was implemented after the Meiji Restoration ushered in a revolution for Japanese society as a whole that included the introduction of modern clothes. Although the government encouraged citizens to dress in a European mode, this did not mean that the new custom immediately, or smoothly, penetrated Japanese society. In Osaka in 1887, for example, only nine per cent of men and 0.2 per cent of women dressed in styles that had originated in the West.[9] The famous Japanese department store, Mitsukoshi, opened a Western clothes division in 1888, but had to close it down again in 1895, because it did not have enough customers, even in Tokyo.[10]

Only upper-class consumers, mainly men, wore Western-style clothes before World War II. While some men had official and social opportunities to wear these garments, only women who were employed as teachers, cashiers, telephone operators, and office clerks changed to a Western style.[11] Some young, upper-class women learned the sewing skills required to make Western clothes at school, along with the traditional skills needed to produce kimonos. These were seen as cultural accomplishments. Nevertheless, these women were still wearing traditional Japanese kimonos, even when they had received Western sewing lessons. A few Western-style dressmaking schools were established in Tokyo and Osaka from around 1920, and some magazines touted the Western lifestyle, including fashion, as an example of modernity.[12]

The start of industrialization in Japan, and the growth of the gross national product (GNP) in the late 1910s, caused the increasing numbers of salaried workers to wear Western-style suits at the office and thus the rise of a new clothing industry. Furthermore, in due course, the Japanese industry that manufactured Western clothing developed and improved. Mitsukoshi, for example, hired Western clothing-manufacturing staff in 1906 at its flagship store in Tokyo to create items that would fit Japanese customers better, while other large department store chains like Takashimaya sent their managers and associated manufacturers to Europe to learn Western engineering and production skills. By the 1930s, demand and supply-side factors had created a market for Western-style clothes in Japanese urban areas.[13]

From a working-class fabric and garment to an American icon

Denim is often portrayed as an American fabric and jeans as a pair of American trousers, respectively. Their histories, though, are much more complicated, multifaceted, and transnational than Levi Strauss & Company, the denim jeans giant, wants us to believe. According to the firm's website, the man Levi Strauss was 'the inventor of the quintessential American garment'.[14] In 1872, Strauss, an immigrant from Bavaria who had become a successful San Francisco wholesale dry-goods merchant, received a letter from one of his customers, Jacob Davis, a tailor. Davis proposed that Strauss should patent his idea of using rivets at the points of strain in a pair of jeans. The tailor needed capital to patent his idea, and the merchant saw a business opportunity. The patent for riveted jeans was granted to Jacob Davis and Levi Strauss & Company on 20 May 1873, which is why the firm still regards this date as the birthday of blue jeans.[15] Workers' trousers made from denim had been around for years, maybe centuries, previously being called 'waste overalls' or 'overalls'; the term 'jeans' was coined after World War II.[16] Nevertheless, riveted blue jeans became a huge success and one of the icons of American industrial history.

According to museum curator Pascale Gorguet Ballesteros, the story is more complicated, as it involves two textiles, jean and denim, and one pair of trousers, formerly called overalls.[17] It is a myth that the blue denim of Levi's jeans came from the French city of Nîmes, although the name is related to the fabric. Lynn Downey, a former archivist of Levi Strauss, maintains that Levi's denim was bought from the Amoskeag Mill in Manchester, New Hampshire in the late 1870s. According to Ballesteros, denim had English roots, but had been made in the United States since the late eighteenth century.[18] The French *serge de Nîmes* was a cotton and wool twill; its woven surface of diagonal parallel ridges can be traced back to eighteenth-century England. There, the fabric was made exclusively from cotton, and its name anglicized to 'denim' to categorize this particular twill and give it a certain sophistication.[19] The related fabric known as 'jean' and worn by Genoese sailors in the seventeenth century was a lighter version of denim and was also made in New England late in the following century. This fabric was less wear-resistant and lost popularity in the nineteenth century, before the name was revived years later to describe denim trousers.[20]

Levi Strauss did not invent denim and jeans, but the company owned the patent for riveted overalls and developed a successful marketing strategy for this garment from the late nineteenth century onwards. Other companies were quick to copy the riveted jean, and before the patent expired in 1890, Levi Strauss sued several competitors for infringements.[21] During World War I, women took factory jobs, and the demand for denim overalls grew because skirts were too dangerous to wear in many war plants. This reality had two lasting effects. Wearing trousers became more acceptable for women, and denim overalls entered the leisure market and were even called 'womanalls'.[22]

Sandra Curtis Comstock maintains that blue jeans became 'a gender- and class-blurring icon of the American people' during the Great

Depression of the 1930s.[23] Changes at the production, distribution, and consumption levels created the massive shift from working-class garment to American icon. On the production side, Levi Strauss suffered tremendously from the economic crisis of the 1930s because expenditures on work clothing plummeted. After the 1934 workers' boycott of Levi Strauss following the represssion of labour protests, the company began to target the middle-class market using Western and frontier advertising campaigns. This eventually led to an article in *Vogue* in 1935 on the Lady Levi, which led to new outlets for denim, including department stores. Moreover, the pro-labour legislation of the New Deal stimulated workers' activism and egalitarianism, and inspired writers, singers, artists, and photographers, many of whom promoted jeans as the new symbol of the American people.[24]

During World War II, wearing jeans became even more of a symbol of patriotism, liberty, and democracy for American women. More college girls began wearing jeans, and working-class women who worked in factory jobs vacated by enlisted men became accustomed to wearing jeans. Rosie the Riveter, wearing denim overalls, was portrayed by the American media as the symbol of feminine wartime patriotism and was turned into a national heroine representing nineteen million women in the United States labour force. As these women were viewed in a positive light, their denim overalls were seen as part of their patriotic uniform and gained greater social acceptance.[25]

The postwar period revealed contradictory tendencies in American fashion. On the one hand, there was a return to elegant, feminine styles such as the New Look, and on the other hand, consumers embraced casual comfort as epitomized by denim and jeans. In particular, middle-class American youth, who had become richer and more demanding, began to wear denim as a token of their individuality. Hollywood helped to immortalize and standardize the casual look by putting Marlon Brando and James Dean in jeans.[26] Nevertheless, denim's image of liberty, egalitarianism, and non-conformism rapidly spread to countries across the globe, including Japan.

From the traditional kimono to jeans

After World War II, the Japanese lifestyle Westernized at an ever-faster pace, particularly in the area of clothing. In the mid-1950s, more European-style clothes were purchased than traditional Japanese garments.[27] Along with high economic growth and industrial development in the late 1950s and early 1960s, the kimono market shrank and Western fashion became a mass phenomenon. Western clothing was introduced, aimed particularly at young Japanese consumers from 1950 to 1970. First came tailor-made clothes for the upper and upper-middle classes, while the mass consumer began making their own Western-style clothing at home. In the 1970s, however, clothing companies rapidly increased their sales, and ready-to-wear garments soon became common among every generation and income group in Japan.[28]

Against this backdrop, the introduction of jeans was revolutionary. Japanese consumers first encountered the garment during the recovery period when they met jean-wearing Americans from GHQ. As the Americans began to introduce the ideals of Western democracy to occupied Japan, young consumers began to identify jeans as a symbol of freedom and individuality, and started buying second-hand versions which were sourced by the US military base in Tokyo. They were happy to adopt the jeans fashion as a form of expression of their acceptance of American working-class informality. Until that time, Japan had a strong culture of honour, tradition, and respect that valued uniformity rather than individuality. A simple pair of jeans symbolized a break from this hide-bound mode of dress.[29] GHQ had thus created a demand for jeans in Japan.

Western fashion including denim and jeans changed the fashion system. For the first time, class no longer mattered in the way that Simmel had analysed it. From the 1950s into the 1960s, a number of American casual modes of dress – West Coast sportswear, the Ivy League style, and the hippie look – gained currency in Japan. In the 1960s, anti-establishment street fashion spread throughout Japan, just as it did in Western Europe and North America.[30] Simultaneously, Parisian brands, such as Christian Dior and Pierre Cardin, launched licensing businesses in Japan to reach the growing luxury market. These styles were all equated with the Western ideals of liberty and democracy, and to one degree or another, their popularity created a demand for jeans. In response, local Japanese manufacturers such as Big John, Edwin, and Kaihara switched from producing traditional fabrics and apparel to denim and jeans during the 1960s and early 1970s.[31]

Growth of Japanese jeans and the denim industry

During the development of the Western fashion industry in Japan, many traditional textile manufacturers suffered due to the introduction of the new styles. Some industrial clusters were forced to convert from the production of traditional kimonos to that of Western-style clothing. The demand plummeted for the cotton kimonos that were everyday attire, but silk kimonos fared better. Even when Western clothing had fully penetrated Japan, silk kimonos for special occasions survived due to their special place in Japanese society.[32] From the start of the Meiji period in 1868, when people gained the freedom of choice in clothing, anyone could wear silk kimonos for weddings, funerals, and anniversaries. Indeed, people enjoyed wearing kimonos on special occasions so these garments were able to survive as luxury products.

Japanese female workers wearing Kasuri while spinning cotton manually in 1954.   **9.2**

The manufacturers of cotton kimonos struggled to compete against the new modern Western styles. One type of cotton kimono, the Kasuri, was particularly problematic, as it could be more expensive to produce and buy than silk versions, due to the high cost of indigo dyeing. It was therefore no longer possible to promote the wearing of cotton kimonos for daily use or work (see figure 9.2). As a result, the market for kimonos shrank and Kasuri textile manufacturers had to transform their business models. A few leading cotton garment companies attempted to produce jeans with imported machines, denim, buttons, zippers, and yarns.[33] The first Japanese denim brand, Big John, had established a school uniform factory in Kojima, Okayama in 1940. It started to import and sell jeans in 1958, sewed the first 'made in Japan' jeans using imported American denim in 1965, and manufactured the first Japanese jeans with Japanese denim in 1973.[34]

Some textile mills started to weave denim, while some dyeing companies began to dye it with techniques they had used for Kasuri kimono cloth. Kaihara was one of the first textile and dyeing companies to adopt these new practices in 1970. Rope dyeing, whereby the warp yarns were dyed with indigo and the filling yarns were left undyed, was the biggest hurdle for these companies. They had to learn the technique by reverse engineering, extracting knowledge or design information by taking apart

American-made jeans and attempting to reproduce the cloth and the colour. In the early days, the quality was poor compared with denim made in the United States. Early Japanese experimenters were able to sell their denim at a lower price, allowing them to compete against labels imported from the United States. Some low-cost denim manufacturers even started to export their cloth in 1973, but they quickly had to improve the quality to measure up against American denim and jeans.[35]

The main manufacturing clusters of the Japanese denim industry were in the provinces of Bingo, Bicchu, and Bizen, which have since been reformed into the Okayama and Hiroshima prefectures (see figure 9.3).[36] As shown in table 9.1, the volume of denim production increased in the early 1980s. The Bizen province including Kojima district was the largest producer, commencing with many small manufacturers in the 1970s. The

9.3   Map of Japan, showing the main manufacturing clusters of the Kasuri and denim industries.

Table 9.1 Volume of denim production (thousands m²), 1976–2001

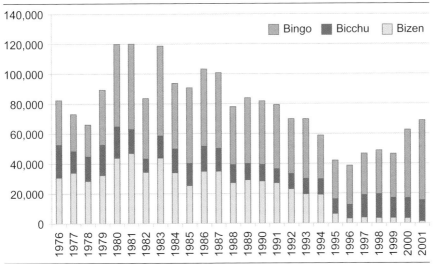

Source: Yano Research Institute.

output in Bizen declined from the late 1980s, when the Bingo province accelerated production. Kaihara is the largest denim manufacturer in the Bingo province, contributing greatly to the area's volume output. Like the denim industry, jeans manufacturers also clustered in the Okayama and Hiroshima prefectures.

So, why did the Okayama and Hiroshima prefectures become hubs of denim and jeans manufacturing in Japan? To answer this, it is necessary to examine the genesis of Japanese denim and jeans manufacturing. The Okayama Prefecture and the Hiroshima Prefecture had been the main producers of cotton kimonos since the Edo period between 1603 and 1868, when Japanese society was under the rule of the Tokugawa shogunate. In 1828, the Bingo province started to produce Kasuri kimonos for daily wear as work clothing, weaving the garments from cotton fabric and dyeing them with indigo. Among the three famous Kasuri clusters – Iyo, Kurume, and Bingo (see figure 9.3), the latter became the largest due to the support of the local government which promoted the production of cotton fabrics and the Kasuri kimono. The production of Kasuri kimonos peaked in 1960, and declined thereafter due to the shrinking of the kimono market.[37]

The main jeans cluster in the Kojima area in Bizen (now in Okayama) had started to grow cotton in the late Edo period, around 1800, and expanded after the late 1850s as a result of local government support.[38] Although most Japanese rural areas grew rice, the land in Kojima was unsuitable for this crop because of the high salt content of the soil caused by the proximity to the sea. As a result, Kojima started to produce cotton obis, a sash-like belt, and cotton textiles for two major types of traditional men's clothing: a formal trouser called Hakama, and elegant waistcoats that were worn by the samurai class on ceremonial occasions under the system of centralized feudalism. After the Meiji Restoration in 1868 (when the Emperor took the supreme position to the detriment of the Tokugawa Shogun and thus changed the political and social system) these traditional clothes were rarely worn, and the Kojima cluster needed to find a new product.

In the late nineteenth and early twentieth centuries, the textile mills of the Kojima cluster diversified their output. In 1877 they started making the Japanese-style socks called Tabi and worn with kimonos; in the 1910s they began sewing work clothes. Later, in the 1920s, the Kojima cluster started to produce Western-style school uniforms, which were increasingly popular.[39] As the Kojima cluster already used advanced cutting and sewing techniques for the thick textiles used to make Tabi, these mills had an advantage when it came to launching new categories of clothing. Existing Tabi sales channels were also used for introducing the new products to market. Kojima thus became the largest producer of school uniforms in Japan, with a ninety per cent market share in 1937. However, the demand for school uniforms fell between 1965 and 1970, because the early generation of baby boomers had passed through school, and some schools decided not to require uniforms any longer. Some manufacturers in Kojima started to produce jeans to make up for the dearth of uniform orders. Although these companies were very small in size, in due course the entire jeans production process from spinning to sewing was completed within the Kojima area.[40]

The different strategies of Japan Blue and Kaihara

As shown by tables 9.1 and 9.2, in Japan the volume of denim production dropped after the late 1980s, and the output of jeans fell after the late 1990s. After the collapse of the Japanese bubble economy in 1991, the clothing market shrank and the jeans market followed suit. At this point, there were three ways for jeans manufacturers to survive. The first was to upgrade the products sold, the second was to outsource production to low-wage economies elsewhere in Asia, and the third was to hook a company's star onto one of the new mass-market fashion chains.

The first option for Japanese jeans and denim manufacturers was the introduction of premium jeans. The 'designer jeans' craze that swept across North America and Europe in the late 1970s and 1980s demonstrated that consumers were willing to pay good money for high-quality denim fashion. The Japanese capitalized on this reality as they rebuilt their jeans industry after the economic bubble burst in 1991. They developed premium jeans, which sold at over 10,000 yen a pair (around $100), including jeans with

Table 9.2 Volume of jeans production (thousands of pairs of jeans), 1987–2012

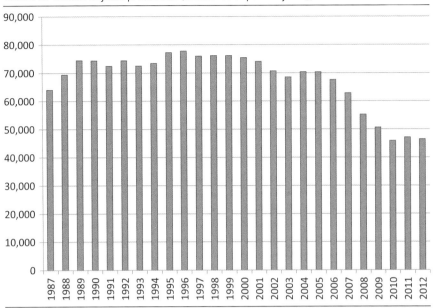

Source: Japan Jeans Association.

visible selvedges, which were made on vintage machines. The premium jeans movement originated on the West Coast of the United States around 2000, led by Adriano Goldschmied and 7 For All Mankind, and then spread to Japan. To meet the demand, a number of newcomers ventured into the Japanese premium jeans market, although most of these disappeared after newer fashions emerged. Japan Blue, however, was one of the success stories that survived the cut-throat competition.

In 1992, Manabe and his business partner, Masahiro Suwaki, set up a textile wholesaler firm called Collect Company, with the aim of creating high-quality indigo fabrics in Kojima in the Okayama Prefecture.[41] The city of Kojima was known for its traditional cotton production and indigo dyeing, as well as for Japanese denim and jeans that had been made by brands such as Big John since the 1960s. Most Japanese denim manufacturers had switched to projectile looms after the 1950s. Compared to shuttle looms, these high-tech machines created wider swaths of fabric at a much lower price. Vintage denim could be recognized by the selvedge, and this was generally seen by denim lovers as a sign of quality. Selvedges thus became a badge of fashionability recognised by denim aficionados, therefore partly reinvesting a Simmelian sense of class. Even if the elites were no longer necessary ruling, yet surely they were ruling on trends. In 1993, Manabe and Suwaki began to use old Toyoda shuttle looms to reintroduce the weaving of selvedge denim. By using the old looms, selvedge denim and jeans could be produced again. Denim consumers were willing to pay a higher price for the selvedge, which looked cool when the jean leg was rolled up into a cuff.[42]

In 1994, Manabe and Suwaki started to use exclusive and expensive Zimbabwean cotton for the production of denim and developed a high-profile fabric. A year later, they invested in research into natural indigo, and created their own blue colour. Named Japan Blue, the new hue was based on the colour of an old cotton kimono.[43] The company that had started as a wholesaler launched its first store in 2003, selling its own, original brand of hand-dyed, hand-woven jeans under the Momotaro label (see figure 9.4). Around this time, many manufacturers in Kojima were using a special washing technique for jeans. Japan Blue's stores, however, specialized in producing authentic with-selvedges jeans made from 100 per cent cotton denim and 100 per cent cotton yarn, and sometimes dyed with traditional Japanese natural indigo. Japan Blue harnessed the Kojima cluster, which included many small production companies, specialized in textiles, dyeing, finishing, and sewing.[44] Japan Blue led the way in terms of product management, and controlled the orders within the cluster. Although the sales of premium jeans in Japan peaked in 2005, Japan Blue continued to increase its sales with its marketing strategy. Premium jeans have therefore been the main driver of the company's expansion, although

9.4   Japan Blue's anchor shop (Momotaro Jeans) in Jeans street, Kojima.

the sale of wholesale items increased from 2008 to 2014, rather than sales in its own stores.[45]

The second option for Japanese manufacturers was to outsource their production to low-cost Asian countries like China. Large garment manufacturers such as Levi Strauss, Big John, and Edwin had moved their production bases to China partly to benefit from lower labour costs after the 1985 Plaza Accord. This was an agreement between France, West Germany, Japan, the United States, and the United Kingdom to depreciate the dollar against the Japanese yen and German mark. It made Japanese and German exports more expensive. Japanese brands that specialized in lower-price jeans also outsourced their production to China and other Asian countries. This was especially true for brands that made jeans for hypermarkets such as Ito Yokado and AEON and for stores specializing in jeans such as JEANS MATE and Right-on. A similar pattern emerged in Japanese denim. The nation's second largest denim company, Kurabo, shifted its production to Hong Kong in 2002 and then established a joint venture in China in 2013. As a result, Kurabo's production capacity expanded and its cost-effectiveness increased. Only its selvedge denim was produced in a domestic plant. In 2011, Nisshinbo, the third-largest denim company in Japan, shifted its production to Indonesia and decided to slash domestic production in an effort to increase efficiency and benefit from lower labour costs.[46]

A third option for Japanese manufacturers was Kaihara's strategy: providing low-price denim, from domestic factories, to the fast fashion retailer UNIQLO while striving to develop a high-quality denim. By doing so, Kaihara increased the scale of its business and became the largest denim manufacturer in Japan, although it was and still is family controlled. It operates four vertically integrated mills in Japan, and opened a new factory in Thailand in 2015. The company caters for more than fifty per cent of the Japanese denim market. It achieved this by integrating its production process so that textiles (from 1978), finishing (1980), and spinning (1991) were added to dyeing (figure 9.5). Indeed, it constructed its business portfolio to reduce the risk directly from other companies in single industry, learning from its experience when the jeans market was saturated as early as 1975 and deeply decreased Kaihara's sales.[47] Then, UNIQLO's orders were the driving force of Kaihara's further expansion, although the retailer's prices were low.

While established brands of jeans suffered from the trend for cheaper products, fast fashion retailers like UNIQLO increased its sales by practicing a strict policy of low prices. In 1998, Kaihara decided to collaborate with UNIQLO, which soon became its biggest customer. In addition to UNIQLO's low prices (for example, 25 Euros for a pair of jeans), it also offered its customers technological innovations such as stretch jeans, raised fabrics, insulating textiles, and UV protective clothing. Kaihara did not want to get involved in price wars with Chinese manufacturers,

9.5   Kaihara's special dyeing machine at Kisa Mill in Bingo (Hiroshima Prefecture).

and so it strived to respond to UNIQLO's requirements for innovation, and for these new fabrics at low prices. Kaihara could provide UNIQLO with high-quality denim at reasonable prices. UNIQLO bought Kaihara's denim at higher prices than it would pay Chinese manufacturers, but the quality of the fabric was much better and so they could use it more efficiently with zero waste in the cutting process. The UNIQLO and Kaihara collaboration was thus innovative, launching low-priced jeans made from high-quality denim.[48] Kaihara continues to prototype about eight hundred kinds of new denims per year. It has the capacity to develop new products, great reproducibility (lot-to-lot consistency), and an ability to use fabric efficiently, creating less waste. The sales and profits of Kaihara and UNIQLO have risen, and so they have succeeded in creating a win–win relationship.

The competitiveness of Japanese denim and jeans manufacturers lies in their ability to produce new materials rather than new designs. Kaihara, for example, created a new denim fabric that it launched in stores within a year, and almost sixty per cent of its sales now come from this. They have the advantage of creating innovations with new, mixed yarns in terms of fit, comfort, and stretch, not only for blue denim, but also denim in different colours. Kaihara's counterstrategy of producing high-quality, but much cheaper denim, was made possible by using fully automated, state-of-the-art manufacturing techniques, and thus economies of scale. Kaihara has invested in automation and robots. Its newest Sanwa mill in Jinseki-gun, Hiroshima Prefecture, is 20,000m^2 and can be run by just eight staff during the night and fifty-three staff during the day.

In the early 1990s, the demand for vintage jeans rose, and the production of vintage denim on old Toyoda looms therefore increased. Kaihara, copying other smaller Japanese denim manufacturers, started to buy back old Toyoda looms, adapted them to modern standards, and began to produce vintage denim. Currently, twenty per cent of Kaihara's sales are of products made on these vintage looms, meaning they amount to only a minor part of Kaihara's total output.[49] The manufacture of vintage denim is the company's second counterstrategy in a highly competitive denim market, and vintage denim provided it with a wonderful marketing tool. Its final counterstrategy was to offshore denim manufacturing to a low-cost nation. In 2014, Kaihara invested $100 million in a new mill in Thailand, thereby eventually following other Japanese denim manufacturers.[50]

Conclusion

The history of Japanese denim and jeans is as much a cultural as an economic story. Indeed, it is impossible to understand this industry without acknowledging both. It was first a demand-driven tale, but demand for denim and jeans rose due to the rapidly changing fashion system in Japan. There is a long history of selective adaptation to Western-style clothes, which began with the Meiji Restoration. The pace of change accelerated during the interwar period, and was completed in the postwar recovery during the 1950s. The demand for traditional cotton products fell due to the transformation of the Japanese lifestyle and economic growth. Demand for denim and jeans increased in this period, initially under the influence of American GIs. This ignited a second-hand market for US-made jeans, led to greater imports of jeans and denim, and eventually, during the 1960s, to the first experiments with Japanese-made denim.

The supply side, which became more important later on, also bore a relationship to cultural factors, especially Japan's long history of producing high-quality indigo cotton products like Kasuri. When demand for traditional indigo-dyed cotton kimonos plummeted, manufacturers had to look for other products. During the early 1970s, Kaihara switched to fully integrated denim production, and was able to survive and even expand. The mentality and traditions of this Japanese family firm matter. Concepts like path dependency and historical continuity can partly explain the success of Kaihara over several decades and its evolution into the largest denim manufacturer in Japan. This case-study fits perfectly within the general pattern, as the firm duly developed into the largest vertically integrated manufacturer of denim in Japan. The location of Kaihara's mills can thus be explained historically, as the Hiroshima Prefecture had been one of the main Kasuri clusters.

However, it was the close collaboration with UNIQLO, when the traditional market for denim fell in the 1990s, that ignited a massive expansion of domestic production and the vertical integration of Kaihara's factories in the Hiroshima Prefecture. Since this collaboration, the firm has focused, like UNIQLO, on the development of innovative fabrics rather than new fashion styles, and aims to fight cut-throat competition on the global denim market. When demand for vintage jeans rose in the early 1990s, and the production of vintage denim on old Toyoda looms increased, Kaihara started to buy these old looms back and produce vintage denim. Simultaneously, the company invested in automation and robots, and most of its denim is made on state-of-the-art machines. Vintage denim is only a minor part of Kaihara's total production and sales. It is not only quality, but also quantity and economies of scale that matter to the company. Indeed, the greater part of its production is based on high, not low, technologies.

Japan Blue is a completely different story of a completely different company. It does not operate fully integrated plants, but it controls an entire supply chain of jeans manufacturing in the Kojima cotton cluster in the Okayama Prefecture. Cotton production goes back to the late-Edo period, when land in Kojima was unsuitable for cultivating rice because of its high salt content. As a result, the city became a cluster for the manufacture of cotton garments, including kimonos, uniforms, and jeans. Although the history of Japanese denim and jeans is not just based on manufacturing on old Toyoda machines, Japan Blue's founder Manabe began to use these old looms in 1993, when demand for vintage denim increased. A year later, he began to use exclusive African cotton to produce a high-profile denim. He also experimented with natural indigo, and created his own blue colour, which he called Japan Blue. Japan Blue began as a vintage manufacturer in 2003, and successfully set up several premium brands of jeans. Clearly, the company sold its high quality vintage denim and jeans in a niche market where prices did not really matter. In this way, Simmel entered the world of so-called egalitarian denim, in which 'the upper classes turn away from this style and adopt a new one, which in its turn differentiates them from the masses.'[51]

Notes

This chapter was partly supported by JSPS KAKENHI Grant Number 15K03751.
I. Finlayson, *Denim: An American Legend* (Norwich: Parke Sutton Publishing, 1990), pp. 18, 27.
2 G. Marsh and P. Trynka (eds), *Denim: From Cowboys to Catwalks: A Visual History of the World's Most Legendary Fabric* (London: Aurum Press, 2002), pp. 107–18.
3 Finlayson, *Denim: An American Legend*, p. 25; P. Fussell, *Uniforms: Why We Are What We Wear* (Boston: Houghton Mifflin Company, 2002), p. 48.

4 The article was translated into English and published in the US in 1957. G. Simmel, 'Fashion', *American Journal of Sociology*, 62:6 (1957), 541–58.

5 Simmel, 'Fashion', 545.

6 R. Ross, *Clothing: A Global History* (Cambridge: Polity, 2008), pp. 149–50.

7 See H. Tamura, *Fashion no Shakai Keizai shi [Socio-Economic History of the Fashion Industry]* (Tokyo: Nihon Keizai Hyoron sha, 2004); Y. Jinno, 'Modern Japan and "Ryukou": transformation of fashion with the advance of social modernization' [in Japanese], *Special Issue of Japanese Society for the Science of Design*, 9:4 (2002), 13–20; and J. Sapin, 'Merchandising art and identity in Meiji Japan: Kyoto Nihonga artists' designs for Takashimaya Department Store, 1868–1912', *Journal of Design History*, 17:4 (2004), 317–36.

8 S. Nakagome, *Nihon no Ifuku Sangyo [Garment Industry in Japan]* (Tokyo: Toyo Keizai Shinpo sha, 1975), pp. 38–9.

9 Youhinkai, *Youhin 100 nen no ayumi [A 100 Year History of Western Clothes]* (Tokyo: Youhinkai, 1968), p. 89.

10 *Mitsukoshi 100 nen no kiroku [A 100 Year History of Mitsukoshi]* (Tokyo: Mitsukoshi, 2005), pp. 33, 67.

11 There is no detailed data about the female labour force in Japan. According to the first Japanese census in 1920, women's participation rate was about fifty per cent and women employed were concentrated mostly in specific sectors such as agriculture (62%). We therefore understand that quite a few working women wore Western-style clothing. (Y. Okazaki, 'Wagakuni no Joshi Rodoryoku: Shugo Keitai to sono Henka (1)' ['Female Labour Force in Japan: Its Employment Structure and Change (1)'], *Journal of Population Problems*, 107 (1968), 1–12).

12 Y. Yoshimoto, 'Hana Hiraku Yosai Gakkou' ['Flowering Western-style sewing school'], in K. Koizumi (ed.), *Yosai no Jidai [The Age of Sewing]* (Tokyo: OM shuppan, 2004), pp. 23–31.

13 Nakagome, *Garment Industry*, pp. 49–50.

14 www.levistrauss.com/our-story/ (accessed 23 June 2016).

15 *Ibid.*

16 According to Ninke Bloemberg, trousers made of a denim-like fabric can be seen in an anonymous Dutch painting from the Golden Age: *Begging woman with two children*. N. Bloemberg, 'Dutch jeans', in N. Bloemberg and H. Schopping (eds), *Blue Jeans* (Utrecht: Centraal Museum 2012), p. 7.

17 In 1994, Pascale Ballesteros curated *Histoires du jeans de 1750 à 1994*, Paris Musées.

18 P. G. Ballesteros, 'Jean and denim, between myth and reality', Denim on Stage: University meets Industry. Enterprise of Culture Conference, Denim City Amsterdam, 30 October 2015. www.enterpriseofculture.leeds.ac.uk/upcoming-events/denim-on-stage-university-meets-industry-at-denim-city-in-amsterdam/speakers/ (accessed 23 June 2016).

19 R. L. Snyder, *Fugitive Denim: A Moving Story of People and Pants in the Borderless World of Global Trade* (New York: W. W. Norton & Company, 2009), p.139.

20 Snyder, *Fugitive Denim*, p. 140.

21 J. Sullivan, *Jeans: A Cultural History of an American Icon* (New York: Gotham, 2007), p. 36.

22 P. Jansen, 'Denimism: denim in the feminist movement and the perception of the American Media, 1915–1975' (Master's Thesis, Erasmus University Rotterdam, 2015), p. 21.

23 S. C. Comstock, 'The making of an American icon: the transformation of blue jeans during the Great Depression', in D. Miller and S. Woodward, *Global Denim* (New York: Berg, 2011), p. 23.

24 Comstock, 'The making of an American icon', pp. 35–8.

25 P. A. Cunningham and S. Voso Lab, *Dress and Popular Culture* (Bowling Green, KY: State University Popular Press, 1991), p. 32.

26 D. Little, *Vintage Denim* (Salt Lake City, UT: Gibbs Smith, 1996), p. 56.
27 T. Kikkawa and M. Takaoka, 'Sengo Nihon no Seikatsu Yoshiki no Henka to Ryutsu heno impact' ['The change of life style and its impact on the distribution business in postwar Japan'], *Shakai Kagaku Kenkyu [Journal of Social Science]*, 48:5 (1997), 115–16.
28 A. Kinoshita, *Apareru Sangyo no Marketing shi [Marketing History of the Garment Industry]* (Tokyo: Dobunkan, 2011), pp. 25–34.
29 Little, *Vintage Denim*, p. 18.
30 W. D. Marx, *AMETORA: How Japan Saved American Style* (New York: Basic Books, 2015), pp. 1–95.
31 S. Sugiyama, *Nihon Jeans Monogatari [The Story of Jeans in Japan]* (Okayama: Kibito Shuppan, 2009), pp. 62–104.
32 T. Hashino, *Luxury Market and Survival: Japan's Traditional Kimono Weaving Industry after 1950*, Kobe University Discussion Paper, No. 1,507 (2015), pp. 1–26.
33 Sugiyama, *Nihon Jeans Monogatari*, pp. 62–9.
34 http://1940.bigjohn.co.jp/history/ (accessed 25 March 2016); www.denimsandjeans.com/news/big-john-journey-of-the-first-japanese-brand (accessed 23 June 2016).
35 Japan External Trade Organization (JETRO), *Okayama ken Jeans Mekâ no Genjo to Oushu Shijo no Doukou ni tsuite [Report on the Jeans Manufactures in Okayama and Market Trends in Europe]* (Okayama: Jetro Kaigai Keizai Jouhou Centre, 1995), p. 3.
36 This chapter focuses on Bizen and Bingo. Regarding Bicchu, see S. Nagata, 'Sanbi Chiku ni okeru Seni Sangyoshuseki no Genjo' ['Analysis on Sanbi Textile Cluster'], *Fukuoka Kenritsu Daigaku Ningen Shakai Gakubu Kiyo*, 21:1 (2012), 23–39; Nihon Shoko Kaigisho [Chamber of Japan], 'Chiiki ga Ichigan to nari Sekai ga Mitomeru Denim no Miryoku wo Hasshin' ['Local manufacturers in the cluster appeal the Japanese high quality denim'], *Ishigaki*, 401 (2013), 25–7.
37 Shinichi Choushi Hensan Iinkai, *Shinichi Choushi [The History of Shinichi cho]* (Hiroshima: Shinichi Cho, 2002), p. 1,088.
38 Okayama Kenshi Hensan Iinkai, *Okayama Kenshi [The History of Okayama Prefecture]* (Okayama: Sanyo Shimbun, 1984), p. 672.
39 D. Fujii, H. Tomae, T. Yamamoto, and J. Inoue, 'Evolving technical capabilities in turmoil: a field research on the value chain network of denim jeans industry in the Setouchi District (2)' [in Japanese], *Okayama Daigaku Keizai Gakkai Zasshi*, 39:3 (2007), 25.
40 JETRO, *Jeans Manufactures*, pp. 7–9.
41 E. Puts, '"Made in Japan". An analysis of the meanings and processes behind a "Japanese" product: denim (Bachelor thesis, University College Ghent, 2016), p. 19.
42 www.artofmanliness.com/2014/04/22/raw-selvedge-denim-introduction/ (accessed 7 July 2016).
43 Puts, 'Made in Japan', p. 19.
44 The wholesalers could connect between the manufacturers to meet demand, e.g., cutting factory and sewing factory, or dyeing factory and weaving factory, and build a mutually dependent relationship. This network has the merit of being in the Kojima cluster. See Fujii, *et al.*, 'Value chain network'; J. Tatemi, 'Okayamaken Kojima Apareru Sanchi no Hatten Mekanizumu' ['Driving force of developing garment industry in Kojima, Okayama'], in H. Ueda (ed.), *Shukusho Jidai no Sangyo Shuuseki [Industrial District under The Depression]* (Tokyo: Sofusha, 2004), pp. 127–51. However, premium jeans manufacturers like Big John have seen a fall in their sales since the late 1990s, and since then small factories within the cluster became dependent on local energetic SMEs (small and medium-sized enterprises) such as Japan Blue.
45 Interviews by Rika Fujioka and Ben Wubs with Japan Blue's CEO, Toshio Manabe, on 5 August 2015 and Rika Fujioka with Toshio Manabe, on 4 August 2016.

46 www.sen-i-news.co.jp/seninews/viewArticle.do?data.articleId=271108&data.news-key=261a97a439d0d3b08aebb1d4e4e1d56b&data.offset=60 (accessed 4 February 2016); www.kurabo.co.jp/news/newsrelease/20020709_48.html (accessed 4 February 2016); www.nisshinbo.co.jp/news/news20110106_692.html (accessed 4 February 2016).

47 J. Kaihara, 'Top Interview Kaihara Junji: Kokunai Seisan ni Kodawari Sekai kara Erabareru Denim Kigyo' ['Interview with Junji Kaihara: appealing to global jeans companies from Japan'], *SQUET*, 253 (2011), 16–18.

48 Zaikai Tsushin sha, 'Koron Rerey Taidan' ['Talk with'], *Gekkan Koron*, 47:8 (2014), 34–42; 'Sekai ga Mitomeru Kokusan Denim' ['Kaihara Denim build a world reputation'], *Nikkei Sangyo Shimbun [Nikkei Industrial Journal]* (11 August 2015).

49 Interview by Rika Fujioka and Ben Wubs with Kaihara's CEO, Yoshiharu Kaihara, on 3 August 2015.

50 www.kaihara-denim.com/english/company/history.html (accessed 9 August 2016).

51 Simmel, 'Fashion', p. 545.

10

Rhythms of production in Scottish textiles and fashion

Shiona Chillas, Melinda Grewar, and Barbara Townley

This chapter analyses culture and enterprise with reference to the Scottish textiles, tartan and tweed. These cloths juxtapose the culturally infused heritage of indigenous textiles with the seasonal rhythms of fashion and enterprise. Although the fashion industry operates in highly structured and differentiated markets, ordered around the symbolic value of garments produced, the distinctive features of the industry render it highly uncertain.[1] It is time-sensitive, notoriously fickle, and increasingly fragmented.[2] By contrast, notions of tradition and authenticity, built up over time and thriving on stable, recognizable patterns in the cloths and in the way they are produced, are central to understandings of tartans and tweeds, thereby constructing an unusual paradox or contradiction. In contrast to the traditional uses of Scottish textiles such as tartan in highland dress and tweed in country clothing, which change only incrementally and express relatively stable social meanings, the fashion industry treats garments as aesthetic forms to be experimented with for visual and immediate effect. Hence, in this social space different approaches to temporality are apparent; as producers of the cloths reach back into history for cultural value, they also look to the contemporary in supplying the fashion industry.

The production and consumption of these cloths beat with contrasting rhythms: while they are interwoven with symbols of an indigenous heritage developed slowly and steadily over centuries, their uses in fashion markets shift with the seasons.

This chapter examines the tensions engendered by these different relationships with time, and considers how rhythms of culture and enterprise are accommodated in the practices of designers, and operated in the production process itself. While heritage and tradition are key to Scottish textile producers' understandings of their purpose, products, and designs, as well as marketing approaches, producers also have a need to engage with the contemporary fashion world as enterprises. Like the warp and weft threads woven within the fabrics, these features pull in contrasting directions but jointly construct the field of practice for the fabrics' producers, fashion designers and the many intermediaries in the chain between production and consumption. We thus investigate the 'fashion as fast' and 'textiles as slow' opposition by examining where and how the material artefacts are produced; the interactions between textile producers and fashion designers; and how and where the symbolic capital of textiles and fashion is manifest and maintained. After a brief description of the textiles, we explain our framework using the work of the French sociologist Pierre Bourdieu, especially his concept of capital, following this with a description of the methods used in this research. We then focus on the symbolic capital of textiles, noting the way that authenticity in the cloth is understood, as producers reach back in time to valorize traditional patterns, modes of production, and traditional garments to express the timeless qualities of the cloths. The second findings section focuses on how this is parlayed into economic capital in the sphere of enterprise. In the concluding section, we discuss symbolic capital in the field of fashion and the place of time in strategies of distinction. We note the exchanges of symbolic capital based on authenticity in product and production, including a romantic view of Scottish heritage that yields dividends in a market zeitgeist that values authenticity and provenance, thus challenging the notion of fast fashion.

Tweed and tartan – indigenous textiles

The word 'tweed' is used generally to describe many woven, woollen cloths, but specifically, to refer to a woollen textile known for its twilled, or diagonally ribbed, texture, and its variety of colour mixtures and patterns. Tweed's name originated with its weave method: the word came from 'tweel' in Scots, or twill, meaning 'woven of double thread', in which both warp and weft threads are manipulated in stepped pairs.[3] The change to 'tweed' may have occurred by association with the River Tweed in the Scottish Borders, or as a misreading of 'tweel' by a London clerk.[4] The fabric can be woven into bold or subtle checks, stripes, herringbones, or 'plain' patterns, although close inspection reveals that even a plain tweed can involve complex mixtures of thread colours. Typical tweeds are heavy cloths and their loosely spun threads make them feel rough in comparison to tartans made for kilts and other clothing, which are usually woven in tightly spun worsted wool. Tartan is a type of tweed, woven in patterns that have an instantly recognizable affiliation with Scotland. Indeed, the Scottish government maintains a registry of tartan, which it defines as: 'a design which is capable of being woven, consisting of two or more alternating coloured stripes which combine vertically and horizontally to form a repeated chequered pattern'.[5]

Researchers Ben Fine and Ellen Leopold note that textile production has been at the heart of industrial development in Scotland.[6] However, the indigenous textile and clothing industries have not been immune to wider pressures such as outsourcing of production to the East, high labour costs, and limited capital investment in new technology and skills development. Traditionally textile producers in Scotland were very location-specific, concentrated in areas near rivers, especially in the Scottish Borders, Aberdeenshire, and the Western Highlands and Islands, as flowing water was an integral feature of hand-production processes and later became the means of powering early machines.[7] In the eighteenth and nineteenth centuries these areas became 'hubs' for the woollen textile industry, and despite a significant postwar decline in production, they remain the homes of Scotland's surviving producers. Some of the mills still producing tartan and tweed include Lochcarron, Johnstons of Elgin, Lovat, and the Harris Tweed mills: Harris Tweed Hebrides, The Carloway Mill and Kenneth MacKenzie. Cloths from Scotland's textile mills and weaving sheds find their way onto international fashion catwalks, particularly those focusing on luxury, and routinely feature in autumn/winter collections by haute couture designers and high street brands such as Chanel, Prada, Marc Jacobs, Topshop, Vivienne Westwood, and Zara.

Both tartan and tweed have historical links to Scotland; tartan to (a geographically based) clan or family and tweed to land holdings in Highland estates.[8] Tartan's original patterns were designed by the weavers who supplied local communities, including family groups and eventually, clans and their chieftains' retainers.[9] Most tartans carry clan names, with some names having multiple tartans representing different geographical areas (e.g., Campbell of Argyll or Campbell of Lochaber). Tartans are also made for different activities (e.g., Hunting Wallace or Dress Wallace), distinguished by having patterns based on similar themes but with different thread counts.[10] Tartan operates on the principle of identifying the wearer as a member of a clan, an organization, or event; this association has to be present to wear the tartan. The first case of a chieftain specifying a 'clan tartan' is believed to have occurred in the early eighteenth century, when a Grant chief decreed his cloth should be 'red and green ... broad springed'.[11] There are also a number of established symbolic associations in tweed. In the army, the London Scottish Regiment, formed in 1859, wore a solid, earthen-coloured tweed rather than the famous red and scarlet of other British soldiers; the 'Elcho mixture' tweed is thus believed to be the origin of military khaki and 'the beginning of all the camouflage uniforms of the armies of the world'.[12] When, in the 1840s, Victorians began to see the Highlands as a tourist destination and to buy its estates or hunting and fishing rights, they sought to continue the clan tradition of wearing an identity cloth. But lacking family associations to tartan,

Highlander John Brown, servant to Queen Victoria, wore archetypal 'Scottish' clothing (here, made of both tweed and tartan).   **10.1**

they commissioned tweeds in checks and stripes, some adapted from the 'shepherd's check' woven in the Borders.[13] Today, some estates maintain several tweed patterns, to camouflage forest workers, deerstalkers, and fishing ghillies in their different work environments.[14]

Textiles thus have symbolic meaning that imbues the garments made from the cloth. Patterns are signals of the artistic design of tweeds, and are also social in the tradition of estate tweeds, which were popularised during the reign of Queen Victoria (see figure 10.1), which continues as a social-class marker by referencing a close relationship with land and sporting pursuits.[15] The patterns are recognized and categorized by estate owners and become a visible code, practiced among the elite, either through the owners wearing the tweed, or dressing estate workers in their tweed.[16] However, the particular patterns are recognizable only to those who are familiar with the history and cultural conventions.

Pierre Bourdieu – understanding capital in enterprise and culture

Our analysis makes reference to Bourdieu's work as being particularly appropriate for the object of our research. We do so for several reasons. Bourdieu was interested in the 'hidden mechanisms of social reality' that are hidden precisely because they are accepted as the natural order of things, of actions, and of practices.[17] We wish to understand the world of textiles and fashion, from textile producers and garment designers, through perspectives that have built up over time and established the 'taken for granted' features of the cloths. Bourdieu's research is also concerned with explanations of reproduction and transformation in the social order, and thus emphasizes the role of temporality as an important aspect of analysis.[18] Finally, his main conceptual tools of field, habitus, and capitals, offer a valuable conceptual framework for the area under study. 'Field' refers to the social space encompassing all those involved in textiles and fashion, from the initial stages of cloth production to its final manifestation as an item of fashion clothing. Thus, although holding different positions in degrees of centrality and periphery, all who potentially engage with, or impact on, this process lie within this particular field. Their understandings, and the taken for granted nature of their practices and activities, constitute the 'habitus' of the field. But it is the concept of 'capital' on which we wish to focus.[19] For Bourdieu, capital is a resource analogous to energy or power, with its use within a field indicating both what is valued in a particular social space and how different positions within that social space are structured.[20]

Capital comes in different forms, having economic, cultural (tacit understanding, knowledge, or qualifications), or social (network) dimensions. Capital may also be symbolic, which is economic or cultural capital that is disavowed as such, becoming recognized instead for its emblematic value; that is, although based on economic or cultural capital, symbolic capital is a recognized resource, legitimized as the currency of the field.[21] Bourdieu's aim was to develop an understanding of how capitals operate and are exchanged in the field in an 'economy of practices', and in particular in the operation of power.[22] Thus, to be specific, both tartan and tweed have histories as cultural goods that have undergone changes in the perception of their symbolic meaning. They are imbued with symbolic associations through inherited and acquired heritage, and through their recognition as symbols of status or national identity. Products manufactured from the textiles acquire symbolic meaning that may or may not confer status on consumers. The recognition and appropriation of these associations informs an embodied cultural capital, able to identify stratified user groups, and 'to manipulate individuals' understandings of themselves, their social and cultural positions'.[23] Hence, the tweed jacket, stereotypically beloved of university professors, is worn as a uniform that declares the wearer to be a member of an elite profession, taken for granted as appropriate dress.

Once recognized, symbolic capital, conferring, as it does, status and prestige in the field, is defended or challenged by players.[24] Dominant players employ conservation strategies to derive profit from their accumulated capitals, while these are relentlessly challenged by newcomers to the field attempting to subvert existing principles of domination for their own interest. Subversion may occur, for example, when a traditional textile such as tartan becomes associated with the punk movement, losing one type of symbolic capital, yet gaining a new audience and cult following.[25] In the economy of cultural goods such as indigenous textiles, symbolic meaning has to be constantly maintained through the 'production of belief' of the value of these goods.[26] Symbolic capital is presented as the intrinsic worth of beauty, value, authenticity, and so on. The autonomy of the field, namely the power to define its own criteria for production and evaluation of its products, measures the extent to which it is able to maintain itself as a field of restricted production, rather than it being dominated by economic criteria as is seen in a field of large-scale production.[27] Producers of cultural objects thus have a vested interest in restricting production, in reinforcing symbolic meanings to articulate the cultural value of their products, and in repudiating changes to both products and their interpretations (see figure 10.2). This tension between aesthetic and commercial values, or between culture and enterprise in the field of restricted production, is often based on rules that are internal to the field, to be used by organizations that are interested in preserving and generating cultural capital for their advantage.[28] We thus focus our analysis on the features of tartans and tweeds that are constructed as legitimate and the strategies employed for deriving profit from their distinction in the marketplace.

A weaver of Harris Tweed operates the treadle loom in her home with foot power and hand controls, as stipulated by the Harris Tweed Act (1993). Master weavers employ production skills and knowledge developed over several centuries.

10.2

Methods

Our fieldwork studied where and how the cloths are produced, paying close attention to how textile producers and fashion designers understand and articulate the key qualities of their products. Our empirical investigation sought to reveal practices in the field in terms of what is valued and how this is exploited in the creation of value. It is based on a mix of primary and secondary data, drawing on thirty-five interviews with textile designers and producers, independent fashion designers, weavers, fashion agencies, and promoters, all recruited by purposive sampling.[29] We also conducted a review of organizational websites and sector reports to understand the history and practices of the field, and visited seven textile mills where we took extensive notes later corroborated in a post-visit researcher meeting. The semi-structured interviews lasted between fifty minutes and two hours, and were taped and transcribed. Two mills refused permission to record because of industrially sensitive processes and materials, indicating commercial competition in the sector. We invited the participants to discuss the sector, their organization and role in it, and their understandings of tweed and tartan as symbolic and material objects. Transcriptions were combined into a large data file of approximately 650 pages and analysed according to the main themes of time and timescales, noting how participants talked about the cloth itself, the narratives they used to describe key features of the cloth, and how the value of cloth was articulated. We then re-coded the data according to cultural, economic, and symbolic capital, paying particular attention to interactions between producers of the cloths and fashion designers.

The rhythms of landscape, heritage, and cultural capital

Understanding the capital of indigenous textiles involves stepping back from the cloth and looking at the cultural and material conditions that have produced contemporary understandings. Scotland's heritage and landscape are key in forming the 'taken for granted' ideas about the cloths and the meanings attributed to them.[30] Meanings have developed over the 'longue durée' such that tartans and tweeds have stable associations connected to a number of historical references and perceptions of the landscape.[31]

Dominant among these is the way in which the Scottish landscape is portrayed. In particular, Scotland is represented pictorially in marketing material and in verbal accounts as a sparsely populated land of mountains, glens, and lochs with occasional ancient castles punctuating the view. This view is timeless, eschewing the harsh realities of an industrial past, social deprivation, and political unrest.[32] However, the romantic view is made material by replicating colours found in the natural environment in the textiles. The inspiration for the design of tweeds and tartans is said to draw on this rural landscape. The simplicity of designs returns to the practical constraints of a cloth originally woven in a particular locality, with a limited range of colours developed from available natural dyes, and the use of local coarse wool which gave the cloth a rough texture. The use of colour continues to be very important, particularly in describing tweeds and in ascribing them to Scotland:

> I think one of the things we've got is great colour. I don't know whether it's the surrounding landscape in Scotland but we've got a reputation for really good colour and part of that is the depth you can achieve in creating some of these yarns that have maybe six component colours, to create one colour.[33]

The reputation of the cloths is thus built on the colours of the surrounding landscape but also the way in which these colours are combined to produce the cloth, which is said to be uniquely Scottish. The words 'made in Scotland' on a label distinguish the garment with reputational capital recognized worldwide and rely in part on this 'look'.[34] The fact that dyes are now sourced from Turkey and India is less important to producers than replicating the 'colours that I see out of that window', binding the cloth to the land where it is produced. However, producers are also keen to establish the endurance of colours by referencing their archives and by drawing attention to the 'eye-popping brights'.[35] Indeed, the mills we visited often made the same point, for example, that 'pre-war wool was unbelievably colourful', proved by showing us archive samples with seemingly current, very bright pinks, greens, yellows, etc.[36] This determination to show that the colour palettes are both historical and modern illustrates that producers are tacitly aware that their product may be seen as old-fashioned, an image they wish to guard against.

Practical traditions also have their place in designing tweeds, with the colours of textiles having a connection with traditional tweed garments. Historical and cultural references bolster the sense that the cloth is designed to blend into the surroundings and is another tie to Scotland and an unchanging temporality:

> You want to be camouflaged in the terrain that surrounds you ... There's been more fashionable requests for estate tweeds but essentially the ones that we remake over and over for the bigger estates, they haven't changed that much over the years ... We make for Balmoral ... Balmoral is quite granitey, it's quite grey because of the surroundings. Whereas you get some of the estates that have a lot of moorland, they'll be quite lodeny and quite brackeny, and you know, you can see actually when you go and look.[37]

The symbolic capital of the landscape and its heritage bestows authenticity on the cloths. It is materially represented in the textile but also embodied within predispositions and propensities of those who wear it, such as lifestyle choices/dress codes.[38] Perceived as camouflage for the country, tweed's practical traditions carry through to form an association, real or imagined, with an elite landowning class. Although traditionally tweed clothing would have been worn by those who had owned hunting estates, this elite status over time has become attached to the cloth and, in particular, the tweed jacket adds a layer of cultural capital to distinguish its wearer as belonging to a certain social group, almost as a type of uniform tacitly understood as bestowing status.[39]

Tartan too has its connotations, most obviously related to a national, and perhaps tribal, identity, that reaches deep into history for its practical genesis, as tartans 'would have been natural dyes and more of the feudal camouflage so that they could identify each other'.[40] Cultural references connecting a particular tartan to a surrounding area or family carry through to the design of the cloths, building capital. For example, when describing the design of a new tartan to celebrate the anniversary of a remote Scottish village, the pattern is connected to influential local families and activities with appropriately Scottish references such as whisky distilling:

> The starting point for that was using the Grant tartan. Grant as a family name was very important. The village was founded by a Charles Grant. Everyone down there is called Grant. And [another] Charles Grant was a very influential teacher at the local school for a long time. A very good man, did a lot of good work ... And there's an existing Grant tartan, of course. And they had a, sort of, heraldic logo that they use on their headed paper and it was specific colours. So we tried to incorporate those colours in to the check. Whisky is a very important part, [the] gold. So it, kind of, evolves that way. It doesn't have to, but I think it's important that there is some sort of raison d'être to what you get.[41]

This 'raison d'être' carries through to an understood authenticity in the patterns produced that is central to the meanings of tartan and tweed. Yet this cultural and symbolic capital can be subverted by fashion designers who are happy to alter extant tartans and to invent new tartans that do not fit with the traditional use and heritage of the material, by commissioning colours that are 'seasonal' or 'fashionable', patterns that are printed rather than woven, or cloths of non-woollen threads. The distinction between the distinguished and the vulgar is key to the field of cultural production.[42] Such 'fashion-first' interpretations of tartan contravene the textile producer's view of authenticity, as suggested by one mill owner's scathing reference to the altered look and feel of contemporary tartans:

> I think the fashion industry's more interested perhaps in the look of the thing. The authenticity of it is probably not as important. You get a lot of printed tartans. You get a lot of, you know, less authentic things happening in the fashion industry. The fashion industry is incredibly transient.[43]

This quotation simultaneously reinforces the 'fact' that key cultural connections are required to give authenticity to the cloth and also that the fashion industry is largely unconcerned about following the rules of this game. Indeed, the fashion industry gets its cachet from deliberately flouting the established ways of doing. Newly minted tartans without traditional Scottish references (such as that designed in one mill for the cartoon character 'Hello Kitty') are treated as 'second class' by the producers relative to historic clan patterns. There is also a sense that the value of the textile diminishes once it has been appropriated by fashion; it is no longer a textile for its own sake and becomes a component of the garment, subject to different criteria.

A tongue-in-cheek use of tartan by fashion designers is particularly evident in the work of the British fashion doyenne Vivienne Westwood, for instance, in her use of authentic tartans in avant-garde garments, and her commissioning of printed tartans – in one case, juxtaposing the Bruce of Kinnaird clan pattern with sea monsters, stars, and hearts. The late Alexander McQueen, too, used his national identity in his designs in a way that explicitly rejected or transformed the Scottish romantic myth. In his 1995 Highland Rape collection, McQueen horrified the critics by showing blood-spattered models in torn clothing and defended himself by saying that the collection was a metaphor for the rape of Scotland by England.[44] The powerful images invoked by the styling and ripped clothing, along with the associated political message, demonstrate key symbolic aspects used to reinforce the artistic aspirations of designers. The 'rules of the game' become different – tartan may be 'the latest trend' or, as with Vivienne Westwood, a 'trademark textile'; however, the recognition and applause are for the 'look' and design, and not the cloth. The subversion employed by Westwood and McQueen is typical of struggles in the field between the avant-garde and the establishment, and is the 'motor of the field', making it dynamic and susceptible to change.[45]

Local connections to place and people are lost when the cloth is seen only as an aesthetic material. The cultural capital that has been built up through its symbolic associations is diminished when these associations are absent. Beliefs about what is a 'true' tartan or tweed create a set of qualities regarding pattern, weight, and 'hand', or tactile feel, of the cloth that are disconnected to monetary value but have, nevertheless, a value of their own. Producers are concerned with maintaining this authenticity and hold themselves as arbiters of what is an authentic tartan.[46] This in turn gives them prestige and authority in the field; the cultural capital of instilled knowledge and tradition becomes translated into symbolic capital.

However, as Bourdieu reminds us, cultural capital and the symbolic capital that accrues from knowing the 'right' way to make and produce authentic examples of tweed or tartan, is negotiable and subject to change, especially when it is exposed to the market for symbolic goods.[47] The true properties of the cloth, its cultural capital, are connected to how it looks and feels and what it was originally designed to do. While textile producers can speak authoritatively on what constitutes a 'true' representation of their cloth, they are not immune to market demands: for example, the rough texture of tweed has been altered over time to make cloths that are more suitable for today's consumer by deviating from production with locally sourced wool:

> Most of our lambswool and merino will come from Australia or New Zealand. The Antipodean nations kind of govern the wool stocks in the world. Also, I guess, historically, as we looked at a bit of heritage, we would have used our own flocks in this country with a much coarser wool, but the demand now in the modern fashion industry is for much softer.[48]

Although new patterns tend to be looked down upon by textile producers, making tweed from luxury fibres such as cashmere and alpaca is seen to enhance the qualities of the material. The look is the same in the finished product but feels more luxurious, an accommodation that is deemed acceptable, if not necessary, by producers.

The capital in these cloths depends on a particular conception of authenticity that establishes a set of rules to identify what is, and what is not, a true tartan or tweed. The justification comes from reaching back into history. This allows different layers and types of cultural and symbolic capital to emerge. Capital is present in the qualities of the cloth, in colours that have their inspiration in the local environment, in patterns that reach back to past uses of the cloth, and in the garments that were made from them. Capital is also apparent in the authority with which producers speak of the cloths' histories; the misreading of 'tweel'; the certainty that tartan must be connected to family and locality. It is consolidated by the assurance with which they can dismiss new tartans that do not conform to these rules. It becomes institutionalized in tartan with the Scottish Register of Tartans, maintained by the Keeper of the National Records of Scotland for the Scottish Government, where patterns are codified and connections to person, place, or event recorded. Similarly, the Harris Tweed Orb Trademark has certified the authenticity of the cloth since 1911, and an Act of Parliament (1993) set out in great detail the material composition and production of Harris Tweed, which has to be made from 100 per cent pure virgin wool, handwoven by islanders on the Outer Hebrides, using yarn which has been dyed and spun there (see figure 10.3).

The rhythms of enterprise and economic capital

While we have so far set out the importance of cultural capital in identifying authentic tartans and tweeds, and also hinted that the rules of the game may be subverted in the face of economic capital, this section focuses more closely on the level of the enterprise and its influence in the field. In textile production, the reputation for quality and the use of highly skilled

Following inspection, the Orb Trademark is stamped onto every length of approved Harris Tweed   **10.3**
to authenticate its origin.

machine operators and designers add value to textiles and garments alike. Quality has a material value manifest in the weight of the textile, in the type and quality of wool used in production, the consistency of pattern and production techniques – craft measurements where the performance of the textile defines its utility. There are constraints in the complex processes of textile production that underlie the slow rhythms of the sector, with twenty-seven independent processes taking place between the wool as a raw material and the finished fabric. These include spinning and dyeing the yarn, designing patterns, and finishing the fabric, all of which require specialist knowledge and skills that have altered very little. Scotland has an estimated 23,250 employees working in the fashion and textiles sector and approximately 5,260 firms. The majority of firms are small businesses (enterprises with fewer than 250 employees) dedicated to a part of the production process. The textile sector has recorded a thirty per cent rise in exports since 2009 and is now worth £375 million annually.[49]

Indeed one interviewee noted that 'there's probably about seventy sets of hands [that] will touch Harris Tweed from start to finish – washing, cropping, carding, spinning, tying, warping, out to weaver, tying in, weaving'.[50] It thus takes a long time to produce a piece of cloth with the return on investment often restricted and protracted, as a mill owner explains:

> It's a very complex industry. There's a long timescale between the buying of the raw material [and] actually getting paid. And the margin is in it for the

fashion industry or for the retailers. Not really in it for the manufacturer too much. And there's a lot of work. Every single process is another stage that something can go wrong.[51]

Long lead times and the risks inherent in such a complex system are problematic in terms of supply. Scottish textile mills simply cannot enter the fast fashion race and therefore have to differentiate themselves in other ways. They do so by emphasizing different features of their product, as a mill manager remarked: 'our lead time's away out to twenty weeks so we're having to put that message out about, you know, this is why the lead time is such, this is why the demand is such and focus on the individual elements'.[52]

The complexity involved in making textiles, however, also represents a business opportunity. Their authenticity, and their having stood the test of time, give economic value to the products, for example:

There's a return also to a British authenticity and I think we've seen that here, but certainly throughout the business, a return to a British product, you know, authenticity, origin, quality The ones that remain – because it is an industry that's been hit hard over the years – are really strong within that context.[53]

Textile mills are often family-owned and run, and are proud of having a continuity of production and quality stretching back across several generations, something that is a mark of distinction giving authenticity to producers.

Differentiation also involves wariness towards wholeheartedly adopting the short-term rhythms of fashion. Mills are reluctant to engage with fashion colours showcased at events such as the Première Vision textile fair in Paris, for economic reasons and also because they don't fit with the long lead times in production and the particular colours that may be associated with the mill:

We keep an eye on trends but we're actually starting before trends begin now. We have our own colour palettes, according to the yarn strings, and we have about twenty yarn strings. They go from Shetland [wool] through to lambswool, merino, merino/cashmere blends, cashmere 100 per cent. The trick is minimizing your stock investment and the yarns that you use. So it has to start right at the beginning, and we're actually now trying to start as early as possible because of the length of time it takes to kind of bring a collection to market.[54]

However much tweed and tartan mills may privately assign value to traditional patterns, they are also keen to display collaborations with high fashion, noting key designers who have used or commissioned textiles from their mill, albeit tartan and tweed that are only produced 'for a collection'. Consequently, a contradiction emerges in the encoding of symbolic goods. On the one hand, a romantic notion of Scotland and its heritage is invoked through 'heather and granite colours used for shooting and deer stalking clothing', while on the other an engagement in the world of fashion is behind the statement that 'the reason Paul Smith is coming here [to Scotland] to photograph his campaign is that tweed is clearly on trend'.[55]

Here we begin to see that stories of heritage have become fashionable in the textiles field, representing a shift in social and cultural perceptions away from fast fashion to an emphasis on sustainability, provenance, and process, akin to the artisanal, 'slow food' ethos. As a textile designer says:

> The sort of current tweed appreciation ... seems to stem from maybe a sort of a values-based approach. It's not so much led by fashion trends. It's a bit more about people looking back, looking at things that are local, that are sustainable certainly; especially things like the Harris Tweed rides where people are going out on their bikes, and it's all celebrating cycling as, you know, and that's sustainable as a form of transport. All these pieces are fitting together as more of almost like a sustainability value-led kind of movement.[56]

Textiles producers have been quick to appreciate how this values-based approach has economic returns, albeit constrained by protracted time for production and a recognition that fashion is temporary, while 'real' heritage is stable and unchanging:

> You can't have heritage in one season and out the other, you know. It's here to stay but it will manifest itself slightly differently. There'll have to be a marriage of heritage and modernity ... Genuine heritage is a kick away from that kind of logo-driven bling, because heritage is not necessarily about the designer or the logo; heritage is about the process. It's about how that finished apparel or accessory or basic textile came to be.[57]

Again this interviewee emphasized what textiles producers can, and cannot do, in terms of providing heritage that can be used as a marketing tool while also turning the long process into a virtue. Fashion is seen as somewhat ethereal. Its business is to persuade, such that when tweed and tartan become 'on trend', it is as much their symbolic associations with heritage and authenticity that are in fashion, as the cloths themselves. This is not lost on textile producers, 'It's something we promote all the time because it's our heritage and it's a sales tool on top of everything else. It's a great story.'[58]

Fashion itself now wants a story behind cloths and uses the cultural connotations originally associated with textiles for economic reasons, as an independent textile designer explains:

> But with tweed having a bit of a renaissance at the moment and having it being kind of quite cool and trendy again, they were really keen to have their own tweed developed ... They really liked that kind of a story [of family and local associations] behind it; and that the specific colours were picked out so that they would blend into the landscape [and] would also work like a kind of camouflage fabric of their time.[59]

This particular interpretation of authenticity opens avenues for innovation, as another designer remarked:

> People are quite obsessed with authenticity at the moment, and especially in this climate for some reason we are going through this time of the huge technological and digital revolution and people are clinging on to things that they feel are authentic, real, and rounded. So we see things on menswear blogs. These can be extremely kind of narrow and very obsessed with authenticity. But you should be designing things that are relevant for the time that you live in and not things that hark back through to a different time.[60]

There is an acute awareness among textile producers of the 'fickleness' of fashion and that they should capitalize on the demand while they can, because it will undoubtedly shift before long. Textile producers have a pragmatic view which understands that demand will be cyclical, 'the traditional tweed look comes round in fashion every few years in a big, big way'.[61] However, any excitement about the opportunities connected to being fashionable comes with the caveat that it is important to maintain authenticity:

> Tartan is particularly fashionable at the moment. It is being used more and more in the fashion world. This is not a bad thing provided it is used in the right way. It doesn't surprise me that it is on the catwalk in Milan as there is quite substantial interest worldwide in authentic tartans with history behind them, rather than fashion checks. What we are keen to see, or want to see, is tartan used in an authentic way, not made fun of.[62]

Change is built into the fashion industry, not from necessity, rather from a desire to be 'in fashion' – however that is interpreted.[63] In contrast to works of art, for example, where permanence and authenticity are key determinants of prestige, garments are more likely to come into vogue if enough (but not too many) people adopt a style. Yet fashion also lacks a command centre with the power to decide what will be in vogue, with the result that consumers are powerful sources of inspiration and future trends.[64] Although the field contains a substantial cadre of 'cultural intermediaries' and commentators, the ultimate arbiter tends to be the consumer. Textile designers are aware of the need to appear innovative to respond to this, to produce collections, and to work with fashion designers to realize a vision, 'to make that story in a garment and in a weave'.[65] New sources of inspiration are particularly important to the fashion designer who uses tweed and tartan while distancing it from its 'stuffy' traditional image and elevating it to fashionable status. Yet the cloths they select for each new season are not entirely new; there has to be a degree of continuity to maintain their cultural capital. For manufacturers, it is also important to review what has sold before, before embarking on new designs: 'we always start the new season by looking at what we sold from the past season'.[66] Thus the 'newness' of fashion is always modified in relation to the past.

Symbolic capital and strategies of distinction

In this section, we unpack the delicate balance between culture and enterprise in textiles by demonstrating how symbolic capital is constructed, appropriated, and exchanged by players in the field.[67] In the struggle to preserve authenticity in textiles and to grapple with the demands of fashion, the tension between textiles and fashion is revealed. The tension is played out in symbolic capital – what matters in the field. We have noted that strategies of distinction in textiles tend towards stability and authenticity steeped in cultural heritage, whereas the demands of enterprise pull players to change and innovate to accommodate prestigious clients, which adds value to contemporary production. The different rhythms of textiles and fashion create tensions between preserving authenticity and maintaining cultural capital built up over the long term, and the demands of contemporary fashion.

Textiles producers tend more towards an appreciation of the quality of the cloth and the production process. The technical aspects of the textile are valorized and held as markers of distinction; mill operators, for example, are more likely to note the properties of different wools and the colours of the tartan than to draw attention to garments made using their textiles. They cleave to the traditional tweed and tartan designs and patterns as being 'true' representations of the textile. Tweed colours reference the landscape to which they are attached and tartans are developed in relation to clans. The underlying materiality of textile production feeds into a denial of 'fashion', based both on structural constraints of long lead times and the rules governing authenticity in each textile. That is not to say that innovation is absent in textiles; to satisfy the market, textile designers are also engaged in creative work to design new selections of colours and patterns in tartans, and in using new materials in tweeds. But symbolic capital is built upon slow rhythms and incremental change. Producers seem less enthusiastic about the colourways in recently commissioned textiles, unless they conform to the traditional patterns of clan or land associations. However, despite the dominant strategy of tradition and authenticity, judgement of new patterns is not entirely censorious; new tartans can be a source of pride for mills and their designers as long as they conform to the 'rules of the game'.[68]

Although textile producers understand that supplying fashion designers with cloths may accumulate key reputational capital, and mills recognize the seasonal nature of fashion and its demands, they are wary of relationships with fashion. The cultural capital of tweed and tartan is manifest in garments designed as sports' clothing or for national celebrations denoting Scottish ancestry. The traditional market may not be as prestigious as high fashion; however, it is more reliable and dependable, and is marked by the authenticity and heritage of the textile. Fashion designers appropriate the markers of quality in textiles and translate that into distinction in the garments that they produce.[69] In the process, the authenticity and longevity of the textile is re-configured, and indeed re-fashioned, to suit the seasonality in the field of fashion. And the refusal to acknowledge the textile designer in this process, except perhaps to establish the provenance of the textile for marketing purposes, reinforces the dominance of aesthetics for the fashion designer and, by association, the fashion label.

We must also accept that textiles are 'aesthetic commodities', 'concerned with properties of beauty, style or design which are categories that change over time across different social spaces'.[70] These properties are clearly visible in tweed and tartan and the aesthetic value generated around the commodity and the businesses selling them.[71] In addition, we would also contend that the associations of tweed to land and tartan to family attest to hidden evaluations by elites who understand the 'correct' representations of these textiles. In markets for symbolic goods, such as those in indigenous textiles, cultural capital plays an important role for agents who draw on authenticity and tradition. The history of the associations of tweed becomes parlayed into sustainability, and the cultural and the symbolic transposed into an economic premium.

The place of Scotland in the field of fashion offers an interesting perspective on cultural capital in aesthetic markets. Here, Scottish identity is a cultural reference in textiles and fashion that gives its holders an economic advantage. 'Made in Scotland' gives a connotation of quality, recognizing the richness of the landscape as an inspiration for colourways in textiles, made by skilled workers, within an industry that has a long history. Yet the same cultural capital that confers economic advantage also appears to present challenges. Interactions in the field reconstitute rhythms of time: 'slow' textiles and 'fast' fashion become tempered by associations. Tweed and tartan are 'fashionable' in short bursts and the fashion industry appropriates symbolic capital in the textiles for economic gain. This struggle over rhythms presents mutual benefits for textiles and for fashion. For textiles, the fashion cycle places tweed and tartan centre-stage, albeit using altered designs. Fabrics become fashionable. And for fashion the symbolic elements of class, culture, and provenance serve to temper the seasonal rhythms of the field. Provenance and authenticity prove lucrative symbols for fashion to play with for economic returns.

Notes

1 P. Aspers, *Orderly Fashion: A Sociology of Markets* (Princeton: Princeton University Press, 2010), pp. 11–13.
2 A. Rocamora, 'Fields of fashion: critical insights into Bourdieu's sociology of culture', *Journal of Consumer Culture*, 2:3 (2002), 341–62.

3 Knockando Woolmill Trust, unpublished manuscript (2014), pp. 5–6; E. Harrison, *Scottish Estate Tweeds* (Elgin: Johnstons of Elgin, 1995), p. 49.

4 *Ibid.*

5 Scottish Register of Tartans Act (2008) Section 2. Details of the Act and illustrations of registered tartan can be found at www.tartanregister.gov.uk. Examples of tweed can be seen at www.harristweed.org and on manufacturers' websites.

6 B. Fine and E. Leopold, *The World of Consumption* (London: Routledge, 1993), pp. 120–37.

7 Knockando Woolmill Trust Scotland, www.knockandowoolmill.org.uk (accessed 30 March 2016).

8 Harrison, *Scottish Estate Tweeds*, p. 25.

9 J. Faiers, *Tartan* (Oxford: Berg, 2008); Harrison, *Scottish Estate Tweeds*, pp. 13–74.

10 N. Fiddes, *Kilts and Tartan Made Easy* (electronic book, www.scotweb.co.uk/kiltsandtartan, 2006) (accessed 5 October 2016).

11 Knockando Woolmill Trust, unpublished manuscript, p. 4.

12 *Ibid.*; Harrison, *Scottish Estate Tweeds*, p. 88.

13 Knockando Woolmill Trust, unpublished manuscript, p. 6; Harrison, *Scottish Estate Tweeds*, p. 88.

14 Harrison, *Scottish Estate Tweeds*, p. 25.

15 *Ibid.*

16 P. Bourdieu, *Distinction* (Abingdon: Routledge, Kegan & Paul, 1984), pp. 3–54.

17 C. Calhoun, 'For the social history of the present', in P. Gorski (ed.), *Bourdieu and Historical Analysis* (Durham, NC and London: Duke University Press, 2013), pp. 36–66.

18 P. Gorski, 'Bourdieusian theory and historical analysis', in Gorski (ed.), *Bourdieu and Historical Analysis*, pp. 327–36.

19 P. Bourdieu, *Outline of a Theory of Practice* (Cambridge: Cambridge University Press, 1977), pp. 143–58; Bourdieu, *Distinction*, pp. 165–222.

20 Bourdieu, *Outline of a Theory of Practice*, pp. 159–77.

21 P. Bourdieu, 'The forms of capital', in J. Richardson (ed.), *Handbook of Theory and Research for the Sociology of Education* (New York: Greenwood, 1986), pp. 241–58.

22 B. Townley, 'Bourdieu and Organization Studies: a ghostly apparition?', in P. Adler, P. du Gay, M. Reed, and G. Morgan (eds), *Oxford Handbook of Sociology, Social Theory and Organization Studies: Contemporary Currents* (Oxford: Oxford University Press, 2015), pp. 39–63.

23 For a discussion of capitals, see Bourdieu, 'The forms of capital' and to locate capitals in Bourdieu's work, see Townley, 'Bourdieu and Organization Studies'.

24 Bourdieu, *Outline of a Theory of Practice*, pp. 159–82.

25 J. M. Percival, 'Rock, pop and tartan', in I. Brown (ed.), *From Tartan to Tartanry* (Edinburgh: Edinburgh University Press, 2010), pp. 195–211.

26 Bourdieu, *Outline of a Theory of Practice*, pp. 164–7.

27 P. Bourdieu, *The Field of Cultural Production* (Cambridge: Polity, 1993), p. 115.

28 L. Oakes, B. Townley, and D. Cooper, 'Business planning as pedagogy: language and control in a changing institutional field', *Administrative Science Quarterly*, 43 (1998), 257–92.

29 M. Miles and A. M. Huberman, *Qualitative Data Analysis: An Expanded Sourcebook* (Thousand Oaks, CA: Sage Publications, 1994), pp. 27–33.

30 B. Graham and P. Howard, 'Heritage and identity', in B. Graham and P. Howard (eds), *The Ashgate Research Companion to Heritage and Identity* (Aldershot: Ashgate, 2008), pp. 1–18.

31 F. Braudel, 'History and the social sciences: the longue durée', *Review (Fernand Braudel Center)*, 32:2 (2009), 171–203.

32 M. Pittock, 'Plaiding the invention of Scotland', in Brown (ed.), *From Tartan to Tartanry*, pp. 32–47.

33 Interviewee M5B.

34 The words 'Made in Scotland' denote that parts but not necessarily all of the production processes happen in Scotland. Labelling of textiles is covered by the Textile Products (Labelling and Fibre Composition) Regulations 2012; country of origin labelling is not compulsory in the EU. Labelling should not, however, mislead the consumer. See UKFT (UK Fashion & Textile Association), 'One Industry. One Voice', at www.ukft.org/business.php (accessed 14 August 2016).
35 Interviewee M5H.
36 Interviewee M3.
37 Interviewee M5B.
38 Bourdieu, *Distinction*, pp. 9–54.
39 *Ibid.*
40 Interviewee M2.
41 Interviewee M4J.
42 Bourdieu, *The Field of Cultural Production*, p. 3.
43 Interviewee M4J.
44 C. Evans, 'Desire and dread: Alexander McQueen and the contemporary femme fatale', in J. Entwistle and E. Wilson (eds), *Body Dressing* (Oxford: Berg, 2001), pp. 201–14.
45 Bourdieu, *Distinction*, pp. 9–54.
46 Bourdieu, *The Field of Cultural Production*, pp. 29–73.
47 Bourdieu, *The Field of Cultural Production*, pp. 74–144.
48 Interviewee M5B.
49 L. Chesters, 'Ta-ta tartan, bonjour haute couture: Scotland's textile trade reinvents itself as a purveyor of luxury goods', *Independent* (2 February 2014), see www.independent.co.uk/news/business/news/ta-ta-tartan-bonjour-haute-couture-scotlands-textile-trade-reinvents-itself-as-a-purveyor-of-luxury-9101653.html (accessed 10 October 2016).
50 Interviewee M6.
51 Interviewee M4J.
52 Interviewee M7.
53 Interviewee M5B.
54 Interviewee M5B.
55 Interviewee FF1.
56 Interviewee D8.
57 Interviewee M6.
58 Interviewee M5B.
59 Interviewee D8.
60 Interviewee D4.
61 Interviewee M5B.
62 Interviewee D12.
63 J. Entwistle, *The Aesthetic Economy of Fashion: Markets and Values in Clothing and Modelling* (Oxford: Berg, 2009), pp. 23–51.
64 Aspers, *Orderly Fashion*, p. 54.
65 Interviewee D4.
66 Interviewee D11.
67 Bourdieu, *Outline of a Theory of Practice*, pp. 183–97.
68 *Ibid.*
69 Bourdieu, *The Field of Cultural Production*, pp. 112–44.
70 Entwistle, *The Aesthetic Economy of Fashion*, p. 55.
71 Entwistle, *The Aesthetic Economy of Fashion*, p. 28.

11

The 'ethical sell' in the Indian luxury fashion business

Tereza Kuldova

In 2007, the fashion media pronounced the Indian fashion designer Samant Chauhan, whose business was established in 2004, to be one of the most promising talents of the Indian fashion industry. Back then Chauhan had just presented his autumn-winter 2007 collection, entitled 'Kamasutra', at the Wills India Fashion Week in New Delhi. The collection featured hand-woven 'ethical' silk garments with digital prints of the erotic statues of Khajuraho (see figure 11.1).[1] The Kamasutra collection played with the notion of ethics as much as with national pride connected to Indian cultural heritage, while also invoking, through digital prints and the persona of the fashion designer (modelled upon the Western counterpart), the 'new India' of technological expertise, progress, and modernity.[2]

Chauhan's approach to value creation in the fashion business is emblematic of the majority of leading Indian fashion designers who operate within a luxury segment catering to wealthy Indian and global elites.[3] Three interconnected engines of value creation drive the work of these luxury fashion designers. First, cultural heritage is transformed into 'artistic nationalism' and infused with a backward-looking sense of national pride.[4] Second, visions of modernity, technological progress, and development are invoked to project the image of a forward-looking, utopian, hyper-modern India. This futuristic narrative is particularly popular with the nation's business and political elites as much as with the aspiring classes. Last but not least, since the mid-2000s, designers have increasingly utilized explicit references to sustainability and ethical business practices.

But why did the luxury Indian fashion industry embrace the 'ethical sell' when the luxury fashion houses in the West did not seem to utilize it to an equal degree? Why is it that ethical fashion in the West still remains a small segment, an upmarket niche of start-ups and small enterprises

11.1   'Kamasutra' collection by Samant Chauhan, Wills India Fashion Week, 2007.

catering to a select clientele of conscious consumers, while in India the top designers are regularly using the 'ethical sell' as an effective and central marketing strategy? This chapter investigates that puzzle.

Value creation in the contemporary aesthetic economy and the 'ethical sell'

The example of Chauhan's collection reveals something about the nature of value creation in the contemporary 'aesthetic economy', as Joanne Entwistle rendered it, 'in which "culture" and "economy" are merged in market practices'.[5] Namely, it shows how influential political currents become translated into elitist aesthetics and thus provide those aesthetics with a very concrete, material shape, while at the same time allowing the elite clients to use these designed garments to express their political and moral sentiments. The 'ethical sell', by which I label any attempt at invoking ethical practices, from Fair Trade to eco-fashion and sustainability, is located precisely between the political and the cultural, while at the same time being deeply economic and profit-oriented. Within the top segment of the Indian fashion market, the 'ethical sell' is often interwoven with both the backward- and forward-looking nationalist narratives, something that has become even more prominent due to the recent rise of Hindu nationalism, as we shall see in due course. 'Indianness' in its multiple forms and shapes became the unique selling point of the Indian fashion industry at nearly the same time as the 'ethical sell' came to gain prominence in the mid-2000s.[6] This points to a conjuncture that needs to be investigated in its own right. The term 'conjuncture' is used here in the way it was developed by the French Marxist philosopher Louis Althusser, namely conjuncture as the meeting of particular ideological, political, economic, and theoretical forces that constitute historical circumstance.[7] But before we get closer to an analysis of this conjuncture, let us first give thought to the dynamics of global and local trends at large.

The peculiarity of the Indian luxury fashion market that emerges here points to the central role of the culturally particular and often also the politically particular framing of what at first sight might appear as unitary global trends, such as the trend of eco-fashion or Fair Trade. In practice, forces that set such trends into motion are multiple, emerging from different locations, but often convergent. Moreover, the logic of enterprise in this part of the world must be considered at the same time.[8] As discussed in Chapter 4, brand narratives, when considered as cultural and ideological forms, can reveal the profoundly global and yet multiply localized cultural mythologies of the present. If we take as our example the 'ethical sell', it is clear that the core of its mythology appeals to and is shared by transnational elites and privileged groups across geographical divides. On a global scale and in an increasingly unequal world, only relatively few individuals have the capital and time to indulge in such concerns, especially given that ethical fashion tends to be priced much higher than fast fashion and is thus far less affordable. Moreover, in India, even the knowledge about the existence of Fair Trade is limited to the upper segments of society; according to one analysis, only seven per cent of urban Indians are familiar with the concept. Fairtrade India, an advocacy organization that supports small-scale farmers and organic agricultural growers, itself first came into existence in 2013.[9] While ethical fashion remains an elitist pastime, we must also consider that business elites and fashion designers in different places of the world face different challenges grounded in local political, economic, and cultural struggles. As a result, the reasons why trends like the 'ethical sell' are embraced and endorsed by businesses and clientele may vary. Hence, the 'ethical sell' today traverses geographical boundaries, but it is also shaped by local specificities.

Brand narratives that embrace the 'ethical sell' might be marginal in terms of turnover and market segments, as the vast majority of the market is flooded by cheap fast fashion, but they are nonetheless symbolically central. As such, brand narratives, which often acquire almost mythological properties, need to be taken seriously. Throughout history, mythologies have been a powerful force, capable of mobilizing people's passions and thus moving them into collective and individual action, while also structuring social reality.[10] Within the contemporary capitalist economy, profit-oriented and commodified brand mythologies and associated ritual-istic practices such as fashion shows fulfil the same function as traditional mythologies. As such they have to be recognized as a powerful cultural force.[11] Value creation in today's fashion market is centred predominantly on such brand mythologies, or else on so-called immaterial value.[12]

Commercial objects have acquired new functions in a world that has lost touch with traditional moralities and a socially imposed strict ethical code of conduct, a world where exploitation of both human labour and of natural resources occurs on an unprecedented scale. In such a world, commercial objects have become endowed with positive moral narratives and can even be said to have become moral on behalf of their owners. Just by displaying one's ownership of an ethical commercial object, people can display their morality and even delegate their morality to the object, and at the same time become relieved from the moral pressures and insecurities they may face in everyday life.[13] In particular, the 'ethical sell' is designed to make people feel good about themselves by publicly displaying their concerns for the environment or fair labour conditions, thus showing to the world not only their cultural capital but also their morality and consumer citizen-ship.[14] Some would argue that this type of feel-good display has replaced real political action or, as the cultural critic Slavoj Žižek more roughly puts it, allows people to buy redemption from the baneful capitalist system that they at the same time reproduce through their acts of consumption.[15]

Often, the 'ethical sell' is precisely that, a carefully constructed and presented narrative, arousing strong passions in its recipients. One exam-ple is Vivienne Westwood's controversial 'Ethical Fashion Africa' collection produced in collaboration with the International Trade Centre. To promote her autumn-winter collection for 2011–12, Westwood posed in the slums of Nairobi with her collection of so-called ethically produced bags made from recycled and waste materials. The image of Westwood selling her recycled bags captures the value creation in the contemporary designer 'ethical sell'. The designer and the narrative are what counts here. The bags are produced by cheap labour from waste material, and yet are sold from about $100 to $500 due to the power of the image of the designer and of the carefully crafted narrative.[16] In contast, the bags designed by Akosua Afriyie-Kumi and ethically produced in Ghana under her brand, A A K S, can be purchased at Urban Outfitters and elsewhere for about $110 to $220 (see figure 11.2).[17] The same product sold on the street by a local woman would fetch no more than $3 on a lucky day. On her website, to celebrate five years of the initiative, Westwood showcased moving images of the happy African women she employed. This example of a Western designer producing a collection in Africa brings us to the question of the role of imagined geographies in the global fashion system and to the power relations between these geographies. The case raises provocative questions. Does Westwood have to engage in the 'ethical sell'

This A A K S bag was designed by Akosua Afriyie-Kumi and woven by a women's cooperative in
Bolgatanga, Northern Ghana; the focus is on using locally sourced materials while also creating
sustainable jobs within Africa. This example is from A A K S's first collection, 2014.

11.2

because she produces in Africa? Or does she produce in Africa in order to
utilize the 'ethical sell'?

Prestige economies of global fashion centres

Before proceeding to these questions, let us turn back to Chauhan and
his career track, which exemplifies another crucial element of the global
fashion system and the influential place of the European fashion capitals within it. While true that in 2007 Chauhan was already hailed by the
Indian fashion industry as an 'ethical' design visionary, it was not before
the Wills India Fashion Week 2010 that his concept of '*ahimsa* silk' (or
non-violent silk) became publicly recognized in India among upper middle
class consumers (i.e., individuals with monthly incomes above 150 000INR
or $2,200) and elite consumers earning even more income.[18] What hap-
pened in the meantime is of crucial importance. In 2008, Chauhan was
invited to present his spring-summer 2009 collection at the prestigious
Ethical Fashion Show at the Carrousel du Louvre in Paris (see figure 11.3).
Established in 2004, the Ethical Fashion Show encourages the industry to
embrace higher ethical standards, in terms of both human labour and the
environment. It has brought together designers from across the world to
showcase their ethical collections. Anita Dongre, who is considered India's

11.3   Gown from Samant Chauhan's spring–summer 2009 collection, presented at the Ethical Fashion Show in Paris.

first eco-designer, was also invited to Paris for the 2010 show. For both Chauhan and Dongre, the presence in Paris sealed their dominance within the Indian star-designer hierarchy as the two designers known as 'ethical'. Being invited to the Ethical Fashion Show in Paris immediately increased their symbolic capital and legitimized their businesses.[19] Only Paris, the 'capital of the nineteenth century' as the cultural theorist Walter Benjamin famously put it.[20] and ever since the epicentre of haute couture, luxury, and art, is capable of providing designers from the fashion peripheries the needed recognition, prestige, and symbolic capital. Often, this cultural capital translates into economic capital as the designer becomes able to attract more clients and wealthier clients. Moreover, it translates into the power to influence consumer choice.

Following Chauhan's success in Paris and his introduction of *ahimsa* silk into luxury fashion, new fashion brands emerged in India imitating his model. Most prominent is Jainam Kumarpal, the eco-entrepreneur behind the high-end Bhu:sattva brand, established in 2009. Kumarpal promotes 'responsible luxury' and works with natural dyes, ecological cotton, *ahimsa* silk, and alternative fibres, such as bamboo, banana fibre from the bark of banana tree, soya, milk protein fibre manufactured by spinning protein fluid, and pineapple fibre. Bhu:sattva is labelled the first certified purely organic designer apparel brand. Chauhan's success owed much to his association with Paris. The symbolic role of cities perceived as cultural and fashion capitals, such as Paris, Milan, or New York, becomes a crucial part of the prestige economy within emerging fashion cities, such as New Delhi, while often also playing an influential role in terms of trendsetting transmitted through the influence of local designers successful elsewhere.

The fact that only certain cities are perceived as capable of providing prestige and recognition becomes obvious if we briefly consider the history of the Ethical Fashion Show in Paris. This history is also indicative of the problematic market for luxury ethical fashion in the West. As a matter of fact, and against the impression of ethical brands being popular, which we might get from the media, the market for ethical fashion has not taken off in France and in Western Europe as the organizers have hoped. Eco- and ethical fashion has been struggling to find buyers, especially in the top segment. In 2010, the Ethical Fashion Show was bought by Messe Frankfurt, the German trade fair company, which ran the last edition of the show in Paris in 2012. In 2013, the Ethical Fashion Show moved to Berlin, a city increasingly perceived in popular imagination as cool, hip, and trendy, with an expanding number of gentrified areas and a booming market for slow fashion, local produce, craft beers, and all other things hip. The Berlin branch of the Ecole Supérieure des Arts et Techniques de la Mode, known as ESMOD Berlin, is the first branch of ESMOD to offer students masters degrees in sustainable fashion design and is now crucially involved with the Ethical Fashion Show. It is a school that caters to a select few; students are often from privileged backgrounds and it churns out small-scale sustainable designer start-ups, much like those seen on stands during the Ethical Fashion Show in Berlin. When Chauhan was asked why he did not show in Berlin, his answer was simple. 'It is too provincial', he said, and hence low on prestige. Here we see yet again that location is crucial in both attracting top designers and in conferring prestige onto them. Chauhan was right about the provinciality of the event in Berlin. According to the count of the labels presented at the Ethical Fashion Show in January 2016, fifty-eight labels were from Germany, followed by eleven from England, seven from the Netherlands, four from Italy, three respectively from Denmark, Portugal, Spain, Austria, Finland, and two respectively from France, Belgium, and Turkey, and only one respectively from Sweden, Bolivia, Peru, India, Estonia, and Portugal. Most of these labels were small niche firms often offering basic apparel in eco-fibres and accessories. Notably, there were no famous designer names on the list of participants. The only Indian-owned label that participated in the Ethical Fashion Show in Berlin in 2016 was Frajorden, run by Pranav Khanna. The name Frajorden translates both in Norwegian and Danish as 'from Earth'. Hence, the brand seeks association with Scandinavian design rather than with its roots in India. Overall, the Ethical Fashion Show has – in terms of status – deteriorated from a fashion week event into a trade fair accompanied by invitational VIP 'public' debates about sustainability and ethical labour practices. The cultural economy of cities, as the geographer Allen J. Scott calls it, with their attached imaginary value, plays a crucial role in the portfolios of fashion designers worldwide.[21]

In 2009, Chauhan was also invited to speak at the London College of Fashion in collaboration with the Centre for Sustainable Fashion and the Shared Talent India initiative.[22] This initiative was funded by British government through the Sustainable Development Dialogue fund of the Department for Environment, Food and Rural Affairs. The objective is to identify sustainable suppliers from India and promote ecological and fair trade fashion across borders. The involvement of a foreign development organization, albeit that of a former colonial master, is not only influential in shaping local policies, but also in bestowing prestige and recognition on designers. From these sketchy introductory remarks, it becomes clear that the recent history of the Indian fashion industry and of the 'ethical sell' is profoundly bound together with the activity of influential fashion centres such as Paris and London.[23] Yet, we must not become too seduced by the immediately visible influences of the West, thus suppressing the role of local business traditions, pre-existing markets, manufacturers, retailers, suppliers, and their cultural logic. Let us now consider some of these particularities that have shaped the Indian luxury fashion industry.

Defining moments of the Indian luxury fashion industry

India has a long history of textile production, textile crafts, and entrepreneurial business.[24] Despite this, the Indian fashion industry proper is a relatively new phenomenon. The first institutions appeared around 1986, when the National Institute of Fashion Technology (NIFT) was established. The Fashion Design Council of India (FDCI) was established in 1998 and its first fashion show took place in 2000 in New Delhi, which has become the capital of Indian fashion. It is said that New Delhi rose to prominence in fashion because it has all four seasons, unlike Mumbai, the seat of the film industry. The Indian luxury fashion industry proper also separates itself from the 'costume design' associated with Bollywood, and only occasionally do elite fashion designers mix with costume designers and work for films.[25] The fashion designer's prestige is dependent on her or his separation from all levels of workers within the traditional Indian textile industry, including those who create costumes for the cinema. The first generation of Indian fashion designers was mostly trained either in the United Kingdom or the United States and often sought initial recognition and prestige by showcasing at fashion weeks in the Western fashion centres. The emergence of the Indian fashion industry is thus not only tightly connected to Western fashion centres, but it also falls within the period of rapid neoliberalization and the sudden penetration of Western brands into the Indian market.[26] The 1990s were marked by a rise of consumerism and a joyful seduction by all things Western, especially among the middle and upper classes.[27] The Bollywood hero of the times was the accomplished 'NRI' (non-resident Indian, typically based in the United States) living a glamorous lifestyle in a Western metropolis. Even the first fashion shows were about liberating women from tradition and from the heavy layers of fabrics, about being playful and sexy, and most importantly, about being modern and Westernized.

However, following more than a decade of running after Western lifestyles and commodities, Western luxury lost its lustre.[28] Around the time of the financial crisis of 2008, the imaginary greatness of the West was undermined in the eyes of many Indians. The West was accused of being reckless, irresponsible, and most especially, devoid of tradition. It had no cultural heritage and lacked anything to be really proud of. Cultural pride, superiority, and excellence became the themes of the day, as India was identified as one of the most rapidly booming economies in the world. Following the financial crisis, which India survived remarkably well – largely due to its heritage of protectionist policies dating back to the 1960s and a resultant low level of involvement in the global market – we can observe a rise of national pride, feelings of superiority, and Hindu nationalism. As one research interlocutor, a businessman, said, 'since the financial crisis, we are high on ourselves'.[29] Suddenly, being stamped as 'Indian' was no longer a bad thing; no feelings of post-colonial inferiority were to be attached to the label 'Indian'. Instead, pride and revelling in national heritage cultivated a sense of cultural superiority. This cultural shift, like any other ideological shift, became directly visible in the realm of fashion as well, where it materialized. Gone were the days of liberating women from tradition. Instead, women were covered up all over again head-to-toe in even heavier, multi-layered, heavily embroidered, lavish, and utterly aristocratic attires, inspired by the maharajas, Mughals, and other rulers of bygone eras and golden ages of the past. The trend of 'royal chic' had established itself.[30]

This backward-looking artistic nationalism, which we have already glimpsed in the work of Chauhan, was accompanied by the forward-looking nationalist imagination of a hyper-modern India: a future superpower and world leader, especially in industry.[31] At around the same time, most Indian designers also understood that India has become one of the largest luxury markets in the world. Rather than running after recognition and sales in what they often perceived as the falling West, Indian designers saw that they would be better off selling their brands at home and close to home. There were large sales to be had among the growing number of wealthy consumers in India, and in emerging markets with a similar taste for neo-royal opulence, such as the Middle East. 'Royal chic' is still the most dominant trend. In fact, it appears that indulgence in heritage extravaganzas has only accelerated, showing no signs of dissipation. An iconic example of this aesthetic is found in the work of Sabyasachi Mukherjee, one of the most famous Indian fashion designers.

This social development culminated in 2014 in the victory of the right-wing Bharatiya Janata Party and its 'muscular' new Prime Minister, Narendra Modi. The Modi campaign slogan – *acche din aane wale hain* (good days are approaching) – promised spectacular economic growth grounded in India's spiritual and cultural heritage. In 2014, Modi launched the 'Make in India' campaign, which reached its publicity peak in early 2016 with a 'Make in India Week' in Mumbai that was visited by more than a thousand companies from around the world. New policies on trade liberalization and reforms to encourage foreign direct investment have completely erased the last remnants of protectionist policies in the textile sector.[32] Reporting on the issue, the *Business of Fashion* website noted that 'billions of dollars of investment is being committed and the mood across the country is *carpe diem* (seize the moment)'.[33] In addition, during the Week's discussions concern was raised about the best global business practices. This acknowledged the tragic death toll of 1,134 resulting from the collapse in 2013 of the Rana Plaza building in the Savar district of Bangladesh, which sparked action among popular fashion chains across the world, as well as new concerns about human-rights responsibilities in the global manufacturing chains. Issues around environmental effects and sustainability were raised as well, India being well known for its increasing pollution levels and use of dangerous pesticides and chemicals in textile production, some of which are outlawed in Europe.[34] Still, such discussions position India as the future textile powerhouse of the world precisely because of its cheap labour. Certainly, Modi's 'Make in India' campaign has been embraced cheerfully by the business sector, no matter how much criticism the government has received for its Hindu nationalist excesses. In 2015, the *Financial Times* pronounced India the world's number one foreign investment destination.[35] This optimism about India's future superpowerdom is shared by business elites and encouraged by the government.

The real consequences of Modi's policies for the textile and fashion industry are yet to be determined. What we know already is that socio-economic inequality has been on the rise, and it has been long clear that the neoliberal policies of the ruling economic elites do not trickle down.[36] Hence, when trying to understand the aesthetic production and brand narratives of leading designers in the Indian fashion industry, we must consider these within the local economic, socio-political, and cultural milieu, as much as within the context of global power relations and interests. Aesthetics are not innocent, and shifts within aesthetics often signal social changes, while ideology is inscribed and reproduced as much through the materiality of the garments. It is no accident that at this moment of

Rohit Bal, called India's master of fantasy, is known for creating lavish attires that mix multiple   **11.4**
crafts and fabrics in one garment, while building on Indian heritage and tradition. This image was
taken at India Bridal Fashion Week, 2013.

rising inequality, 'royal chic' and neo-feudal aesthetics are taking over the
fashion catwalks, allowing the wealthy elite to imagine itself as the new
capitalist aristocracy. At the same time, it is no accident either that the
rich, rather than paying their taxes, present themselves as ethical benevolent patrons. This behaviour is also visible among elite Indian designers who, increasingly, have been collaborating with non-governmental
organizations or NGOs, embracing different causes and joining in with
charitable activities in times of crisis. In 2014, Rohit Bal, a prominent
Indian designer (see figure 11.4) whose garments retail for up to $10,000,
teamed up with the NGO Insaniyat (which translates as 'human dignity') to
help build houses for flood victims in his native Kashmir. Another leading
fashion designer, JJ Valaya, also known for his designs inspired by roy-
alty and by traditional crafts, has created the Valaya Magic Foundation,
which provides education and meals for around two hundred girls with
disabilities. Overall, most designers either collaborate on collections with
different NGOs or run their own foundations, often aimed at the workers
they employ. But we should not be naive here, as using benevolence is also
a way of exerting power in the world, reproducing hegemony and stable
class relations that benefit the elite.[37] Within charitable and philanthropic
discourses, designers represent the artisans and workers as skilled but not
creative, as labourers without imagination, as poor people who need to be

guided by their design genius.[38] In a moment, we will see how this ties up with the problem of legitimization within the luxury fashion industry.

Elite Indian fashion designers often legitimize their position precisely through their benevolence towards the thousands of craftspeople who work for them and continue to live in poverty.[39] This brings us back to the image of Westwood in the Nigerian slum, where a similar dynamic is at play, only more readily discernible. It is important here to not be fooled by the lens of post-colonial critique that divides the world along the lines of East and West, and which would thus postulate a difference between the white woman in Africa patronizing slum dwellers and the Indian designer patronizing poor Indian artisans. No, we must insist that the logic is exactly the same. The lines of division are formed along *class* interests and *class* difference. The fact is that the elite class transgresses any national boundaries no matter how much it indulges in its own artistic nationalism and no matter how much it celebrates local traditions. Unlike the labouring class of craftspeople and workers, this powerful, cosmopolitan, global class can at anytime dispose of these local symbols. Hence, in this respect we must at all times keep in mind that the lines of division are not West versus East, but instead, as the historian David Cannadine convincingly argued in his work on the British colonial empire, the meaningful lines of division follow class antagonism.[40] It is a matter of the top versus the bottom, something that is becoming increasingly obvious in a globalized and networked world. If we accept this argument, it will also raise a question mark in relation to discussions about so-called cultural appropriation. The Indian fashion designers cannot possibly be accused of such an act; this is deemed heretical and yet they indulge in it daily. This would suggest that it is not cultural appropriation that is the problem, but the relation between the powerful and the powerless, and the fact that unequal structural relations and hegemony are being reproduced in such practices. But how does this matter when thinking about the 'ethical sell'?

'Ethical sell' in the Indian fashion business as a response to crises of legitimacy

Having now gained a basic understanding of the Indian fashion industry, we need to ask the question why ethical fashion has become so pronounced among Indian business elites and certain segments of customers since the mid-2000s. We are dealing with a confluence of factors, which pertain, on the one hand, to businesses on a global scale, and on the other hand, to local struggles specific to the industry. These invocations of 'ethicality' and the insertion of morality into the market are a consequence of several interconnected crises of legitimacy.[41]

The surge in claims to ethical business, and the rise of Corporate Social Responsibility (CSR) policies and 'humane capitalism', are directly linked to the financial crisis, even if similar tendencies predate it. Ethical fashion movements date back to the 1970s and the hippie era, a time when environmental sustainability entered the political consciousness through the influential 1972 Conference on the Human Environment in Stockholm, Sweden. This led to the creation of the United Nations Environmental Program (UNEP), followed by the Brundtland Commission in 1983, which effectively established the concept of sustainable development.[42] The first influential book in business theory written about business ethics appeared in 1982, but it was not until the early 1990s that companies, especially in the West, began to demonstrate ethical practices.[43] More often than not, such efforts were linked to attempts to distance oneself from the business scandals of the day, as in the case of The Bill & Melinda Gates Foundation, which was established as a direct response to a crisis of legitimacy, following accusations of unlawful monopolization that crippled competitors throughout the 1990s.[44]

Yet it was not until after the financial crisis of 2008 that business at large, and the fashion industry in particular, fully embraced the 'ethical sell'. Designers were operating NGOs alongside their businesses, raising awareness during their fashion shows, and sharing their benevolent actions through profit-oriented clicktivism on social media (that is, exploiting digital activism that embraced the logic of the marketplace). It is no coincidence that this embrace of ethics and morality coincides with the period of intense neoliberalization, accompanied by the rise of inequality, the exploitation of cheap labour, and widespread environmental destruction. The financial crisis became a crisis of legitimacy for big business. The business elite felt delegitimized and feared the breakdown of the established order. As one of my elite Indian business interlocutors once pointed out to me, 'around the financial crisis, greed was bad, terribly bad, even the Indian businessmen were perceived as reckless; then we had to create the image that greed is good, that it can change the world into a better place'.[45]

The global fashion industry faced a similar crisis. The discovery of sweatshops, child labour, and chemical pollution in the production processes in India and across Asia created its own crisis of legitimacy. All fashion eyes were turned towards humanitarian trespass in the so-called 'Third World'. As a result, practices within Europe remained unexamined by the media. Hence, the European luxury fashion industry evaded the charges of foul play as long as it labelled the goods as 'Made in Europe'. Ever since, India as a textile producer has been connected in the imagination with exploitation of labour and the environment. This left a profound mark on the Indian luxury fashion industry. As one designer noted, 'you cannot be in the industry and ignore the suffering that goes on in the production, people (i.e., the rich) know it, they see the poor around every day, even if they try to ignore them; so yes, you have to deal with this and say you do something about that'.[46] Precisely because of this positioning of India on the global map of fashion production, almost every Indian fashion designer relates in one way or another to the question of morality. It is particularly difficult for things 'Made in India' to be glamorous and luxurious, when they are associated with cheap labour, low quality, and poor finishing.[47] In the Western fashion industry, Brunello Cucinelli, the Italian 'King of Cashmere' and the chief executive officer of one of the most successful luxury brands, is an exception to the rule that luxury brands normally do not utilize the 'ethical sell'. Cucinelli is a promoter of a 'humanist capitalism' grounded in neo-humanistic business ethics centred on providing human and economic dignity to the workers.[48] The fact that he is a bit lonely in his endeavour within the luxury segment is at first surprising, given that several major luxury brands – Gucci, Dolce & Gabbana, and Prada – were found to be using illegal Chinese immigrants in sweatshops in Italy from 2007 onwards.[49] However, we have already seen that this disinterest in the 'ethical sell' within the luxury segment was also one of the reasons for the failure of the Ethical Fashion Show in Paris and its relocation to Berlin, where it serves a niche market of hipsters rather than wealthy buyers of haute couture. Again, we see that the often-imaginary cultural prestige and economy of cities and countries play a crucial role in shaping the luxury fashion industry in different places of the world.

Another reason for the disinterest in the West is the underlying assumption that if the consumer pays a premium price for a luxury product, it must have been made under ethical conditions. In practice, this 'illusion without owners' – an illusion that no one really believes in – structures the Western luxury market.[50] Research has shown that the correlation between price and ethical standards is practically non-existent. The British activist-journalist Tansy E. Hoskins has revealed that luxury fashion is produced in the same establishments, factories, and workshops around the world that produce goods for Primark and other fast fashion chains.[51] Moreover, the bottom line is not sweatshops, but the fabric producers and the cotton farmers, who serve the entire industry, not just one brand. The idea that luxury goods are somehow inherently sustainable because they are made to last, an idea promoted by the Western fashion industry, does not really resonate with the Indian market. The fact is that most Indian elite women would rather stay home than be seen publicly in the same designer outfit twice; if they ever repeat their party wear, ideally there is a gap of at least four years between wears.[52]

Overall, due to the numerous scandals within big business at large and within the global fashion industry in particular, morality had to be inserted back into the Indian fashion market. The billionaires, who following the financial crisis were cast as greedy and reckless by the media, were suddenly relaunched as philanthropic heroes or as ethical heroes with a strong sense of conscience. The tainted image had to be improved, and it was only through morality that the business elite could regain an appearance of legitimacy and capitalism could be rendered good again, a 'capitalism with a human face' capable of fixing its own evils.[53] The business elite's fears of delegitimization in India, connected to the crisis of capitalism that emerged after the 2008 financial crisis, reinforced their views of the impoverished Other and reiterated the elitist desire to perpetuate the status quo of strict divisions of class and caste. Ironically, this has occurred in a country with millions of artisans and skilled textile workers.

Here we are getting to the particularities of the Indian luxury fashion business. The relationship between a few rather wealthy designers at the top and the masses of poor cotton farmers, weavers, and artisans at its core has been particularly tense within the Indian fashion industry, more so precisely because the idea of 'the designer' was imported from the West, along with the creative individual's relatively high socio-economic position. The first generation of designers struggled to establish fashion design in India as a respectable profession. When in 1975 Rohit Khosla, the heavily mythologized founding father of the Indian fashion fraternity, said that he wanted to become a fashion designer, he was met with laughter: '*Bade hokar darzi banna hai kya*?' or 'Do you want to be a tailor when you grow up?' When decoded, it means, 'Do you want to be a low-class person?' In response, Khosla set out to prove that fashion design is something more elevated than tailoring. It is a profession that deserves recognition, and tailoring practitioners should belong to the upper middle class and social elite, as opposed to the country's millions of artisans, who, as the design practitioners claim, do not possess the same imagination, creativity, and drive for innovation. Claiming that fashion design is a superior practice akin to high art is the most common strategy of legitimization of the position of the designer within the social hierarchy, whether in France, or in India.

Another effective strategy to deal with the problem of one's position in society is the 'ethical sell'. This legitimization strategy allows the designer to present herself or himself as a knowledgeable and benevolent patron caring for workers and typically giving them recognition. Within this logic, it is the designer who benevolently gives certain limited importance to the artisan, an importance that remains imaginary for the artisan but translates into financial capital for the designer. In reality, it is the designer who would not exist without the artisan and who is dependent on the worker's labour.[54] Indeed, such legitimization strategies are at the same time strategies of value creation, and thus serve a double purpose. A recent example of this widespread practice is the work produced by the house of Anita Dongre (see figure 11.5). The image is reminiscent of Westwood in Nigeria, and follows the same logic. The poor workers are given the privilege of being showcased on a runway and afforded 'recognition' for their

11.5   Anita Dongre (left), presenting her 'Grassroots' collection with the Bollywood actress Dia Mirza (second from right). The showstopper at Lakme Fashion Week winter/festive 2015 collections, Dongre remarked that 'it is high time we should respect our own legacy'.

craft skill. Yet it is Dongre, the designer, who owns the aesthetic sensibility that they produce and who capitalizes on her own benevolence to maintain the status quo and established class relations. Rather than empowering the women to become fashion designers, all such initiatives have a tendency to reproduce the gap of inequality by setting limits on the possibilities, such as a decent living wage. As such, they never allow a radical break and true emancipation of craftswomen, precisely because they always speak on the workers' behalf. There is massive profit in injustice. While the Western notion of expertise serves here as a legitimization of this visible inequality, the ethical business creates the illusion that the maximum is done to elevate the needy and hence any critique of such business practices is typically eliminated from the outset. After all, who could argue against a designer doing 'good'?

Conclusion

Throughout this chapter, we have seen that if we are to understand the rise of the 'ethical sell' in the Indian luxury fashion industry, we are forced to take into account both global and local challenges, as much as cultural and political forces. These, as we have seen, form a particular conjuncture that involves forces such as (a) the global crisis of capitalism (economic, environmental, and humane), (b) the global rise of socio-economic inequality, and (c) the rise of Hindu nationalism in India with associated forms of nationalism. It also entails the relationships between Indian luxury designers and their workers in light of the scandals in the global fashion industry, which has also shaped Narendra Modi's 'Make in India' initiative within the garment sector. Moreover, the 'ethical sell' in the Indian luxury fashion industry, as has been shown, cannot be understood without examining the relationships between geographical places and their associated cultural prestige and meanings within the hegemonic imaginations of the global map. These historically constituted imaginary geographies play a crucial role in both how the world sees the Indian fashion industry and how the industry sees itself. The 'ethical sell' in the Indian fashion industry is in this sense not only a response to the global and local crises of legitimacy, but also to the persistent casting off (but also self-perception) of India as inferior, which has dominated much of the postcolonial period up until the mid-2000s, when the idea of India's inevitable future superpowerdom took hold. The 'ethical sell', in combination with the dominant aesthetics of 'royal chic', thus facilitates the re-positioning of India as a proud country with a vast heritage, one that also is morally superior to the West – against all odds. This allows local fashion designers to be publicly cast and celebrated as entrepreneurial heroes, the antithesis of predatory, exploitative brands from the West. The material aesthetics of Indian designer-products, and the associated brand narratives, are powerful expressions of these global and local relations. As one of the Indian fashion designers, who prefers to remain anonymous, remarked:

> I design pride, I want my clients to wear India's greatness, just look at our heritage, all the fabrics, all the crafts, that is our superb nation … I also want them to be modern, to care for development, that's why I show I care, to create kind of a movement, inspire others, especially the rich. That's why we run an NGO, help the poor and source ecologically, no chemicals … We have to show the world that India can lead. India is superior in all respects to the West, in terms of culture and morality. The West is out. India is the future leader.[55]

The final two sentences could have been said by Prime Minister Modi. Fashion, being both a cultural expression and a business, is always closer to politics than we might think.

Notes

1 A group of Jain and Hindu temples in Madhya Pradesh built between 950–1050 by the Chandela dynasty, famous for the intricate erotic sculptures incorporated in the architecture; the temple complex is a UNESCO world heritage site and a popular tourist destination.
2 For the discussion of the notion of the 'new India' see in particular: R. Kaur, 'Nation's two bodies: rethinking the idea of "new" India and its Other', *Third World Quarterly*, 33:4 (2012), 603–21.

3 The biggest market for the Indian designers is India, followed by the Middle East and Russia. T. Kuldova, *Luxury Indian Fashion: A Social Critique* (London: Bloomsbury, 2016).

4 M. Ciotti, 'Post-Colonial renaissance: "Indianness", contemporary art and the market in the age of neoliberal capital', *Third World Quarterly*, 33:4 (2012), 637–55; T. Kuldova, 'Forcing "good" and the legitimization of informal power: philanthro-capitlism and artistic nationalism among the Indian business elite', *Asienforum: International Quarterly for Asian Studies* (2017, forthcoming); T. Kuldova, 'Designing an illusion of India's future superpowerdom: of the rise of neo-aristocracy, Hindutva and philanthrocapitalism', *The Unfamiliar: An Anthropological Journal*, 4:1 (2014), 15–22.

5 J. Entwistle, *The Aesthetic Economy of Fashion: Markets and Values in Clothing and Modelling* (Oxford: Berg, 2009), p. 11.

6 T. Kuldova, 'On fashion and illusions: designing interpassive Indianness for India's rich', in E. Mora and M. Pedroni (eds), *Fashion Tales* (New York: Peter Lang, 2017), pp. 273–90.

7 L. Althusser, *Machiavelli and Us* (London: Verso, 2000).

8 T. Kuldova, '"The maharaja style": royal chic, heritage luxury and the nomadic elites', in T. Kuldova (ed.), *Fashion India: Spectacular Capitalism* (Oslo: Akademika Publishing, 2013), pp. 51–70.

9 'How ethical is fashion in India? Abhishek Jani, CEO, Fairtrade India', at social. yourstory.com/2015/04/fairtrade-india/ (accessed 18 January 2016).

10 Y. Citton, *Mythocratie: Storytelling et imaginaire de gauche* (Paris: Editions Amsterdam, 2010); F. Lordon, *Willing Slaves of Capital: Spinoza and Marx on Desire* (London: Verso, 2014); T. Kuldova, 'Directing passions in New Delhi's world of fashion: on the power of ritual and "illusions without owners"', *Thesis Eleven*, 133:1 (2016), 96–113.

11 D. B. Holt, *How Brands Become Icons: The Principles of Cultural Branding* (Cambridge, MA: Harvard University Press, 2004); J. Cayla and E. J. Arnould, 'A cultural approach to branding in the global marketplace', *Journal of International Marketing*, 16:4 (2008), 86–112.

12 A. Arvidsson, *Brands: Meaning and Value in Media Culture* (London: Routledge, 2006), 7.

13 M. Walz, S. Hingston, and M. Andehn, 'The magic of ethical brands: interpassivity and the thievish joy of delegated consumption', *Ephemera: Theory and Politics in Organization*, 14:1 (2014), 57–80.

14 R. A. Lukose, *Liberalization's Children: Gender, Youth, and Consumer Citizenship in Globalizing India* (Durham, NC: Duke University Press, 2009); M. Scammel, 'The internet and civic engagement: the age of the citizen-consumer', *Political Communication*, 17:4 (2000), 351–5; L. Cohen, *A Consumers' Republic: The Politics of Mass Consumption in Postwar America* (New York: Knopf, 2003); K. K. Sklar, 'The consumers' white label campaign of the National Consumers' League, 1898–1918', in S. Strasser, C. McGovern, and M. Judt (eds), *Getting and Spending: European and American Consumer Societies in the Twentieth Century* (Cambridge: Cambridge University Press, 1998), pp. 17–35.

15 S. Banaji and D. Buckingham, 'The civic sell: young people, the internet and eth-ical consumption', *Information, Communication & Society*, 12:8 (2009), 1,197–223; S. Žižek, *First as Tragedy, Then as Farce* (London: Verso, 2009).

16 While some media outlets reported that the number of people helped by the project amounted to 7,000, Vivienne Westwood's website cites the more modest number of 1,558 individuals, whose incomes rose from double to ten times their previous income. See Vivienne Westwood, 'Celebrating Five Years: Made in Africa Bags', 6 June 2015, at www.viviennewestwood.com/blog/celebrating-five-years-made-afri ca-bags (accessed 21 February 2016). Considering that most were slum dwellers,

    this increase within the local economy often still means poverty and marginaliza-
tion. Moreover, there is no guarantee that this project will continue in the future.

17 www.aaksonline.com/about/

18 Non-violent silk refers to silk that is produced without killing the silkworm; it is wild
silk produced in and around Bhagalpur in Bihar. No dyes are used in the process.
The idea of non-violent silk appeals to the eco-friendly consumers, but the concept
of *ahimsa* also immediately evokes Gandhi's political project of non-violent resistance and thus endows the designer products also with a backward-looking nationalist pride. The concept of *ahimsa*, which translates from Sanskrit as 'compassion'
or 'doing no harm', is central to leading Indian religions, namely Hinduism, Jainism,
and Buddhism.

19 Kuldova, 'Forcing "good" and the legitimization of informal power'.

20 W. Benjamin, 'Paris: Capital of the nineteenth century', *Perspecta*, 12 (1969), 163–72.

21 A. J. Scott, *The Cultural Economy of Cities: Essays on the Geography of Image-
Producing Industries* (London: SAGE, 2000).

22 H. Higgison, N. Saio, A. Swinnerton, and D. Williams, 'Promoting sustainable Indian
textiles: final report to the Department for Environment, Food and Rural Affairs
(Defra), London, UK', *Centre for Sustainable* Fashion, 5 (2009),, brochure available at: sustainable-fashion.com/wp-content/uploads/2010/11/CSF_Promoting_
Sustainable_Indian_Textiles_5_0.pdf (accessed 19 February 2016).

23 A. Sandhu, *Indian Fashion: Tradition, Innovation, Style* (London: Bloomsbury, 2014);
Kuldova, *Luxury Indian Fashion*. See also M. Khaire, 'The Indian fashion industry
and traditional Indian crafts', *Business History Review*, 85:2 (summer 2011), 345–66.

24 R. Crill (ed.), *Textiles from India: The Global Trade* (Calcutta: Seagull Books, 2006).

25 C. M. Wilkinson-Weber, *Fashioning Bollywood: The Making and Meaning of Hindi
Film Costume* (London: Bloomsbury, 2013).

26 W. Mazzarella, *Shoveling Smoke: Advertising and Globalization in Contemporary
India* (Durham, NC: Duke University Press, 2006).

27 C. Brosius, *India's Middle Class: New Forms of Urban Leisure, Consumption and
Prosperity* (New Delhi: Routledge, 2010); Lukose, *Liberalization's Children*.

28 D. Thomas, *Deluxe: How Luxury Lost its Luster* (New York: Penguin, 2007).

29 Anonymous source, informal interview by author, New Delhi, India, December
2011.

30 Kuldova, *Luxury Indian Fashion*.

31 Kuldova, 'Designing an illusion of India's future superpowerdom'.

32 Make in India, 'Textiles and Garments', at www.makeinindia.com/sector/textiles-
and-garments (accessed on 18 February 2016).

33 B. Tewari, 'India, the fashion world's next manufacturing power house?', *Business
of Fashion* (22 February 2016), at www.businessoffashion.com/articles/india-
inc/india-fashion-world-manufacturing-powerhouse-garment-textile-industry
(accessed 23 February 2016).

34 'Developing nations urged to follow EU in banning toxic pesticide', *EurActiv.com*,
31 July 2013, at www.euractiv.com/section/development-policy/news/developing-
nations-urged-to-follow-eu-in-banning-toxic-pesticide/ (accessed 20 January 2016).

35 C. Fingar, 'India grabs investment league pole position', *Financial Times* (29
September 2015).

36 On this see the influential Oxfam report: Oxfam, 'Even It Up: Time to End Extreme
Inequality' (2014), www.oxfam.org/sites/www.oxfam.org/files/file_attachments/
cr-even-it-up-extreme-inequality-291014-en.pdf (accessed 12 January 2016).

37 T. R. Bates, 'Gramsci and the theory of hegemony', *Journal of the History of Ideas*,
36:2 (1975), 351–66; T. Kuldova, 'Fatalist luxuries: of inequality, wasting and anti-
work ethic in India', *Cultural Politics*, 12:1 (2016), 110–29.

38 T. Kuldova, 'Heads against hands and hierarchies of creativity: Indian luxury
embroidery between craft, fashion design and art', in M. Svašek and B. Meyer

(eds), *Creativity in Transition: Politics and Aesthetics of Circulating Images* (Oxford: Berghahn Books, 2016), pp. 61–85.

39 According to unofficial estimates, there are around 200 million craftspeople in the textile industry in India, with a turnover of $4.5 billion.

40 D. Cannadine, *Ornamentalism: How the British Saw Their Empire* (Oxford: Oxford University Press, 2002).

41 Kuldova, 'Forcing "good" and the legitimization of informal power'.

42 T. Benton, *The Greening of Machiavelli: The Evolution of International Environmental Politics* (London: Royal Institute of International Affairs, 1994).

43 M. G. Velasquez, *Business Ethics: Concepts and Cases* (New Jersey: Prentice Hall, 1982).

44 L. McGoey, *No Such Thing as Free Gift* (London: Verso, 2015).

45 CEO and a client of one of the leading Indian fashion designers, anonymized interview by author, New Delhi, 12 December 2012.

46 Indian top designer, anonymized interview by author, 10 November 2012.

47 While cotton production, silks and other fabrics, and weaving have always been of high quality, the problem (notoriously) for the Indian textile industry is stitching and finishing.

48 I. Amed, 'CEO Talk/ Brunello Cucinelli, founder and Chief Executive, Brunello Cucinelli', *Business of Fashion* (1 July 2014), at www.businessoffashion.com/arti cles/ceo-talk/ceo-talk-brunello-cucinelli-founder-chief-executive-brunello-cucinelli (accessed 10 January 2016); D. LaRocca, 'A new philosophy of clothes: Brunello Cucinelli's neohumanistic business ethics', *Journal of Religion and Business Ethics*, 3:10 (2014), 1–24.

49 T. E. Hoskins, *Stitched Up: The Anti-Capitalist Book of Fashion* (London: Pluto Press, 2014).

50 R. Pfaller, *On the Pleasure Principle in Culture: Illusions without Owners* (London: Verso, 2014).

51 Hoskins, *Stitched Up*.

52 Kuldova, *Luxury Indian Fashion*.

53 Žižek, *First as Tragedy, Then as Farce*.

54 Kuldova, 'Fatalist luxuries'.

55 Top Indian fashion designer, anonymized interview by author, New Delhi, 8 October 2012.

12

A bag of remembrance: a cultural biography of Red-White-Blue, from Hong Kong to Louis Vuitton

Wessie Ling

Stamped with its renowned logo, could the 2007 Louis Vuitton laundry bag – a replica of the ubiquitous plaid plastic carrier bag – be an ironic visual pun in response to the countless Chinese market stalls that had relentlessly ripped off their infamous 'LV' design? With its little-known origin in Hong Kong via Japan and Taiwan, the striped polyethylene material of the laundry bag, or migrant bag, was first used for burlap-type sacks or tarpaulin in the construction industry of Hong Kong, where it was subsequently made into carrier bags. In the 1970s and 1980s, plaid plastic carrier bags were often used to transport food and necessities from Hong Kong to mainland China through Shenzhen, the first city after crossing the British-Chinese border. Today, it is the plaid carrying bag that continues to be used widely in China and throughout the world.

Commonly known as 'Red-White-Blue' in Hong Kong, the bag is imbued with symbolic meaning associated with the 'local spirit' of an industrious, trading city built by a 'hardy and hard-working people'.[1] In Hong Kong, the bag is emblematic of the city's colonial days and serves as a potent symbol of an ever-changing city that seems to be perpetually under construction. The shortage of land and rising property prices in Hong Kong restricted the cluster of small producers of Red-White-Blue bags, who could not expand to develop economies of scale. Over the past two decades, the manufacturing of the bag has moved to mainland China to take advantage of low-cost labour and cheaper production facilities. The worldwide dissemination of inexpensive products made in China means that the Red-White-Blue carrier bag has found a global audience. Its little-known origin in Hong Kong permits new users to imagine new meanings for the bag; because of its low retail price and widespread availability, Red-White-Blues primarily suit the needs of the migrant, and is found in different corners of the world. The bag has different names in different countries, and has taken on new meanings in various localities. In the United States, it is called the 'Chinatown tote'; in Trinidad, the 'Guyanese Samsonite'; in Germany, 'Türkenkoffer', which translates as the 'Turkish suitcase'; in the United Kingdom, 'Bangladeshi bag'; in South Africa, 'Zimbabwe bag'; in Thailand, 'Rainbow bag', and in Nigeria and Ghana, 'Ghana must go bag'.[2]

This chapter discusses the extent to which a Chinese export has played a part in the realities and identities of varied communities, as well as the re-fashioning of Chinese exports into a fashion commodity. It traces the origin and development of Red-White-Blue, and its connotations and cultural significance to Hong Kong and communities across several continents. Through its biography, this chapter unpacks how various communities adopted and (re)interpreted their versions of Red-White-Blue bags. The chapter concludes with a discussion of Louis Vuitton's replica of this plaid bag. The questions addressed here include authenticity, cultural identity, and the power dynamic between high and low culture. Specifically, the chapter juxtaposes Western fashion institutions and Asian street culture, and examines the relationship of Chinese production to the European-American fashion system. The analysis draws on empirical and ethnographic research, including interviews with makers and users, and detailed readings of the contemporary global fashion scene as represented in the traditional press and on the Web.

The origin of the Red-White-Blue

It is believed that the Red-White-Blue sheeting was first manufactured in Japan in the 1960s and was imported to Hong Kong through a Taiwanese manufacturer in 1975.[3] Composed of materials from the outset synthetic in nature, the bag is made from plastic sheeting woven from either polyethylene (PE) or polypropylene (PP) threads in a crisscross weave. The low cost, strength, and durability of these plastics resulted in their widespread use in industry and construction during the 1960s. Eventually, these plastics supplanted canvas for many different industrial purposes. As Japan became unable to meet this demand, in the 1970s Taiwan overtook it to become the major manufacturer and exporter of Red-White-Blue.[4]

The reason why this plastic sheeting is called Red-White-Blue in Hong Kong is unknown. In the manufacturing industry, it was referred to as Red-Blue-White or 'grass-mat cloth', because its weave is similar to that of the grass mat.[5] However, these terms were rarely used outside of the plastics industry. A direct reading would put it down to its combination of colours, but in fact a variety of colours are available such as red, black, white, blue, green, and orange, with other colour combinations such as white-blue and red-white stripes. Some believe that the choices or combinations of colour have no definite origin and appear to be the result of economic imperatives rather than aesthetic considerations.[6] However, it is generally believed that, traditionally, Taiwan people held funerary and prosperity rites at home using temporary pavilions covered with blue-and-white striped fabric. Later, red – representing luck and fortune in China – was added to the colour scheme for celebratory occasions, resulting in the typical Red-White-Blue.[7] Although such colour combinations are common to many national flags, the evocation of national identity from the plastic sheeting had not arisen from its colour scheme but from the endowed symbolic meaning of the material itself. More importantly, the representation and cultural affiliation of this plastic sheeting have close associations with the social reality of Hong Kong. Given the mundane nature of the material, the bag seems to have been named out of convenience. Widely circulated among the locals, 'Red-White-Blue' has consequently become the bag's official name.

In the 1970s, Red-White-Blue sheeting made in Taiwan was imported to Hong Kong to meet the huge demand of local construction projects then being undertaken (see figure 12.1). Hong Kong was undergoing an economic boom and new buildings were going up at an astonishing rate. This created great demand for Red-White-Blue on construction sites, where it was used as a covering material for scaffolding to prevent falling debris. Red-White-Blue plastic sheeting is ubiquitous in Hong Kong's landscape. It is used for temporary shelters in Hong Kong's squatter areas, where immigrants and the poor live, and in rural areas as protective covers for farmers' plots. Although large-scale construction projects have declined over recent years, numerous ongoing, small-scale city renovation projects sustain the demand for Red-White-Blue tarpaulins in Hong Kong.[8]

In addition to its industrial usage, the Red-White-Blue sheeting was made into cheap, lightweight carrier bags in Hong Kong itself, and popularized among Hong Kong's working class. One of its many connotations has evolved from the use of the carrier bag by ordinary Hong Kong citizens, who frequently travel between Hong Kong and mainland China. The low-cost Red-White-Blue carrier bag has thus become synonymous with endurance, owing in part to the material's sturdy qualities and industrial usage. The bag also symbolizes the act of border crossing, thus embodying the relationship between Hong Kong and mainland China. The image and nature of border-crossing travellers carrying a Red-White-Blue bag has developed especially since the 1980s, when mainland China adopted an open policy encouraging population flow between the two regions.[9] Red-White-Blue bags thus have an intimate connection with the social history of Hong Kong and the lives of its people. As a piece of material culture, the bag embodies Hong Kong's collective creativity while serving as a symbol of frequent border crossings.[10]

Despite the fact that this transnational textile originated in Japan, the fabric has garnered its authenticity as the quintessence of Hong Kong, where it became instilled into the everyday life of the locals. Even the profile of the bag's creator, Mr. Lee Wah – now in his ninetieth year – encompasses the enduring and industrious image of postwar Hong Kong. There, equipped with a Singer household sewing machine, Lee Wah established his Red-White-Blue bag business in 1953. He made his name with the manufacture of canvas bags, most of which were made into school bags for schoolchildren. When polyethylene was imported from Taiwan in the 1970s, Lee responded to the practical needs of industry and individuals by making the material into bags. The bag's success was due to its light-weight and water-resistant material, which made it particularly suitable for transporting goods by trucks and for use as a personal tote. Despite producing over seventy bags per day at peak times, Lee's enterprise never incorporated nor became a financial partner in a corporation. His devoted crew was a humble family of eight, equipped with a tiny shop front of less than ten square metres. All of his children were essentially raised by his bag manufacturing business.[11]

Building Hong Kong: Redwhiteblue

However, it was not until recently that the Red-White-Blue material came to represent the identity of Hong Kong's people. In 2004, Hong Kong designer and artist Stanley Wong (otherwise known as 'Anothermountainman') curated a thematic exhibition, entitled *Building Hong Kong: Redwhiteblue,* in the Hong Kong Heritage Museum. The exhibit took the plastic material as its medium and as a subject matter. Numerous artists and designers participated, along with cultural scholars, writers, and poets, in an effort to interpret the meaning of the Red-White-Blue fabric. The material was promoted as a representation of Hong Kong's identity, referring in particular to a collective image of Hong Kong's working class in the 1960s and 1970s.[12]

The Red-White-Blue was further associated with Hong Kong's culture and people through the popular press, which published responses to the artworks in the exhibition. Moreover, the link between Red-White-Blue-inspired works of art and a unitary notion of Hong Kong's identity was further enforced by institutional discourse. For example, the museum curator maintains that this 'mundane and banal Red-White-Blue material popularized by artists' has 'assumed an illustrative visual identity through different conceptual interpretations to represent the spirit of the Hong Kong people'.[13]

The collective initiative saw artists, scholars, and cultural critics join forces to imbue Red-White-Blue cloth with symbolic meaning. According to cultural scholar Matthew Turner, 'red-white-blue stripes may be imagined as an unofficial kind of flag of the people'. The neatly reserved stripes 'take on an almost caricature symbolism of proletarian purity'. Accordingly, the bag is 'defiantly local and prudently patriotic', 'innocently authentic and internationally sophisticated', 'wickedly illegitimate and institutionally legitimatized'. The ubiquitous textile draws on the colonial promotion of 'the Hong Kong Story'.[14] Between the lines and stripes of the bag lies the perfect symbol of Hong Kong cultural identity.

Social fabrication

The Red-White-Blue carrier bag is a chameleon. The multiple symbolic meanings of the Red-White-Blue bag are characterized by the particular social reality of a specific moment, and a specific community that has a history of migration, that is hardworking, and is hoping for a better future. It gained the name 'the rural worker's bag' to represent frugality, affiliated with working-class identity in Hong Kong. The highly utilitarian fabric was invested with the symbolic meanings associated with the modern Hong Kong lifestyle, leading to its establishment as a cultural icon in the city.

The rise of Red-White-Blue in post-colonial Hong Kong has much to do with the city's struggle to incorporate and negotiate itself under the iron governance of Chinese authority. Following ninety-nine years of British colonization, Hong Kong returned to the People's Republic of China (PRC) in 1997. It is now a Chinese special administrative region (SAR) under the regime of 'one country, two systems'. Formulated by Deng Xiaoping, this constitutional principle allows Hong Kong to continue to have its own political system to oversee legal, economic, and financial affairs (including external relations with foreign countries) for fifty years following the handover of Hong Kong's sovereignty to China in 1997.[15] Hong Kong is a society that combines the legacy of British colonialism with a heavy Chinese influence. The economic and political separation from the Chinese mainland during the colonial era meant that Hong Kong was greatly exposed to Japanese and Western cultures. Hong Kong's culture is often described as a hybrid and sharply different from Chinese orthodoxy. The disparity in ideological and material conditions set the people of Hong Kong apart from their mainland counterparts on issues such as identity, politics, nationalism, and patriotism. Hong Kong's people have an ambiguous and complicated relationship with their nation. They have an undeniable cultural attachment to the mainland. However, their varied political ideologies are tainted with scepticism.

Tensions caused by political and cultural differences cast long shadows across the mainland–Hong Kong divide. Human rights violations and corruption are widespread in China: one high-profile example is the Tiananmen crackdown on 4 June 1989, which has left a deep historical wound.[16] Although the inhabitants of Hong Kong started to appropriate a new dual Hong Kong-Chinese identity and came to rely on the mainland for economic advancement,[17] many sensitive political issues and dubious public events disappointed the locals.[18] Among the many Hong Kong–mainland conflicts are those over the erosion of colonial heritage sites; the reinterpretation of the Basic Law to undermine the freedom and rights of Hong Kong residents; and the implementation of national education in which the communist and nationalist ideology of China's government are acknowledged in the curriculum. The administrative government of Hong Kong failed to represent and fight for its people. The temptation to please the Beijing authorities saw SAR officials cooperate with the pro-mainland forces at the expense of their own citizens.

All these controversial issues have led to rising fears that Hong Kong is losing touch with its traditional values. In 2004, the year of the exhibition *Building Hong Kong: Redwhiteblue*, more than two hundred professionals and academics signed a declaration calling for the defence of Hong Kong's core values, which they believed were being eroded. Published as an advertisement in several local newspapers, the manifesto included values such as 'liberty, democracy, human rights, rule of law, fairness, social justice, peace and compassion, integrity and transparency, plurality, respect for individuals, and upholding professionalism'.[19] The organizers claimed a strong sense of helplessness and rising frustration in the community; Beijing's then-recent interference in Hong Kong's affairs had undermined trust and social freedom. The foregrounding of Red-White-Blue as a cultural symbol in the museum exhibition was set against a backdrop of social unrest. The popularity of the bag, the cloth, and the exhibition coincided with the fear of losing one's soul, the call for unity in Hong Kong, and a need for a space of belonging at a time when local identity and principled values were under threat.

Mobilizing Red-White-Blue

In 2005, the year following the museum exhibition, the Red-White-Blue bag was proudly displayed in the Hong Kong pavilion at the 51st Venice Biennale. Stanley Wong was chosen as one of the two artists to represent Hong Kong with a Red-White-Blue art installation. The pavilion featured a Hong Kong-style teahouse with window frames and walls entirely covered in Red-White-Blue fabric. The exhibition's theme was an 'investigation of a journey to the West by micro and polo'.[20] It loosely referenced Marco Polo's travels from Europe to East Asia. In this regard, the two selected Hong Kong artists travelled west in the computer age. Wong represented 'micro' while the other artist embodied 'polo'. By creating an installation based on Hong Kong's teahouses – another important symbol of the city – Wong addressed the importance of face-to-face communication for society in the micro-technological age.[21] Accordingly, the teahouse was intended to re-establish human contact in the hope that interacting with others over a cup of tea would help people to reflect on societal issues and to regain focus. The juxtaposition of tea drinking on the one hand, and Red-White-Blue on the other, further fortified the material's iconic status to the world.

Following Wong's successful revamping of Red-White-Blue, more local artists were inspired to use it as a material in their artistic productions, leading to a mushrooming effect that reinforced its cultural significance. Popular culture has also taken its inherent symbolic meaning to an expanded audience. In 2013, a social enterprise called rwb330 was established to promote the spirit of 'Positive Hong Kong' through Red-White-Blue. This non-profit organization is a collaborative project between the New Life Psychiatric Rehabilitation Association (New Life) and the Urban Renewal Authority of Hong Kong. It supports holistic health and helps people recovering from mental illness to integrate into society, and hence to achieve self-reliance. Products made from Red-White-Blue sheeting are hand crafted by participants in New Life's sheltered workshops, and then sold in stores.[22] Here, the textile is taken to represent the organizational idea of a positive Hong Kong. In the words of the rwb330 collective, Red-White-Blue

> is omnipresent, at construction sites, hawkers' stalls, Lowu border, and everywhere. It witnesses the economic boom in the 60s–70s when Hong Kong people were striving for life. Accordingly, the rwb homecoming bag evokes collective memories embodying the industrial story of Hong Kong.[23]

Here again, to the people of Hong Kong, Red-White-Blue is seen as a metaphor for fortitude, adaptability, and industriousness.

An attempt to foster holistic health by means of a piece of cloth endowed with symbolic meanings may seem novel, even wacky. The case in point is that during the process of indigenization, Red-White-Blue cloth was widely embraced by the people of Hong Kong as being emblematic of their collective memory.[24] When the city faced the possible loss of its cultural identity, the preservation of values and portrayal of a common destiny were called in as saviour. When history has been misrepresented and partially erased, holding on to old artefacts, monuments, and historic sites allows the community to affirm its own past and its sense of belonging to a particular geographic locale.[25] The transformation of Red-White-Blue into an artefact from Hong Kong's industrial past – first as a manufacturing hub with gigantic clothing and textile industries in the 1960s and 1970s, and then, having overtaken Italy, as the world's largest clothing exporter in 1973 – was completed as Hong Kong became a white-collar city with major financial and professional services starting in the 1980s. Since then, Hong Kong has become an important financial centre and international metropolis. The economic success of the city has led to a considerable rise in people's incomes and the consumption of international fashion.[26] The substantially improved standard of living, and the rise of the urban land-scape, stood in stark contrast to the economically retrograde mainland. In addition, Hong Kong's unique creative identity gradually took shape in the 1960s alongside the emergence of its own cultural industries, notably in art, design, fashion, literature, film, music, and television, all of which fed the daily appetites of Hong Kong audiences.[27] The affirmation of history and the memory of the post-colonial city thus saw Red-White-Blue framed within the city's collective memory as a fabric of remembrance, and in many ways, as a 'bag of remembrance'. It held out the hope that restoring historical memory can be achieved through engaging with the imaginings stirred by the bag. In this regard, rehabilitation through Red-White-Blue functions as a safeguard for a distinctive cultural identity, invigorating its cultural heritage to imbue Hong Kong with a strength and determination that can favourably position the city internationally, nationally, regionally, and locally.

Consuming Red-White-Blue bags

Since the late 1990s, the manufacture of Red-White-Blue carrier bags has moved to mainland China, where lower labour and manufacturing costs prevail. However, users have noted a decline in quality as demonstrated by a looser weave, resulting in a material now less sturdy. For example, Zhejiang Daxin Industry Co. Ltd, a firm situated in an eastern province of China, mass-manufactures tens of thousands of bags per order, and distributes them around the world. Now a cheaply made export from China, Red-White-Blue carrier bags have found a global audience. Because China has remained economically competitive in low-end production, the vast majority of mainland exports that reach retail consumers are mass-market products. This includes the carrier bag, offered in a wide range of plaids and colours. It can be found in all corners of the world, in a variety of outlets, such as pound shops, hardware stores, corner shops, liquor stores, street markets, and so on. Costing less than £2 each, the bag has been established as a mass-consumption product for all walks of life.

While China made cheap products available to the rest of the world, they depended, in return, on the world consuming goods from China. From textiles to home appliances, consumer goods, particularly those made in the United States and Western Europe, were generally more expensive prior to China becoming the new workshop of the world. The affordable products made in China fuelled mass consumption globally, giving rise to an increasingly wide class of mass consumers.[28] The abundance of Chinese consumer goods in our daily lives has made China an inexorable part of our social reality. The consumer no longer calls the origin of the product into question.

Polyethylene production at Benzene Enterprise Corporation, a Taiwanese factory in Taichung.   **12.1**

Localizing Red-White-Blue bags

Despite its manufacture in China, the Red-White-Blue bag's longstanding cultural and economic association with Hong Kong allows novel sensibilities, re-imagination, and representation to take place. The versatility, low retail price, and easy availability of the bag means that it has a place in countless households. It is being used in travel and transporting goods across generations, class, and ethnicities, and is not exclusive to non-Western consumers. Although to some it is not regarded as a flattering item, when it comes to practicality, users admire its limitless functionality. In particular, its reputation captured the attention of the migrant, who uses the bag for travel, and the transportation of personal effects, across borders. Red-White-Blues have been adopted as utility bags in strikingly similar ways in different parts of the world. The migrant's use of the bag has subsequently increased the visibility of Red-White-Blue. As we have seen, the bag goes by different nicknames in different places. At first glance, the common denominator in these names is their relationship to the embedded cultures of migration in the various locales. Colonialization, border control, free movement, immigration law, political turmoil, socio-economic difficulties; the paraphernalia of exile, the experience of living abroad, a sense of belonging, and identity politics: all are intrinsically woven into the bag.

Upon closer examination, each regional nickname for the bag reflects a different migration story. For instance, the 'Ghana must go' bag is entwined with a history of politics, immigration, dislocation, fear, fracture, and sudden enforced exile. It entails the various expulsions of immigrants that Ghana and Nigeria engaged in between the 1960s and 1980s. The phrase 'Ghana must go' was directed in Nigeria at incoming Ghanaian refugees during the political unrest of the 1980s, and it was applied to the plaid carrier bags during the 1983 Expulsion Order, when illegal immigrants were given fourteen days to leave Nigeria.[29] Around two and a half million Ghanaians and other foreigners used the bags as makeshift luggage when they were forcibly deported. Many were barely able to pack their belongings before fleeing, expelled with only a few hours' or a few days' notice. During this tumultuous time, the 'Ghana must go' bag was exceedingly practical as luggage because of its generous capacity, light weight, and affordability. Packed in a hurry for fear of safety, the bag provided an immediate necessity for the Ghanaians. Pointing to repeated upheavals in Ghana and Nigeria, the cheap, practical, and functional 'Ghana must go' bag is now associated by many people with loss and division.[30]

Today, the bag continues to be used for transportation of goods and personal belongings in Nigeria and Ghana. The 'Ghana must go' bag is as familiar to the locals as world-famous celebrities. Using the phrase as a title, in 2013 author Taiye Selasi published a novel in which she told the complicated story of an African-American family.[31] Exploring the theme of family via the lens of immigration, the book provides insight into the cultures in Nigeria and Ghana. A metaphor for Ghanaian immigration, 'Ghana must go', while largely entailing movement within or between Ghana and Nigeria, is also about their socio-political realities. In 2016, the Nigerian film director Frank Rajah Arase released an award-wining movie using the phrase 'Ghana must go' as its title, albeit unrelated to the novel.[32] A light-hearted comedy featuring the conflicts between Nigerians and Ghanaians, the movie unfolds the story of the refusal of a Ghanaian father to let his daughter marry a Nigerian due to the 'Ghana must go' saga. In one dramatic scene of house-moving day, in which a pile of the signature bags has a notable presence, the character chants, 'Ghana must go bag in this house!' Not only has the bag a noticeable presence in the movie poster (see figure 12.2), it was also used as a prop for the celebrities who attended the movie premiere. Some three decades after the expulsion, Red-White-Blue bags, or 'Ghana must go' bags in this instance, are still a potent symbol of the unfortunate treatment of Ghanaian migrants in their adopted country.

It is telling that the bag acquired distinctive names only within communities of migrants and immigrants. Elsewhere in popular culture, it remains nameless or is merely referred to by its origin or functionality. In Sri Lanka, for example, the bag is referred to simply as 'China bag'.[33] It is

Ghana Must Go film premiere poster, 2016, featuring several 'Ghana must go' bags alongside the Desamour Film Company's movie actors and actresses.

very useful in the transportation of goods due to its durability and water-resistant properties, much appreciated given the island nation's unpredictable weather conditions. The plastic material itself is widely available and is largely used to protect street stalls and rooftops from the heady sun and drenching rain. For Sri Lankans, the material, as well as the bag, is part of everyday experience. They might not come to acknowledge the cloth and the bags as identity markers, but in a nuanced way, they have acquired meaning because the material is closely associated with the local daily life.[34] In Africa, the bag is imbued with the emotions of a family member's homecoming after a long day of work in a faraway place.[35] The bag is a symbol of their hard work in the city. This diffusion of commodities and cultural practices, as analysed by Arjun Appardurai, may paradoxically enhance cultural differentiation under the rubric of globalization.[36] The Red-White-Blue bag is local everywhere and simultaneously global.[37]

The Louis Vuitton replica bag

The embedded stories of the Red-White-Blue bag in various regions are nearly infinite. Yet the fame of the bag has stretched beyond migrant and immigrant communities and ventured into the fashion marketplace. The most notable and perhaps controversial example of this new iteration of Red-White-Blue is the Louis Vuitton plaid bag of 2007, by Demna

Gvasalia, bag designer under the artistic direction of Marc Jacobs, who was working for Louis Vuitton at the time (see figure 12.3). This new artefact by a high-end producer of luxury handbags and other fashionable items is a leather replica of the ubiquitous Red-White-Blue bag, labelled with the well-known Louis Vuitton logo in a passport-stamp style. This is not the first time that the Red-White-Blue motif has been adopted to make a high-fashion commodity. Several brands have refashioned the look to suit their collections: Helmut Lang for the spring-summer 2003 men's wear, Comme des Garçons for a handbag in 2004, and Jack Spade for his 'Chinatown' Collection in 2005. However, Louis Vuitton's adoption of the plaid bag in its authentic pattern and shape as a fashion commodity was a one-of-a-kind venture. The bag's release immediately generated a worldwide response. The international fashion media generally praised its creativity, boldness, and clever interpretation of a mundane item. By 2006 in Hong Kong, it was generally understood that the now-omnipresent Red-White-Blue bag was originally from China. There was a certain irony in Vuitton copying cheap Chinese produce to be sold under their label for large sums of money, given the countless counterfeit Vuitton handbags for sale on the Chinese black market.

The critics of the Red-White-Blue replica bag described it as the quintessential example of the fashion industry's practice of 'slumming' (also discussed in relation to Vivienne Westwood in Chapter 11). One fashion blogger, Koranteng Ofosu-Amaah, called it 'a trope in the rarefied heights of *haute couture*', claiming that 'we have seen much appropriation of the sort' in recent years.[38] The watchdogs who monitor the ethics of the fashion industry put this particular creation for Vuitton under scrutiny. In essence, two antagonists – Western capitalism and the 'Third World' slum – are at play in this case of plagiarism.

Vuitton's version of Red-White-Blue bags assumed centre stage in debates on geo-cultural power relations, raising serious questions about race, gender, class, and most importantly, the inequalities as to who controls and benefits from the exploitation of cultural resources.[39] Such 'exploitation chic', as critics described the Vuitton reinterpretation, essentially shores up differences and fortifies cultural boundaries between rich and poor, or North and South. Another group of observers denounced the practice of cultural appropriation as 'smuggling'. Accordingly, it can only operate on a one-way power flow from the top down, from the hegemonic West to the Other.[40]

In Hong Kong, comments on Red-White-Blue Vuitton replicas were mixed. Detractors called it 'irrelevant' and a 'copycat'. Others, however, praised the Red-White-Blue spin-off in the belief that it would spark a trend that other global brands would follow. For its part, the Vuitton brand unreservedly denied its connection with either the original Red-White-Blue bag or with the popular culture of Hong Kong. There, pride and

Louis Vuitton's replica of a Red-White-Blue bag in tightly-woven leather; spring–summer collection 2007. Photo: François Guillot/AFP/Getty Images.

12.3

patriotism were engendered by this incident of plagiarism, so much so that the Red-White-Blue bag's iconic status was even more firmly embedded in its own locality. The 2005 representation of Red-White-Blue material in the 51st Venice Biennale had been a defining moment for the city of Hong Kong, showcasing its ownership to the world, so that by 2007, the authentic Red-White-Blue bag had been elevated to the status of a cultural icon and a major part of the Hong Kong community's 'feel-good' factor, which could be shared only among local people. Despite the many versions and interpretations by artists, designers, and commercial labels, for many people around the world the essence of the Red-White-Blue lies in its authenticity and its association with Hong Kong. In the eyes of local people in Hong Kong, if Vuitton could adopt their bag for commercial advancement, so could local retailers. For example, one of Hong Kong's household product retailers, called G.O.D. and known for incorporating local cultural icons and images into its product range, offered a variation of the Red-White-Blue in the form of a handbag in a contemporary style back in 2002.[41] In another example, the multi-brand store based in Hong Kong, The CLOT, teamed up with Adidas to release RWB sneakers, resulting in a 2015 collaboration under the name CLOT Consortium x Adidas ZZ Flux. Their promotions featured ordinary Hong Kong citizens in RWB sneakers posing against the backdrop of local scenes, including a symbolic Hong Kong teahouse.[42] The focus was on the enduring celebration of local identity, ordinary culture, pride, and belonging within the community.

In mainland China and Ghana, responses to the Vuitton reinterpretation of Red-White-Blue were not so generous. Anger, bitterness, and a sense of injustice were expressed. Comments such as 'cheap', 'working class', and 'distasteful' were recorded.[43] Far from the Western catwalk, countless people in mainland China continued to use traditional Red-White-Blue carrier bags as they always had, filling them with personal belongings, consumables, and gifts. Chinese factory workers who lived apart from their loved ones for much of the year saw the traditional carrier bag as a symbol of their exhaustion and their longing to see their families. The bag accompanied their stressful journey home, and denoted hardship and poverty. It did not speak to choice, joy, or celebration. In Africa, the Ghanaians learned of the Vuitton bag and called it 'another colonial invasion rip-off'.[44] The bag pointed to the 'Ghana must go' saga and an era of political unrest, the consequences of which many were still living through. The 'Ghana must go' bag, to the Ghanaians, is an emblem of suffering, exigency, and division. Vuitton's rendition dug up the painful memories of exile.

Further criticism pointed to the materiality of the bag and its lack of utility as luggage. The Vuitton replica contradicted the functionality of the original. It is made of two square metres of tightly woven leather, marketed at a retail price of £1,400. In another words, it is heavy, heftily priced, and impractical. If resilience and a long lifespan were meant to be part of the bag's DNA – to borrow a phrase used increasingly in high-fashion marketing – the replica was likely a faddish mutation; forgivable, perhaps, if it had been a collaboration with a Hong Kong artist. The thought process behind the bag remained a mystery: no rationale behind Vuitton's version was explained by LVHM (the French holding company discussed in Chapter 3).[45] The hefty price tag of the Vuitton replica distances this interpretation of Red-White-Blue from any hint of social inequality. The replica would never withstand enduring use, underscoring its irrelevance given the short life of any fashion craze. The expensive Vuitton bag was the antithesis of the cheap Red-White-Blue. It was high-end fashion created to be discarded when the brand-conscious consumer grew tired of the look. While fashionistas took pride in their latest Vuitton creation, the users of the original bag looked on with a grim sense of humour at a distance. Vuitton's replica bag is ironic at best, mocking at worst.

Why Red-White-Blue matters

Red-White-Blue bags have been endowed with meanings by artistic production, commodification, and popular culture in the specific local context of Hong Kong. The carrier bag, together with the plastic sheeting of which it is made, has come to denote the spirit of the city (see figure 12.4). It serves as the material expression of locality and is a popular cultural icon embraced by Hong Kong residents. This highly symbolic textile artefact has mobilized local communities into responding to cultural, social, and

The now-iconic Red-White-Blue bag included in a wall mural celebrating 'All Things Hong Kong', photographed in 2014.   **12.4**

political issues, which in turn has transformed the cultural dynamics of a city once historically perceived as apolitical. The association between Red-White-Blue and Hong Kong is unquestionable: the Hong Kong-ness of Red-White-Blue lies in its meanings as assigned by the people of Hong Kong.

With the worldwide distribution of Red-White-Blue bags made in China, the little-known origins of the authentic artefact allows it to become part of the everyday realities of many communities, especially among particular migrants and immigrants. Around the globe, bag users invest Red-White-Blues with their collective memories and experiences that address specific social, political, and economical conditions. The Red-White-Blue has been localized worldwide, with many a place assigning a name that speaks only for the community at hand and of its particular struggles and hardship. When Western fashion turned the bag into a luxury item, communities that understood the original artefact to be part of their cultural identities responded with vitriol. Through the process of indigenization, the original Red-White-Blue bag has been endlessly reconstructed and reimagined in ways that embodied patriotism, belonging, and cultural identities. The beauty of Red-White-Blue bags lies in the eye of the beholders. In their eyes, its fullest expression is to be found in the 'four M's' of fashion – Mode: the way it is adopted; Manners: the way it serves as a means of expression for the communities concerned; Mores: the way in which it unfolds the life of the individuals in those communities; and Markets: the way these communities are defined demographically and psychologically.[46] Red-White-Blue bags are not considered to be fashion items for these communities, and it inarguably withstands the currency of fashionable trends. Unlike the infamous chop suey, which accentuates Chinese sensibilities only when eaten in the United States, the 'glocalization' of Red-White-Blue bags makes it at once indigenous to user localities and an artefact with universal appeal.

Postscript

The trend of 'Chinatown chic', or 'migrant worker chic', continues to hit the headlines in the fashion press. Autumn 2013 ready-to-wear collections, as shown in New York City by Céline and by Stella McCartney, included outfits that featured bright, graphic plaid prints reminiscent of Red-White-Blue. Céline denied any relation to Hong Kong or China but referred to the plaid of Tati, a bazaar-like department store situated in a section of Paris inhabited by African migrants. Tati uses a distinctive pink plaid on its store logo and on its shopping bags. On close examination, the plaid that was used by Céline clearly resembles the many different colour combinations of the Red-White-Blue material. Further, had Tati's plaid been plagiarized, the Paris fashion label would not easily get away with it.

As luxury brands venture deeper into exploitation chic, Balenciaga was the newcomer that adopted a Red-White-Blue bag into its autumn-winter collection for 2016. The press discussed the issue from the perspective of fashion law, but nothing came of the chatter about intellectual property rights and ethics. One headline that read 'Balenciaga did not "copy" traditional Thai shopping bags for F/W16' was telling in its denial of imitation.[47] Asian street culture and non-institutionalized practice continue to be expropriated by the Western fashion system. To the amusement of some and the dismay of others, the drawing of the ever-finer line between mere appropriation and (illegal) copying in high fashion is bound to continue.

Acknowledgements

The author would like to thank the following individuals for their contributions to this chapter: Carmen Au, Mary Chan, Gary Chang, Chien-Ming Lee, Kung-Chiu Tse, Kris Wong, Stanley Wong, Michael Miller Yu. Special thanks to Travis Kong and Tommy Tse for inviting me to the University of Hong Kong as Visiting Scholar (Sociology, January–February 2017), enabling me to conduct further fieldwork in Hong Kong. This research received further support from the Research Institute for Languages and Centres of Asia (RILCA) at Mahidol University (Bangkok), where a Research Fellowship (2018) is granted for the study of the Thai version of the bag.

Notes

1 S. Wong (ed.), *Redwhiteblue Here/There/Everywhere: To All Those Hong Kongers Who Have Given Their Hearts and Souls to Their City* (Hong Kong: MCCM Creations, 2005).
2 Koranteng's Toli, 'Bags and Stamps' (13 April 2007), at koranteng.blogspot.co.uk/2007/04/bags-and-stamps.html (accessed 16 September 2016); L. Hunt, 'Immigrants Have Bags of Ambition', *Telegraph* (2 June 2007), at www.telegraph.co.uk/comment/personal-view/3640310/Immigrants-have-bags-of-ambition.html (accessed 15 September 2016); S. Mansfield, 'Art in the bag', *Scotsman* (28 September 2010).
3 Wong (ed.), *Redwhiteblue*.
4 N. Lui, 'Red-White-Blue and Hong Kong Installation Art' (MA dissertation, Lingnan University, 2011).
5 Wong (ed.), *Redwhiteblue*.
6 Lui, 'Red-White-Blue and Hong Kong Installation Art'.
7 Lee, Chien Ming, Red-White-Blue plastic sheeting manufacturer in Taiwan, interview with author, Taichung, 16 March 2017; Tse, Kung Chiu, Red-White-Blue plastic sheeting importer in Hong Kong, interview with author, Hong Kong, 23 January 2017.
8 Lui, 'Red-White-Blue and Hong Kong Installation Art'.
9 *Ibid.*; Wong (ed.), *Redwhiteblue*.
10 Y. Chen, 舊時風光:香港往事回味 (Hong Kong: Arcadia Press, 2006).
11 J. Chan, *Building Hong Kong: Redwhiteblue.* Exhibition Pamphlet (Hong Kong: Leisure and Cultural Service Department, 2005).

12 Wong (ed.), *Redwhiteblue*; Stanley Wong, interview with the author, Hong Kong, 20 December 2016.

13 Chan, *Building Hong Kong*.

14 M. Turner, 'Reading Between the Lines', in Wong (ed.), *Redwhiteblue*.

15 Deng Xiaoping was the Paramount Leader of the People's Republic of China (PRC) for the reunification of China during the early 1980s.

16 G. Matthews, K. W. Ma, and T. L. Lui, *Hong Kong, China: Learning to Belong to a Nation* (London: Routledge, 2008); T. Wang and W. Po Shan, 'Re-imagining China: the continuity and change of identity in post-1997 Hong Kong', in S. K. Lau, K. Y. Wong, and P. S. Wan (eds), *Society and Politics in Hong Kong: Continuity and Change* (Hong Kong: Hong Kong Institute of Asia-Pacific Studies, Chinese University of Hong Kong, 2004), pp. 213–41.

17 A. Fung, 'Postcolonial Hong Kong identity: hybridizing the local and the national', *Social Identities*, 10:3 (2004), 99–414.

18 S. Vag, 'Hong Kong's enduring identity crisis', *Atlantic* (16 October 2013), at www.theatlantic.com/china/archive/2013/10/hong-kongs-enduring-identity-crisis/280622/ (accessed 15 September 2016).

19 A. Leung, 'Push to defend city's core values', *South China Morning Post* (7 June 2004), at www.scmp.com/article/458500/push-defend-citys-core-values (accessed 15 September 2016).

20 Hong Kong Arts Development Council, 'Hong Kong's participation in La Biennale di Venezia' (16 June 2005), at www.venicebiennale.hk/vb2005/eng/press_20050616.htm (accessed 15 September 2016).

21 The Hong Kong teahouse, known as *Cha chaan teng* in colloquial terms, is synonymous with the city's hybrid culture and has long been the symbol of Hong Kong. Emerging in the 1950s, it is beloved by citizens and has an eclectic and affordable menu that includes many dishes typical of Hong Kong cuisine, and Hong Kong-style Western cuisine. Its popularity supports more than 2,000 teahouses across town. A public poll in 2007 found that seven out of ten people in Hong Kong believed it deserves a UNESCO cultural listing. Lawmaker Choy So Yuk subsequently lobbied for it to be an 'intangible cultural heritage of humanity' by UNESCO. See V. Chong, 'Keeping alive a tea café culture', *Straits Times* (23 December 2007), 28.

22 Carmen Au, Workshop Manager at New Life Psychiatric Rehabilitation Association, interview with author, Hong Kong, 8 February 2017; Kris Wong, General Manager (Social Enterprise) of New Life Psychiatric Rehabilitation Association, interview with author, Hong Kong, 8 February 2017.

23 rwb330, 'About rwb330', at rwb330.hk/about-rwb330/about-rwb/?lang=en (accessed 16 September 2016)

24 A. Abbas. *Hong Kong: Culture and the Politics of Disappearance* (Minneapolis: University of Minnesota Press, 1997).

25 C. Cartier, 'Culture and the City: Hong Kong, 1997–2007 ', *China Review*, 8:1 (2008), 59–83.

26 W. Ling, 'From "Made in Hong Kong" to "Designed in Hong Kong": searching for an identity in fashion', *Visual Anthropology*, 24:1 (2011), 106–23.

27 M. Turner, *Hong Kong Sixties: Designing Identity* (Hong Kong: Hong Kong Arts Centre, 1994).

28 K. Gerth, *As China Goes, So Goes the World: How Chinese Consumers are Transforming Everything* (New York: Hill and Wang, 2011); K. Pomeranz, *The Great Divergence: China, Europe, and the Making of the Modern World Economy* (Princeton: Princeton University Press, 2000).

29 Retaliation for a similar expulsion from Ghana also took place in the 1960s. See Koranteng's Toli, 'Bags and Stamps'.

30 *Ibid.*; A. Chia's Gringingles, 'Ghana Must Go: Nigera's Expulsion of Immigrants'

(20 April 2015), at annechia.com/2015/04/20/ghana-must-go-nigerias-expulsion-of-immigrants (accessed 15 September 2016).

31 T. Selasi, *Ghana Must Go* (Toronto: Penguin, 2013).

32 R. F. Arase (dir.), *Ghana Must Go* (Desamour Film Company Ltd, Ghana, 2016).

33 C. Greru, informant from Sri Lanka, email exchange with author, 4 April 2016.

34 C. Greru, informant from Sri Lanka, email exchange with author, 12 April 2016.

35 L. V. Rovine, 'History, art and plastic bags: viewing South Africa through fashion', in A. Jansen and J. Craik (eds), *Modern Fashion Traditions: Negotiating Tradition and Modernity Through Fashion* (London: Bloomsbury, 2016), pp. 165–84.

36 A. Appadurai, *Modernity at Large: Cultural Dimensions of Globalisation* (Minneapolis: University of Minnesota Press, 1996).

37 For further discussion in relation to the bag and contemporary art see Rovine, 'History, art and plastic bags'. Liese Van Der Watt, 'The chequered history of checks: contemporary African artists speak about plaid', *Selvedge*, 72 (September–October 2016), 52–6.

38 Koranteng's Toli, 'Bags and Stamps'.

39 M.-H. T. Pham, 'Fashion's cultural-appropriation debate: pointless', *Atlantic* (15 May 2014), at www.theatlantic.com/entertainment/archive/2014/05/cultural-appro priation-in-fashion-stop-talking-about-it/370826/ (accessed 16 September 2016).

40 *Ibid.*

41 G.O.D. a Hong Kong household furniture store, stands for Goods Of Desire. The lifestyle furniture store is widely known for its name in its abbreviated form.

42 See for example www.highsnobiety.com/2015/03/21/clot- adidas-consortium-zx-flux-rwb-video/ (accessed 10 October 2016).

43 AMZINGdeal, 'Freaky Friday: Luis Vuitton – Who's Shanzhai'ing who?' at amz-ingdeal.com/geeker/freaky-friday-luis-vuitton-–who's-shanzhai'ing-who.html (accessed 15 September 2016).

44 Koranteng's Toli, 'Bags and Stamps'.

45 S. Rushton, 'It's in the bag – Louis Vuitton air their laundry', *Independent* (8 October 2006), at www.independent.co.uk/news/world/europe/its-in-the-bag-louis-vuitton-air-their-laundry-419282.html (accessed 15 September 2016).

46 R. L. Blaszczyk (ed.), *Producing Fashion: Commerce, Culture, and Consumers* (Philadelphia: University of Pennsylvania Press, 2008).

47 The Fashion Law, 'Balenciaga did not "copy" traditional Thai shopping bags for F/W16' (10 March 2016), at www.thefashionlaw.com/home/shk1uxb7w8en33x62s-0j1th5ns3nos (accessed 16 September 2016).

Select bibliography

Abbas, A., *Hong Kong: Culture and the Politics of Disappearance* (Minneapolis: University of Minnesota Press, 1997).

Agins, T., *The End of Fashion: How Marketing Changed the Clothing Business Forever* (New York: William Morrow Paperbacks, 2nd edn 2000).

Ammah, O. Koranteng, *Koranteng Toli* (13 April 2007).

Andersson, B., *Swedishness* (Stockholm: Positive Sweden, 1993).

Appadurai, A., *Modernity at Large: Cultural Dimensions of Globalisation* (Minneapolis: University of Minnesota Press, 1996).

Arase, R. F. (director), *Ghana Must Go* (Desamour Film Company Ltd, Ghana, 2016).

Arnault, B. and Y. Messarovitch, *La passion créative* (Paris: Plon, 2000).

Aspers, P., *Orderly Fashion: A Sociology of Markets* (Princeton: Princeton University Press, 2010).

Assouly, O. (ed.), *Le luxe : Essais sur la fabrique de l'ostentation* (Paris: IFM, 2011).

Badel, L., *Un milieu libéral et européen: Le grand commerce français 1925–1948* (Paris: Comité pour l'histoire économique et financière de la France, 1999).

Balfour-Paul, J., *Indigo: Egyptian Mummies to Blue Jeans* (London: British Museum Press, 2011).

Barthes, R., *Système de la mode* (Paris: Seuil, 1967).

Becker, H. S., *Art Worlds* (Berkeley and Los Angeles: University of California Press, 1982).

Belfanti, M. and F. Giusberti (eds), *La Moda, Storia d'Italia, Annali*, 19 (Turin: Einaudi, 2003).

Bengtsson, M., *The Art of Replicating* (Linköping: Department of Management and Engineering, Linköping University, 2008).

Bentley, L., J. Davis, and J. C. Ginsburg (eds), *Copyright and Piracy: An Interdisciplinary Critique* (Cambridge: Cambridge University Press, 2010).

Berger, S., *Making in America: From Innovation to Market* (Cambridge: MIT Press, 2015).

Bergeron, L., *Les industries du luxe en France* (Paris: Odile Jacob, 1998).

Berghoff, H. and T. Kühne (eds), *Globalizing Beauty: Consumerism and Body Aesthetics in the Twentieth Century* (New York: Palgrave Macmillan, 2013).

Berghoff, H. and U. Spiekermann (eds), *Decoding Modern Consumer Societies* (New York: Palgrave Macmillan, 2012).

Blaszczyk, R. L., *Imagining Consumers: Design and Innovation from Wedgwood to Corning* (Baltimore: Johns Hopkins University Press, 2000).

Blaszczyk, R. L., 'Styling synthetics: DuPont's marketing of fabrics and fashions in postwar America', *Business History Review*, 80:3 (2006), 485–538.

Blaszczyk, R. L. (ed.), *Producing Fashion: Commerce, Culture, and Consumers* (Philadelphia: University of Pennsylvania Press, 2008).

Blaszczyk, R. L., *American Consumer Society, 1865–2005: From Hearth to HDTV* (Hoboken, NJ: Wiley, 2009).

Blaszczyk, R. L., *The Color Revolution* (Cambridge, MA: MIT Press, 2012).

Blaszczyk, R. L., *Fashionability: Abraham Moon and the Creation of British Cloth for the Global Market* (Manchester: Manchester University Press, 2017).

Blaszczyk, R. L. and P. B. Scranton (eds), *Major Problems in American Business History: Documents and Essays* (Boston: Houghton Mifflin, 2006).

Blaszczyk, R. L. and U. Spiekermann (eds), *Bright Modernity: Color, Commerce, and Consumer Culture* (New York: Palgrave Macmillan, 2017).

Blaszczyk, R. L. and B. Wubs (eds), *The Fashion Forecasters: A Hidden History of Color and Trend Prediction* (London: Bloomsbury Academic, 2018).

Blum, D., *Shocking! The Art and Fashion of Elsa Schiaparelli* (Philadelphia, PA: Philadelphia Museum of Art, 2003).

Bonin H., 'A reassessment of the business history of the French luxury sector: the emergence of a new business model and renewed corporate image (from the 1970s)', in L. Segreto, H. Bonin, A. K. Kozminski, C. Manera, and M. Pohl (eds), *European Business and Brand Building* (Brussels: Peter Lang, 2012), pp. 113–35.

Bonvicini, S., *Louis Vuitton: Une saga française* (Paris: Fayard, 2004).

Bossuat, G., *Faire l'Europe sans défaire la France, 60 ans de politique d'unité européenne des gouvernements et des présidents de la République française (1943–2003)* (Brussels: PIE Peter Lang, 2006).

Bourdieu, P., *Outline of a Theory of Practice* (Cambridge: Cambridge University Press, 1977).

Bourdieu, P., *La distinction: Critique sociale du jugement* (Paris: Minuit, 1979).

Bourdieu, P., *Distinction* (Abingdon: Routledge, Kegan & Paul, 1984).

Bourdieu, P., 'The forms of capital', in J. Richardson (ed.), *Handbook of Theory and Research for the Sociology of Education* (New York: Greenwood, 1986), pp. 241–58.

Bourdieu, P., *The Field of Cultural Production* (Cambridge: Polity, 1993).

Bourdieu, P., *Questions de sociologie* (Paris: Éditions de Minuit, 2002).

Brachet, F., M. Allera, and S. Desvaux, *Du Grand Bazar de l'Hôtel de Ville au BHV Marais, le grand magasin préféré des parisiens* (Paris: Assouline, 2016).

Brachet Champsaur, F., 'Aux Galeries Lafayette, 1893–1919: Naissance d'un leader de la distribution dans le secteur de la mode' (Master's thesis dissertation, École des hautes études en sciences sociales, Paris, 2005).

Brachet Champsaur, F. and L. Cailluet, 'The Great Depression? Challenging the periodization of French business history in the Interwar period', *Business and Economic History*, 8 (2010), 16–17.

Braudel, F., 'History and the social sciences: the longue durée', *Review (Fernand Braudel Center)*, 32:2 (2009), 171–203.

Breward, C., *The Culture of Fashion: A New History of Fashionable Dress* (Manchester: Manchester University Press, 1995).

Breward, C., *Fashioning London: Clothing and the Modern Metropolis* (Oxford: Berg, 2000).

Breward, C., *The Suit: Form, Function and Style* (London: Reaktion Books, 2016).

Breward, C. and D. Gilbert (eds), *Fashion's World Cities* (New York: Berg, 2006).

Brosselin, C. and C. Sordet, *La grande histoire des regroupements dans la distribution* (Paris: L'Harmattan, 2011).

Brown E., C. Gudis, and M. Moskowitz (eds), *Cultures of Commerce: Representation and American Business Culture, 1877–1960* (New York: Palgrave Macmillan, 2006).

Brown, I. (ed.), *From Tartan to Tartanry* (Edinburgh: Edinburgh University Press, 2010).

Brunnström, L., *Svensk Industridesign: En 1900-talshistoria* (Stockholm: Prisma, 1997).

Cannadine, D., *Ornamentalism: How the British Saw Their Empire* (Oxford: Oxford University Press, 2002).

Cartier, C., 'Culture and the City: Hong Kong, 1997–2007', *China Review*, 8:1 (2008), 59–83.

Chan, J., *Building Hong Kong: Redwhiteblue.* Exhibition Pamphlet (Hong Kong: Leisure and Cultural Service Department, 2005).

Chan, W.-S., '集體回憶袋袋相傳紅白藍之父李華', *Ming Pao* (4 April 2007).

Chandler Jr., A. D., *Strategy and Structure: Chapters in the History of the American Industrial Enterprise* (Cambridge, MA: MIT Press, 1962).

Chandler Jr., A. D., *The Visible Hand: The Managerial Revolution in American Business* (Cambridge, MA: Belknap Press of Harvard University Press, 1977).

Chandler Jr., A. D. and T. Hikino, *Scale and Scope: The Dynamics of Industrial Capitalism* (Cambridge, MA: Harvard University Press, 1994).

Chatriot, A., 'La construction récente des groupes de luxe français: Mythes, discours et pratiques', *Entreprises et histoire*, 46:1 (2007), 143–56.

Chen, Y., 舊時風光：香港往事回味 (Hong Kong: Arcadia Press, 2006).

Chevalier, M. and G. Mazzalovo, *Luxury Brand Management: A World of Privilege* (Singapore: John Wiley & Sons, 2012).

Chong, V., 'Keeping alive a tea café culture', *Straits Times* (23 December 2007), 28.

Clark, H. and A. Palmer (eds), *Old Clothes, New Looks: Second-Hand Fashion* (London: Berg, 2004).

Clarke, S., 'Managing design: the Art and Colour Section at General Motors, 1927–1941', *Journal of Design History*, 12:1 (1999), 65–79.

Clemence, R. (ed.), *Essays of J. A. Schumpeter* (Cambridge, MA: Addison-Wesley, 1989).

Clemente, D., *Dress Casual: How College Students Redefined American Style* (Chapel Hill: University of North Carolina Press, 2014).

Cordobes, S. and P. Durance, *Attitudes prospectives: Eléments d'une histoire de la prospective en France après 1945* (Paris: L'Harmattan, 2007).

Cortada, J., *Before the Computer: IBM, NCR, Burroughs, and Remington Rand and the Industry They Created, 1865–1956* (Princeton: Princeton University Press, 1993).

Crane, D., *Fashion and Its Social Agendas: Class, Gender, and Identity in Clothing* (Chicago: University of Chicago Press, 2000).

Cunningham, P. A. and S. Voso Lab, *Dress and Popular Culture* (Bowling Green, KY: State University Popular Press, 1991).

Daria, I., *The Fashion Cycle* (New York: Simon & Schuster, 1990).

de Grazia, V., *Irresistible Empire: America's Advance through Twentieth-Century Europe* (Cambridge, MA: Harvard University Press, 2009).

de la Haye, A. and V. Mendes, *The House of Worth: Portrait of an Archive* (London: V&A Publishing, 2014).

Demornex, J., *Madeleine Vionnet* (Paris: Éditions du Regard, 1990).

Djelic, M.-L., *Exporting the American Model: The Post-War Transformation of European Business* (Oxford: Oxford University Press, 1998).

Donzé, P.-Y., *Les patrons horlogers de La Chaux-de-Fonds (1840–1920): Dynamique sociale d'une élite industrielle* (Neuchâtel: Alphil, 2007).

Donzé, P.-Y., *Histoire du Swatch Group* (Neuchâtel: Alphil, 2012).

Donzé, P.-Y., *A Business History of the Swatch Group: The Rebirth of Swiss Watchmaking and the Globalization of the Luxury Industry* (Basingstoke: Palgrave Macmillan, 2014).

Donzé P.-Y and R. Fujioka, 'European luxury big business and emerging Asian markets, 1960–2010', *Business History*, 57:6 (2015), 822–40.

Entwistle, J., *The Aesthetic Economy of Fashion: Markets and Values in Clothing and Modelling* (Oxford: Berg, 2009).

Entwistle, J. and E. Wilson (eds.), *Body Dressing* (Oxford: Berg, 2001).

Evans, C., *Fashion at the Edge: Spectacle, Modernity and Deathliness* (New Haven: Yale University Press, 2003).

Eveno, P., 'La construction d'un groupe international, LVMH', in J. Marseille (ed.), *Le luxe en France, du siècle des Lumières à nos jours* (Paris: Association pour le développement de l'histoire économique, 1999), pp. 291–321.

Faiers, J., *Tartan* (Oxford: Berg, 2008).

Fauchart, E. and E. von Hippel, 'Norms-based intellectual property systems: the case of French chefs', *Organization Science*, 19:2 (2008), 187–201.

Feydeau, E. de, *Les Parfums: Histoire, Anthologie, Dictionnaire* (Paris: Laffont, 2011).

Fine, B. and E. Leopold, *The World of Consumption* (London: Routledge, 1993).

Finlayson, I., *Denim: An American Legend* (Norwich: Parke Sutton Publishing, 1990).

Florida, R., *The Rise of the Creative Class: And How It's Transforming Work, Leisure, Community, and Everyday Life* (New York: Basic Books, 2002).

Font, L. M., 'International couture: the opportunities and challenges of expansion 1880–1920', *Business History*, 54:1 (2012), 30–47.

Fontana, G. L. and J. A. Miranda, 'The business of fashion in the nineteenth and twentieth centuries', *Investigaciones de Historia Economica – Economic History Research*, 5:2 (2016), 1–9.

Forden, S. G., *The House of Gucci: A Sensational Story of Murder, Madness, Glamour, and Greed* (New York: Morrow, 2000).

Forestier, N. and N. Ravai, *Bernard Arnault ou le goût du pouvoir* (Paris: OlivierOrban, 1993).

Friedman, W. A., *Birth of a Salesman: The Transformation of Selling in America* (Cambridge, MA: Harvard University Press, 2005).

Friedman, W. A. and G. Jones (eds), 'Creative industries in history' special issue, *Business History Review*, 85:2 (summer 2011), 237–366.

Frykman, J. and O. Löfgren, *Den kultiverade människan [The Cultured Man]* (Malmö: Gleerups Utbildnings AB, 1979).

Fung, A.,'Postcolonial Hong Kong identity: hybridizing the local and the national', *Social Identities*, 10:3 (2004), 99–414.

Galvez-Behar, G., *La République des inventeurs: Propriété et organisation de l'innovation en France (1791–1922)* (Rennes: Presses Universitaires de Rennes, 2008).

Gerth, K., *As China Goes, So Goes the World: How Chinese Consumers are Transforming Everything* (New York: Hill and Wang, 2011).

Gill, T. M., *Beauty Shop Politics: African American Women's Activism in the Beauty Industry* (Urbana, IL: University of Illinois Press, 2010).

Gimeno Martinez, J., 'Restructuring plans for the textile and clothing sector in post-industrial Belgium and Spain', *Fashion Practice*, 3:2 (2011), 197–224.

Godley, A., 'Selling the sewing machine around the world: Singer's international marketing strategies 1850–1920', *Enterprise and Society*, 7:2 (2008), 266–314.

Golbin, P. (ed.), *Madeleine Vionnet, puriste de la mode* (Paris: Les Arts Décoratifs, 2009).

Goldstein, C., *Creating Consumers: Home Economists in Twentieth-Century America* (Chapel Hill: University of North Carolina Press, 2012).

Gorski, P. (ed.), *Bourdieu and Historical Analysis* (London: Duke University Press, 2013).

Gråbacke, C., *Kläder, shopping och flärd [Clothes, Shopping and Flair]* (Stockholm: Stockholmia Förlag, 2015).

Graham, B. and P. Howard (eds.), *The Ashgate Research Companion to Heritage and Identity* (Aldershot: Ashgate, 2008).

Green, N., *Du Sentier à la Septième Avenue: La confection et les immigrés, Paris-New York, 1880–1980*, trans. P. Ndiaye (Paris: Editions du Seuil, 1998).

Green, N. L., *Ready-to-Wear and Ready-to-Work: A Century of Industry and Immigrants in Paris and New York* (Durham, NC: Duke University Press, 1997).

Grimm, J. and W. Grimm, *The Original Folk and Fairy Tales of the Brothers Grimm: The Complete First Edition*, trans. J. Zipes (Princeton and Oxford: Princeton University Press, 2014).

Grossiord, S. (ed.), *Roman d'une garde-robe: Le chic d'une Parisienne, de la Belle Epoque aux années 30* (Paris: Paris-musées, 2013).

Guillaume V., *Jacques Fath* (Paris: Adam Biro, 1993).

Hansen, K. T., *Salaula: The World of Secondhand Clothing and Zambia* (Chicago: University of Chicago Press, 2000).

Hansen, P. H., 'Business history: a cultural and narrative approach', *Business History Review*, 86:4 (winter 2012), 693–717.

Harlaftis, G., *A History of Greek-Owned Shipping: The Making of an International Tramp Fleet, 1830 to the Present Day* (London: Routledge, 2005).

Harrison, E. (1995). *Scottish Estate Tweeds* (Elgin: Johnstons of Elgin, 1995).

Heilbronn, M. and J. Varin, *Galeries Lafayette, Buchenwald, Galeries Lafayette* (Paris: Economica, 1989).

Hill, J. and P. Church-Gibson (eds), *World Cinema: Critical Approaches* (Oxford: Oxford University Press, 1995).

Hobsbawm, E. and T. Ranger (eds), *The Invention of Tradition* (Cambridge: Cambridge University Press, 1983).

Holmes, D. and A. Smith (eds), *100 Years of European Cinema: Entertainment or Ideology?* (Manchester: Manchester University Press, 2000).

Holt, D. B., *How Brands become Icons: The Principles of Cultural Branding* (Cambridge, MA: Harvard University Press, 2004).

Honeyman, K., *Well Suited: A History of the Leeds Clothing Industry, 1850–1990* (Oxford: Oxford University Press, 2000).

Hoskins, T. E., *Stitched Up: The Anti-Capitalist Book of Fashion* (London: Pluto Press, 2014).

Howard, V., *Brides, Inc.: American Weddings and the Business of Tradition* (Philadelphia: University of Pennsylvania Press, 2006).

Howard, V., *From Main Street to Mall: The Rise and Fall of the American Department Store* (Philadelphia, University of Pennsylvania Press, 2015).

Hunt, L., 'Immigrants have bags of ambition', *Telegraph* (2 June 2007).

Jackson Lears, T. J., *Fables of Abundance: A Cultural History of Advertising in America* (New York: Basic Books, 1994).

Jaumain, S. and G. Crossick (eds), *Cathedrals of Consumption: The European Department Store 1850–1939* (London: Ashgate, 1999).

Jessen, R. and L. Langer (eds), *Transformations of Retailing in Europe after 1945* (Farnham: Ashgate, 2016).

John, R., 'Elaborations, revisions, dissents: Alfred D. Chandler Jr.'s *The Visible Hand* after twenty years', *Business History Review*, 71:2 (summer 1997), 151–200.

Jones, G., *Beauty Imagined: A History of the Global Beauty Industry* (Oxford: Oxford University Press, 2010).

Jones, G. and V. Pouillard, *Christian Dior: A New Look for Haute Couture*, Harvard Business School Case No. 809–159 (2009, revised 2013).

Jones, G. and J. Zeitlin (eds), *The Oxford Handbook of Business History* (Oxford: Oxford University Press, 2007).

Judt, T., *Postwar: A History of Europe Since 1945* (London: Penguin, 2005).

Kapferer, J. N. and V. Bastien, *The Luxury Strategy: Break the Rules of Marketing to Build Luxury Brands* (London: Kogan Page, 2nd edn 2012).

Kawamura Y., *Fashion-ology: An Introduction to Fashion Studies (Dress, Body and Culture)* (London: Bloomsbury, 2nd edn 2005).

Kidwell, C. and V. Steele (eds), *Men and Women: Dressing the Part* (Washington, DC: Smithsonian Institution Press, 1989).

Kinoshita, A., *Apareru Sangyo no Marketing shi [Marketing History of the Garment Industry]* (Tokyo: Dobunkan, 2011).

Kipping, M. and O. Bjarnar (eds), *The Americanization of European Business: The Marshall Plan and the Transfer of US Management Models* (London and New York: Routledge Studies in Business History, 1998).

Kirke, B., *Madeleine Vionnet* (San Francisco: Chronicle Books, 1998).

Klein, N., *No Logo: Taking Aim at the Brand Bullies* (Toronto: Alfred A. Knopf Canada, 1999).

Kloosterman, R. and J. Rath, 'Immigrant entrepreneurs in advanced economies: mixed embeddedness further explored', *Journal of Ethnic and Migration Studies*, 27:2 (2001), 189–201.

Kristoffersson, S., *IKEA: En kulturhistoria* (Stockholm: Bokförlaget Atlantis AB, 2015).

Kuisel, R., *Capitalism and the State in Modern France: Renovation and Economic Management in the Twentieth Century* (Cambridge: Cambridge University Press, 1981).

Kuldova, T., *Luxury Indian Fashion: A Social Critique* (London: Bloomsbury, 2016).

Laird, P. W., *Advertising Progress: American Business and the Rise of Consumer Marketing* (Baltimore: Johns Hopkins University Press, 2001).

Lanzmann J. and P. Ripert, *Cent ans de prêt-à-porter: Weill* (Paris: P.A.U, 1992).

Larsson, M., *Det svenska näringslivets historia 1864 – 2014* (Stockholm: Dialogos förlag / Centrum för Näringslivshistoria, 2014).

Lau, S. K., K. Y. Wong, and P. S. Wan (eds), *Society and Politics in Hong Kong: Continuity and Change* (Hong Kong: Hong Kong Institute of Asia-Pacific Studies, Chinese University of Hong Kong, 2004).

Laver, J. and A. de la Haye, *Costume and Fashion: A Concise History* (London: Thames & Hudson, 4th edn 1995).

Leach, W., *Land of Desire: Merchants, Power, and the Rise of a New American Culture* (New York: Pantheon Books, 1993).

Lerner, P., *The Consuming Temple: Jews, Department Stores, and the Consumer Revolution in Germany, 1880–1940* (Cornell, NY: Cornell University Press, 2015).

Leung, A., 'Push to Defend City's Core Values', *South China Morning Post* (7 June 2004).

Levi, M., 'L'évolution et la structure des échanges commerciaux de la France avec l'étranger de 1951 à 1955', *Politique étrangère*, 5 (1956), 567–86.

Lhermie, C., *Carrefour ou l'invention de l'hypermarché* (Paris: Vuibert, 2001).

Ling, W., 'From "Made in Hong Kong" to "Designed in Hong Kong": searching for an identity in Fashion', *Visual Anthropology*, 24:1 (2011), 106–23.

Lipartito, K. J., 'Culture and the practice of business history', *Business and Economic History*, 24:1 (winter 1995), 1–41.

Lipovetsky, G., *L'empire de l'éphémère: La mode et son destin dans les sociétes modernes* (Paris: Gallimard, 1987).

Lipovetsky, G., *The Empire of Fashion* (Princeton: Princeton University Press, 1994).

Lipovetsky, G., *Hypermodern Times* (Cambridge: Polity Press, 2005).

Little, D., *Vintage Denim* (Salt Lake City, UT: Gibbs Smith, 1996).

Lopes, T. S., *Global Brands: The Evolution of Multinationals in Alcoholic Beverages* (Cambridge: Cambridge University Press, 2007).

Lordon, F. *Willing Slaves of Capital: Spinoza and Marx on Desire* (London: Verso, 2014).

Lui, N.-Y., 'Red-White-Blue and Hong Kong Installation Art' (MA dissertation, Lingnan University, 2011).

Lukose, R. A., *Liberalization's Children: Gender, Youth, and Consumer Citizenship in Globalizing India* (Durham, NC: Duke University Press, 2009).

Madeleine Vionnet (1876–1975): L'art de la couture (Marseilles: Direction des Musées, 1991).

Madeleine Vionnet: Les années d'innovation, 1919–1929 (Lyon: Musée des Tissus, 1994).

Madeleine Vionnet: 15 dresses from the collection of Martin Kramer (London: Judith Clark Costume Centre, 2001).

Mansfield, S., 'Art in the bag', *Scotsman* (28 September 2010).

Marchal, A., 'Prospective par Gaston Berger, Louis Armand, François Bloch-Lainé, Pierre Chouard, Marcel Demonque, Jacques Parisot et Pierre Racine', *Revue économique*, 11 (1960), 973–5.

Marchand, R., *Advertising the American Dream: Making Way for Modernity, 1920–1940* (Berkeley: University of California Press, 1986).

Marchand, R., *Creating the Corporate Soul: The Rise of Public Relations and Corporate Imagery in American Big Business* (Berkeley: University of California Press, 2001).

Marsh, G. and P. Trynka (eds), *Denim: from Cowboys to Catwalks: A Visual History of the World's Most Legendary Fabric* (London: Aurum Press, 2002).

Marx, W. D., *AMETORA: How Japan Saved American Style* (New York: Basic Books, 2015).

Matthews, G., K. W. Ma and L. T. Lui, *Hong Kong, China: Learning to Belong to a Nation* (London: Routledge, 2008).

Maul, D. R., 'The International Labour Organization and the struggle against forced labour from 1919 to the present', *Labor History*, 48:4 (2007): 477–500.

Mazzarella, W., *Shoveling Smoke: Advertising and Globalization in Contemporary India* (Durham, NC: Duke University Press, 2006).

McGoey, L., *No Such Thing as Free Gift* (London: Verso, 2015).

McNeill, P. and G. Riello, *Luxury: A Rich History* (New York: Oxford, 2016).

Mears, P. (ed.), *Ivy Style: Radical Conformist* (New Haven: Yale University Press, 2012).

Mendelsohn, A. D., *The Rag Race: How Jews Sewed Their Way to Success in America and the British Empire* (New York: New York University Press, 2015).

Merlo, E. and F. Polese, 'Turning fashion into business: the emergence of Milan as an international fashion hub', *Business History Review*, 80:3 (autumn 2006), 415–47.

Meyerowitz, J. (ed.), *Not June Cleaver: Women and Gender in Postwar America, 1945 1960* (Philadelphia, PA: Temple University Press, 1994).

Milbank, C. R., *Couture: The Great Designers* (New York: Stewart, Tabori & Chang, 1985).

Milbank, C. R., *New York Fashion: The Evolution of American Style* (New York: Harry N. Abrams, 1996).

Miller, D. and S. Woodward, *Global Denim* (New York: Berg, 2011).

Miller, M. B., *The Bon Marché: Bourgeois Culture and the Department Store, 1869–1920* (Princeton: Princeton University Press, 1981).

Milward, A., *The European Rescue of the Nation State* (London: Routledge, 2000).

Montégut, P., 'Boué Sœurs: the first haute couture establishment in America', *Dress*, 15:1 (1989), 79–86.

Moore, C. M. and G. Birtwistle, 'The nature of parenting advantage in luxury fashion retailing: the case of Gucci group NV', *International Journal of Retail & Distribution Management*, 33:4 (2005), 256–70.

Moskowitz, M., *Standard of Living: The Measure of the Middle Class in Modern America* (Baltimore: Johns Hopkins University Press, 2009).

Moutet, A., *Les logiques de l'entreprise: La rationalisation dans l'industrie française de l'entre-deux-guerres* (Paris: Editions de l'Ecole des hautes études en sciences sociales, 1997).

Nakagome, S., *Nihon no Ifuku Sangyo [The Garment Industry in Japan]* (Tokyo: Toyo Keizai Shinpo sha, 1975).

Oakes, L., B. Townley and D. Cooper, 'Business planning as pedagogy: language and control in a changing institutional field', *Adminstrative Science Quarterly*, 43 (1998), 257–92.

Offerlé, M., 'L'action collective patronale en France, 19ᵉ–20ᵉ siècles : organisations, répertoires et engagements', *Vingtième Siècle. Revue d'Histoire*, 114 (2012), 83–97.

Okonkwo, U., *Luxury Fashion Branding: Trends, Tactics, Techniques* (Basingstoke: Palgrave Macmillan, 2007).

Omnès, C., *Ouvrières parisiennes : Marché du travail et trajectoires professionnelles au 20ᵉ siècle* (Paris: Editions de l'EHESS, 1997).

Pagliai, L., *La Firenze di Giovanni Battista Giorgini* (Florence: OMA, 2011).

Palmer, A. *Couture and Commerce: The Transatlantic Fashion Trade in the 1950s* (Vancouver, BC: University of British Columbia Press, 2001).

Palmer, A., *Dior: A New Look, A New Enterprise* (London: V&A Publishing, 2009).

Palmer, A. (ed.), *The Cultural History of Dress and Fashion. Vol. 6: The Twentieth Century* (London: Bloomsbury, 2016).

Pareja-Eastaway, M., 'Creative industries', *Journal of Evolutionary Studies in Business*, 1:1 (2016), 40–3.

Parpoil, C. (ed.), *Paul Poiret, couturier-perfumer* (Paris: Somogy, 2013).

Paulicelli, E., *Fashion Under Fascism: Beyond the Black Shirt* (Oxford and New York: Berg, 2004).

Peiss, K. L., *Hope in a Jar: The Making of America's Beauty Culture* (New York: Metropolitan Books, 2000).

Peiss, K. L., *Zoot Suit: The Enigmatic Career of an Extreme Style* (Philadelphia: University of Pennsylvania Press, 2011).

Perrault, C., *Old-Time Stories told by Master Charles Perrault*, trans. A. E. Johnson (New York: Dodd, Mead, 1921).

Perrot, P., *Les dessus et les dessous de la bourgeoisie: Une histoire du vêtement au XIXᵉ siècle* (Paris: Fayard, 1981).

Pettersson, B., *Handelsmännen [The Businessmen]* (Stockholm: Ekerlids Förlag, 2003).

Pfaller, R., *On the Pleasure Principle in Culture: Illusions without Owners* (London: Verso, 2014).

Pham, M.-H. T., 'Fashion's cultural-appropriation debate: pointless', *Atlantic* (15 May 2014).

Pierre Balmain, 40 années de création (Paris: Musée Galliera, 1985).

Piketty, T., *Le capital au XXIᵉ siècle* (Paris: Seuil, 2013).

Pochna M.-F., *Christian Dior* (Paris: Flammarion, 2004).

Polan, B. and R. Tredre, *The Great Fashion Designers* (London: Bloomsbury, 2009).

Polese, F. and R. L. Blaszczyk (eds), 'Fashion' special issue, *Business History*, 54 (February 2012), 6–115.

Pomeranz, K., *The Great Divergence: China, Europe, and the Making of the Modern World Economy* (Princeton: Princeton University Press, 2000).

Potvin, J., *Bachelors of a Different Sort: Queer Aesthetics, Material Culture, and the Modern Interior in Britain* (Manchester: Manchester University Press, 2015).

Pouillard V., *Hirsch & Cie Bruxelles (1869–1962)* (Brussels: Editions de l'Université Libre de Bruxelles, 2000).

Pouillard, V., 'American advertising agencies in Europe: J. Walter Thompson's Belgian business in the interwar years', *Business History*, 47:1 (2005), 44–58.

Pouillard, V., *La publicité en Belgique: Des courtiers aux agencies internationales, 1850–1975* (Brussels: Académie Royale de Belgique, 2005).

Pouillard, V., 'Design piracy in the fashion industries of Paris and New York in the interwar years', *Business History Review*, 85:2 (summer 2011), 319–44.

Pouillard V., 'Keeping designs and brands authentic: the resurgence of post-war French fashion business under the challenge of US mass production', *European Review of History*, 20:5 (2013), 815–35.

Pouillard, V., 'Managing fashion creativity: the history of the Chambre Syndicale de la Couture Parisienne during the interwar period', *Investigaciones de Historia Economica – Economic History Research*, 12:2 (2016), 76–89.

Przybyszewski, L., *The Lost Art of Dress: The Women Who Once Made America Stylish* (New York: Basic Books, 2014).

Rappaport, E., *Shopping for Pleasure: Women and the Making of London's West End* (Princeton: Princeton University Press, 2000).

Refait M., *Moët & Chandon: De Claude Moët à Bernard Arnault* (Reims: Dominique Guéniot, 1998).

Rivoli, P., *Travels of a T-Shirt in the Global Economy: An Economist Examines the Markets, Power and Politics of World Trade* (Hoboken, NJ: John Wiley & Sons, 2005).

Robbins, D., *Bourdieu and Culture* (London and Thousand Oaks, CA: Sage Publications, 2000).

Rocamora, A., 'Fields of Fashion: critical insights into Bourdieu's sociology of culture', *Journal of Consumer Culture*, 2:3 (2002), 341–62.

Rocamora, A. and A. Smelik (eds), *Thinking Through Fashion* (London: I. B. Tauris, 2016).

Roche, D., *La culture des apparences: Une histoire du vêtement, XVII –XVIIIe siècle* (Paris: Fayard, 1989).

Rose, C., *Making, Selling and Wearing Boys' Clothes in Late-Victorian England* (Farnham: Ashgate, 2010).

Ross, R., *Clothing: A Global History* (Cambridge: Polity, 2008).

Routier A., *L'ange exterminateur: La vraie vie de Bernard Arnault* (Paris: Albin Michel, 2003).

Rovine, L. V., 'History, art and plastic bags: viewing South Africa through fashion', in A. Jansen and J. Craik (eds), *Modern Fashion Traditions: Negotiating Tradition and Modernity Through Fashion* (London: Bloomsbury, 2016).

Rushton, S., 'It's in the bag – Louis Vuitton air their laundry', *Independent* (8 October 2006).

Salmon C., *Storytelling: La machine à fabriquer des histoires et à formater les esprits* (Paris: La Découverte, 2007).

Sandemose, A., *En flykting korsar sitt spår: Espen Arnakkes kommentarer till Jantelagen* (Stockholm: Forum, 1968).

Savignon, J., *L'esprit Vionnet et ses influences de la fin des années vingt à nos jours* (Lyon: Association pour l'Université de la mode, 2009).

Scafidi, S., *Who Owns Culture? Appropriation and Authenticity in American Law* (New Brunswick, NJ: Rutgers University Press, 2005).

Scarpellini, Emanuella, *Material Nation: A Consumer's History of Modern Italy* (Oxford: Oxford University Press, 2011).

Schwarzkopf, S., 'The consumer as "voter", "judge", and "jury": historical origins and political consequences of a marketing myth', *Journal of Macromarketing*, 31:1 (March 2011), 8–18.

Scott, A. J., *The Cultural Economy of Cities: Essays on the Geography of Image-Producing Industries* (London: SAGE, 2000).

Scranton, P. B. and P. Fridenson, *Reimagining Business History* (Baltimore: Johns Hopkins University Press, 2013).

Selasi, T., *Ghana Must Go* (Toronto: Penguin, 2013).

Servais, J.-M., *International Labor Organization* (Alphen aan de Rijn, Neth.: Wolters Kluwer, 2011).

Shirley, K., *Pucci: A Renaissance in Fashion* (New York: Abbeville Press, 1991).

Sicilia, D. B., 'Cochran's legacy: a cultural path not taken', *Business and Economic History*, 24:1 (fall 1995), 27–39.

Simmel, G., 'Fashion', *American Journal of Sociology*, 62:6 (1957 [1904]), 541–58.

Sluiter, L., *Clean Clothes Campaign: A Global Movement to End Sweatshops* (London: Pluto Press, 2009).

Smith, M. O. and A. Kubler, *Art/Fashion in the Twenty-first Century*, (London: Thames & Hudson, 2013).

Snyder, R. L., *Fugitive Denim: A Moving Story of People and Pants in the Borderless World of Global Trade* (New York: W. W. Norton & Company, 2009).

Stanfill, S., *New York Fashion* (London: V&A, 2007).

Stanfill, S. (ed.), *The Glamour of Italian Fashion Since 1945* (London: V&A Publishing, 2014).

Steele, V., *Fashion and Eroticism: Ideals of Feminine Beauty from the Victorian Era to the Jazz Age* (New York: Oxford University Press, 1985).

Steele, V., *Paris Fashion: A Cultural History* (Oxford: Berg, 1998).

Steele, V., *The Corset: A Cultural History* (New Haven: Yale University Press, 2001).

Steele, V. and T. A. Long, *Chic Chicago: Couture Treasures from the Chicago History Museum* (New York: Museum at FIT, 2007).

Steinwall, C. and Å. Crona, *Moderouletten* [*The Fashion Roulette*] (Stockholm: Bonniers, 1989).

Stewart, M. L., 'Copying and copyrighting haute couture: democratizing fashion', *French Historical Studies*, 28:1 (2005), 103–30.

Stewart, M. L., *Dressing Modern Frenchwomen: Marketing Haute Couture, 1919–1939* (Baltimore: Johns Hopkins University Press, 2008).

Strasser, S., C. McGovern, and M. Judt (eds), *Getting and Spending: European and American Consumer Societies in the Twentieth Century* (Cambridge: Cambridge University Press, 1998).

Sugiyama, S., *Nihon Jeans Monogatari* [*The Story of Jeans in Japan*] (Okayama: Kibito Shuppan, 2009).

Sullivan, J., *Jeans: A Cultural History of an American Icon* (New York: Gotham, 2007).

Tatli, A., M. Özbilgin, and M. Karatas-Özkan (eds), *Pierre Bourdieu, Organisation, and Management* (New York and London: Routledge, 2015).

Tedlow, R., *New and Improved: The Story of Mass Marketing in America* (New York: Basic Books, 1990).

Thil, E., *Combat pour la distribution: D'Édouard Leclerc aux supermarchés* (Paris: Arthaud, 1964).

Thil, E., *Les inventeurs du commerce moderne: Des grands magasins aux bébés-requins* (Paris: Arthaud, 1966).

Thomas, D., *Deluxe: How Luxury Lost its Luster* (New York: Penguin, 2007).

Three Women: Madeleine Vionnet, Claire McCardell, and Rei Kawakubo (New York: Fashion Institute of Technology, 1987).

Tiersten, L., *Marianne in the Market: Envisioning Consumer Society in Fin-de-Siècle France* (Berkeley: University of California Press, 2001).

Townley, B., 'Bourdieu and Organization Studies: a ghostly apparition?' in P. Adler, P. du Gay, M. Reed, and G. Morgan (eds), *Oxford Handbook of Sociology, Social Theory and Organization Studies: Contemporary Currents* (Oxford: Oxford University Press, 2015), pp. 39–63.

Townley, B. and N. Beech (eds), *Managing Creativity: Exploring the Paradox* (Cambridge and New York: Cambridge University Press, 2010).

Troy, N., *Couture Culture: A Study in Modern Art and Fashion* (Cambridge, MA: MIT Press, 2003).

Trueb, L. F., *The World of Watches: History, Industry, Technology* (New York: Ebner Publishing, 2005).

Turner, M., *Hong Kong Sixties: Designing Identity* (Hong Kong: Hong Kong Arts Centre, 1994).

Ugolini, L., *Men and Menswear: Sartorial Consumption in Britain, 1880–1939* (Aldershot: Ashgate, 2007).

Vag, S., 'Hong Kong's enduring identity crisis', *Atlantic* (16 October 2013).

Van Derr Watt, Liese. 'The Chequered History of Checks: Contemporary African artists speak about plaid', *Selvedge*, 72 (September–October 2016), 52–6.

Veblen, T., *The Theory of the Leisure Class: An Economic Study in the Evolution of Institutions* (New York: Macmillan, 1899).

Veillon D., *La mode sous l'Occupation* (Paris: Payot, 1990).

Von Drehle, D., *Triangle: The Fire that Changed America* (New York: Atlantic Monthly Press, 2003).

White, N., *Reconstructing Italian Fashion: America and the Development of the Italian Fashion Industry* (Oxford: Bloomsbury, 2000).

Wilcox, C. (ed.), *The Golden Age of Haute Couture: Paris and London, 1947–1957* (London: V&A Publishing, 2007).

Wilson, E., *Adorned in Dreams* (London: I. B. Tauris, 2003).

Wong, S. [Anothermountainman] (ed.), *Redwhiteblue Here/There/Everywhere: To All Those Hong Kongers Who Have Given Their Hearts and Souls to Their City* (Hong Kong: MCCM Creations, 2005).

Worth, R., *Fashion For the People: A History of Clothing at Marks & Spencer* (Oxford: Berg, 2007).

Zamagni, V., *The Economic History of Italy 1860–1990* (Oxford: Clarendon Press, 2nd edn 2003).

Zdatny, S. (ed.), *Hairstyles and Fashion: A Hairdresser's History of Paris, 1910–1920* (Oxford: Berg, 1999).

Index

Note: Italicized page numbers refer to illustrations.